The NEUROGES® Analysis System for Nonverbal Behavior and Gesture

Hedda Lausberg

The NEUROGES® Analysis System for Nonverbal Behavior and Gesture

The Complete Research Coding Manual including an Interactive Video Learning Tool and Coding Template

PETER LANG

Bibliographic Information published by the Deutsche Nationalbibliothek
The Deutsche Nationalbibliothek lists this publication in the Deutsche Nationalbibliografie; detailed bibliographic data is available online at http://dnb.d-nb.de.

Library of Congress Cataloging-in-Publication Data
A CIP catalog record for this book has been applied for at the Library of Congress.

The development of the NEUROGES analysis system was supported by the German Research Association Grants DFG LA 1249/1-1, 1-2, 1-3.

Cover image: © Jana Bryjovà
Cover design: Olaf Glöckler, Atelier Platen, Friedberg

ISBN 978-3-631-77172-3 (Print)
E-ISBN 978-3-631-77852-4 (E-PDF)
E-ISBN 978-3-631-77853-1 (EPUB)
E-ISBN 978-3-631-77854-8 (MOBI)
DOI 10.3726/b15103

Peter Lang – Berlin · Bern · Bruxelles · New York ·
Oxford · Warszawa · Wien

This publication has been peer reviewed.

www.peterlang.com

For Elisabeth and Dietrich

Preface

Nonverbal interaction and gesture researchers can proudly look up on a long and multi-disciplinary history of their research field. Currently, research on nonverbal interaction and gesture is conducted among others in medicine, psychology, neuroscience, linguistics, anthropology, sociology, or computer science. Given the long history, documented since the ancient Greek, and the broad spectrum of research areas, nowadays a substantial body of knowledge on body movement, gesture, and nonverbal interaction research is available.

However, while the exploration of the field by many different scientific disciplines extends the understanding of nonverbal interaction and gesture, the spread across many different scientific disciplines also bears the risk of isolated areas of specialized knowledge caused by a lack of communication between the different disciplines. Unfortunately, this often applies and one important reason for the scant exchange between the scientific disciplines is that many different methods are used. Researchers of different disciplines often do not understand each other's terminology, methodology including coding systems, and consequently, findings. This condition constitutes a severe obstacle for comparing and relating the results of different studies and for gradually building up a common inter- or even trans-disciplinary corpus of knowledge on body movement, gesture, and nonverbal interaction. Furthermore, many studies in the field still lack a reliable methodology and an operationalization of the behavioral units and gesture types submitted to investigation. As units and types are often not clearly defined, it remains vague what kind of phenomenon had actually been investigated. Different researchers might use the same term, e.g. "symbolic" gesture, but actually refer to different phenomena, or vice versa – a fact that constitutes a severe obstacle in developing a reliable body of knowledge on body movement, gesture, and nonverbal interaction.

The development of the NEUROGES® system, which was made possible by a long-lasting funding of the German Research Association from 1999–2017 (grants LA 1249/1-1, 1-2, 1-3, 2-1), responds to this situation in research. On the one hand, NEUROGES® has become an objective, reliable and user-friendly analysis system for body movements and gestures. A recent review of 18 empirical studies using NEUROGES® in combination with ELAN demonstrated a good objectivity and reliability of the system. On the other hand, NEUROGES® suits as a basic analysis system that can be used across scientific disciplines and thereby facilitates interdisciplinary exchange. Recent studies using NEUROGES® cover a broad range of different scientific disciplines, e.g. linguistics/psycholinguistics, psychology, neuropsychology, medicine, evolutionary anthropology, or criminology. Thus far, altogether more than 500 individuals from different cultures of five continents have been investigated, Germans, British, US Americans, francophone and anglophone Canadians, Suisse, Koreans, Kenyans, and Papua New Guineans, including healthy adults and children as well as individuals with brain damage and with mental illness. Furthermore, NEUROGES® has been used for studies on non-human primates. Finally, NEUROGES® can be combined with other more specialized coding systems such as the Linguistic Annotation System for Gestures (LASG) or the Movement Psychodiagnostic Inventory (MPI).

The present book follows up on the first book "Understanding Body Movement" published 2013 in Peter Lang Academic Research, in which the theoretical background and design of the NEUROGES® system are presented. This second book contains the complete coding manual for the application of the system in research. It further includes an interactive video learning tool that illustrates the assessment algorithm and provides video examples of all NEUROGES® -registered hand movement and gesture types. In addition, four training videos are provided that enable readers to train the application of NEUROGES® and to compare their analyses with a correct solution. Thus, the present book provides all materials needed for an effective self-study of the NEUROGES® system and it enables to a reliable application of the system in research.

I would like to thank the German Research Association for the long-lasting funding of this project and the Peter Lang Company, notably Benjamin Kloss, for publishing the two books on the NEUROGES® system. Furthermore, over the past two decades, discussions with many colleagues from different scientific disciplines have influenced the development to the NEUROGES® system and have made it a truly interdisciplinary tool, notably with Martha Davis, Robyn Flaum Cruz, Miriam Roskild Berger, Norbert Freedman, Georg Goldenberg, Alain Ptito, Eran Zaidel, Joachim Hermsdörfer, Cornelia Müller, Sotaro Kita, Irene Mittelberg, Ellen Fricke, Katja Liebal, Mandana Seyfeddinipur, Janka Bryjovà, Marianne Eberhard-Kaechele, Peter Joraschky, Angela v. Arnim, Harald Skomroch, Ingo Helmich, Robert Rein, Melanie Seiler, Konrad Juszczyk, Oliver Schreer, Ippokrates Konstantinidis, Katharina Reinecke, Niklas Neumann and the many students of the NEUROGES® seminars that have been held since 2007. In particular, the scientific exchange with Han Slöetjes, the main software developer of the ELAN video and audio annotation tool, has been inspiring for the elaboration of the NEUROGES® algorithm and resulted in a highly efficient combination of NEUROGES® and ELAN. Janka Bryjovà has made major contributions to the interactive learning tool, not only by collecting numerous video examples of participants willing to give their consent to publication but also with regards to the aesthetic design of the learning tool. Corinna Klabunde has formatted the manuscript and designed and over the years repeatedly updated the figures of the algorithms in the course of the NEUROGES® development.

Finally, I am thinking of my husband Lothar Stemwedel whose insights were always an inspiration. I miss him deeply.

Cologne, August 2018
Hedda Lausberg

In order to receive your individual password for the login area on the NEUROGES® website www.neuroges-bast.info please send the code of this book to c.klabunde@dshs-koeln.de and h.lausberg@dshs-koeln.de.

Code: x12ynd14jeieng

Contents

I. Introduction to the NEUROGES® analysis system

1 How to use the system in research

The NEUROGES® analysis system is an objective and reliable analysis tool for kinesic[1] behavior and gesture. While it is typically used for the analysis of kinesic behavior and gesture in interaction, it can also be applied to examine the individuals' nonverbal behavior in non-interactive situations, such as thinking during a math task, waiting in a waiting room, etc.

NEUROGES® analyzes kinesic behavior and gesture based on the movement form of the body movements. The movement criteria on the basis of which the movement behavior is segmented into units and classified with values are valid with regards to neural, cognitive and emotional processes. This implies that the values are also sensitive to more complex phenomena such as spatial cognition, language and other neuropsychological functions, or stress, alterations in mental states and mental disease, but also gender and culture, and interaction. The system has been tested with the NEUROGES® archive, a video corpus of more than 500 individuals from different cultures of five continents, including healthy adults and children as well as individuals with brain damage and with mental illness, and furthermore, of non-human primates.

The aims, the theoretical background, and the development of the system are described in detail in the first book "Understanding Body Movement" published 2013 in Peter Lang Academic Research (hereafter referred to as: book I). Developments of the system since 2013 are reported in detail in the manuscript "The revised NEUROGES® -ELAN system–An objective and reliable interdisciplinary analysis tool for nonverbal behavior and gesture" by Lausberg & Slöetjes, published in Behaviour Research Methods, 48(3), 973–93, 2016. NEUROGES® is registered as a European trademark by the European Union Intellectual Property Office.

The NEUROGES® system is characterized by a user-friendly and flexible structure that allows the researcher to tailor the analysis according to her/his research requirements. The flexibility is achieved by the combination of a vertical and a horizontal dimension of analysis (Fig. 1) and by selectivity of the part(s) of the body submitted to the analysis.

The vertical dimension of the analysis is composed of seven assessment steps that build up on each other. The researcher is guided through an algorithmic

1 The term kinesic is adopted from Birdwhistell (1952) to specify the aspect of nonverbal behavior that is subject of the NEUROGES® analysis.

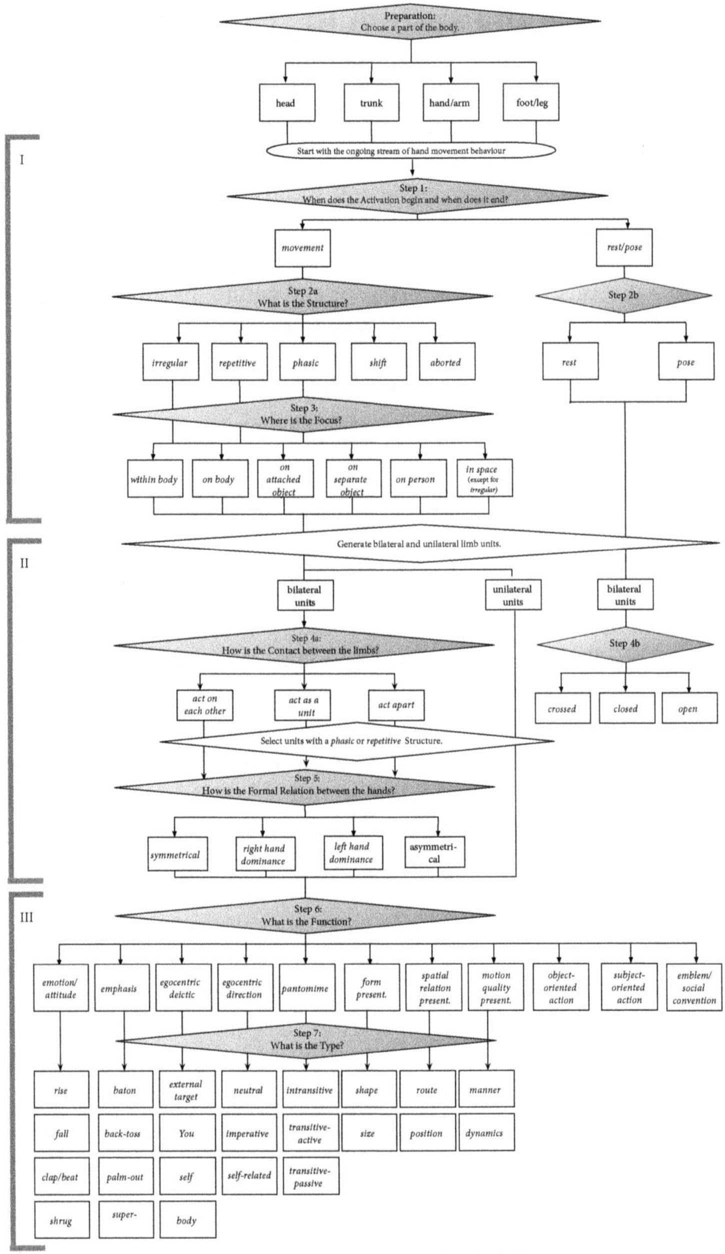

Fig. 1: The analysis algorithm of the NEUROGES® system

assessment, in the course of which the ongoing stream of body movement is segmented into more and more fine-grained movement units, which represent conceptually more and more complex phenomena.

However, each assessment step does not only serve to achieve a more fine-grained segmentation and classification, but furthermore, it constitutes a conceptually valid category per se, e.g. Step 3 constitutes the Focus category. Within each category, the category values are systematically organized, e.g. in the Focus category the values *within body, on body, on attached object, on separate object, on person, in space* (see Fig. 1, from left to right). This horizontal dimension of the NEUROGES® analysis reflects its developmental approach.

The seven assessment steps and seven main categories, respectively, are grouped into three modules that have different foci of analysis: Module I comprising Steps 1 – 3 the Kinesic analysis; Module II comprising Steps 4 – 5 the Laterality analysis; and Module III comprising Steps 6 – 7 the Gesture and Action analysis. Thus, the system consists of several categories and modules, the assessment of which altogether has strong synergetic effects (in the vertical dimension), but which can also be used independently of each other (because of the horizontal dimension). Therefore, the NEUROGES® system can be employed in a flexible manner according to the researcher's objectives.

Furthermore, in line with the researcher's requests, the body movements are grouped according to anatomy of the body into the four parts hand/arm/shoulder, foot/leg, head, and trunk movements. As these parts can be analyzed altogether or independently of each other, even more flexibility in the use of NEUROGES® is achieved.

To summarize, the design of the NEUROGES® system bears the advantage that the system can be used in a flexible manner according to the researcher's requirements. On the one hand, the vertical dimension provides a highly operationalized systematic and comprehensive analysis, on the other hand, the horizontal dimension entails that already the assessment of a single category offers a conceptually valid analysis. Furthermore, the researcher can analyze all parts of the body or just select one. As the complete analysis comprises three modules that comprise altogether eight main categories that are each are meaningful per se, the complete analysis can be broken up into the algorithmic analysis of one or more modules and the analysis of one or more categories. Thus, depending on her/his research question the researcher decides if (s)he wants to conduct the complete algorithmic analysis, or apply only one module, one main category, or one supplementary category (see below). Aims, advantages and limitations of the three different approaches are described below.

1.1 Complete algorithmic analysis

The complete analysis is recommended for researchers who aim at a comprehensive exploration of kinesic behavior and gesture. The complete analysis is particularly suitable for exploratory research, for pattern detection, for research questions requiring a high quantitative reliability, and for investigations including all parts of the body.

First, the complete analysis is ideal for exploratory research as it provides the full analysis of kinesic behavior. It registers the classical types of kinesic behavior, such as gestures, actions, head motions, trunk shifts, self-touches, foot movements, rest positions, etc.. In addition, it sheds light on certain dimensions of body movement across these movement types that reflect mental processes: the combination of motion, position and muscle contraction shows the extent of motor activity (Activation category), the trajectory and its structure reflects different types of mental states, such as dysregulated unproductive versus regulated productive states (Structure category), or the locus where the hand/foot acts (on) reveals the locus of sensory stimulation (Focus category). The detailed investigation of the laterality of limb movements provides insight into the neural basis of movement production, i.e., hemispheric specialization, interhemispheric cooperation, and complexity of neural control (Contact and Formal Relation categories). Finally, the complete analysis includes the elaborate analysis of the function and meaning of gestures and actions (Function and Type categories) as well as the analysis of rests and poses. Thus, as it is so comprehensive, the complete analysis is particularly suitable for exploratory research.

Second, as the complete ongoing stream of kinesic behavior is analyzed and thereby all movements and rests/poses are registered and classified, the output of the complete analysis provides the perfect basis for the detection of intraindividual and intradyadic kinesic and gestural patterns (see book I, 2.3).

Third, as the whole stream of kinesic behavior is registered and analyzed, the complete analysis offers a high quantitative precision concerning information about the frequency (number / minute), duration (seconds / unit), and the overall proportion of time (seconds / minute) of the different movement types (see book I, 2.4). Notably, as all kinesic phenomena are registered, also movements that are hard to classify at first glance are obligatorily submitted to the analysis and that challenge the researcher to deal with difficult kinesic phenomena. This further implies that the registered frequency of certain kinesic and gesture types is more accurate (Lausberg & Slöetjes, 2016, Introduction).

Fourth, all four parts of the body can be submitted to the complete analysis with the exception of the laterality assessment (Contact and Formal Relation categories) that only applies to limb movements.

Procedurally, the complete analysis is based on an assessment algorithm that includes seven assessment steps (Fig. 1). The algorithm enables to segment the ongoing stream of body movement into more and more fine-grained units.

Practically, at each assessment step, the units of the previous step are adopted, i.e., they become the 'to-be-coded' units for the next assessment step in which they are reassessed with new movement criteria. If according to the reassessment, the kinesic behavior changes within the adopted unit, the unit is segmented into subunits. These subunits then constitute the 'to-be-coded' units for the assessment step. As this principle of (sub-) unit generation applies to all coding steps, the multi-step evaluation process results in more and more fine-grained kinesic units that represent more and more complex phenomena. Thus, at steps 6 and 7, when complex decisions concerning the function and meaning of a gesture or action are required, fine behavioral units are available that are based on a highly operationalized step-wise segmentation of behavior. As the set of movement criteria (e.g. presence of physical contact + quality of physical contact + object/subject of dynamic contact) that is employed in an assessment step represents a specific aspect of neural, cognitive, or emotional processes (e.g. locus of sensory stimulation and attention), each assessment step constitutes a conceptually valid category. According to the conceptual main theme, the eight categories are grouped in three modules.

The Activation category (Fig. 1, Step 1) segments the ongoing stream of movement behavior into *movement* units and *rest/pose* units. The *movement* units are further assessed with the Structure category (Step 2a) regarding the movement trajectory, and classified with five Structure values (*irregular, repetitive, phasic, shift, aborted*). The *rest/pose* units are further classified (Step 2b) according to muscle relaxation/contraction with two R/PStructure values (*rest, pose*). In the Focus category (Step 3), *phasic, repetitive,* and *irregular* Structure units are further assessed and classified with six Focus values (*within body, on body, on attached object, on separate object, on person, in space*). The kinesic assessment in Module I (Kinesic Module) is finalized with the concatenation of the Structure values and the Focus values of the units (e.g. *phasic in space*). The StructureFocus units represent classical kinesic behavior types at a highly operationalized level.

As a preparatory step for Steps 4 and 5 (Module II: Laterality Module), based on the StructureFocus units and the R/PStructure units of the limbs unilateral and bilateral units are generated. In the Contact category, the bilateral StructureFocus units are analyzed regarding the physical contact between the right and left limbs and classified with three Contact values (*act on each other, act as a unit, act apart*). The bilateral RestPose units are classified with three R/P Contact values (*crossed, closed, open*). The subsequent Formal Relation category (Step 5) concentrates on conceptual bilateral limb movements, which are defined by a *phasic* or *repetitive* structure (the complex phase is the realization of an idea or a concept). It assesses symmetry and dominance in bilateral limb movements and classifies the units with four Formal Relation values (*right hand dominance, left hand dominance, symmetrical,* and *asymmetrical*). The Contact and Formal Relation assessments can be concatenated with the StructureFocus units and thereby provide highly differentiated information about the laterality of kinesic behavior types. Furthermore, the Step 5 codings determine whether in Step 6 the function is assessed for both hands together, e.g. both hands together pantomime drumming, or whether it is assessed separately for the right hand and for the left hand, e.g. one hand scratches the leg while the other hand points to an external location.

In Steps 6 and 7 (Module III: Gesture and Action Module) the bilateral Formal Relation unit, the unilateral limb units (and optionally the *phasic* and *repetitive* head and trunk units) are analyzed with regards to emotional, cognitive, instrumental, and practical functions. In the Function category (Step 6),on the basis of 10 movement criteria, gestures and actions are classified with eleven Function values are defined (*emotion/attitude, emphasis, egocentric deictic, egocentric direction, pantomime, form presentation, spatial relation presentation, motion quality presentation, emblem/social convention, object-oriented action, subject-oriented action*). In the Type category (Step 7), most of the Function values are further specified with Type values.

Supplementary categories are provided for the examination of specific aspects of kinesic behavior: Technique of Presentation, Efforts, Temporal Structure, Target Hemi-Space, Execution Hemi-Space, Referent, and Trigger/Motive. The supplementary categories are assessed for specific values of the main categories. For some main values several supplementary categories may be applied, e.g. for the Function value *motion presentation* the supplementary categories Technique of Presentation, Target Hemi-Space, Execution Hemi-Space, Techniques of Presentation, and Referent. Thus, the decision to analyze a specific supplementary category depends on the research question.

While among the three approaches (complete, module, category) the complete analysis is the most time-consuming option in terms of total time invested, it is nevertheless the most efficient option with regards to the ratio of invested time and gained output. The complete analysis is characterized by strong synergy effects as each assessment step profits from the assessments of the previous steps. As an example, in the Function category assessment the already existing assessments of the Activation, Structure, Focus, Contact and Formal Relation categories are re-used.

1.2 Algorithmic analysis of one module

The analysis of one module is recommended for researchers who want to focus either on kinesic behavior, laterality of limb movements, or gestures and actions. Within a module the algorithmic assessment approach is preserved.

The Kinesic module (Module I) serves to analyze all body movements that are displayed in a certain context. According to defined movement criteria, the ongoing stream of kinesic behavior is segmented into units and these units are then classified. Thus, any movement such as shifts, actions, gestures, self-touches, etc. is registered. Precise analyzes about the frequency, duration, and proportion of time spent with certain kinesic behaviors are obtained and kinesic patterns can be detected. The kinesic analysis can be applied to hand/arm/shoulder, foot/leg, head, and trunk movements. The right and left limbs are assessed separately. The Kinesic module consists of three categories: Activation, Structure, and Focus (see 1.1). The Kinesic module analysis is compatible with automatized techniques for movement recognition (see book I).

The Laterality module (Module II) provides a differentiated analysis of the laterality of limb movements and rests/poses (hand/arm/shoulder and foot/leg). The laterality analysis is relevant for research on the neuropsychology of movement and rest/pose production. It allows the researcher to determine which cerebral hemisphere predominantly contributes to the production of a movement type, e.g. if a specific gesture type is predominantly generated in the right or left hemisphere. Furthermore, it assesses interhemispheric cooperation and the complexity of neural control (see book I). In the Laterality module, all bilateral limb movements and rests/poses are analyzed. The Laterality module consists of two categories: Contact and Formal Relation.

The Gesture and Action module (Module III) includes a classical gesture analysis, mostly in the tradition of Efron (1941) (see book I). The name of the NEUROGES® system historically originates from this module: NEUROpsychological GESture analysis system. As compared to other gesture coding systems, the NEUROGES® Gesture and Action module provides a very fine-grained and highly operationalized classification of gesture types. Furthermore, it includes actions as well as motor correlates of emotional experience. The Gesture and Action module is applied to all conceptual body movements. Most researchers have used the Gesture and Action module for the analysis of hand/arm/shoulder movements. However, likewise gestures and actions of the feet and the head can be submitted to Module III analysis. The Gesture and Action module consists of two categories: Function and Type.

1.3 The analysis of one category

NEUROGES® consists of seven main categories (Activation, Structure, Focus, Contact, Formal Relation, Function, Type) and seven supplementary categories (Techniques of Presentation, Efforts, Temporal Structure, Target Location, Execution Hemi-Space, Referent, Trigger/Motive). The theoretical and empirical background of each main category is described in detail in book I and in the literature cited below in section 1.6. The researcher chooses the category that is most suitable for her/his research question.

In terms of total time spent for the analysis, the analysis of one category is the best option as it focuses on one category only. However, the limitations of this approach are that the ad hoc identification of the to-be-coded units is less reliable than the generation of to-be-coded units based on the algorithmic procedure. The ad hoc identification implies that a specific movement or gesture type, which is the focus of research interests, is picked out of the stream of kinesic behavior. For instance, all movements that match the prototype of a pointing gesture are selected. While this methodological approach is efficient with regards to the expenditure of time, it has the limitation that movements are neglected that do not at first glance perfectly match the target prototype, e.g. a small pointing gesture with the thumb. Ambiguous forms of a movement type might, however, provide valuable information about the movement type itself and about the associated cognitive, emotional, and interactive processes. If the ongoing stream of behavior is submitted to the analysis, the researcher is forced to thoroughly consider each movement and to attribute a value to it. Thereby, the precision of the analysis and the gain in knowledge are substantially improved. Furthermore, hand movement and gesture analyses that are based on the segmentation and classification of an ongoing stream of movement behavior rather than on an a priori selection provide a more reliable basis for quantitative analyses, since the variations of the target movement type are also considered.

1.4 Objectivity of the NEUROGES® values

The NEUROGES® analysis system is objective as its values are defined by highly operationalized movement criteria. Some of these movement criteria can be measured with kinematic methods. The objectivity of the NEUROGES® analysis is further evidenced by the fact that the NEUROGES® value definitions have been successfully used for the development of automatic analysis approaches (HHI NEUROGES® video recognizer and KINEMO).

In this research coding manual, for each category and each value the precise definitions based on movement criteria are given.

1.5 Reliability of the NEUROGES® values

A recent review of 18 empirical studies using NEUROGES® in combination with ELAN for the analysis of hand/arm movements demonstrated a good objectivity and reliability of the main categories and values (Lausberg and Slöetjes, 2016).

In this book, for each NEUROGES® value the reliability score is reported. For the binary Activation category, the interrater reliability is assessed with overlap-merge ratio scores (book I, chapter 14) and for all other categories with EasyDIAg (Holle & Rein, 2015; and book I, chapter 15). The means and standard deviations of the reliability scores of the values provide a frame of reference for the researcher to assess the reliability in their own studies (see also book I, chapters 12 and 16).

1.6 Validity of the NEUROGES® values

With regards to validity, recent studies using NEUROGES® have covered a broad range of different scientific disciplines, e.g. neurology, linguistics/psycholinguistics, psychology, neuropsychology, psychosomatic medicine, evolutionary anthropology, primatology, criminology. Thus far, altogether more than 500 individuals from different cultures of five continents have been investigated, Germans, British, US Americans, francophone and anglophone Canadians, Suisse, Koreans, Kenyans, and Papua New Guineans, including healthy adults and children as well as individuals with brain damage and with mental disorders. Further, NEUROGES® has been used for studies on non-human primates. The multidisciplinary use of the system has demonstrated its applicability for a numerous research questions.

As examples, while NEUROGES® values register universal behavioral phenomena, i.e., all NEUROGES® values were found to occur in all cultures, cultures differ in the frequency of the display of certain values (Skomroch et al., 2013; Kim, 2016; Kim & Lausberg, 2018a, Kim & Lausberg, 2018b). Furthermore, NEUROGES® evidences gender differences in nonverbal behavior (Lausberg et al., 2016; Skomroch et al., 2013). Several studies have demonstrated the sensitivity of the NEUROGES® system to conditions of stress, among others in children and adolescents (e.g. Densing et al., 2017; Bryjovà et al., 2013; Heubach, 2016) and to happy versus sad stimuli (Kim, 2016). NEUROGES® is sensitive to personality traits and mental disorders (Reinecke et al., 2018a; Lausberg et al, 2016; Helmich et al., 2011; Lausberg et al., 2010) as well as to improvement in mental health in psychotherapy (e.g. Reinecke et al., 2018b; Neumann et al., 2017; Kreyenbrink et al., 2017; Dvoretska et al., 2014; Gabor et al., 2014; Kryger, 2010), and it shows the quality of interactive processes (Gabor et al., 2015; Dvoretska et al., 2013; Lausberg 2011; Dvoretska, 2009).

Furthermore, NEUROGES® differentiates between different locations of brain damage and associated neuropsychological deficits (Hogrefe et al, 2016; Lausberg et al., 2003) and it is sensitive to alterations in kinesic behavior secondary to mild head trauma (Helmich et al., 2018). It is effective for investigating the neuropsychology of gesture and hand movement in relation to spatial cognition and other cognitive processes (Helmich & Lausberg, 2014; Lausberg et al., 2007; Lausberg & Kita, 2003; Lausberg et al., 2003; Lausberg & Kita, 2002; Lausberg et al., 2000), including speech (Helmich et al., 2014; Skomroch et al., 2013; Skomroch & Lausberg 2013; Lausberg & Kita, 2003), and in relation to intelligence (Dvoretska & Lausberg, 2013; Sassenberg et al, 2011; Sassenberg & van der Meer, 2010; Wartenburger et al., 2010).

Finally, NEUROGES® is suitable for the development of automatic approaches (Juszczyk & Ciecierski, 2016, Postma-Nilsenová et al., 2013; Rein 2013; Masneri et al., 2010).

Research on the validity of the NEUROGES® categories and values is an ongoing process. The interested researcher finds the permanently updated overview on the publications on the website http://neuroges.neuroges-bast.info/publications.

1.7 Occurrence, frequency, and duration of the NEUROGES® values

Data on the occurrence, the frequency, and the duration of the NEUROGES® values (movement types) are based on the NEUROGES® archive. Six empirical studies with different experimental settings including 191 healthy individuals (99 females, 92 males) from Germany, United States, Canada, Korea, and Papua New Guinea were included in the analyses. The statistical analyses were conducted by Dr. Melanie Seiler and the author.

Occurrence refers to how many individuals in the sample show the NEUROGES® value in their nonverbal kinesic behavior. As some NEUROGES® values were not examined in all studies, for some values the sample size is smaller than 191. Reported is the percentage of individuals in the sample who display the respective value. As an example, only 37 % of individuals in the sample show the value *on attached object* as part of their kinesic repertoire.

Frequency refers to how often in a minute a unit with the respective value is displayed. Reported is the Mean number per minute (M) ± Standard Deviation (SD) as well as the Median. The calculation of the Mean frequency is based on all individuals of the sample including those who do not display the value. As an example, the mean frequency of right hand *repetitive* units is 2.28 ± 1.71; 1.95 units per minute.

Duration refers to how many seconds a unit with the respective value lasts. Reported is the Mean duration in seconds (M) ± Standard Deviation (SD) as well as the Median. As the duration of a behavioral phenomenon can only be determined if the phenomenon is displayed by an individual, the calculation of the Mean duration of a value unit is based only to those individuals in the sample who display the value (compare occurrence). As an example, the Mean duration of left hand *in space* units is 2.81 ± 1.02; 2.55 seconds per unit.

In this book, data on the occurrence, the frequency, and the duration of the Module I values are provided separately for the right and left hands. Given that Module II only assesses bilateral units, the data on the occurrence, the frequency, and the duration of the Module II values refer to bilateral hand movements. Finally, data on the occurrence, the frequency, and the duration of the Module III values are provided separately for the right hand, the left hand, and bimanual movements. Note that these data are only approximate, since in some studies of the NEUROGES® archive *right hand dominance* and *left hand dominance* units (rarely occurring values based on the Formal Relation assessment) were further coded as right hand units and left hand units while in other studies they were coded as both hand units (see explanation in 8.2.2).

1.8 How to use the coding manual

In this book, each category is dealt with in a separate chapter. This enables researchers who want to use only one category or only one module of the NEUROGES® system to directly find the desired information. Each chapter can be understood by itself and it is not necessary to read the other chapters (only occasionally, there is reference to specific sections in other chapters).

The coding manuals of the categories are consistently structured as follows:

- **Definition of the category**: An overview on the category with short definitions of the values and their reliability scores is provided.

- **Generation of to-be-coded category units**[2]: This section informs researchers who conduct the complete algorithmic analysis or the algorithmic analysis of Module I, how the to-be-coded units for the assessment step are generated based on the units from the previous step.
- **Alternative generation of to-be-coded category units:** This section provides recommendations for researchers who conduct the analysis of one category or who start with Module II or III, i.e., who have no units from previous steps to start with, how to generate units from the scratch.
- **Criteria for the definition of the category values**: In this section, the movement criteria that are used to define the values of the category are defined in a highly operationalized manner.
- **Definitions of the category values**: With reference to the movement criteria, each category value is precisely defined
  - o Short definition
  - o Definition
  - o Meeting the criteria (definition according to the movement criteria)
  - o Data on occurrence, frequency, and duration of the value
  - o ♦ Examples: In the Modules I and II, each value is illustrated by several examples, separately for the four parts of the body. For space-saving reasons, for the 35 Module III values and the 29 values of the Supplementary categories no written examples are given. However, in the Formal Relation category, which in the complete algorithmic analysis is the last assessment step before Module III, as an illustration, the examples include information about the Module III coding. Note that the interactive video learning tool provides video examples for all values (see 1.9).
  - o Differentiate the value from…: Having been most appreciated by many raters, this section informs how to distinguish the value from other values that share certain movement features and that, therefore, may be mixed up.
- **Procedure in NEUROGES® -ELAN**: In this section, it is described step by step how researcher realizes the assessment in the NEUROGES® -ELAN template.

2 Only in the first step, the Activation category, this section is named: "Data submitted to the Activation assessment".

1.9 How to use the interactive video learning tool, the NEUROGES® template file for the multimedia annotation ELAN, and the annotated NEUROGES® training videos

The interactive video learning tool, the NEUROGES® template file, and four annotated NEUROGES® training videos are provided on the NEUROGES® website www.neuroges-bast.info in the password protected login area. In order to receive your individual pass word for the login area please send the code of this book (see page X) to c.klabunde@dshs-koeln.de and h.lausberg@dshs-koeln.de.

The development and application of the interactive video learning tool is described in detail in book I, Chapter 13. The use of the interactive video learning is self-explanatory. The user is guided through the NEUROGES® algorithm in which each NEUROGES® value is illustrated by one or more video examples.

For the practical application of the NEUROGES® analysis it is recommended to use the system together with the multi-medial annotator software ELAN. In numerous aspects, ELAN provides the perfect software environment for applying the NEUROGES® analysis system. Therefore, since 2006, NEUROGES® has been combined with ELAN and in their developments the NEUROGES® system and the annotation tool ELAN have mutually influenced each other (Lausberg & Slöetjes, 2009; Lausberg & Slöetjes, 2016). For its application with ELAN, the NEUROGES® algorithm has been translated into a ready-to-use NEUROGES® -ELAN template, which is basically an electronic rating scale. Tab. 1 shows how the NEUROGES® categories are represented as tiers in the NEUROGES® -ELAN template.

Tab. 1 evidences that the NEUROGES® -ELAN template is very comprehensive. However, if additional tiers are needed for very specific research question, e.g. the Type analysis of head movements, the tier simply has to be duplicated and relabeled.

The use of the NEUROGES® -ELAN template is described in detail in book I, Chapter 9 (Step by Step Instruction in NEUROGES® Coding with ELAN). General guides how to use ELAN are available on the website https://tla.mpi.nl/tools/tla-tools/elan/.

Furthermore, four annotated NEUROGES® training videos are provided on the NEUROGES® website that enable the researcher to train analyzing videos with NEUROGES® -ELAN. The labels of the videos, i.e., Beginner, Intermediate, Advanced, and Expert, indicate the degree of difficulty. There is an instruction how to use the training videos (written by Harald Skomroch).

Tab. 1: Modules, categories, corresponding ELAN tiers, and values in the NEUROGES®-ELAN template

Module	Category	ELAN tiers	Values
I	Activation	rh_Activation_R0 lh_Activation_R0 rh_Activation_R1 lh_Activation_R1 rf_Activation_R0 lf_Activation_R0 rf_Activation_R1 lf_Activation_R1 trunk_Activation_R0 trunk_Activation_R1 head_Activation_R0 head_Activation_R1	*movement* *rest/pose* *?*
I	Structure	rh_Structure_R0 lh_Structure_R0 rh_Structure_R1 lh_Structure_R1 rf_Structure_R0 lf_Structure_R0 rf_Structure_R1 lf_Structure_R1 trunk_Structure_R0 trunk_Structure_R1 head_Structure_R0 head_Structure_R1	*irregular* *repetitive* *phasic* *aborted* *shift* *r/p rest* *r/p pose* *(rest/pose)** *?*
I	Focus	rh_Focus_R0 lh_Focus_R0 rh_Focus_R1 lh_Focus_R1 rf_Focus_R0 lf_Focus_R0 rf_Focus_R1 lf_Focus_R1	*within body* *on body* *on attached object* *on separate object* *on person* *in space* *(aborted)** *(shift)** *?*
II	Contact	bh_Contact_R0 bh_Contact_R1 bf_Contact_R0 bf_Contact_R1	*act on each other* *act as a unit* *act apart* *prep-retract* *r/p crossed* *r/p closed* *r/p open* *?*

Tab. 1: Continued

Module	Category	ELAN tiers	Values
II	Formal Relation	bh_Formal Relation_R0 bh_Formal Relation_R1 bf_Formal Relation_R0 bf_Formal Relation_R1	*symmetrical* *right hand dominance* *left hand dominance* *asymmetrical* *(prep-retract)**
III	Function	bh_Function_R0 rh_Function_R0 lh_Function_R0 bh_Function_R1 rh_Function_R1 lh_Function_R1 bf_Function_R0 rf_Function_R0 lf_Function_R0 bf_Function_R1 rf_Function_R1 lf_Function_R1 head_Function_R0 head_Function_R1 trunk_Function_R0 trunk_Function_R1	*emotion/attitude* *emphasis* *egocentric deictic* *egocentric direction* *pantomime* *form presentation* *spatial relation* *presentation* *motion quality* *presentation* *object-oriented action* *subject-oriented action* *emblem/social convention* *different functions* *(prep-retract)**
III	Type	bh_Type_R0 rh_Type_R0 lh_Type_R0 bh_Type_R1 rh_Type_R1 lh_Type_R1	*rise* *fall* *clap/beat* *shrug* *other e-motion* *baton* *superimposed* *back-toss* *palm-out* *external target* *You* *self* *body* *neutral* *imperative* *self-related* *transitive* *intransitive* *passive* *shape*

(*continued on next page*)

Tab. 1: Continued

Module	Category	ELAN tiers	Values
			size *route* *position* *manner* *dynamics*
S (Supplementary)	Technique of Presentation	bh_Technique of Presentation_R0 rh_Technique of Presentation_R0 lh_Technique of Presentation_R0 bh_Technique of Presentation_R1 rh_Technique of Presentation_R1 lh_Technique of Presentation_R1	*hand-as-object* *enclosure* *palpating* *tracing*
S	Effort	bh_Effort_R0 rh_Effort_R0 lh_Effort_R0 bh_Effort_R1 rh_Effort_R1 lh_Effort_R1	*free* *bound* *light* *strong* *heavy* *sustained* *sudden* *indirect* *direct*
S	Temporal Structure	bh_Temporal Structure_R0 rh_Temporal Structure_R0 lh_Temporal Structure_R0 bh_Temporal Structure_R1 rh_Temporal Structure_R1 lh_Temporal Structure_R1	*single accents* *metrical* *rhythmical*
s	Target Location	bh_Target Location _R0 rh_Target Location_R0 lh_Target Location _R0 bh_Target Location _R1 rh_Target Location_R1 lh_Target Location _R1	*right side* *left side* *body-midline* *both sides*
S	Execution Hemi-Space	bh_Execution Hemi-Space_R0 rh_Execution	*ipsilateral* *contralateral* *body-midline* *ipsi-contra*

Tab. 1: Continued

Module	Category	ELAN tiers	Values
		Hemi-Space_R0 lh_Execution Hemi-Space_R0 bh_Execution Hemi-Space_R1 rh_Execution Hemi-Space_R1 lh_Execution Hemi-Space_R1	
S	Referent	bh_Referent_R0 rh_Referent_R0 lh_Referent_R0 bh_Referent_R1 rh_Referent_R1 lh_Referent_R1	*material* *non-material*
S	Trigger/ Motive	bh_Trigger/Motive_R0 rh_Trigger/Motive_R0 lh_Trigger/Motive_R0 bh_Trigger/Motive_R1 rh_Trigger/Motive_R1 lh_Trigger/Motive_R1	*physical regulation* *visual appearance* *mental regulation* *trigger/motive unknown*
	Phases	***_Phases_R0 _Phases_R1	*complex static* *complex motion* *transport complete* *transport partial* *retraction complete* *retraction partial*

Notes:
R0 These are the tiers for Rater A
R1 These are the tiers for Rater B
bh These are the tiers for both hands movements
rh These are the tiers for right hand movements
lh These are the tiers for left hand movements
r/p These values serve the analysis of *rests* and *poses*
()* These values are provided only in the template for re-coding of a unit.
? In the template, the value***?*** is provided for work-in-progress. If you are not sure about the beginning or end of a unit or the value of the unit and you want to get back to this unit later again, mark the unit preliminarily with this value.
*** Researchers who use the tier Phases have to adapt its label according to the Structure tier that they want to specify, e.g. rh_Phases_R0 or lf_Phases_R0. The definitions of the phases are given in 4.3.

1.10 How to acquire the NEUROGES® certificate

The NEUROGES® certificate is registered as European Union trademark by the European Union Intellectual Property Office. The acquisition of the certificate is recommended as it guarantees a reliable application of the NEUROGES® system in research. The certification is given after successful passing of the exam. Applicants should thoroughly study the category coding manuals in this book, the interactive video learning tool, and the four NEUROGES® training files before registering for the exam. The exam can be taken for single categories, single modules, or the whole system. For more information about the exam and certificate see http://neuroges.neuroges-bast.info/training and contact c.klabunde@dshs-koeln.de and h.lausberg@dshs-koeln.de.

2 Parts of the body submitted to the analysis

The NEUROGES® system analyzes the kinesic behavior of the body. For the purpose of the analysis and based on anatomical and neuroanatomical grounds, the body is divided in four parts: upper limbs, lower limbs, head, and trunk. The NEUROGES® system allows the researcher to choose if (s)he wants to code all four parts of the body or to select one, two, or three parts (see Fig. 1).

In a natural context, often more than one part of the body or even the whole body is involved in a movement. For many research questions, however, it is efficient to focus on one part of the body, as the different parts of the body fulfil different functions. As an example, a researcher who is interested in cognitive processes and wants to study gestures might want to focus on the upper limbs, as gestures are most often executed by the hands, and more rarely by the head and feet. On the other hand, a researcher, who is interested in openness and rapport in a therapy session might include the analysis to trunk movements in his study (see book I, 2.1.4). Thus, the research question determines if all parts of the body or just one or two parts are studied. Finally, sometimes the video material only allows for the examination of one or two parts of the body, e.g. if the video only shows the upper body.

2.1 Upper limbs

The upper limbs comprise the fingers, hands, arms, and shoulders. Upper limb movements are anatomically defined by motions in the finger, hand, wrist, elbow, and shoulder articulations including those with the collarbone and shoulder blade relative to the trunk. Thus, not only movements of the mere shoulder joint, i.e., inward and outward rotation, adduction and abduction, anteversion and retroversion, but also lifting and lowering, and moving backward and forward of the shoulder are coded as upper limb movements.

Note that in upper limb movements involving the shoulder joints, the upper arm is moved relative to the trunk, e.g. the arm is lifted, while in the rare case of isolated trunk movements involving the shoulder joint, the trunk is moved relative to the upper arm, e.g. leaning forward in a chair but without changing the positions of the arms on the armrests.

The distal muscles of the upper limbs (fingers, hands) can be controlled only by the motor cortex of the contralateral cerebral hemisphere, i.e., the right hand by the left hemisphere. In contrast, the proximal muscles of an upper limb, i.e., the shoulders and upper arms can be controlled by both cerebral hemispheres via contralateral and ipsilateral pathways.

In upper limb movements, often, fingers, hand, arm, and shoulder move together. However, either subpart can move isolated, such as a thumb toss or a shoulder shrug. Therefore, simultaneous isolated movements of the finger(s) or hand and of the shoulder may occur, e.g. a thumb toss simultaneously with a shoulder shrug. With regards to the practical coding with NEUROGES®, in this rare case only **one** *movement* unit is tagged.

2.2 Lower limbs

The lower limbs comprise the toes, feet, legs, hips, and buttocks. Lower limb movements are anatomically defined by motions in the toe, foot, ankle, knee and hip articulations relative to the trunk.

Note that in lower limb movements involving the hip joint, the thigh is moved relative to the trunk, e.g. the thigh is lifted, while in trunk movements involving the hip joint, the trunk is moved relative to the thigh, e.g. leaning forward with the trunk when sitting.

As for the upper limbs, the distal muscles, i.e., the toes and feet can only be controlled by the contralateral cerebral hemisphere, while the proximal muscles of the lower limbs, i.e., the thigh can be controlled by the motor cortex of both cerebral hemispheres. With regards to the practical coding, the same rules apply as for the upper limbs.

2.3 Head

Head and neck movements are anatomically defined by motions in the atlanto-occipital joints (between lower surface of the skull and the first vertebra), i.e., nodding, and in the cervical spine relative to the thoracic spine, i.e., turning the head, bending it forward, backward, and sideward.

Head and neck muscles are controlled by both cerebral hemispheres, with a stronger impact of the contralateral hemisphere.

2.4 Trunk

The trunk is the central part of the body from which extend the neck with head and the limbs. It includes the abdomen, the back, the thorax, and the pelvis. Trunk movements are motions in the thoracic, lumbar and sacral spine and in the hip and shoulder joints relative to the limbs. Included are motions of joints within the pelvis and ribcage.

Trunk movements are leaning forward, backward, and sideward, rotating, or contracting, expanding, tilting the pelvis forward, backward, and sideward.

At the level of the spine, the trunk is controlled by different neural pathways than the limbs. While it shares with the lower limbs the innervation of anti-gravity muscles, it differs especially from the control of the upper limbs, neck and head.

In NEUROGES®, the four parts of the body are coded independently of each other. However, the movements and rests, respectively, of the four parts can be related to each other, which is technically realized by a concatenation procedure. The concatenation procedure delivers complex *movement* units, e.g. simultaneous turning of head, turning of trunk, and pointing with right hand, or *rest/pose* units, e.g. upper limbs and lower limbs crossed in rest. The concatenation procedure for the four parts of the body is described in Chapter 3.

With regards to the upper and lower limbs, in Module I the right and left limbs are coded separately of each other, and in the Modules II and III, the movements of the right and left limbs are related to each other.

It has to be noted that thus far, the large majority of researchers has used NEUROGES® to analyze the upper limbs. Only few publications deal with an analysis of all four parts of the body, i.e., the whole body (Lausberg, 2011). The researchers' preference for the analysis of upper limb movements entails that the reliability of the NEUROGES® system has been established on the basis of empirical studies using NEUROGES® for the analysis of upper limb movements. There is, however, little reason to assume that the reliability of NEUROGES® might differ for the other three parts of the body, as the categories and values are the same for all four parts of the body. However, as a precautionary measure, researchers who aim at investigating head, trunk, or lower limbs are recommended to carefully control the reliability in their studies.

II. The Kinesic Module (Module I)

The Kinesic Module (Module I) analyses all body movements that are displayed in a certain context. Thus, it serves to register classical types of kinesic behavior, such as gestures, head motions, trunk shifts, self-touches, repetitive foot movements, closed rest positions, etc. (see book I). These types emerge at the end of the Kinesic Module analysis as StructureFocus values, which are fine-grained types of kinesic behavior.

The StructureFocus values are based on an algorithmic three steps analysis. The three categories Activation, Structure, and Focus focus on certain dimensions of body movement that are valid with regards to mental processes: the analysis of the combination of motion, position, and muscle contraction provides information about the individual's extent of motor activity (Activation category), the analysis of the trajectory and of its structure about mental states and processes (Structure category), and the analysis of the locus of limb movement about sensory stimulation patterns (and if it applies to attention processes) (Focus category). The final concatenation of the analyses of these basic components of body movement results in the StructureFocus values.

Technically, according to defined movement criteria, the ongoing stream of body movements is segmented into units and these units are then classified with values. Precise analyses about the frequency, duration, and proportion of time spent with certain kinesic behaviors are obtained and kinesic patterns can be detected. The kinesic analysis can be applied to hand/arm/shoulder, foot/leg, head, and trunk movements. The right and left limbs are assessed separately.

3 The Activation category

3.1 Definition of the Activation category

The Activation category segments the ongoing stream of kinesic behavior into *movement* and *rest/pose* units (see Fig. 2). The Activation category assessment can be applied to all four parts of the body (upper limbs, lower limbs, head, and trunk).

The two values *movement* and *rest/pose* are defined by the three criteria motion vs. stillness, actively held position vs. gravity-aligned / supported position, muscle contraction vs. relaxation. Tab. 2 shows the short definitions of the two Activation values and the interrater reliability scores (from Lausberg & Slöetjes, 2016).

Thereby, the Activation category measures the extent of an individual's (psycho-)motor activity (see book I, section II). While the analysis of all four parts of the body enables to register motor activity of the whole body, for many research questions the analysis of only the upper limbs has been sufficient.

In the clinical domain, the Activation category enables to operationalize hypo- and hyperactivity (e.g. as listed in the International Classification of Diseases ICD and in the Diagnostic and Statistical Manual of Mental Disorders DSM) by providing data about the frequency (number / minute), the duration (seconds / unit) and proportion of time (seconds / minute) of *movement* versus *rest/pose* units. With the exception of severe pathological states of hyper- or hypoactivity, in most individuals, there is a permanent alternation between *movement* units and *rest/pose* units. ♦ Example: the right hand rests on the arm rest (*rest/pose* unit) ⇒ the hand rises, traces a circle, moves back to lap (*movement* unit) ⇒ rests on the knee (*rest/pose* unit) ⇒ knee moves and hand is passively moved with the knee (continuation of the *rest/pose* unit) ⇒ hand rises again, forms a fist, moves back to waist and is put on the hip, while trunk becomes erect and other hand as well is put on the hip (*movement* unit) ⇒ posing with erect trunk and hands put on the hips (*rest/pose* unit) ⇒ rises again, forms a fist, moves back to lap (*movement* unit) ⇒ rests in lap (*rest/pose* unit).

3.2 Data submitted to the Activation assessment

In the Activation category (Step 1 of Module I), for each part of the body, i.e., the upper limbs, the lower limbs, the head, and the trunk, the ongoing flow of the

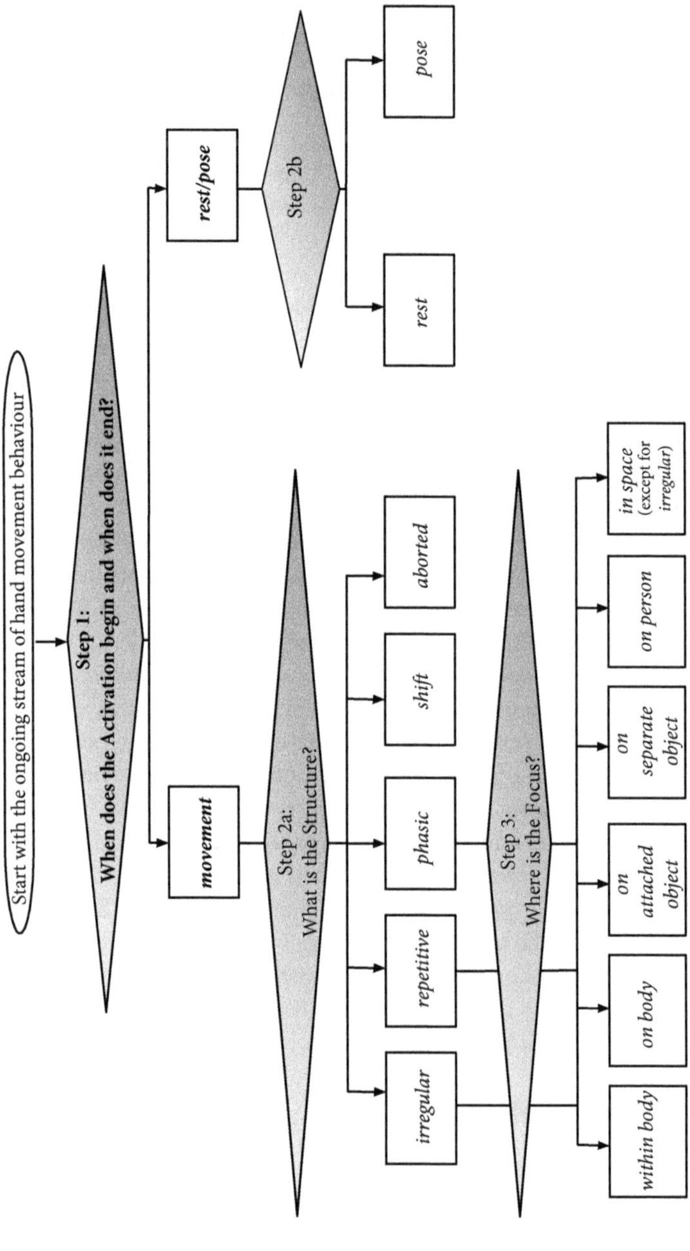

Fig. 2: The analysis algorithm for the Kinesic module (Module I) with the Activation category (Step 1) in fat print

Tab. 2: Short definitions and reliabilities of the Activation values

Activation value	**Short definition**	**Reliability * M ± SD**
movement	part of the body in active motion, potentially including transient motionless phases in an actively held position	.80 ± .05
rest/pose	part of the body rests or poses	idem

* Interrater reliability as measured with Merge-Overlap (from Lausberg & Slöetjes, 2016)

movement behavior is screened for *movement* versus *rest/pose*. The upper and lower limbs, respectively, are coded separately for the right and left sides.

Procedurally, only the *movement* units need to be tagged, as the *rest/pose* units are defined by the absence of a *movement* unit (for the technical procedure of the *rest/pose* unit generation in NEUROGES® -ELAN see 3.5).

3.3 Criteria for the definition of the Activation values

The Activation values are defined according to the following criteria[3]:

Motion vs. Stillness: Motion is defined as a change in position of the part of the body with respect to time. In contrast, in stillness the part of the body remains in a constant position.

Actively Held Position vs. Gravity-Aligned / Supported Position: In case of stillness, the part of the body can be either in a position that is aligned in gravity or supported against gravity (aligned / supported position) or it can be held against gravity (actively held position).

The gravity-aligned position requires no additional muscle activation other than that of the antigravity muscles. Antigravity muscles are muscles, mainly extensors of the knees, hips, and back, that by their tone resist the constant pull of gravity in the maintenance of a normal posture, e.g. as in upright standing or upright sitting. In the supported position the part of the body is supported by a physical entity, e.g. hand/arm resting in the lap or trunk leaning against the back of the chair. Thus, the aligned / supported position requires no additional muscle activation.

3 Note that the definition of the terms in NEUROGES® may deviate from the general definition of these terms, as they are adapted to the requirements of movement behavior analysis.

In contrast, in an actively held position the part of the body is in a position that requires muscle contraction other than that of the antigravity muscles, e.g. holding the arm or the leg stretched out. The actively held position implies isometric contraction of muscles. An actively held position can occur within a *movement* unit, e.g. a pointing gesture in which the extended arm with the shaped hand is held for a moment before being retracted. The actively held position within a *movement* unit serves emphasis or it indicates a hesitation, dysfluency, or disruption.

In rare cases, the actively held position may constitute a *pose* unit. It often contributes to a whole body pose and in case of the limbs, they are typically held in the body near space (near kinesphere, see 8.3). The actively held position in a *pose* is held for a much longer period of time than the actively held position within a *movement*, as a *pose* is kind of a settlement. While it is the theoretical claim of NEUROGES® to not operate with absolute / arbitrary time frames, however, based on the NEUROGES® archive data it is suggested to consider a *pose* if the actively held position is held for longer than four seconds.

Muscle Contraction vs. Relaxation: Muscle contraction can be isometric or isotonic. In isometric activation the muscle length does not change during contraction. This results in an actively held constant position of the limb. In contrast, in isotonic activation, the tension remains unchanged but the muscle length changes, resulting in a motion.

In NEUROGES®, contraction is defined as the visible or inferred contraction of muscles other than the antigravity muscles. When analyzing videos a muscle contraction may be visible, i.e., the observer can actually see how specific muscle groups contract. However, in most cases the contraction is not directly visible and the observer infers from the actively held position or the displacement of the part of the body that the muscles must be contracted because the position or the displacement of that part of the body cannot be explained otherwise.

In a *movement* unit, motion is associated with isotonic muscle contraction. Note that the rare case of the combination of motion and muscle relaxation is passive motion, i.e., the part of the body **is** moved. For conceptual reasons, i.e., as the Activion category serves to register an individual's level of motor activity, a passive motion is coded as a *rest/pose* unit.

Note that the normal activity of the antigravity muscles is not coded as *movement*. Thus, researchers who analyze the lower limbs in a standing person do not code the antigravity function of the lower limb as a *movement*. If there is a supporting leg and a free leg, only the activity of the free leg is coded as *movement*. As an example, if the person stands on the left leg and points with the right foot, this is coded as right limb *movement* unit and left limb *rest/pose* unit.

3.4 Definitions of the Activation values

3.4.1 *movement*

Short definition

THE PART OF THE BODY IN ACTIVE MOTION, POTENTIALLY INCLUDING TRANSIENT MOTIONLESS PHASES IN AN ACTIVELY HELD POSITION

Definition

A *movement* unit is defined by motion and muscle contraction. The combination of motion and muscle contraction (active motion) matches the general definition of a movement.

Short motionless phases with an actively held position may be embedded in the *movement* unit, e.g. pointing with the hand and holding still the shaped hand against gravity for a moment. In other words, a transient motionless phase is part of the *movement* unit if the part of body is held against gravity and if the motionless phase is framed by motion phases.

At the end of a *movement*, the moving person might need some time to find a comfortable *rest* position or to establish a *pose*. The searching of the *rest/pose* position happens during the retraction phase and it is therefore coded as part of the *movement* unit, i.e., the *rest/pose* unit only starts when the part of the body has come to stillness and remains in a constant position. Technically, the transition from a *movement* unit to a *rest/pose* unit is coded according to Seyfeddinipur (2006). It is identified by the transition from the last blurred video frame to the first clear video frame. Vice versa, the transition from a *rest/pose* unit to a *movement* unit is identified by the transition from the last clear video frame to the first blurred video frame.

In a natural context, especially for the limbs, often more than one subpart of the limb is involved in a movement. As an example, fingers, hand, arm, and shoulder move together. However, each subpart can move isolated, such as a thumb toss or a shoulder shrug. Therefore, rarely, simultaneous isolated movements of the fingers or hand and of the shoulder (or toes and thigh) may occur, e.g. a hand toss and a simultaneous shoulder shrug. No matter if the two subparts of one limb move together or isolated, for that limb only **one** *movement* unit is coded and the assessments of the subsequent NEUROGES® categories refers to the more prominent one of the two isolated movements, e.g. the shoulder shrug. In the

NEUROGES® -ELAN, the researcher can use the tier Notes to note that simultaneous isolated movements within the limb occurred.

Meeting the criteria

Motion vs. Stillness: In most *movement* units, there is motion. Stillness is only compatible with a *movement* unit, if there is an actively held position.

Actively Held Position vs. Gravity-Aligned / Supported Position: If there is an actively held position, in which the part of the body is held against gravity within the *movement,* the holding is of short duration (according to the NEUROGES® archive data less than four seconds).

Muscle Contraction vs. Relaxation: There is visible or inferred muscle contraction. It is isotonic in motion and isometric in an actively held position.

Occurrence (see 1.7): Right hand *movement* units are displayed by 100 % of the individuals in the NEUROGES® archive sample (n = 163), and left hand *movement* units by 100 %.

Frequency (see 1.7): In the NEUROGES® archive sample, right hand *movement* units were displayed with a frequency (Mean ± Standard Deviation; Median) of 6.06 ± 2.93; 5.60 units per minute, and left hand *movement* units with a frequency of 6.07 ± 3.02; 5.78.

Duration (see 1.7): The duration (Mean ± Standard Deviation; Median) of right hand *movement* units was 8.67 ± 9.24; 4.94 seconds per unit, and that of left hand *movement* units 8.70 ± 9.09; 5.75 seconds per unit.

Examples for *movement* units

- ◆ upper limbs: hand displaying self-touch movements
- ◆ lower limbs: shifting the legs to a crossed position
- ◆ head: turning the head
- ◆ trunk: shifting the trunk from the right side to the left side

Differentiate *movement* from…

🖉 no movement in *rest/pose*: Human observers have individually different thresholds concerning the perception of body movement. Some raters are very sensitive and they perceive fine movements of the fingers, while other raters notice only rather big movements. Factors that influence a rater's movement perception are his/her experience in coding movement behavior, his/her own movement experience, and his/her motivation. To improve the raters' sensitivity and the inter-rater agreement, raters should aim at coding any movement they perceive.

- passive motion in *rest/pose* (subtype: *rest*): In passive motion, the part of the body **is moved**, i.e., the motion is secondary to the movement of another agent. As an example, the hand rests on the knee, which moves repetitively up and down. In this case, the knee moves but the hand is in *rest*. Or, when a person with a floppy muscle tonus drops the arm over an armrest with the hand hanging free in space, a rebound movement of the forearm might occur. These passive motions are not coded as *movement* units, since the criterion of muscle contraction is not fulfilled. They are coded as *rest/pose* units (subtype: *rest*). Novice raters, who often focus primarily on the criterion motion, may oversee this aspect. However, they will typically recognize (and correct) the error when they assess the Structure category.
- an actively held position in *rest/pose* (subtype: *pose*): In rare cases, in a *pose*, there is an actively held position, in which the part of the body is held against gravity. The actively held position is held longer than the actively held position within a *movement,* it is more often held in the body-near space, and it may contribute to a static whole body expression, i.e., a whole body pose.

3.4.2 *rest/pose*

Short definition

THE PART OF THE BODY RESTS OR POSES

Definition

A *rest/pose* unit is primarily defined by stillness and a gravity-aligned/supported position of the part of the body.

Only in rare cases, there is a long actively held position (subtype: *pose*) or passive motion (subtype: *rest*).

Meeting the criteria

Motion vs. Stillness: There is stillness. The exception is passive motion in a *rest*.

Actively Held Position vs. Gravity-Aligned / Supported Position: There is a gravity-aligned / supported position of the part of the body. The exception is an actively held position in a *pose*. It is of a long duration and the part of the body often contributes to a whole body expression and in case of the limbs, they are often held in the body-near space.

Muscle Contraction vs. Relaxation: This is the criterion that distinguishes the two subtypes *rest* and *pose* (see Chapter 4: R/P Structure values). In *rest*, there is muscle relaxation. In *pose*, there is isometric muscle contraction.

Examples for *rest/pose* units

- upper limbs: arms/hands rest on the arm rests (aligned/supported position) (*rest*)
- upper limbs: hands and arms contribute to the "thinker pose" (aligned/supported position) (*pose*)
- lower limbs: sitting person with legs crossed, relaxed muscles except from activation of the antigravity muscles (aligned/supported position) (*rest*)
- lower limbs: sitting person with legs crossed, muscles tensed with the foot held in flexed position (actively held position) (*pose*)
- head: sitting person with head in normal upright position, relaxed muscles except from activation of the antigravity muscles (aligned/supported position) (*rest*)
- head: sitting person, head rests in the hand of the vertically positioned forearm (aligned/supported position) (*rest*)
- head: holding the head tilted in an "flirtatious" attitude (actively held position) (*pose*)
- trunk: sitting person in normal upright position, relaxed muscles except from activation of the antigravity muscles (aligned/supported position) (*rest*)
- trunk: sitting person with trunk leaning against back of the chair (aligned/supported position) (*rest*)
- trunk: sitting upright with trunk erect and chest out in an "arrogant pose" (actively held position) (*pose*)

Differentiate *rest/pose* units from…

- *irregular movement*: In continuous *irregular movements* such as hand-to-hand fidgeting, it may be hard to distinguish retarded or sustained *movements* or spatially minimal *movements* from *rests*. As *irregular* movements tend to be an ongoing background motor activity that fluctuates, do **not** code a *rest/pose* unit if you cannot clearly detect a stillness of the hand.
- actively held position in a *movement* unit: An actively held position in a *movement* unit is typically executed isolated by a limb and only held for a short time, e.g. a gesture, in which the hand is transported in the gesture/action space and held for a movement to emphasize the message, e.g. showing a form. In contrast, an actively held position in a *pose* is often part of a whole body expression. If it occurs in an isolated limb, e.g. sitting with crossed legs and the foot flexed, it is typically held longer than an actively held position in a *movement* unit and it is held in the body-near space.

***Rest/pose* positions**

Researchers who analyze more than one part of the body are able to identify *rest/pose* positions. A *rest/pose* position is defined as a specific static arrangement of two, three, or all four parts of the body, e.g. sitting comfortably with crossed legs in a chair with the arms resting on the arm rests. Thus, the part of the body does not *rest/pose* in isolation but it rests together with other parts of the body, and together they form a *rest/pose* position.

Since *rest/pose* positions might contain *rests* of some parts of the body and *poses* of other parts, e.g. foot flexed but rest of the body relaxed, the two subtypes *rest* (muscle relaxation) and *pose* (isometric muscle contraction) are not separated in the Activation category analysis, which technically in NEUROGES® -ELAN serves as the basis for the concatenation of simultaneous *rest/pose* units of the four parts of the body in order to generate *rest/pose* position (see below 3.5). The differentiation between *rest* and *pose* will be conducted in the Structure category assessment.

3.5 Procedure for Step 1 / Module I in NEUROGES® -ELAN

It is strongly recommended to use the NEUROGES® analysis system in combination with the annotation software ELAN: https://tla.mpi.nl/tools/tla-tools/elan/. Different versions of user guides are available on the ELAN website, e.g. a practical overview in the "How-to Guide". A step-by-step instruction that is specifically tailored to the use of ELAN in combination with NEUROGES® is published in book I, section III.

Download the NEUROGES® -template from the login area on the NEUROGES® website www.neuroges-bast.info (in order to receive your individual password for the login area on the NEUROGES® website please send the code of this book on page X to c.klabunde@dshs-koeln.de and h.lausberg@dshs-koeln.de). Open the template in ELAN. Note that in this book, instructions for ELAN refer to the version 5.0.

If you code the NEUROGES® training eafs, you do not need to download the template, but you open the eaf files directly in ELAN.

To code the Activation category with the NEUROGES® -template proceed as follows:

First, attribute your initials and the identification of the videotaped participant whom you are going to analyze to the Activation tiers in the template:

Go to the function Tier > Change Tier Attributes:

Click on the tier rh_Activation_R0 (Rater 0).

In the field Tier Name, change the template initials R0 into your initials (for instance: RX)

In the field Participant enter the identification of the videotaped person whose behavior you are going to analyze.
In the field Annotator enter your name.

Proceed analogously for the lh_Activation tier.

(Go to the function Tier > Change Tier Attributes:

Click on the tier lh_Activation_R0.

In the field Tier Name, change the template initials R0 into your initials (hereafter RX)

In the field Participant enter the identification of the videotaped person whose behavior you are going to code.
In the field Annotator enter your name.)

Then start coding. In the template, the following values are provided for the Activation category:

movement

rest/pose

?

On the tier rh_Activation_RX tag all right hand *movement* units and mark them with the value *movement.*

Once you have finished tagging all right hand movements, on the tier lh_Activation_RX tag all left hand *movement* units and mark them with the value *movement.*
The value*?* is provided for work-in-progress. If you are not sure about the beginning or end of a unit or the value of the unit and you want to go back to this unit later again, mark the unit preliminarily with the value*?*.

Technically, there is no need to tag and label the *rest/pose* units, as they can be generated automatically by the Create Annotations from Gaps function:

Apply the function Tier.

Create Annotations from Gaps.

Select Tier: rh_Activation_RX.

Create annotations on ⊙ the same tier.

Value for the new annotations ⊙ Specific value: Enter *rest/pose.*

OK.

Select Tier: lh_Activation_RX.

Create annotations on ⊙ the same tier.

Value for the new annotations ⊙ Specific value: Enter *rest/pose.*

OK.

Note: If you want to conduct the R/P Contact assessment for *rest/pose* units (or for *rest* and *pose* units, as coded in Step 2) later on, you have to save the *rest/pose* units on a separate tier, i.e., separate from the *movement* units:

Apply the function Tier.

Create Annotations from Gaps.

Select Tier: rh_Activation_RX.

Create annotations on ⊙ a new tier.

Enter rh_Rest/Pose_RX.

etc.

For researchers who analyze also the lower limbs, the head, and the trunk
Proceed analogously for the template tiers rf_Activation_R0, lf_Activation_R0, head_Activation_R0, and trunk_Activation_R0.

You might aim at creating concatenated units of the four (or only two or three) parts of the body, i.e., units in which head, trunk, upper and lower limbs *rest/pose* simultaneously (*rest/pose* position units) or units in which trunk, head, and upper and lower limbs move simultaneously (whole body *movement* units). These units are technically the overlaps of *movement* and *rest/pose* units of the tiers rh_Activation_RX, lh_Activation_RX, rf_Activation_RX, lf_Activation_RX, head_Activation_RX, and trunk_Activation_RX. The overlap procedure can be conducted for multiple eafs at a time.

File > Multiple file processing > Annotations from Overlaps.

Step 1/4: File and Tier Selection.

Select files to use for computation:

⊙ Select files from domain. Click on the button Domain.

Select an existing domain. Load.

Select tiers to use for computation:

rh_Activation_RX, lh_Activation_RX, rf_Activation_RX, lf_Activation_RX, head_Activation,_RX and trunk_Activation_RX.
Next.

Step 2/4: Overlaps Computation Criteria.

Create annotation when annotations overlap

⊙ and their annotation values are equal.
Next.

Step 3/4: Destination Tier Name Specification.

Enter name for destination tier: wholebody_Activation_RX.

⊙ Destination tier is a root tier.

Select a linguistic type for destination tier: Notes OR other Linguistic Type.
Next.

Step 4/4: Destination Tier Value Specification.

⊙ Value from a specific tier: rh_Activation_RX

Finish.
Now you have the following new tier that contains whole body *movement* units and *rest/pose* position units in which all parts of the body *move* or *rest/pose*, respectively, simultaneously: wholebody_Activation_RX.

4 The Structure category

4.1 Definition of the Structure category

The Structure category further specifies *movement* units and *rest/pose* units. *Movement* units are classified according to the trajectory with five Structure values: (i) *irregular*, (ii) *repetitive*, (iii) *phasic*, (iv) *shift*, and (v) *aborted* (Fig. 3, Step 2a). *Rest/pose* units are classified according to muscle contraction with two R/P[4] Structure values: (i) *rest*, and (ii) *pose* (Fig. 3, Step 2b). The Structure category assessment can be applied to all four parts of the body.

Short definitions of the Structure values and their reliabilities as well the short definitions of the R/P Structure values are given in Tab. 3. The most relevant movement criterion for the classification of *movement* units is the trajectory. It is defined by the path and more specifically, by the absence or presence of phases within the path.

Since the trajectory reflects the absence or presence and complexity of motor planning process (see 4.3), the first three Structure values *irregular, repetitive* and *phasic* as shown in Fig. 3 represent a continuum with an increase in complexity from motor arousal to formative motor processes. The value *shift* registers transitions between still positions (and as such it belongs to the resting/posing behaviors, but since it is a movement it is listed among the Structure values). Finally, the value *aborted*, which is at the end of the horizontal order in Fig. 3, registers the abortion of movements, independently of whether they could have potentially become repetitive, phasic or shift movements (book I, section II).

The Structure category enables to differentiate mental states as reflected in kinesic behavior: motion states dominated by dysregulation (*irregular*), motion states reflecting productive processes (two levels: *repetitive* and *phasic*), transitions between still states (*shift*), the abortion of these processes (*aborted*), as well as still states of relaxation (*rest*) and tension (*pose*). Thus, the Structure category is sensitive to changes in mental states in healthy individuals (including changes elicited by experimental conditions), as well as to alterations of mental states in mental disease or brain damage (see book I, section II).

4 R/P values serve the further classification of *rest/pose* units.

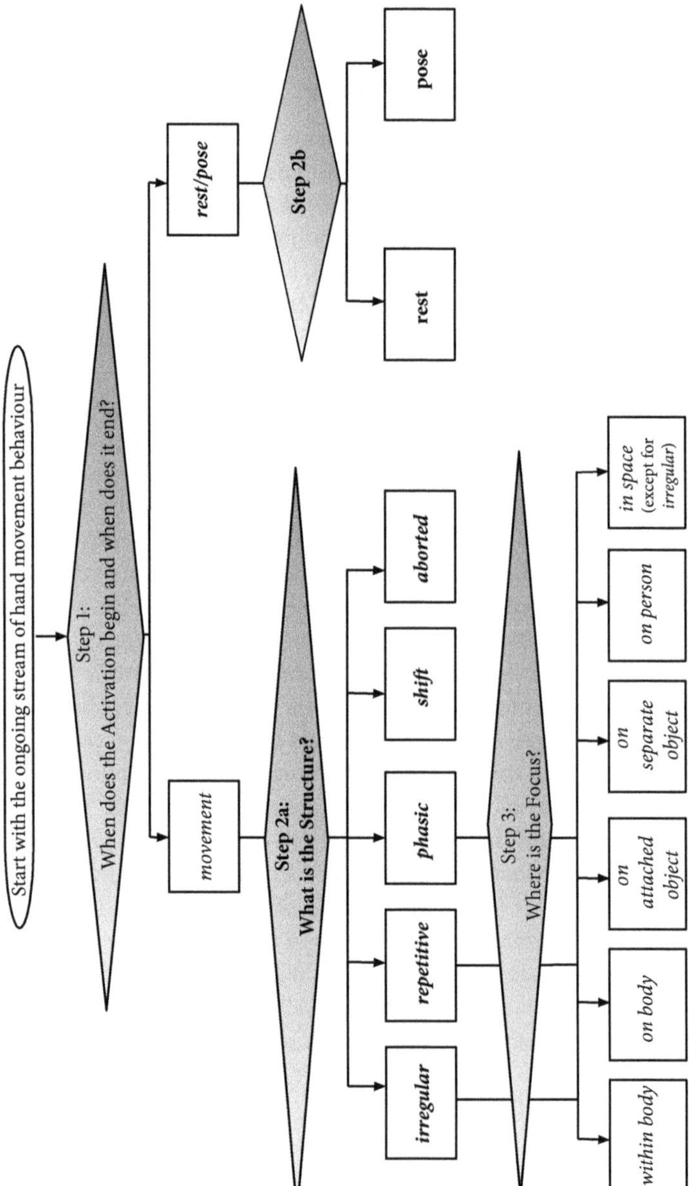

Fig. 3: The analysis algorithm for the Kinesic module (Module I) with the Structure category (Step 2) in fat print

Tab. 3: Short definitions and reliabilities of the Structure values and the R/PStructure values

Structure value / R/P Structure value	Short definition	Reliability* M ± SD
irregular	movement with no phase structure; trajectory with short paths in various directions; practically no displacement between beginning and end of unit; potentially continuous in time	.84 ± .09
repetitive	movement with a phase structure: one-dimensional–complex–one-dimensional; during the complex phase the same movement path is used repetitively; discrete in time	.79 ± .14
phasic	movement with a phase structure; the complex phase can be dynamic or static: in a dynamic complex phase there is a one-way movement path, in a static complex phase there is transient motionlessness, in which the part of the body is actively held against gravity; discrete in time	.77 ± .17
shift	movement with no phase structure; direct displacement of the part of the body from a *rest/pose* position to another one; the trajectory equals the displacement; discrete in time	.83 ± .14
aborted	movement with no phase structure; transport and retraction phase only with no complex phase; discrete in time; often no displacement	.67 ± .27
r/p rest	the part of the body rests	no data yet available
r/p pose	the part of the body poses	no data yet available

* Interrater reliability as measured with EasyDIAg (from Lausberg & Slöetjes, 2016)

4.2 Generation of the 'to-be-coded' Structure and R/PStructure units

4.2.1 Generation and assessment of to-be-coded Structure and R/PStructureunits

The *movement* units that have been generated in the Activation category assessment are directly adopted for the Structure category evaluation. They are termed 'to-be-coded' Structure units and are classified with the five Structure values. Once they are classified, the units are termed Structure units.

Researchers who also investigate *rest/pose* units, generate the 'to-be-coded' R/P Structure units with the same procedure as the 'to-be-coded' Structure units and classify them with the two R/P Structure values *rest* and *pose*.

If there is a change of the Structure value, e.g. first *phasic*, then *repetitive*, within a 'to-be-coded' Structure unit, then the structural change demarcates two new Structure units. However, if there are two or more different movements within a *movement* unit but the Structure value remains the same, e.g. a *repetitive* in space movement (gesture) followed by a *repetitive* on body movement (self-touch), there is no new Structure unit starting, as the mental mode of *repetitive* processes remains the same. In other words, in the Structure category assessment there can never be two Structure units with the same Structure value immediately following each other, i.e., with no *rest/pose* unit inbetween. As an example, a *repetitive* unit cannot be followed immediately by another *repetitive* unit as these two units remain in one Structure unit as long as they have the same Structure value.

In the case that within a to-be-coded unit a *repetitive* unit directly follows a *phasic* unit, or vice versa, the transport phase of the second unit often starts immediately after the complex phase of the first unit, e.g. Structure unit 1 [transport phase ⇒ *phasic* complex phase] ⇒ Structure unit 2 [transport phase ⇒ *repetitive* complex phase] ⇒ Structure unit 3 [transport phase ⇒ *phasic* complex phase ⇒ complete retraction to *rest position*]. In rare cases, foremost in the upper limbs, there is a partial retraction, i.e., after the complex phase, the hand is partially retracted, that is, it is stopped half-way on its way back to rest position and starts a new transport phase, e.g. Structure unit 1 [transport phase ⇒ *repetitive* complex phase ⇒ partial retraction] ⇒ new Structure unit 2 [transport phase ⇒ *phasic* complex phase ⇒ complete retraction to *rest/pose*] (see examples in the NEUROGES® training videos Intermediate 00:00:25.000, and Advanced 00:00:41.000).

Furthermore, as already described in the Activation category chapter, regarding the limbs, a *movement* unit may contain simultaneous isolated movements of different subparts of the limb, e.g. a thumb toss co-occurring with a shoulder shrug. These independent simultaneous movements within one limb require consideration in Structure coding (and in Focus coding) if the Structure values differ between the two parts, e.g. a shoulder shrug (Structure value *phasic*) occurs while fidgeting with the hands (Structure value *irregular*). In this case, the spatially and dynamically more complex movement is coded. For instance, if the *phasic* shoulder shrug is performed with emphasis while the *irregular* fidgeting is less prominent, the value of the unit is *phasic*. On the other hand, if the *irregular* fidgeting is more intensive it will determine the value of the unit. However it should be noted that in a natural context, if isolated non-synchronized movements with different Structures values seem to co-occur, a closer look often reveals that there is a short interruption of the movement in one subpart of the upper limb when the movement of the other subpart is displayed. As an example, the *irregular* activity of the fingers stops during the *phasic* shoulder shrug and continues after the shrug.

4.2.2 Alternative generation of 'to-be-coded' Structure and R/PStructure units

Researchers who start with the Structure category, i.e., who have not coded the Activation category before, identify movements and rests/poses, respectively, in the ongoing flow of behavior and classify them directly with the Structure and R/PStructure values according to the rules described in 4.2.1 (see also 4.5.3 Alternative procedure in NEUROGES® -ELAN). This approach probably saves time but it is more challenging than the stepwise procedure. Furthermore, it does not provide data on the individual's general extent of motor activity in terms of *movement* units.

4.3 Criteria for the definition of the Structure values

The Structure values are defined according to the criteria below.

Trajectory: The trajectory is defined as the path that is generated by the moving part of the body. For the limbs, the point of reference for the evaluation of the trajectory is the subpart of the limb that displays the most complex spatial movement and dynamics. For the upper limbs, this is typically the hand.

The trajectory can be straight, angular, curved or in other terms, one-, two-, three-dimensional. Most importantly, in some *movement* units the trajectory can be subdivided into phases[5]. The identification of distinct phases is characteristic for *phasic* and *repetitive* units (therefore, termed units with a phase structure),

5 In fact, the method of identifying phases within a movement is adopted from gesture research. Gestures are described to consist of a preparation phase, a stroke phase, and a retraction phase (e.g. Kendon, 1972; McNeill, 1992; Seyfeddinipur, 2006). In gesture research, the phases are defined functionally, i.e., the function of the "preparation phase" phase is to prepare the stroke, the function of the stroke phase is to carry the content of the gesture, and the function of the retraction phase is to bring the hand back to rest position. Similar concepts are used in kinematographic research. Based on kinematographic criteria such as trajectory, displacement, and velocity, Hermsdörfer et al. (1996) distinguishes a transport phase (equivalent to the preparation phase in gesture research) and an adjustment phase (equivalent to the stroke phase). In

as well as to a lesser extent for *aborted* units. *Irregular* units and *shift* units are characterized by the fact that there are no phases, i.e., the trajectorial pattern remains unchanged during the unit. In a prototypical *phasic* or *repetitive* unit, three phases can be distinguished:

(i) transport phase (T): There is a one-dimensional trajectory (a straight movement path), in which the part of the body is transported directly to a location, where it is going to act (complex phase). Therefore, functionally the transport phase is a preparation phase. It may start from a *rest/pose* unit, from a preceding complex phase, or from a partial retraction phase. Transport phases are part of *phasic, repetitive,* and *aborted* units.

(ii) complex phase (C): There is high complexity with regard to the trajectory, the effort factors, and in case of the upper limbs the hand orientation and the hand shape. Functionally, the complex phase serves the realization of a concept. Therefore, with regards to the function, it can also be termed conceptual phase. There are two subtypes of complex phases:

  (α) motion complex phase (mC): The trajectory is spatially complex. There may be a dynamics as defined by the degree of variation in the effort factors (see below). In the upper limbs, often a hand orientation and a hand shape is fully developed. The transition from the transport phase to the complex phase may be demarcated by a turn-point in the trajectory, by an increase in spatial complexity of the trajectory, and by an increase of the dynamics.

  (β) static[6] complex phase (sC): The trajectory is stopped and the limb is held against gravity with a distinct orientation and shape. The static complex phase is mostly found in gestures (as defined in the Function category). The gestural information is conveyed by a still image, i.e., a photo could capture the relevant information (see 8.4.6). A static complex phase may follow directly after a motion complex phase, and vice versa.

---

contrast to gesture research, in NEUROGES®, the concept of phases is applied to classify movements in general, e.g. actions, shifts, self-touches, and not only gestures. As the term "stroke phase" has been coined specifically for gestures and it defines a phase by its function rather than by movement parameters, in NEUROGES® the term is not adopted.

6 The term static (stroke) is adopted from M. Seyfeddinipur (personal communication) who suggests using it instead of stroke hold. The corresponding term dynamic was not used to describe the complementary type of complex phase, as this term is reserved for changes in the effort factors. Instead, the term motion complex phase was introduced.

Complex phases are obligatorily part of *phasic* and *repetitive* units, but not of *aborted* units.

(iii) retraction (R): The part of the body is moved back to *rest/pose* position. The transition from the complex phase to the retraction phase is often demarcated by a turn-point in the trajectory. The hand relaxes while retracting. The retraction phase can include searching for a new *rest/pose* position, e.g. some adaptations may be necessary until the hand has found a comfortable *rest* position. In these cases, the path is not one-dimensional (straight). The reaching of the *rest/pose* position is marked by stillness (see 4.4.6 and 4.4.7). Retraction phases are part of *phasic, repetitive,* and *aborted* units.

While the prototypical phase structure is *rest/pose* ⇒ Transport ⇒ Complex ⇒ Retraction ⇒ *rest/pose*, in natural data, there are often variations of this structure:

A *movement* unit can contain more than one complex phase and accordingly, more than one transport phase and more than one retraction phase, e.g. *rest/pose* ⇒ complete Transport (cT) ⇒ Complex (C) ⇒ partial Transport (pT) ⇒ Complex (C) ⇒ partial Retraction (pR) ⇒ partial Transport (pT) ⇒ Complex (C) ⇒ complete Retraction (cR). The complete transport phase starts from *rest/pose*, the complete retraction phase goes back to *rest/pose.* The partial transport phase starts after a complex phase and leads directly to the next complex phase. Alternatively, there can be a partial retraction after a complex phase, before the partial transport phase to the next complex phase starts. Thus, the retraction phases within the *movement* unit are partial retraction phases (pR), in which the hand retracts but it is stopped half-way on its way back in order to start a new transport phase, which is also only partial as is starts half-way (see 4.4.2 *repetitive* Example ♦ iv). In partial retraction, the hand is often held – without a distinct shape or orientation – for a moment against gravity before the new partial transport phase starts (see example in the NEUROGES® training video Advanced 00:00:41.000, right hand movement).

In rare cases, in the upper limbs, a complex phase starts without a preceding transport phase directly from *rest/pose* position. This is only possible if the *rest/pose* position, in which the hand rests, comfortably allows free moving of the hand right away (see 4.4.2 *repetitive* Example ♦ v; 4.4.3 *phasic* Example ♦ v), such that it is not necessary to first transport the hand to a location where it can act. Furthermore, the trajectory of the complex phase has to be compatible with a start from the *rest/pose* position, e.g. the hand rests on an armrest and then the index traces a circle.

Researchers who want to code the phases of *phasic, repetitive,* and *aborted* units in NEUROGES® -ELAN use the tier Phases that provides the following values: *complex static, complex motion, transport complete, transport partial, retraction complete, and retraction partial.*

Presence / Absence of Efforts: The five Structure values *irregular, repetitive, phasic, shift,* and *aborted* can be displayed with dynamics. The consideration of the movement dynamics is especially helpful for the identification of units with a phase structure, as the complex phase is often marked by an increase in dynamics as compared to the transport and retraction phases. It is evident that this criterion only applies to the subtype motion complex phase and not to the subtype static complex phase.

The movement dynamics are described with the Efforts as defined by Laban (1988). Efforts are the inner impulses from which movement originates. Four Effort factors, flow, weight, time, and space are distinguished. Each factor is a continuum with 2 polarities, i.e., flow changes between free or bound, weight between strong or light, time between sustained or quick, and space between direct or indirect. These effort qualities result from the inner attitude (conscious or unconscious) towards the four Efforts. Movement dynamics result from variation in one or more Effort factors.

The following definition is taken from Robyn Cruz's lecture material based on Dell (1979).

(i) Flow: variations in bodily tension representing ease or restraint of movement
  (α) free: going with, allowing energy to go through our and beyond body boundaries; indulgent / expansive use of flow.
  (β) bound: restricted, controlled, keeping energy flow within body boundaries; fighting / condensing use of flow.
(ii) Weight: force or pressure exerted in movement
  (α) light: rarified, delicate, fine touch, overcoming the body weight; indulgent / expansive intention in weight
  (β) strong: having impact, penetrating, getting behind the body weight; fighting / condensing intention in weight (to be distinguished from heavy, i.e., passive giving into gravity)
(iii) Time: compensation to outward time demands, or attitude toward duration of action
  (α) sustained: stretching out time, leisurely, actively indulging in time; indulgent / expansive decision in time (to be distinguished from slow movement and from evenness of bound flow)
  (β) sudden: urgent, instantaneous, a sense of urgency recreated each time; fighting / condensing decision in time (to be distinguished from fast movement)

(iv) Space: attention or orientation to space, how energy is focused in action, selective versus free-floating attention
  (α) indirect: multi-overlapping foci, multi-faceted attention, active meandering; indulgent / expansive attention in space
  (β) direct: channeled, pin-pointing; fighting / condensing attention in space

Upper limbs: Presence / Absence of Hand orientation: During the complex phase of a *phasic* or *repetitive* Structure unit, the hand may (α) adopt a distinct orientation, and (β) remain in neutral orientation (see also 8.3).

(α) The hand adopts a specific orientation relative to the body and to the body-external space. The body-external space (i.e., the gesture/action space, see also 8.3) is the space outside the body-surface and within the personal reach of the fingers tips when the arms are extended. The point of reference for defining the hand orientation is the palm or the back of the hand, respectively, or the orientation of the finger tips. The sagittal, horizontal, and frontal planes are used to describe the orientation of the hand, e.g. flat hand in frontal plane, finger tips pointing upward, palm facing the body.
(β) The hand has a neutral orientation and no distinct orientation is adopted. The anatomically most economic orientation is maintained, e.g. in up-down movements of the lower arm the flat hand is in line with the sagittal plane in the ipsilateral hemi-space. A neutral orientation is typically combined with a relaxed hand (no distinct hand shape).

Upper limbs: Presence / Absence of Hand shape: During the complex phase of a *phasic* or *repetitive* Structure unit, the hand may (α) adopt a distinct shape, or (β) remain relaxed or unshaped (see also 8.3).

(α) The hand adopts a distinct shape that is maintained during the complex phase such that a still picture of the hand shape emerges. The configuration of the fingers substantially contributes to the shape, e.g. index and thumb form a ring, a hand with an extended index.
(β) There is no active shaping of the hand and the hand often remains relaxed (flat hand with slightly flexed fingers).

The R/PStructure values *r/p*[7] *rest* and *r/p pose* are defined according to the criteria **Motion vs. Stillness, Actively Held Position vs. Gravity-Aligned / Supported Position,** and **Muscle Contraction vs. Relaxation** described in section 3.3.

---

7 abbreviation for *rest/pose*

4.4 Definitions of the Structure and R/PStructure values

4.4.1 *irregular*

Short definition

SMALL MOVEMENTS WITHOUT DISTINCT TRAJECTORY, POTENTIALLY ONGOING IN TIME

Definition

An *irregular* unit is characterized by the fact that the movement starts and ends at the place where the hand[8] (part of the body) happens to be in *rest* position. Thus, there are no transport and retraction phases and in general, no phases can be distinguished within the unit. There is no distinct trajectory, no distinct hand orientation and no distinct hand shape. The movement seems going by itself and it is potentially ongoing in time.

Meeting the criteria

Trajectory: The trajectory lacks any clear spatial direction. The imaginary trace that is left by the movement would look like a muddle of thread that is fallen in one spot on the ground. Thus, the movement stays in one area (see book I, 6.5).

Irregular units do not have phases. The occurrence of a transport phase, which is distinct from a complex phase, would per definition exclude the occurrence of an *irregular* unit. Thus, an *irregular* unit is characterized by the fact that there is no transport phase and that the movement starts at the place where the hand (part of the body) happens to have *rest*ed before.

---

8 As the large majority of the researchers has used NEUROGES® for the analysis of the upper limbs and as the NEUROGES® categories and values are identical for all four parts of the body, in order to facilitate reading, in the coding manual the definition are formulated for hand/arm/shoulder movements. However, any specificity of foot/leg, head, and trunk movements that deviates from the definitions for hand/arm/shoulder movements are noted, and in the **Examples ♦** sections for each NEUROGES® value, examples are provided separately hand/arm/shoulder, foot/leg, head, and trunk movements.

Efforts: There is a broad range of variation in efforts[9] in *irregular* units, e.g. light (e.g. gently sensing the skin), strong (e.g. kneading or squeezing the muscles), sudden (e.g. tic-like short irregular moves), etc.

Hand orientation: During the *irregular* unit, the hand does not adopt a distinct orientation.

Hand shape: During the *irregular* unit, the hand does not adopt a distinct shape.

Occurrence (see 1.7): *Irregular* units were investigated in 164 individuals of the NEUROGES® archive. Right hand *irregular* movements were displayed by 95 % (155/164) of the individuals, and left hand *irregular* movements by 99 % (163/164).

Frequency (see 1.7): In the NEUROGES® archive sample (n = 164), right hand *irregular* units were displayed with a frequency (Mean ± Standard Deviation; Median) of 2.77 ± 1.77; 2.60 units per minute, and left hand *irregular* units with a frequency of 3.10 ± 1.74; 2.88.

Duration (see 1.7): The duration (Mean ± Standard Deviation; Median) of right hand *irregular* units was 3.92 ± 3.72; 2.86 seconds per unit, and that of left hand *irregular* units 4.07 ± 3.71; 3.36 seconds per unit.

Examples for *irregular* units

- ♦ i) hand rests on knee ⇒ (no transport phase) hand starts massaging the knee in a sustained manner, movement seems going by itself ⇒ (no retraction phase) hand comes to rest again
- ♦ ii) hands rests on lap, hands loosely folded ⇒ fingers of the two hands start fidgeting on each other in an irregular manner ⇒ (no retraction phase) come to rest again
- ♦ iii) the lower arm rests on the thigh and the hand hangs free and relaxed ⇒ (no transport phase) fingers started stretching in various manners while hand remains hanging ⇒ (no retraction phase) fingers relax again
- ♦ iv) hand rests on table ⇒ fingers start moving around on table while hand remains in the same location, for a certain period of time there are repetitive-like

9 More precisely, precursors of effort described by Kestenberg (1965a,b, 1967) may better define what is observed: tension flow rhythms (sucking, snapping/biting, twisting, strain/release, running/drifting, starting/stopping, swaying, surging/birthing, jumping, spurting/ramming p. 27) and tension flow attributes (flow adjustment/even flow, low intensity/high intensity, graduality/abruptness p. 65) and possibly pre-efforts (flexibility/channeling, gentleness/vehemence-straining, hesitation/suddenness, p. 79). (Eberhard, pers. communication, 2012).

back and forth movements of the fingers, then the fingers move around again ⇒ hand rests again

- ◆ lower limbs: legs *rest* in a crossed position ⇒ now and then occasionally with no temporal structure, the foot of the upper leg displays small tic-like movements ⇒ foot *rests* again
- ◆ lower limbs: legs are crossed and the foot of the upper leg is held flexed against gravity (*pose*) ⇒ the foot then starts moving with small movements in an irregular manner ⇒ then *poses* again
- ◆ head: head in *rest* position ⇒ small erratic tic-like movements ⇒ head rests again
- ◆ trunk: sitting in a chair in an upright erect position (*pose*) ⇒ stirs of the trunk ⇒ again upright erect position (*pose*)

Differentiate *irregular* units from…

- ✎ *rest*: Raters might sometimes disagree on whether the *irregular* movement is ongoing with moments of retardation or whether there are actually interruptions of the *irregular* movement activity with short *rests*. As an example, one rater might observe a 3 seconds break in the *irregular* movement and code two *irregular* and one *rest* units, while the other rater who perceives only a retardation within the *irregular* activity with the hand remaining activated codes one long *irregular* unit instead. As *irregular* movement activity tends to be an ongoing motor back-ground activity, if in doubt, the rater should rather code one long *irregular* unit than several short ones.
- ✎ transport phase: If one observes something similar to a transport phase before an *irregular* movement starts, e.g. the two hands are brought together and then start fidgeting, the detailed analysis will reveal that the supposed transport phase is, indeed, a *shift*, and that there is a short *rest* before the *irregular* movement starts. In other words, the hands are not brought together for the purpose of fidgeting (which would functionally be a transport phase and thereby exclude the occurrence of an *irregular* unit), but rather the new *rest* position triggers the fidgeting. However, if there is a clear transport phase preparing a complex phase, code *phasic* or *repetitive*.
- ✎ *repetitive*: Within an *irregular* unit, the movements may become seemingly repetitive now and then. However, these repetitive intermezzos differ from real *repetitive* units, as they tend to have shorter trajectories and they never have a transport phase. Functionally, while in *repetitive* units the movement is goal-directed, e.g. scratching to stop the itching (motor-sensory), in *irregular* units the intermittent repetitive movement tends to follow the tactile sensation (sensory-motor). Thus, a seemingly repetitive movement that is

embedded in an *irregular* unit is part of the *irregular* unit and it does **not** constitute a *repetitive* unit (see Example ◆ iv). However, if researchers want to identify *irregular* units that become temporarily more structured, i.e., intermittently repetitive, they can use the supplementary category Temporal Structure to register this phenomenon with the value *metrical*.

- ✎ *phasic* or *repetitive* (here: of sensing nature): In rare cases, a *phasic* or a *repetitive* movement can be of sensing nature, e.g. the gesturer moves the hand to the hair (transport phase) in order to sense it. In this case, during the complex phase the trajectory of the fine movement might appear to be irregular, but the transport phase indicates the existence of an underlying motor plan. Therefore, the unit is coded as *phasic* or *repetitive* (see examples in NEUROGES® training video Beginner 00:00:14 ff.).
- ✎ *phasic* (here: short pC): In contrast to short *phasic* movements (pC), *irregular* tic-like movements are not synchronized with other body movements. They occur suddenly and erratically.

4.4.2 *repetitive*

Short definition

MOVEMENT WITH A PHASE STRUCTURE AND A REPETITIVE MOTION COMPLEX PHASE

Definition

Repetitive units are units with a phase structure, i.e., prototypically they consist of a transport phase, a complex phase, and a retraction phase (but see variations described in 4.3). The complex phase of a *repetitive* unit (rC) is always a motion complex phase. It is characterized by the fact that the hand (part of the body) moves at least twice in the same direction, i.e., forth – back – forth in the same dimension (see NEUROGES® training videos Intermediate 00:47–00.49 and 00:55–00:57, and Expert 00.08–00:10). Therefore, a repetitive complex phase (rC) can be segmented into sub-phases. Any time, the hand (part of the body) starts moving again in the same direction, a new sub-phase will start.

The paths of the sub-phases can be identical, i.e., actually moving back and forth on the same path, or they may be displaced relative to each other in one dimension, i.e., moving back and forth in the same dimension but with a displacement in another dimension, e.g. moving repetitively up and down while moving from left to right. However, the hand orientation and the hand shape remain constant between the sub-phases. The temporal distance between the sub-phases of the complex phase may differ, but the hand never *rests* or *poses* between the sub-phases. Equal duration between the sub-phases results in a meter, and varying duration in a rhythm.

Meeting the criteria

Trajectory: In the complex phase of a *repetitive* unit (rC), the hand (part of the body) moves repetitively on a defined one-, two- or three-dimensional spatial path. Repetition is defined as moving at least twice in the same direction of the same dimension. The paths of the sub-phases may be identical or they may be displaced relative to each other in one dimension. As an example, there may be a repetitive up-down movement of the hand, while it moves sidewards (Example ◆ iv).

Efforts: In the complex phase (rC), there are often variations in the effort factors time, flow, weight, and space. If there is a specific dynamics, this can be repeated in all sub-phases, e.g. in each sub-phase the downward movement is executed with direct space and strong weight, e.g. pantomiming hammering. However, likewise, the dynamics can increase or decrease across the subphases, e.g. moving faster and faster from subphase to subphase.

Hand orientation: In the complex phase (rC), the hand may or may not adopt a distinct orientation. If there is a distinct orientation, it remains constant between the sub-phases. In rare cases, there may be two or more hand orientations which are executed in a repetitive sequence, e.g. palm up – palm down–palm up – palm down–palm up – palm down. In this case, the sequence constitutes a sub-phase, i.e., in the example, there are three sub-phases with the new subphase always starting with the palm down.

Hand shape: In the complex phase (rC), the hand may or may not adopt a specific shape. If there is a distinct shape, it remains constant between the sub-phases. In rare cases, there may be two or more hand shapes which are executed in a repetitive sequence, e.g. ring – flat–ring – flat–ring – flat. In this case, the sequence constitutes a sub-phase, i.e., in the example, there are three sub-phases with the new subphase always starting with the ring shape.

As the five fingers of a hand represent anatomically a quasi repetitive structure, the sequential use of the five fingers constitutes a repetitive complex phase. Therefore, sequential movements of the fingers such as galloping from the small finger to the index or counting from 1 to 5 with the fingers, are coded as one *repetitive* unit (see also Example ◆ vi).

Occurrence: *Repetitive* units were investigated in 164 individuals of the NEUROGES® archive. Right hand *repetitive* movements were displayed by

95 % (156/164) of the individuals, and left hand *repetitive* movements by 96 % (157/164).

Frequency: In the NEUROGES® archive sample (n = 164), right hand *repetitive* units were displayed with a frequency (Mean ± Standard Deviation; Median) of 2.28 ± 1.71; 1.95 units per minute, and left hand *repetitive* units with a frequency of 2.02 ± 1.62; 1.52.

Duration: The duration (Mean ± Standard Deviation; Median) of right hand *repetitive* units was 3.55 ± 1.66; 3.41 seconds per unit, and that of left hand *repetitive* units 3.45 ± 1.76; 3.41 seconds per unit.

Examples for *repetitive* units

- ♦ i) hand rests on lap (*rest* position) ⇒ hand rises (complete T) ⇒ moves down and up several times on the same trajectory with downward emphasis and with the same dynamics, e.g. in each sub-phase downward acceleration, then change from free to bound flow to stop the movement (rC) ⇒ hand moves back to *rest* (complete R)
- ♦ ii) hand rests on table ⇒ hand moves to the other arm (complete T) ⇒ performs repetitive back and forth movements on the other arm (rC) ⇒ moves back to armrest (complete R)
- ♦ iii) hand rests on lap ⇒ hand rises to right upper gesture space (complete T) ⇒ performs on the same path repetitive up and down movements rhythmically with downward emphasis (1rst rC) ⇒ retracts to level of shoulder (partial R) ⇒ hand rises to left upper gesture space (partial T) ⇒ performs on the same path repetitive up and down movements rhythmically with downward emphasis (2nd rC) ⇒ hand moves back to rest (complete R) (Note: This is coded as **one** *repetitive* unit with 2 complex phases rC.)
- ♦ iv) hand rests on armrest ⇒ hand moves to the mouth while index extends (complete T) ⇒ makes repetitive small up-down movements while moving from the right to the left side of the mouth (1rst rC with variation in one dimension) ⇒ moves to the hair (partial T) ⇒ makes repetitive back and forth movements in the hair (2nd rC) ⇒ moves back to a new *rest* position (complete R) (Note: This is coded as **one** *repetitive* unit with 2 complex phases rC.)
- ♦ v) hand rests on knee ⇒ (no transport phase) fingers rise up (and down) with upward accent several times on the same path (rC) ⇒ (no retraction phase) rest again in same *rest* position
- ♦ vi) hands rest on lap ⇒ hands rise to meet each other (complete T) ⇒ the right index touches the fingers of the left hand one after the other by performing up and down movements with displacement in one dimension; in the left hand, first the thumb is extended (sub-phase 1), then the index (sub-phase 2), then

the middle finger (sub-phase 3), then the ring finger (sub-phase 4), and then the little finger (sub-phase 5) (rC) ⇒ hands moves back to *rest* position (complete R) (Note: As the left hand fingers are actively presented one after the other, this is coded not only as a *repetitive* unit in the right hand but also as a *repetitive* unit in the left hand)

- vii) right hand rests on table ⇒ right hand moves to left side of head (complete T) ⇒ strokes hair repetitively backwards while moving from the left side of the head to the right (1rst rC with displacement in one dimension), then curls up hair repetitively (2nd rC), moves back to the left side of the head (partial T), then strokes hair again repetitively backwards while moving from the left side of the head to the right (3rd rC with displacement in one dimension), then curls up hair repetitively (4th rC) ⇒ moves back to rest (complete R) (Note: This is coded as **one** *repetitive* unit with 4 complex phases rC)
- viii) hand rests on lap ⇒ hand rises (complete T) ⇒ makes repetitive circulating movements while moving hand downward (rC with displacement in one dimension) ⇒ moves back to rest (complete R)
- lower limbs: *rest* position with crossed legs, right leg above the left one ⇒ (no transport phase) repetitive rhythmical wagging with the right foot ⇒ (no retraction phase) foot *rests* again
- lower limbs: standing person ⇒ *pantomimes* (see 8.4.5) walking, i.e., without actual locomotion, staying in one place (motion pC) ⇒ back to standing
- head: head in *rest* position ⇒ head is raised up (complete transport) ⇒ repetitive nodding with downward accent (see 9.4.9 *emblems*) (motion pC) ⇒ back to neutral position to *rest* (complete retraction)
- trunk: sitting with trunk leaning at the back of the chair ⇒ moving trunk to upright position (complete transport) ⇒ repetitive rocking with the trunk with forward accent (motion pC) ⇒ back to *rest* position (complete retraction)

Differentiate *repetitive* from …

- passive rebound movements: A rebound movement may occur, when people have a relaxed muscle tonus. As an example, when a person with a floppy muscle tonus drops the arm over an armrest with the hand remaining free in space, a rebound movement of the hand might occur. This is not coded as a *repetitive* movement but as a *rest* unit, since it is a passive movement (actually, in the Activation category this rebound movement should have already been identified as a *rest/pose* unit).
- *phasic* (here: a sequence of *phasic* units): As the complex phase of a *repetitive* unit (rC) contains sub-phases, some raters may mistake it as several *phasic* units in a row. However, as long as the sub-phases of rC are identical with

regard to dimension, hand orientation, hand shape, and effort (see exceptions above), there is no doubt that this is one *repetitive* unit even if the temporal distances between the sub-phases differ. However, if there are a short *rests* or *poses* between one-way *phasic* movements, these are several *phasic* units, e.g. the hand rises, turns out, retracts, rests shortly, rises, turns out, retracts, rests shortly, rises, turns out, retracts, rests (in the example, there are three *phasic* units).

- *irregular*: Within an *irregular* unit, for a short moment the movement may become repetitive. However, as long as the repetitive intermezzo is embedded in an *irregular* unit and it is not preceded by a transport phase nor followed by a retraction phase, this is coded as part of the *irregular* unit. If a researcher wants to identify *irregular* units that become temporarily more structured, i.e., that include repetitive moments, they can apply the Supplementary category Temporal Structure.
- repetitive pattern: A *repetitive* unit has to be distinguished from a repetitive pattern. The latter contains a repetitive sequence of units with different Structure value, e.g. *phasic* unit – *rest* unit – *repetitive* unit – *rest* unit – same *phasic* unit – *rest* unit – same *repetitive* unit – *rest* unit – same *phasic* unit – *rest* unit – same *repetitive* unit. In the example, in the Structure category, six Structure units are coded (see example in the NEUROGES® training video Beginner 00:00:20.000). Depending on the research aim, it might, however, be worth registering that these units constitute a repetitive pattern. Technically, in the NEUROGES® -template the rater notes in the tier Notes that there is a repetitive pattern of units.

4.4.3 *phasic*

Short definition

MOVEMENT WITH A PHASE STRUCTURE AND A STATIC OR PHASIC MOTION COMPLEX PHASE

Definition

Phasic units are units with a phase structure, i.e., prototypically they consist of a transport phase, a complex phase, and a retraction phase (but see variations described in 4.3). The complex phase of a *phasic* unit (pC) may be static or motion. The motion complex phase of a *phasic* unit is characterized by the fact that the hand (part of the body) moves on a one-way path, i.e., with no repetition of the same direction and at most once in opposite directions in the same dimension, i.e., once back and forth but – in contrast to a *repetitive* unit – never twice in the same direction in the same dimension, i.e., forth – back – forth.

Meeting the criteria

Trajectory: In a motion complex phase of a *phasic* unit (motion pC), the hand (part of the body) moves forth one-way or at most forth and back on a defined one-, two- or three-dimensional spatial path. One could imagine that the path leaves a clear trace. On this trace, the hand moves once in one direction (forth one-way) or two times but in opposite directions (forth and back).

In a static complex phase (static pC), there is no trajectory.

Efforts: During the motion complex phase (motion pC), the movement may become more dynamic as compared to the transport phase, i.e., there are variations in the effort factors time, flow, weight, and space.

Hand orientation: In the static complex phase (static pC), the hand adopts a distinct orientation. In the motion complex phase (motion pC), the hand may or may not adopt a distinct orientation.

Hand shape: In the static complex phase, the hand adopts a distinct shape. In motion complex phases (motion pC), the hand may or may not adopt a distinct shape.

Occurrence: *Phasic* units were investigated in 164 individuals of the NEUROGES® archive. Right hand as well as left hand *phasic* movements were displayed by 100 % (164/164) of the individuals.

Frequency: In the NEUROGES® archive sample (n = 164), right hand *phasic* units were displayed with a frequency (Mean ± Standard Deviation; Median) of 4.63 ± 2.80; 4.09 units per minute, and left hand *phasic* units with a frequency of 4.41 ± 2.67; 3.85.

Duration: The duration (Mean ± Standard Deviation; Median) of right hand *phasic* units was 3.08 ± 1.65; 2.48 seconds per unit, and that of left hand *phasic* units 3.13 ± 1.51; 2.54 seconds per unit.

Examples for *phasic* units

- ◆ i) hand rests on lap (*rest*) ⇒ hand rises (complete Transport) ⇒ traces the form of a circle (motion pC) ⇒ hand moves back to same *rest* position (complete Retraction)
- ◆ ii) hand rests on lap ⇒ hand rises (complete T) ⇒ touches the chin and strokes along the chin (motion pC) ⇒ hand retracts to same *rest* position (complete R)

- ♦ iii) hand rests on lap ⇒ (no transport phase) while wrist remains resting, short movement up and out with back of hand leading, hand falls back (motion pC) ⇒ (no retraction phase) rests in same *rest* position
- ♦ iv) hand rests on lap ⇒ hand moves forward on a centrifugal, straight trajectory to the right (complete T) ⇒ is held with a distinct hand orientation and a distinct hand shape with index extended (static pC) ⇒ retracts to level of breast and is held relaxed for a short moment (partial R) ⇒ moves forward on a centrifugal, straight trajectory to the right again (partial T) ⇒ draws the circle (motion pC) ⇒ retracts to *rest* position (complete R)
- ♦ v) palm rests on lap ⇒ (no transport phase) index draws a circle, while palm remains resting (motion pC) ⇒ (no retraction phase) rests in same *rest* position
- ♦ lower limbs: *rest* position with crossed legs, right leg above the left one ⇒ right lower leg is raised (complete T) ⇒ points with the foot by holding it for a moment (static pC) ⇒ moves back to *rest* position (complete R)
- ♦ lower limbs: standing person ⇒ moves the right leg forward (complete T) ⇒ kicks away some trash on the floor (motion pC) ⇒ moves back to standing position (complete R)
- ♦ head: head in *rest* position ⇒ head is turned to the right (complete transport) ⇒ looks at something (static pC) ⇒ back to neutral position to rest (complete R)
- ♦ head: head in *rest* position ⇒ performs an *egocentric direction* gesture (see 8.4.4) ⇒ back to neutral position to rest (complete R)
- ♦ trunk: sitting in a chair, trunk leaning against right arm rest ⇒ bending the trunk forward (complete T) ⇒ from that forward leaned position of trunk (static pC of trunk) hand grasps something (motion pC of hand) ⇒ trunk back to *rest* position (complete R)

Differentiate *phasic* from …

- ✐ transport phase only or a retraction phase only: A simple straight one-way move on a one-dimensional straight path, with no dynamics, no distinct hand orientation, nor a distinct hand shape does not constitute a *phasic* unit. This is either a transport phase or a retraction phase.
- ✐ *repetitive*: If during a motion complex phase, the hand moves forth-back-forth or more often in the same direction in the same dimension (often even on the same path), the criteria for a repetitive complex phase (rC) are fulfilled.
- ✐ *aborted*: The static complex phase of a *phasic* unit is characterized by the fact that the hand is held with a distinct orientation and a distinct shape. An *aborted* unit may also contain a hold that, however, is a pausing after the disruption of the transport phase. The hand is held relaxed and undeveloped with regards to orientation and shape.

- ✎ *irregular*: *Irregular* movements are often ongoing continuous movements but there can also be single movements that might be mistaken as *phasic* units. However, the single *irregular* movements are very short and tic-like with a sudden, impulsive dynamics and no spatial complexity. There is no transport, complex and retraction phase.
- ✎ *shift*: A simple one-way move on a one-dimensional straight path between two *rest/pose* positions does not constitute a *phasic* unit. It is a *shift* as it is a mere transition between two *rest/pose* positions.

4.4.4 *shift*

Short definition

DIRECT DISPLACEMENT FROM ONE REST/POSE POSITION TO ANOTHER ONE

Definition

In a *shift* unit, the hand (part of the body) is moved **directly,** i.e., without any detour, from one *rest/pose* position to another *rest/pose* position. Thus, the movement path is typically straight. Only if the hand (part of the body) does not immediately find a comfortable new *rest/pose* position, the path is not entirely straight but at the end there is a short adjustment movement. As an example, when a *rest* position with folded hands is aimed at, the fingers might not immediately find the inter-digital gap between the fingers of the other hand and there are searching movements of the fingers. Since the only purpose of these searching/adjustment movements is to find the new *rest/pose* position, they are part of the *shift* unit.

Note that especially *phasic* and *repetitive* units (and more rarely *aborted* or *irregular* units) may start from one *rest/pose* position and end in another *rest/pose* position. These changes that occur quasi as by-products after *phasic, repetitive, aborted,* or *irregular* movements are **not** marked with the value *shift,* because a *shift* unit is strictly defined as a **direct** transition from one *rest/pose* position to another one with no *phasic, repetitive, aborted,* or *irregular* movement inbetween. Changes in *rest/pose* positions that occur after *phasic, repetitive, aborted,* or *irregular* movements are registered indirectly with the R/P Structure values *r/p rest* and *r/p pose* and the R/P Contact values and, if desired, remarks in the tier Notes.

Shifts are often whole body phenomena, e.g. shifting from a *rest* position with the back leaning at the back of the chair and open legs and arms to a *rest* position with trunk leaning forward, crossed arms placed on the table, and legs closed. Therefore, researchers might be interested to merge the *shift* units of the upper limbs, the lower limbs, the head, and the trunk.

Meeting the criteria

Trajectory: The hand moves one-way on a straight trajectory. The path is the shortest way from one *rest/pose* position to another one.

The exception is searching movements that may become necessary when a comfortable *rest/pose* position is not found right away. These searching movements can result in that towards the end of the *shift* the movement path is no longer straight. However, any other form of detour in the trajectory is not compatible with the value *shift*.

As a *shift* is a transition from one *rest/pose* position to another one, technically in NEUROGES® -ELAN, a *shift* unit is always framed by *rest/pose* units.

Efforts: *Shifts* to *rest* positions are often displayed without variation in the effort factors. In contrast, *shifts* to *poses* are often performed with variation in the effort factors (see Example ◆ iii).

Hand orientation: During the *shift*, the hand does not adopt a specific orientation.

Hand shape: During the *shift*, the hand does not adopt a specific shape.

Occurrence: *Shift* units were investigated in 191 individuals of the NEUROGES® archive. Right hand *shift* movements were displayed by 84 % (160/191) of the individuals, and left hand *shift* movements by 86 % (165/191).

Frequency: In the NEUROGES® archive sample (n = 191), right hand *shift* units were displayed with a frequency (Mean ± Standard Deviation; Median) of 0.82 ± 0.83; 0.58 units per minute, and left hand *shift* units with a frequency of 0.89 ± 0.93; 0.67.

Duration: The duration (Mean ± Standard Deviation; Median) of right hand *shift* units was 1.28 ± 0.83; 1.21 seconds per unit, and that of left hand *shift* units 1.29 ± 0.89; 1.25 seconds per unit.

Examples for *shift* units

- ◆ i) hand rests on the thigh (*rest* position A) ⇒ hand moves forward on a straight path (*shift*) ⇒ hand stops on knee and rests there (new *rest* position B)
- ◆ ii) both hands rest on table (*rest* position A) ⇒ both hands shift to arm rests (*shift*) ⇒ stop there and rest (new *rest* position B)
- ◆ iii) arms are folded, erect trunk, head tilted (*pose* position) ⇒ trunk moves forward and the arms open and move towards the right and left armrests, but as they do not immediately find a stable position, they display adjustment movements (*shift*) ⇒ hands / arms come to rest on the armrests, trunk leans against the back of the chair (*rest* position)

- iv) hands rests on the thigh (*rest* position) ⇒ with strength and directness, the hands move on a straight path to the hips (*shift*) ⇒ the hands are placed on the hips, elbows pointed out, trunk and head erect (*pose* position)
- lower legs: sitting person, legs open (*rest* position A) ⇒ moves left leg above the right one (*shift*) ⇒ legs rest in a crossed position (new *rest* position B)
- head: head in upright neutral position (*rest* position A) ⇒ head is tilted to the left to where the lower left arm is held upright (*shift*) ⇒ head rests on left hand (new *rest* position B)
- trunk: trunk leaning against the right arm rest (*rest* position A) ⇒ trunk is shifted to the left (*shift*) ⇒ trunk leaning against the left arm rest (*rest* position B)

Differentiate *shift* from …

- *phasic, repetitive,* or *aborted* (here: the retraction phase): In *phasic, repetitive,* and more rarely *aborted* units, the hand might not return to the same *rest/pose* position from which it started, but instead, it might come to rest in a new *rest/pose* position. In these cases, the change of the *rest position* is a byproduct of the *phasic,* the *repetitive,* or the *aborted* unit. As the new *rest position* is only by-product but not the main and only goal of the unit, it is not to be confused with a *shift* unit (see above).
- *irregular* (here: the ending of the *irregular* unit): In *irregular* units, the hand sometimes does not come to rest in the same *rest position* from which it started but in a new *rest position.* In these cases, the change of the *rest position* is part of the *irregular* unit.
- being shifted: In hemiparetic subjects, the healthy hand might shift the paralyzed hand. This is coded as a *phasic (on body)* unit only for the healthy hand. The passive movement of the paralyzed hand is not coded (actually, the passive movement must have been coded as a *rest/pose* unit in the Activation category).

4.4.5 *aborted*

Short definition

DISRUPTED TRANSPORT PHASE OR SHIFT FOLLOWED BY RETRACTION

Definition

An *aborted* unit is a movement that is disrupted. The disruption occurs either during the transport phase of movements that could have become *phasic* or *repetitive* or during a shift movement that could have ended in a new *rest/pose* position[10]. Thus, functionally, an *aborted* unit can be a disrupted *phasic* unit, a disrupted *repetitive* unit, or a disrupted *shift*. However, the original motor plan cannot be determined since the movement is disrupted before the complex phase or the new *rest/pose* position is displayed.

Thus, an *aborted* unit consists of two phases, a transport phase/shifting movement and a retraction phase. It is characterized by the fact that the transport phase is **not** followed by a complex phase and the shift movement is **not** followed by a new *rest/pose* position, respectively. Instead, the hand (part of the body) is retracted. Often, the movement dynamics give the impression that the transport phase/shift movement is disrupted halfway. The retraction can take place immediately after the disruption, or the hand (part of the body) is held for a moment and then retracted. If the hand is held for a moment, there is no distinct hand orientation and no distinct hand shape.

Many *aborted* units occur during bilateral hand movements. Both hands start with a transport phase, but then only one hand performs the complex phase, while the other hand, which displays the *aborted* unit, either retracts immediately or it is simply held – as if forgotten – with no distinct shape or orientation during the complex phase of the dominant hand and then retracts together with the dominant hand.

Per definition, an *aborted* unit can**not** directly (i.e., with no *rest/pose* in between) precede nor follow a *phasic*, a *repetitive*, or a *shift* unit, as in that case the ostensible abortion would in fact only be an interruption but not a disruption. As an example, the hand rises half-way, stops for a moment, then continues to rise and then starts with complex phase. This is an interrupted, but not a disrupted transport phase. Likewise, an interruption can occur during the retraction phase of a *phasic* or *repetitive* unit, e.g. hand retracts half-way, stops for a moment, and then continues to retract to *rest/pose* position. Furthermore, conceptually, an interruption – in contrast to a disruption as during an *aborted* unit – in the course of the *phasic, repetitive,* or *shift* unit is no obstacle for the Structure category assessment, as the relevant information which is necessary to assess the Structure, i.e., the complex phase and the new *rest* position, is provided.

---

10 A *rest/pose* position is quasi the position system equivalent of the complex phase of *phasic* and *repetitive* units. Therefore, *shifts* can be compared to transport phases. *Shifts* that are performed to move to a new *pose* position or a new *rest* position share movement features with transport phases, e.g. to shift the hands from the lap to the arm rests (the exception is *shifts* that are performed to move away from a *rest* position, e.g. when the location on which the hand rests becomes hot. They might resemble more retraction phases).

Meeting the criteria

Trajectory: An *aborted* unit is characterized by a one-dimensional straight spatial path starting from *rest/pose* position, followed by another one-dimensional straight spatial path back to *rest/pose* position.

Efforts: Immediately before the hand stops, the movement flow becomes bound (with the consequence that the movement is stopped).

Hand orientation: During the *aborted* unit, the hand does not adopt a distinct orientation.

Hand shape: During the *aborted* unit, the hand does not adopt a distinct shape.

Occurrence: *Aborted* units were investigated in 191 individuals of the NEUROGES® archive. Right hand *aborted* movements are displayed by 51 % (97/191) of the individuals, and left hand *aborted* movements by 55 % (104/191).

Frequency: In the NEUROGES® archive sample (n = 191), right hand *aborted* units were displayed with a frequency (Mean ± Standard Deviation; Median) of 0.29 ± 0.49; 0.06 units per minute, and left hand *aborted* units with a frequency of 0.42 ± 0.66; 0.10.

Duration: The duration (Mean ± Standard Deviation; Median) of right hand *aborted* units was 1.66 ± 1.48; 1.73 seconds per unit, and that of left hand *aborted* units 1.80 ± 1.61; 1.81 seconds per unit.

Examples for *aborted* units

- i) hand rests on table ⇒ hand rises (T) ⇒ then stops ⇒ hand moves back to *rest* position on table (R)
- ii) hand rests on armrest ⇒ hand rises (T) ⇒ then stops and is held against gravity for a while as if it were forgotten ⇒ hand moves back to table and rests (R)
- iii) both hands rest on arm rests ⇒ both hands rise (T) ⇒ right hand (here: dominant hand) traces a circle (pC), while left hand remains held unshaped ⇒ both hands retract (R) (right hand: *phasic* unit; left hand: *aborted* unit)
- iv) both hands rest folded in lap ⇒ both hands open, fingers spread (T) ⇒ right hand (here: dominant hand) rises and moves repetitively up and down (rC), while left hand remains in lap with fingers spread ⇒ right hand moves back to left hand and both hands fold again (R) (right hand: *repetitive* unit; left hand: *aborted* unit). Note in the example, the hand that displays the *aborted* unit "freezes" in the configuration as it is and does not adopt a distinct shape.
- v) both arms rest on table ⇒ both arms start to shift in the direction of the armrests (T) ⇒ stop half-way ⇒ both hands move back to old *rest* position on table (R)

- ♦ lower legs: sitting person, legs crossed with the left leg above the right one ⇒ starts to shift left leg towards open *rest* position ⇒ stops half-way ⇒ moves left leg back to old *rest* position
- ♦ head: head in upright neutral position ⇒ head starts to turn to left ⇒ stops half-way ⇒ moves back
- ♦ trunk: trunk leaning against the right arm rest ⇒ trunk starts shifting leftwards (as a tendency towards to the left arm rest) ⇒ stops half-way ⇒ moves back to old *rest* position

Differentiate *aborted* from …

✎ *phasic*: In a *phasic* unit in which the hand moves forth and back on a one-dimensional path, there is always dynamics that develop, often with endpoint accent, and there is a distinct hand orientation. Often there is also a distinct hand shape, e.g. a pointing gesture with index extended. In contrast, in an *aborted* unit, the dynamics diminish and there is no distinct hand orientation and no distinct hand shape.

4.4.6 *r/p rest*

Short definition

THE PART OF THE BODY RESTS

Definition
A *rest* of a part of the body is defined by stillness, gravity-aligned/supported position, and muscle relaxation.

If several or all parts of the body *rest*, they form a *rest* position, which is a specific static arrangement of the resting parts of the body (compare 3.4.2).
Meeting the criteria

Motion vs. Stillness: There is stillness.

The exception is passive movement (see 3.3), where there is motion in combination with muscle relaxation. The part of the body is moved.

Actively Held Position vs. Gravity-Aligned / Supported Position: The part of the body is resting in a gravity-aligned or supported position.
Muscle Contraction vs. Relaxation: There is muscle relaxation.

Examples for *rest* units

- ♦ upper limbs: standing person in normal upright position with arms hanging

- upper limbs: sitting person with arms resting on the arm rests
- lower limbs: sitting person with legs fallen to an open position
- lower limbs: sitting person with relaxed legs crossed, with no additional muscular contraction except from those of the antigravity muscles in that position
- lower limbs: standing person with no additional muscular contraction except from those of the antigravity muscles in that position
- head: standing person with head in normal (aligned) upright position, no muscular contraction except those of antigravity muscles
- head: sitting person, head is resting on the right hand (right elbow rests on arm rest and the lower arm is held vertically against gravity), no muscular contraction except those of antigravity muscles
- trunk: standing person in normal (aligned) upright position, no muscular contraction except from those of antigravity muscles

Differentiate *rest* units from…

- *irregular*: In continuous *irregular* hand movements such as hand-to-hand fidgeting, it may be hard to distinguish retarded or sustained movements or spatially minimal movements from *rests*. As continuous small hand movements tend to be an ongoing background motor activity, do **not** code a *rest* unit if you cannot clearly detect a stillness and relaxation of the hand.
- *pose*: Some individuals display *rest* positions in which the elbow rests on something and the lower arm is held vertically against gravity. The upright holding of the lower arm requires rather little muscle energy and therefore, this position can serve as a *rest* position. In this case, the hand always relaxes. In contrast, in a *pose*, the hand would be shaped and activated. In order to get an impression of what a relaxed hand would look like bring your own hand in the same position and relax it. Furthermore, if later in the course of the video sample you observe that the individual's hand relaxes it will be evident that the hand was activated before.

4.4.7 *r/p pose*

Short definition

THE PART OF THE BODY POSES

Definition

A *pose* of a part of the body is defined by stillness and muscle contraction. In most *pose* units, there is a gravity-aligned/supported position of the part of the body. In rare cases, the part of the body is in a position in which it is actively held against gravity.

If several or all parts of the body *pose*, they form a *pose* position, which is a specific static arrangement of the posing parts of the body (compare 3.4.2). A *pose* position is an activated or expressive position in which the person can remain for a longer period of time, e.g. the thinker pose, the arrogant pose, etc.

Meeting the criteria

Motion vs. Stillness: There is stillness.

Actively Held Position vs. Gravity-Aligned / Supported Position: Given that a *pose* is adopted for a longer period of time, there is typically a stable gravity-aligned/supported position of the part of the body. In rare cases, the part of the body is held actively held against gravity.

Muscle Contraction vs. Relaxation: There is isometric muscle contraction.

Examples for *pose* units

- upper limbs: in a standing or sitting person, the hands are pressed into the waist with the elbows pointed out
- lower limbs: standing with tensioned legs apart in a "fighter pose"
- lower limbs: sitting person with legs crossed, holding the upper foot in a tensed flexed position
- head: holding the head lowered in a "thinker pose", in contact with the hand (but not resting on the hand)
- trunk: sitting upright with trunk erect and chest out in an "arrogant pose"

Differentiate *pose* from...

Confusions between *poses* and other values mainly occur for those rare *poses* in which a part of the body is actively held against gravity. In these cases, the actively held part of the body often contributes to an expressive whole body pose. Specifically for posing limbs, they are typically held in the body near space (near kinesphere, see 8.3). As a *pose* is kind of a settlement, the actively held position in a *pose* is held for a longer period of time than the actively held position within a *movement* (see static complex phase). While it is the theoretical claim of NEUROGES® to not operate with absolute / arbitrary time frames, however, based on the NEUROGES® archive data on the duration of the value units is suggested to consider a *pose* if the actively held position is held for more than four seconds.

✎ a static complex phase of a *phasic* unit with an actively held position: In a static complex phase of a *phasic* unit, the hand (part of the body) may be held against gravity for a moment. The hand is typically held in the middle or far kinesphere of the gesture space. As an example, in a gesture showing the

Peace sign the shaped and oriented hand is held for a moment in the upper gesture space. The holding serves the emphasis.

- ✎ a hold during a transport phase or a retraction phase: A moment of stillness with an actively held position against gravity may occur as a hesitation during transport or retraction. The hold is substantially shorter than the hold in a *pose* with an actively held position. Furthermore, there is no distinct hand shape or hand orientation, while in a *pose* there is typically a distinct hand shape and hand orientation.
- ✎ a hold in an *aborted* unit: An *aborted* unit is a disruption of a transport phase or of a shift movement. The movement is stopped halfway, and before the part of the body is retracted, it may be actively held against gravity for a moment. The holding is rather a hesitation and therefore it is of a substantially shorter duration than an active holding in a *pose*. Furthermore, in an *aborted* unit, there is no distinct hand shape or hand orientation, while in a *pose* there is typically a distinct hand shape and hand orientation.
- ✎ an individually high rest muscle tonus in a *rest* unit: Some individuals who are psychologically tense or who have a neurological, psychosomatic, or psychiatric disease might have a high rest muscle tonus. In these individuals, the high rest muscle tonus is easy to diagnose as no further relaxation can be observed in the video sample. Furthermore, in individuals with a neurological disease the increased tonus is often more pronounced in or even limited to one side of the body, e.g. a person with a stroke and a spastic paresis of one arm or a person with a Parkinson's syndrome in whom the rigor is stronger on one side of the body than on the other. In these individuals, the **persistent** holding of a limb against gravity, e.g. the holding of the flexed forearm, is coded as *rest* as further muscle relaxation is physiologically not possible. In contrast, if the holding of a limb against gravity constitutes a *pose* unit, there should be evidence in the video material that the individual actually can relax the limb.

4.5 Procedure for Step 2 / Module I in NEUROGES® -ELAN

4.5.1 Generation of the 'to-be-coded' Structure and R/P Structure units

The 'to-be-coded' Structure units are generated by copying the *movement* units.

Researchers who have also generated *rest/pose* units in Step 1 and kept them on the same tier as the *movement* units, i.e., on the tiers rh_Activation_RX and lh_Activation_RX, copy the *rest/pose* units together with the *movement* units in the same procedure to the new tiers rh_Structure_RX and lh_Structure_RX.

Researchers who have generated *rest/pose* units in Step 1 but saved them separate from the *movement* units, i.e., on the tiers rh_Rest/Pose_RX and lh_Rest/Pose_RX, have to copy the *rest/pose* units in a separate procedure to the new tiers rh_R/PStructure_RX and lh_R/PStructure_RX. This route is obligatory if you want to conduct the R/P Contact assessment for *r/p rest* and *r/p pose* units later on (see 3.5).

Open the eaf file with the Activation units (Step 1 codings), then proceed as follows:

Apply the function: Tier > Copy Tier.

Select a tier to copy: click on rh_Activation_RX.

Next.

Select the new parent tier: skip this step.

Next.

Select another linguistic type: click on Structure.

Finish.

Apply the function: Tier > Copy Tier.

Select a tier to copy: click on lh_Activation_RX.

Next.

Select the new parent tier: skip this step.

Next.

Select another linguistic type: click on Structure.

Finish.

When the two operations are finished,

apply the function: Tier > Change Tier Attributes.

Scroll down in the list of Current Tiers to the end:

Click on rh_Activation_RX-cp.

Enter the Tier Name: rh_Structure_RX ('RX' = your initials).

Enter the Annotator: your name.

Enter the Participant: the identification of the person whom you are going to code.

Change.

Click on lh_Activation_RX-cp.

Enter the Tier Name: lh_Structure_RX ('RX' = your initials).

Enter the Annotator: your name.

Enter the Participant: the identification of the person whom you are going to code.

Change.
Close.

Now, you have the following new tiers:

rh_Structure_RX

lh_Structure_RX

Proceed analogously for the other parts of the body.

4.5.2 Coding of the 'to-be-coded' Structure and R/P Structure units

The units on the tiers rh_Structure_RX and lh_Structure_RX are now taken as the basis for the coding of the Structure category (therefore, they are termed 'to-be-coded' Structure units). These units still have the copied values *movement* and *rest/pose*, respectively. The 'to-be-coded' Structure units are assessed with the Structure values listed below. Technically, by double-clicking on the unit and clicking on the correct Structure value, the old *movement* values are replaced by the Structure values:

irregular

repetitive

phasic

shift

aborted

The old *rest/pose* values are replaced by the R/PStructure values:

r/p rest

r/p pose

In the template the value (*rest/pose*) marked by brackets is provided for manual unit generation (see 4.5.3) for researchers who do not want to further classify *rest/pose* units.

The value**?** is provided for work-in-progress. If you are not sure about the value of the unit and you want to get back to this unit later again, mark the unit preliminarily with the value?.

For the final statistical data evaluation, the value? is only accepted as a final code for those units in which the hand is not fully visible, e.g. if the hand is hidden beneath the table, but it is evident from the arm movements that there must be a hand movement. In the statistical evaluation, these values count as not sufficiently visible movements.

Especially in long 'to-be-coded' units, the Structure value might change within the unit (see 4.2.1). Then divide the old unit in the new subunits. As an example, the 'to-be-coded' unit turns out to contain to three different Structure values, e.g. *repetitive – phasic – irregular*. Delete the unit and replace it by the three new subunits. With regard to the precise segmentation of a unit into subunits (where to segment the unit), the procedure is described in detail in 4.2.1.

Important: Code first the units of the rh_Structure_RX, then the units of the tier lh_Structure_RX. It is essential to obey this order of coding, as a simultaneous coding of the right and left hand creates the tendency to adapt the values of the two hands to each other.

4.5.3 Alternative procedure: Manual generation of Step 2 / Module I units and coding

If you start with the Structure category, i.e., you have not coded the Activation category, use the alternative procedure of manual unit generation. In this procedure, the tiers rh_Structure_R0, lh_Structure_R0, rf_Structure_R0, lf_Structure_R0, trunk_Structure_R0, and head_Structure_R0 are used that are provided in the template. Directly tag and code the Structure value of the movement or the rest/pose.

Likewise, for short video clips you might prefer the manual unit generation, even if you have coded the Activation category before. Click on the first unit in the tier rh_Activation_R0. A blue vertical bar appears. Follow the bar to the level of the tier rh_Structure_R0, double click, and a tag appears. Thereby, you have copied the unit from the tier rh_Activation_R0 to rh_Structure_R0. Proceed with copying the next unit on the tier rh_Activation_R0. After having copied all units of the tier rh_Activation_R0, you recode them with the Structure values. You repeat the same procedure for the units of the tier lh_Activation_R0. It is essential to obey this order of coding, as a simultaneous coding of the right and left hand creates the tendency to adapt the values of the two hands to each other.

5 The Focus category

5.1 Definition of the Focus category

The Focus category classifies *phasic, repetitive,* and *irregular* units according to the locus where the part of the body acts (on). The assessment is limited to these three Structure values as per definition in *shift* and *aborted* units there is no acting (on something). Six Focus values are distinguished: (i) *within body*, (ii) *on body*, (iii) *on attached object*, (iv) *on separate object*, (v) *on person*, and (vi) *in space* (Fig. 4).

The Focus category assessment is typically applied to the limbs, and most often to the upper limbs. Therefore, the Focus definitions are formulated for the upper limbs, but they apply likewise to the lower limbs[11]. Only in specific settings with bodily contact, e.g. parent-infant interaction or body-oriented psychotherapy, it might be useful to apply the Focus category to all four parts of the body[12].

The Focus category refers to the locus where the hand/arm or foot/leg (hereafter often only referred to as 'hand') acts (on). It is operationalized by four criteria: presence of physical contact with something/someone (presence vs. absence), quality of physical contact (dynamic vs. static), the object/subject of dynamic contact, and orientation in absence of dynamic contact (body-external vs. body-internal). Short definitions of the Focus values and their reliabilities are given in Tab. 4.

Thereby, the Focus category registers loci of sensory stimulation. These can be ordered from body-internal to body-external as reflected in the order of the six Focus values from left to right in Fig. 4. A second aspect of the Focus category is that it provides information about attention processes as at least overt goal-directed (voluntary *phasic* and *repetitive*) hand movements are preceded by a shift of attention towards the goal, i.e., here the locus of sensory stimulation (but

11 As the large majority of the researchers has used NEUROGES® for the analysis of the upper limbs and as the NEUROGES® Focus category is identical for the upper and lower limbs, in order to facilitate reading, the definitions are formulated for hand/arm/shoulder movements. However, in the **Examples ♦** sections for each NEUROGES® value, examples are also provided for foot/leg movements.

12 However, the differentiation of intransitive movements into *within body* and *in space* is conceptualized specifically for limb movements, as–with the exception of some elaborate dance performances–only the limbs are moved to a specific location in order to act there (*in space*).

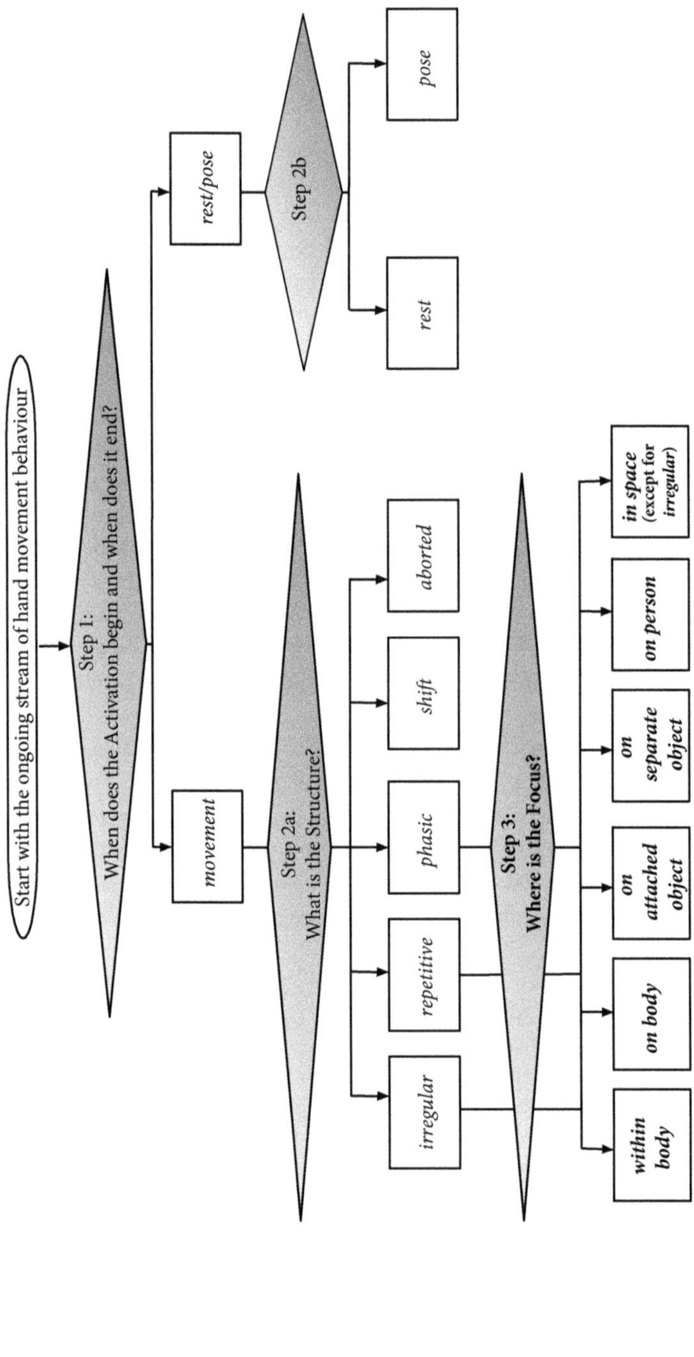

Fig. 4: The analysis algorithm for the Kinesic module (Module I) with the Focus category (Step 3) in fat print

Tab. 4: Short definitions and reliabilities of the Focus values

Focus value	**Short definition**	**Reliability* M ± SD**
within body	1. acting on body-internal structures, i.e., muscles, tendons, joints, by moving them without touching them; 2. movements of the shoulders and hips	.62 ± .21
on body	acting on the body surface	.83 ± .13
on attached object	acting on an object that is attached to the body	.87 ± .23
on separate object	acting on an object that is separate from the body	.57 ± .23
on person	acting on another person's body	1.00 (only 1 study)
in space	acting in the body-external free space without touching anything	.89 ± .08

* Interrater reliability as measured with EasyDIAg (from Lausberg & Slöetjes, 2016)

see also book I, section II). Finally, the Focus category indirectly provides information about the individual's body image.

It is recommended to concatenate the Focus value of a movement with the Structure value of that movement. The concatenation delivers StructureFocus units, which constitute fine-grained types of kinesic behavior (see 5.5).

5.2 Generation of the 'to-be-coded' Focus units and selection of the unit phases submitted to Focus assessment

5.2.1 Generation of the 'to-be-coded' Focus units

The *phasic, repetitive,* and *irregular* Structure units that result from the Step 2 / Module I coding are adopted for the Focus category assessment. They are then termed 'to-be-coded' Focus units and they are further classified with the six Focus values.

If there are one or more changes of the Focus within a 'to-be-coded' Focus unit, e.g. first *on body*, then *in space*, then the Focus changes demarcate new Focus units, e.g. new Focus unit 1 *on body*, new Focus unit 2 *in space*.

If the Structure value of the 'to-be-coded' Focus unit that contains two or more new Focus units is *phasic* or *repetitive*, then the segmentation of the 'to-be-coded' Focus unit into new Focus units is determined by the beginning of the transport phase (T). The procedure is the same procedure as for the Structure category assessment (see 4.2.1, second paragraph; see examples in the NEUROGES® training videos Pre-Intermediate 00:00:25.000; Intermediate 00:00:41.000).

5.2.2 Selection of the unit phases submitted to Focus assessment

For the Focus assessment two types of 'to-be-coded' Focus units have to be distinguished:

(i) 'to-be-coded' Focus units with a *phasic* or *repetitive* Structure: The Focus assessment refers only to the complex phase (pC or rC), and **not** to the transport phase (T) nor the retraction phase (R).
(ii) 'to-be-coded' Focus units with an *irregular* Structure: The Focus assessment refers to the whole unit.

(*Shift* and *aborted* units are not submitted to the Focus assessment).

Furthermore, as already described for the Activation category and the Structure category, a 'to-be-coded' Focus unit may contain simultaneous isolated movements of different parts of the upper limb, e.g. a thumb toss co-occurring with a shoulder shrug. These independent simultaneous movements within one limb require consideration in the Focus coding if the values between the two segments differ, e.g. a shoulder shrug (StructureFocus value: *phasic within body*) co-occurs with a thumb toss (StructureFocus value: *phasic in space*). In this case, the spatially and dynamically more complex movement is coded (compare 4.2.1).

5.2.3 Alternative generation of 'to-be-coded' Focus units

Researchers who start with the Focus category, i.e., who have not coded the Activation and Structure categories before, identify *phasic, repetitive*, and *irregular* movements (see definitions in the Structure category chapter) in the ongoing flow of kinesic behavior and classify them directly with the Focus values according to the rules described in 5.2.2. This approach saves time but it is more challenging than the stepwise procedure and it provides information only about the Focus category.

5.3 Criteria for the definition of the Focus values

The Focus values are defined according to the following criteria:

Presence of Physical Contact: This criterion refers to the presence or absence of physical contact between the moving parts of the limb and something/-one. The acting parts of the upper limb are most often the hand or only the fingers (and for the lower limb the foot). It is evident that the hand can most easily reach other parts of the body, attached or separate objects, or other persons, while it less comfortable to establish contact with the elbow and especially the shoulder. This can be observed only in exceptional cases, e.g. if the hands are dirty and there is an itching at the cheek, lissom persons might use the lower arm or even the shoulder to rub the face.

During the *irregular* unit or during the complex phase of a *phasic* or *repetitive* unit, the moving part of the limb has...

(i) no contact: There is no physical contact of the limb with anything/-one.
(ii) contact: There is physical contact of the limb with something/-one (primary contact). This thing can be in further contact with another thing or person (secondary contact), e.g. hand holds a hammer that hits a nail.

Quality of Physical Contact: In case of the presence of physical contact, this criterion refers to the quality of that contact. During the *irregular* unit or during the complex phase of a *phasic* or *repetitive* unit, the primary and/or secondary physical contact of the moving parts of the limb is...

(i) dynamic: The hand or foot **acts on** something. After having established the contact, the spatial relation between the hand and the object/subject of contact changes, e.g. the hands strokes on the arm rest. The hand or foot action is directed at something and potentially changes it, e.g. the right foot scratches the lower left leg. Note that during repetitive complex phases (rC), the dynamic contact might include short phases of separation, e.g. the hand claps repetitively on the thigh.
(ii) static: The hand or foot **acts with** something. After having established the contact, the spatial relation between the hand and the object/subject of contact does not change. The hand has an actively fixated relation to the object/subject of contact, e.g. the hand holds a hammer. Note that, however, that especially in tool use there can be a secondary contact that is dynamic, e.g. hand writes with a pen (primary static contact) on a piece of paper (secondary dynamic contact). The dynamic contact no matter if it primary or secondary determines the Focus value. Thus, the Focus value is always determined by the object/subject that the gesturer **acts on** (dyamic contact) and **not** by the object/subject that the gesturer **acts with** (static contact).

Object/Subject of Dynamic Contact: In case of the dynamic physical contact, this criterion refers to the object/subject that the moving part of the limb is in contact with. During the *irregular* unit or during the complex phase of a *phasic* or *repetitive* unit, the moving part of the hand is in dynamic physical contact with …

(i) a part of the body: any part of the body including the hand itself. Thus, finger-to-finger movements within one hand are included here.

(ii) an attached object: any object that is attached to the body. These are typically clothes, jewelry, or medical devices, e.g. a finger ring, a tie, a necklace, glasses, trousers. Objects are classified as attached objects as long as they are connected with the body. If they are removed from the body, e.g. glasses are put on the table, the objects are classified as separate objects.

(iii) a separate object: any object that is separate from the body, e.g. a pen, a table, an arm rest. Objects are classified as separate objects as long as they are not connected with the body. If they are attached to the body, e.g. glasses are put on the nose, the objects are classified as attached objects.

(iv) a person: any person that is touched, typically the interactive partner or a bystander.

Orientation in Absence of Dynamic Contact: In case of the absence of dynamic physical contact, this criterion specifies the space that the movement is directed at. Two spaces are distinguished:

(i) body-external free space: The body-external space is the space outside the body-surface and within the reach of the fingers tips when the arms are extended (see also 8.3. definition of gesture/action space). The body-external **free** space is the space within the body-external space that is free of an object/subject. The free space is filled with air. Theoretically, it could also be filled with water, e.g. if someone gestures or acts under water. The body-external free space includes the gesture space (see 8.3), which is in front of the thorax. There needs to be a transport phase to move the hand into the body-external free space so that it can act there. Thus, the use of the body-external free space requires a *phasic* or *repetitive* Structure of the movement.

(ii) body-internal space: The body-internal space is the space within the body, i.e., inside the surface. The body-internal space is modified by changes in muscle length, tendons, and joint position. In contrast to the body-external free space, the body-internal space can be used in *phasic, repetitive* and *irregular* movements.

Structure: This criterion refers to if a Focus value is typically associated with a specific Structure value. Vice versa, the Structure values partly pre-determine the Focus values:

(i) If the Structure value is *phasic*, all Focus values may occur.

(ii) If the Structure value is *repetitive*, all Focus values may occur.
(iii) If the Structure value is *irregular*, all Focus values with the exception of the value *in space* may occur.
(If the Structure value is *shift* or *aborted*, no Focus is coded).

5.4 Definitions of the Focus values

5.4.1 *within body*

Short definition

ACTING ON BODY-INTERNAL STRUCTURES

Definition

1. During the complex phase of a *phasic* or *repetitive* unit or during the *irregular* unit, the hand movement focuses on the body-internal space. This is the space within the body-surface that is modified among others by changes in muscle length and joint position.
2. All shoulder (and hip) movements are coded as *within body*.

Meeting the criteria

Presence of Physical Contact: In most cases, during the complex phase, or during the irregular unit the hand is not in contact with anything/-one.
If it is in contact with something, then the contact is static:
(i) Together with the other hand as a unit (see also 6.4.2 Contact value *act as a unit*), the hand acts *within body*, e.g. the palms of folded hands are turned outwards and the arms are extended, such that the medial muscles and tendons of the hands and lower arms are stretched.
(ii) With an attached object in hand, the hand acts *within body*, e.g. circulating in the wrist while holding the worn scarf.
(iii) With a separate object in hand, the hand acts *within body*, e.g. performing weight training.

Quality of Physical Contact: The hand is not in primary or secondary dynamic contact with something/someone.

Object/Subject of Dynamic Contact: There is no object/subject with which/whom the hand is in primary or secondary dynamic contact.

Orientation: The movement always focuses on the body-internal space.

Structure: Most frequently, the Structure of *within body* units is *irregular*. In rare cases, the Structure of *within body* units is *phasic* or *repetitive* but then often without a transport phase: As the focus is on body-internal structures, the hand does not need to be transported anywhere in the body-external space, e.g. opening and closing the fingers of the hand in order to stretch them.

Occurrence: *Within* body units were investigated in 191 individuals of the NEUROGES® archive. Right hand *within body* movements were displayed by 57 % (109/191) of the individuals, and left hand *within body* movements by 62 % (118/191).

Frequency: In the NEUROGES® archive sample, right hand *within body* units were displayed with a frequency (Mean ± Standard Deviation; Median) of 0.60 ± 1.22; 0.18 units per minute, and left hand *within body* units with a frequency of 0.61 ± 0.98; 0.26.

Duration: The duration (Mean ± Standard Deviation; Median) of right hand *within body* units was 1.10 ± 0.86; 0.99 seconds per unit, and that of left hand *within body* units 1.37 ± 1.06; 0.93 seconds per unit.

Examples *for phasic within body, repetitive within body,* and *irregular within body* units

- ◆ i) hands rest in lap (*rest position*) ⇒ fingers are stretched and then relax again (pC *within body*) ⇒ rest again
- ◆ ii) hand rests ⇒ repetitive isolated rolling in the hand wrist (rC *within body*) ⇒ rest again
- ◆ iii) hand rests ⇒ fingers start little movements in various manners (*irregular within body*) ⇒ rest again
- ◆ iv) hands/arms/shoulders rest ⇒ shoulders start moving in an irregular manner (*irregular within body*) ⇒ rest
- ◆ v) hand rests on arm rest ⇒ short, tic-like movements of the fingers (*irregular within body*) ⇒ rest
- ◆ lower limbs: *rest* position with crossed legs, right leg above the left one ⇒ repetitive circulating with the foot to stretch the tendons and muscles (rC *within body*) ⇒ foot *rests* again
- ◆ lower limbs: *rest* position with sitting with open legs ⇒ small tic-like erratic movements of the foot (*irregular within body*) ⇒ foot *rests* again

Differentiate *within body* from…

🖉 *in space*: In *in space* units, the complex phase is typically preceded by a transport phase. In contrast, in *within body* units, the complex phase usually starts where the limb rests.

In settings with physical exercises it has to observed carefully, if the Focus of the exercise is more on a demonstration in space, e.g. as in dance, or on the effect on body-internal structures, e.g. Feldenkrais exercises.

✐ *on separate object, on attached object, on body*: In these units, the Focus is on the object or the part of body. In *within body* units, the Focus is on body-internal structures (even if the hand is in static contact with a separate object, with an attached object, or with a part of the body).

5.4.2 *on body*

Short definition

ACTING ON THE BODY SURFACE

Definition

During the complex phase of a *phasic* or *repetitive* unit or during an *irregular* unit, the acting parts of the hand act on the body. The primary or secondary contact between the hand and the body part is dynamic. Included here are dynamic within-one-hand movements, i.e., finger-to-finger movements of one hand.

Meeting the criteria

Presence of Physical Contact: The hand is always in physical contact with the body.
Quality of Physical Contact: The hand is always in primary or secondary dynamic contact with the body.
Object/Subject of Dynamic Contact: The object of the primary or secondary dynamic contact is the surface of a part of the body.

If the dynamic contact on the body surface is primary, the hand directly acts on it, e.g. stroking the cheek.

If the dynamic contact on the body surface is secondary, there is a primary static contact:

(i) Together with the other hand (see also 6.4.2 Contact value *act as a unit*), the hand acts on the body, e.g. the folded hands scratch the belly.
(ii) With an attached object in hand, the hand acts on the body, e.g. rotating the finger ring on the finger.
(iii) With a separate object in hand, the hand acts on the body, e.g. scratching the face with a pen.

Orientation: -

Structure: *On body* units may have a *phasic*, a *repetitive*, or an *irregular* Structure.
Occurrence: *On body* units were investigated in 191 individuals of the NEUROGES® archive. Right hand *on body* movements were displayed by 99 % (189/191) of the individuals, and left hand *on body* movements by 99 % (189/191).

Frequency: In the NEUROGES® archive sample (n = 191), right hand *on body* units were displayed with a frequency (Mean ± Standard Deviation; Median) of 3.96 ± 2.66; 3.76 units per minute, and left hand *on body* units with a frequency of 3.46 ± 2.59; 2.84.

Duration: The duration (Mean ± Standard Deviation; Median) of right hand *on body* units was 2.89 ± 2.62; 2.14 seconds per unit, and that of left hand *on body* units 3.00 ± 2.25; 2.45 seconds per unit.

Examples for *phasic on body, repetitive on body,* and *irregular on body* units

- ◆ i) hand rests on the thigh (*rest position*) ⇒ moves to the face (complete T) ⇒ strokes the face (pC *on body*) ⇒ moves back to the thigh (complete R) ⇒ rests
- ◆ ii) hand rests on the thigh ⇒ moves on the thigh towards the knee (rare case of transport phase with a trajectory on the body) ⇒ strokes the knee once (pC *on body*) ⇒ rests on the knee (no R, new *rest position*)
- ◆ iii) left side hemiparetic subject sitting with left leg crossed over, right hand rests on table ⇒ right hand moves to left paretic leg (complete T) ⇒ right hand moves the left paretic leg to another position (pC *on body*) ⇒ right hand retracts (complete R) ⇒ rest
- ◆ iv) hands rest on the thighs ⇒ both hands rise to meet each other (complete T) ⇒ the hands clap once (pC *on body*) ⇒ move back to thigh (complete R) ⇒ rest
- ◆ v) hand rests on the knee with palm down ⇒ fingers rise while palm remains on the knee (complete T) ⇒ fingers perform repetitive up-down movements with downward accent on knee (rC *on body*) ⇒ rest (no R, old rest position). Note that ss the dynamic emphasis of the hand movement is directed on the body, the movement is coded as *repetitive on body*. Compare *in space* example ◆ v.
- ◆ vi) hand rests on table with palm down ⇒ radial side of hand turns up, while ulnar side rests on table (complete T) ⇒ repetitively snaps one's fingers (rC *on body*) ⇒ moves back (complete R) ⇒ rest
- ◆ vii) hands rest on the thighs ⇒ both hands rise to meet each other (complete T) ⇒ hands clap repetitively (rC *on body*) ⇒ move back to the thighs (complete R) ⇒ rest
- ◆ viii) hands rest ⇒ both hands rise to meet each other (complete T) ⇒ right index touches the digits of the left hand one after other (rC *on body*) ⇒ move back to the thighs (complete R) ⇒ rest
- ◆ ix) folded hands rest ⇒ folded hands rise (complete T) ⇒ folded hands rub the face (rC *on body*) ⇒ folded hands move back to the lap (complete R) ⇒ rest

- ◆ x) hand on knee ⇒ (no T) hand starts erratically squeezing the knee (*irregular on body*) ⇒ (no R) hand comes to rest again
- ◆ xi) hand on armrest ⇒ (no T) the fingers of the hand start fidgeting on each other (*irregular on body*) ⇒ (no R) fingers comes to rest
- ◆ xii) hands rest folded ⇒ (no T) right hand fingers start rubbing on the left hand in an irregular manner (*irregular on body*) ⇒ (no R) fingers rest again
- ◆ xiii) hand rests with pen in hand (*rest position* with a separate object in hand) ⇒ moves hand with pen to ear (complete T) ⇒ strokes repetitively with pen behind the ear (rC with separate object *on body*) ⇒ moves hand with pen back (complete R) ⇒ rests. Note that the contact with the pen is static, and therefore, it does not determine the Focus value.
- ◆ xiv) hand holds a pen, arms are crossed ⇒ hand moves with pen to knee (complete T) ⇒ repetitively hits the knee with pen (rC with separate object *on body*) ⇒ moves hand with pen back to old rest position (complete R) ⇒ rests with pen in hand. Note that the contact with the pen is static, and therefore, it does not determine the Focus value.
- ◆ lower limbs: *rest* position with open legs ⇒ right foot moves to left shin (complete T) ⇒ repetitive scratching the left shin with the right foot (rC *within body*) ⇒ right foot moves to open rest position (complete R) ⇒ *rests* again

Differentiate *on body* from…

- ✐ *in space*: *On body* units may be confused with *in space* units in which there is a static contact of the hands. *In space* units may include a static contact with the other hand. In unity with the other hand, the hand acts *in space*, e.g. hands in prayer position perform a *deictic*. It is evident that the Focus is on acting in the body-external free space (here: gesture space) and not on the other hand. The same applies to the static contact between the fingers of one hand, e.g. when displaying the ring gesture.
- ✐ *on person:* If the gesturer acts on the other person's body, i.e., on the other person, the value *on person* is given.
- ✐ *on separate object*: *On body* units may be confused with *on separate object* units in which there is a static contact of the hands. In an *on separate object* unit, the Focus is on the separate object. Included here are those rare movements in which the hands as a unity act on the separate object, e.g. the hands are in prayer form and as a unit, they beat on the table. The contact between the two hands is static.

In contrast, in an *on body* unit, the hand may act with a separate object on the body, e.g. rubbing the head with a pen.

- *on attached object*: In an *on attached object* unit, the Focus is on the attached object. Included here are those rare units in which in unity with the other hand, the hand acts on an attached object, e.g. the folded hands adjust the pullover.

In contrast, in an *on body* unit, the hand may act with an attached object on the body, e.g. rubbing the face with a scarf.

As body-attached objects are very close to the body and therefore, most actions on the attached object also stimulate the body, it has to be observed carefully if the attached object is used as a tool to stimulate the body or if the Focus of action is primarily on the attached object.

- *within body:* Movements that focus on internal structures such as muscles, tendons, and joints may be performed while a static contact between the hand and the part of the body is kept, e.g. circling the shoulders with folded hands. In the example, the Focus is determined by the dynamic movement directed at the body-internal structures of the shoulders and not by the static contact between the hands.
- *rest/pose* (here: *rest/pose* with body contact): During *rest/poses* there may be a static contact of the hand with a part of the body, e.g. the hand rests on the lap or the hands rest folded. Actually, such *rest/pose* units should not appear as 'to-be-coded' Focus units. If they do, this error should be corrected.

5.4.3 *on attached object*

Short definition

ACTING ON AN OBJECT THAT IS ATTACHED TO THE BODY

Definition

During the complex phase of a *phasic* or *repetitive* unit or during an *irregular* unit, the hand is in primary or secondary dynamic contact with objects that are attached to the body. The hand manipulates attached objects, such as a watch, clothes, jewelry, or glasses. Objects are classified as attached as long as they are connected to the body. If they are removed from the body, the objects are classified as separate, e.g. glasses are put on the table.

Meeting the criteria

Presence of Physical Contact: The hand is always in physical contact with something.

Quality of Physical Contact: The hand is always in primary or secondary dynamic contact with something.

Object/Subject of Dynamic Contact: The object of the primary or secondary dynamic contact is an attached object.

If the dynamic contact on the attached object is primary, the hand directly acts on it, e.g. playing with the necklace.

If the dynamic contact on the attached object is secondary, there is a primary static contact:

(i) Together with the other hand (see also 6.4.2 Contact value *act as a unit*), the hand acts on an attached object, e.g. the folded hands touch the shoe.

(ii) With an attached object in hand, the hand acts on another attached object, e.g. rubbing with a worn scarf on the watch. Note that the *value on attached object* refers to the action on the watch.

(iii) With a separate object in hand, the hand acts on an attached object, e.g. tapping with a pen on the watch.

Orientation: -

Structure: *On attached object* units may have a *phasic*, a *repetitive*, or an *irregular* Structure.

Occurrence: *On attached object* movements were investigated in 73 individuals of the NEUROGES® archive. Right hand *on attached object* movements were displayed by 37 % (27/73) of the individuals, and left hand *on attached object* movements by 37 % (27/73).

Frequency: In the NEUROGES® archive sample (n = 73), right hand *on attached object* units were displayed with a frequency (Mean ± Standard Deviation; Median) of 0.17 ± 0.31; 0.00 units per minute, and left hand *on attached object* units with a frequency of 0.19 ± 0.40; 0.00.

Duration: The duration (Mean ± Standard Deviation; Median) of right hand *on attached object* units was 2.69 ± 1.80; 2.08 seconds per unit, and that of left hand *on attached object* units 2.25 ± 0.90; 2.13 seconds per unit.

Examples for *phasic on attached object, repetitive on attached object,* and *irregular on attached object* units

- ◆ i) hand rests on the thigh (*rest position*) ⇒ moves to the earring (complete T) ⇒ strokes along the earring (pC *on attached object*) ⇒ moves back to the thigh (complete R) ⇒ rests
- ◆ ii) hand rests on the thigh ⇒ moves along the leg to a sock (rare case of transport phase with a trajectory on the body) ⇒ adjusts the sock (pC *on attached object*) ⇒ moves back on the leg to the knee (rare case of complete retraction phase with a trajectory on the body) ⇒ rests

- ◆ iii) hand rests on the thigh ⇒ moves to the tie (complete T) ⇒ strokes along the tie (pC *on attached object*) ⇒ moves back to the thigh (complete R) ⇒ rests
- ◆ iv) hand in rest position ⇒ moves to glasses that are on the nose (complete T) ⇒ moves the glasses upwards on the nose (pC *on attached object*) ⇒ moves back to rest position (complete R)
- ◆ v) hand rests on the thigh ⇒ rises and moves to tie (complete T) ⇒ repetitively pulls on tie (rC *on attached object*) ⇒ moves back to the thigh (complete R) ⇒ rests
- ◆ vi) hands rest on table ⇒ right hand moves to pullover (1rst, complete T) ⇒ grasps pullover (1rst pC 1 *on attached object*) ⇒ moves with pullover in hand to the watch on the left wrist (2nd, partial T) ⇒ cleans the face of the watch with the pullover in repetitive circular movements (2nd rC with an attached object *on attached object*) ⇒ moves back to the table (complete R) ⇒ rests
- ◆ vii) hand rests on lap on a pullover ⇒ (no T) starts fidgeting continuously with the pullover (*irregular on attached object*) (no R) ⇒ rests
- ◆ lower limbs: *rest* position with crossed legs, the left trouser leg has got out of place ⇒ right foot moves to left trouser leg (complete T) ⇒ moves down the trouser leg (pC *on attached object*) ⇒ right foot moves back to rest position with crossed legs (complete R) ⇒ rests
- ◆ lower limbs: *rest* position with sitting with open legs ⇒ removing with the left foot the shoe of the right foot

Differentiate *on attached object* from…

- ✐ *in space*: In general, *in space* units are easy to distinguish from *on attached object* units. However, it may occur that with an attached object in hand, the hand acts *in space*, e.g. gesturing with a scarf, which is worn, in hand. This is coded as *in space*, because the Focus of the hand movement is not on the attached object but on the action in the body-external free space.
- ✐ *on separate object*: In *on separate object* units, the Focus of the action is on an object that is separate from the body. In general, it is unambiguous if an object is separate from or attached to the body. The only cases that require consideration are those, in which the status of the object changes, i.e., a separate object can become attached to the body, and vice versa, an attached object can become separate from the body. If objects that are separate from the body are attached to the body, they become attached objects. Technically, the Focus value changes within the 'to-be-coded' Focus unit. As an example, the glasses on the table are grasped (Focus value *on separate object*) and then put on (Focus value *on attached object*). Or vice versa, the glasses on the nose are grasped (Focus value *on attached object*) and then put on the table (Focus value *on separate object*).

Furthermore, *on separate object* units may include a static contact with an attached object. With an attached object in hand, the hand acts on a separate object, e.g. the gesturer cleans the table with the tie that he wears. This is an *on separate object* unit because the Focus is on cleaning the table, and not on the attached tie, which is held in hand and with which the hand acts.

- *on body*: In *on body* units, the Focus of the action is on the body and not on the attached object. This is unambiguous for those units, which the hand is in direct dynamic contact with the skin. However, as the biggest part of the body surface is covered with clothes, naturally, one has to be in contact with the clothes, to stimulate the skin. For example, a gesturer, who wears trousers, strokes his leg. This happens naturally via the trousers, i.e., in physical contact with the trousers. As the gesturer acts on the body and not the trousers, this is coded as *on body*.

In contrast, when a gesturer, who wears trousers, stretches the trousers, this is coded as *on attached object*. Furthermore, if a gesturer puts glasses on the nose, there is no primary stimulation of the body, but the action focuses on the positioning of the glasses. Therefore, the value *on attached object* is given.

However, as body-attached objects are very close to the body and therefore, most actions on the attached object also stimulate the body, it has to be observed carefully if the attached object is used as a tool to stimulate the body or if the Focus of the action is primarily on the attached object.

- *within body*: Movements that aim at moving muscles, tendons, and joints may be performed with an attached object that is held in hand, e.g. circling the shoulders while holding the jacket. The contact with the jacket is static, the Focus is on the body-internal space. Thus, the unit is coded as *within body*.
- *rest/pose*: During *rest/pose* the hand may be in contact with an attached object, e.g. when the hand rests on the watch. Actually, such *rest/pose* units should not appear as 'to-be-coded' Focus units. If they do, this error should be corrected.

5.4.4 *on separate object*

Short definition

ACTING ON AN OBJECT THAT IS SEPARATE FROM THE BODY

Definition

During the complex phase of a *phasic* or *repetitive* unit or during an *irregular* unit, the hand is in primary or secondary dynamic contact with objects that are separate from the body, such as a table.

Meeting the criteria

Presence of Physical Contact: The hand is always in physical contact with something.

Quality of Physical Contact: The hand is always in primary or secondary dynamic contact with something.

Object/Subject of Dynamic Contact: The object of the primary or secondary dynamic contact is a separate object.

If the dynamic contact on the separate object is primary, the hand directly acts on it, e.g. stroking over the table.

If the dynamic contact on the separate object is secondary, there is a primary static contact:

(i) In unity with the other hand (see also 6.4.2 Contact value *act as a unit*), the hand acts on a separate object, e.g. folded hands beat on the table.

(ii) With an attached object in hand, the hand acts on another separate object, e.g. rubbing with a scarf that is being worn on the table. In the example, the value *on separate object* refers to the table, and not to the scarf.

(iii) With a separate object in hand, the hand acts on another separate object, e.g. writing with a pen on the paper, or tapping a pen on the table. In the examples, the value *on separate object* refers to the table and to the paper, and not to the pen.

Orientation: -

Structure: *On separate object* units may have a *phasic*, a *repetitive*, or an *irregular* Structure.

Occurrence: *On separate object* movements were investigated in 73 individuals of the NEUROGES® archive. Right hand *on separate object* movements are displayed by 30 % (22/73) of the individuals, and left hand *on separate object* movements by 33 % (24/73).

Frequency: In the NEUROGES® archive sample (n = 73), right hand *on separate object* units were displayed with a frequency (Mean ± Standard Deviation; Median) of 0.37 ± 1.13; 0.00 units per minute, and left hand *on separate object* units with a frequency of 0.36 ± 0.90; 0.00.

Duration: The duration (Mean ± Standard Deviation; Median) of right hand *on separate object* units was 5.90 ± 8.59; 2.58 seconds per unit, and that of left hand *on separate object* units 5.29 ± 7.43; 2.84 seconds per unit.

Examples for *phasic on separate object, repetitive on separate object,* and *irregular on separate object*

- i) hand rests on the thigh (*rest position*) ⇒ moves to the table (complete T) ⇒ strokes over the table (pC *on separate object*) ⇒ moves back to the thigh (complete R) ⇒ rests
- ii) hand rests on the thigh ⇒ moves to the table, where the glasses are (1^{rst}, complete T) ⇒ grasps the glasses (pC *on separate object*) ⇒ moves with the glasses in hand to the nose (2nd, partial T) ⇒ puts the glasses on (pC *on attached object*) ⇒ moves back to the thigh (complete R) ⇒ rests. Note that the second complex phase is coded as on attached object because the object is attached to the body.
- iii) hand rests ⇒ moves to a pen on the table (1^{rst}, complete T) ⇒ grasps the pen (1^{rst} pC *on separate object*) ⇒ moves hand with pen to ear (2nd, partial T) ⇒ strokes with pen behind the ear (2nd pC *on body*) ⇒ moves hand with pen back (complete R) ⇒ rests
- iv) hand rests ⇒ moves to a pen on the table (1^{rst}, complete T) ⇒ grasps the pen (1^{rst} pC *on separate object*) ⇒ moves hand with pen to the watch (2nd, partial T) ⇒ repetitively taps with the pen on the watch (2nd rC *on attached object*) ⇒ moves hand with pen back (complete R) ⇒ rests
- v) hand rests on table ⇒ moves to a pen on the table (1^{rst}, complete T) ⇒ grasps the pen (1^{rst} pC *on separate object*) ⇒ moves with pen to a piece of paper (2nd, partial T) ⇒ writes with the pen on a piece of paper (2nd pC *on separate object*) ⇒ moves with pen to a table (3rd, partial T) ⇒ puts the pen down (3rd pC *on separate object*) ⇒ retracts to rest position (complete R) ⇒ rests
- vi) hand rests on the thigh ⇒ moves to the table (complete T) ⇒ repetitively gallops on the table (rC *on separate object*) ⇒ rests on the table (no R, new *rest position*)
- vii) hand rests ⇒ moves to a pen on the table (complete T) ⇒ grasps the pen and repetitively manipulates it (pC *on separate object*) ⇒ rests with pen in hand on the table (no R, new *rest position* with a separate object in hand)
- viii) hand rests with pen in hand ⇒ hand with pen moves to table (complete T) ⇒ taps with the pen repetitively on the table (rC with separate object *on separate object*) ⇒ hand with pen moves back (complete R) ⇒ rests with pen in hand
- ix) hand rests on the table ⇒ (no T) starts drumming rhythmically on the table (rC *on separate object*) ⇒ (no R) rests on table in old rest position
- x) hand rests on arm rest ⇒ (no T) starts fidgeting on the arm rest in an irregular manner (*irregular on separate object*) ⇒ (no R) rests.
- xi) hand rests with pen in hand ⇒ (no T) starts fidgeting with the pen in an irregular manner (*irregular on separate object*) ⇒ (no R) rests.

- ♦ lower legs: moving away something on the floor, e.g. waste, with the foot; or stamping on the floor with anger
- ♦ lower limbs: sitting with open legs (*rest*) ⇒ right leg moves to a piece of waste that is on the floor (complete T) ⇒ kicks away the waste (pC *on separate object*) ⇒ right foot moves back to rest position (complete R) ⇒ rests
- ♦ lower limbs: sitting with crossed legs (*rest*) ⇒ right foot moves to left shoe (complete T) ⇒ removes the left shoe from the left foot (pC *on separate object*) ⇒ right foot moves back to rest position (complete R) ⇒ rests. Note that the removal of the left shoe from the foot is coded as *on separate object* because the shoe becomes a separate object.

Differentiate *on separate object* from…

- ✎ *in space*: In general, *in space* units are easy to distinguish from *on separate object* units. However, it may occur that with a separate object in hand, the hand acts *in space*, e.g. gesturing with a cigarette in hand. This is coded as *in space*, because the Focus of the hand movement is not on the separate object, but on the action in the body-external free space (here: gesture space).
- ✎ *on attached object*: In *on attached object* units, the Focus of the action is on an object that is attached to the body. In general, it is unambiguous if an object is separate from or attached to the body. The only cases that require consideration are those, in which the status of the object changes, i.e., a separate object can become attached to the body, and vice versa, an attached object can become separate from the body. If objects that are separate from the body are attached to the body, they become attached objects. Technically, the Focus value changes within the 'to-be-coded' Focus unit. As an example, the glasses on the table are grasped (Focus value *on separate object*) and then put on (Focus value *on attached object*). Or vice versa, the glasses on the nose are grasped (Focus value *on attached object*) and then put on the table (Focus value *on separate object*).

Furthermore, *on attached object* units may include a static contact with a separate object. With the separate object in hand, the hand acts on an attached object, e.g. touch-pointing with a pen on the watch that is tied around the wrist. This is an *on attached object* unit as the Focus is on the attached object.

- ✎ *on body*: In *on body* units, the Focus of the action is on the body. This is unambiguous for those units, which the hand is in direct dynamic contact with the body. However, also with the separate object in hand, the hand may act on the body, e.g. writing or tapping with a pen on the hand. This case is coded as *on body*, because the Focus of the action is on the body and not on the object itself.

- *within body*: Movements that aim at moving muscles, tendons, and joints may be performed with a separate object held in hand, e.g. circling the shoulders with a cigarette held in hand. The contact with the cigarette is static, the Focus is on the body-internal space. Thus, these units are coded as *within body*.
- *rest/pose:* During a *rest position* or *posture,* the gesturer may hold a separate object in hand, e.g. when the hand rests on the table and embrace a glass. Actually, such *rest/pose* units should not appear as 'to-be-coded' Focus units. If they do, this error should be corrected.

5.4.5 *on person*

Short definition

ACTING ON ANOTHER PERSON'S BODY

Definition

During the complex phase of a *phasic* or *repetitive* unit, the hand acts on another person, i.e. physically on the other person's body. This is a person who is within the gesturer's reach, typically the interactive partner or a bystander. Dynamic contact with objects that are attached to the other person's body is coded as well with the value *on person.*

Meeting the criteria

Presence of Physical Contact: The hand is always in physical contact with someone.

Quality of Physical Contact: The hand is always in primary or secondary dynamic contact with someone.

Object/Subject of Dynamic Contact: The subject of the primary or secondary dynamic contact is a person who is in reach.

If the dynamic contact on person is primary, the hand directly acts on the other person's body, e.g. displaying the High Five emblem, in which the two persons batter their hands at the level of their heads.

If the dynamic contact on person is secondary, there is a primary static contact the other person's body:

(i) The hand acts together as a unit with the other hand (see also 6.4.2 Contact value *act as a unit*), e.g. the folded hands touch on the other person.

(ii) The hand acts indirectly with an attached object on the other person, e.g. with his/her scarf the gesturer rubs the other person's hand.

(iii) The hand acts indirectly with a separate object on the other person, e.g. with a pen the gesturer touches the other person.

Orientation: -

Structure: The Structure is *phasic* or *repetitive.*

The exceptional occurrence of *irregular on person* units may be observed in intimate relationships, e.g. when a little baby is sitting on the mother's lap and the mother plays with the baby's hair.

Occurrence, Frequency, and Duration: Thus far, no data are available, since empirical studies that have been conducted so far did not investigate settings with body contact.

Examples for *phasic on person, repetitive on person,* and *irregular on person*

- ◆ i) hand rests on the thigh (*rest*) ⇒ moves to the other person (complete T) ⇒ gently strokes over the other person's hair (pC *on person*) ⇒ moves back to the thigh (complete R) ⇒ rests
- ◆ ii) hand rests with pen in hand ⇒ hand with pen moves to the other person (complete T) ⇒ taps with the pen repetitively on the other person's shoulder (rC with separate object *on person*) ⇒ moves hand with pen back (complete R) ⇒ rests with pen in hand
- ◆ iii) hand rests on lap ⇒ moves to a worn scarf (1rst, complete T) ⇒ grasps the scarf (1rst pC *on attached object*) ⇒ moves hand with scarf to the other person (2nd, partial T) ⇒ repetitively rubs with the scarf on the other person's dress to remove a blob (2nd rC *on person*) ⇒ hand with scarf back moves back (3rd, partial T) ⇒ drops scarf (3rd pC) ⇒ hand moves back to lap (complete R) ⇒ rests
- ◆ iv) parent's hand rests on baby's head ⇒ (no T) starts gently and slowly moving on baby's hair in an irregular manner, hand seems to move beyond the ges parent's awareness, as if going by itself (*irregular on person*) ⇒ (no R) rests.
- ◆ lower limbs: sitting at a table, legs hidden under the table (*rest*) ⇒ left foot moves to the neighbor's right foot (complete T) ⇒ gently touches the neighbor's right foot (pC *on person*) ⇒ left foot moves back to rest position (complete R) ⇒ rests

Differentiate *on person* from…

✐ *on attached object:* This value refers to units in which the gesturer acts on objects that are attached to her/his own body. In contrast, if the gesturer acts on objects that are attached to another person's body, the value *on person* is given.

- *on body:* This value refers to units in which the gesturer acts on her/his own body. In contrast, if the gesturer acts on the other person's body, the value *on person* is given.
- *rest/pose:* During *rest,* the gesturer may have her/his hand rest on another person, e.g. the gesturer's hand rests on another person's lap. Actually, such *rest/pose* units should not appear as 'to-be-coded' Focus units. If they do, this error should be corrected.

5.4.6 *in space*

Short definition

ACTING IN SPACE WITHOUT TOUCHING SOMETHING

Definition

During the complex phase of a *phasic* or *repetitive* unit, the hand acts in the free space that is external to the body surface and within the personal reach (see criterion body-external space).

Most often, the hand acts in the body-external free space in front of the thorax (gesture space). It is moved towards there with a transport phase. In rare cases, only the fingers move out into the space while the wrist or the palm remain resting.

Rarely, the hand acts **on** the air (or on the water) as a physical substrate, e.g. fanning the air.

Meeting the criteria

Presence of Physical Contact: In most cases, during the complex phase, the hand is not in contact with anything/-one.

If it is in contact with something, then the contact is static:

(i) Together with the other hand as a unit (see also 6.4.2 Contact value *act as a unit*), the hand acts *in space*, e.g. hands in prayer position perform an *egocentric deictic*. This is coded as *in space*, because the Focus of the hand movement is not on the other hand but on the action in the space.

(ii) With an attached object in hand, the hand acts *in space*, e.g. gesturing with a necklace in hand. This is coded as *in space*, because the Focus of the hand movement is not on the attached object but on the action in space.

(iii) With a separate object in hand, the hand acts *in space*, e.g. gesturing with a cigarette in hand. This is coded as *in space*, because the Focus of the hand movement is not on the separate object but on the action in space.

Quality of Physical Contact: The hand is not in primary or secondary dynamic contact with something/someone.

Object/Subject of Dynamic Contact: There is no object/subject with which/whom the hand is in primary or secondary dynamic contact.

Orientation: The movement always focuses on the body-external free space.

Structure: The value *in space* can only occur in *phasic* and *repetitive* units, since in *irregular* units, the hand is not oriented to the body-external space.

Occurrence: *In space* movements were investigated in 191 individuals of the NEUROGES® archive. Right hand *in space* movements were displayed by 100 % (190/191) of the individuals, and left hand *in space* movements by 100 % (190/191).

Frequency: In the NEUROGES® archive sample (n = 191), right hand *in space* units were displayed with a frequency (Mean ± Standard Deviation; Median) of 6.22 ± 4.13; 5.46 units per minute, and left hand *in space* units with a frequency of 5.48 ± 3.63; 4.44.

Duration: The duration (Mean ± Standard Deviation; Median) of right hand *in space* units was 3.02 ± 2.22; 2.41 seconds per unit, and that of left hand *in space* units 2.81 ± 1.02; 2.55 seconds per unit.

Examples for *phasic in space* and *repetitive in space* units

- ◆ i) hand rests on the thigh (*rest*) ⇒ rises (complete T) ⇒ traces a circle (pC *in space*) ⇒ moves back to the thigh (complete R) ⇒ rests
- ◆ ii) hands rest on the thighs ⇒ rise to meet each other (complete T) ⇒ touch of the tips of the indices (as starting point for symmetrical semicircles) (pC *on body*) ⇒ the right index draws the right half of the circle and the left index the left half of the circle (pC *in space*) ⇒ touch of the finger tips to close the circle (pC *on body*) ⇒ move back to thighs (complete R) ⇒ rest
- ◆ iv) hand rests on the thigh ⇒ rises (complete T) ⇒ several repetitive up-down movements in the air with downward accent (rC *in space*) ⇒ moves back to the thigh (complete R)
- ◆ v) hand rests on the knee with palm down ⇒ palm remains on the knee, while fingers perform repetitive up-down movements with upward accent (rC *in space*) ⇒ move down to knee (complete R) ⇒ rest. Note that as the dynamic emphasis of the hand movement is directed away from the body, the movement is coded as *repetitive in space*. Compare *on body* example ◆ v.
- ◆ vi) hand rests with pen in hand ⇒ rises with pen in hand (complete T) ⇒ performs repetitive up-down movements with downward accent in the air with pen held in hand (rC with separate object *in space*) ⇒ moves hand with pen back (complete R) ⇒ rests with pen in hand

- ♦ vii) hand rests ⇒ rises (complete T) ⇒ repetitively with a flat hand moves up and down to fan the embers (rC *in space*) ⇒ moves back (complete R) ⇒ rests. Note that as the hand is in primary dynamic contact with the air, the Focus is *in space* and not *on separate object.*
- ♦ lower limbs: standing (*rest*) ⇒ right foot moves to the left (complete T) ⇒ points to a location on the left (*egocentric deictic*, see 8.4.3) (pC *in space*) ⇒ right foot moves back to rest position (complete R) ⇒ rests
- ♦ lower limbs: sitting with crossed legs (*rest*) ⇒ right foot moves up (complete T) ⇒ performs a movement as if kicking something (*pantomime*, see 8.4.5) (pC *in space*) ⇒ right foot moves back to rest position (complete R) ⇒ rests

Differentiate *in space* movements from…

✐ *on separate object, on attached object, on body* (here: static contact): In *on body, on attached object,* and *on separate object units*, the hand is in dynamic contact with these parts of the body or objects, respectively. The Focus of the movement is on the body or the objects.

In *in space* movements, the hand may be only in static contact with a separate object, with an attached object or with the other hand (as a co-agent). The Focus of the movement is **not** on the objects or the hand but on the action in the body-external free space, e.g. gesturing with a glass held in hand or gesturing with folded hands.

✐ *on separate object, on attached object, on body* (here: short accidental contact): In *on body, on attached object,* and *on separate object units*, the establishment of contact and the subsequent display of dynamic contact (complex phase) is typically preceded by a transport phase.

In rare cases, *in space* movements may include a short, quasi accidental random physical contact of the body, an attached object, or a separate object. However, the physical contact does not constitute the complex phase, i.e., there is no long duration and no dynamic emphasis on the touch. Furthermore, there is no transport phase before the touch. The short touch represents only a (accidental) point on the trajectory of a constant dynamic movement which otherwise is *in space.*

✐ *on body*: In *on body* movements, the two hands may act dynamically on each other.

When the hands are folded but the thumbs are turned out and in again during the complex phase, this is coded as *in space*, because the acting parts (here: the thumbs) act in space.

✎ *within body*: A *within body* movement with a *phasic* or *repetitive* Structure has no transport phase, in which the hand is transported anywhere. In an *in space* movement the hand is transported to a specific location in the body-external free space.

In settings with physical exercises it has to observed carefully, if the Focus of the exercise is more on a demonstration in space, e.g. as in dance, or on the effect on body-internal structures, e.g. Feldenkrais exercises.

5.5 Generation of StructureFocus units

In the final evaluation step of Module I, the Structure units and the Focus units are concatenated (Fig. 5). This procedure produces units with StructureFocus values.

The data on the occurrence, the frequency, and the duration of the StructurFocus values given in Tab. 5 are based on the NEUROGES® archive. While the original NEUROGES® archive analysis included six empirical studies (total of 191 healthy individuals), not in all of these empirical studies StructureFocus values were created. Thus, as the raw occurrence data in Tab. 5 reveal, the number of individuals for whom StructureFocus values are available ranges between 71 and 151, because some StructureFocus values are simply only displayed by some individuals and not by others. Therefore, it is recommended to statistically conduct a descriptive statistics on the frequency distribution of the StructureFocus values (see 5.6.4 at the end).

5.6 Procedure in for Step 3 / Module I in NEUROGES® -ELAN

5.6.1 Generation of the 'to-be-coded' Focus units

The 'to-be-coded' Focus units are generated by copying the Structure units.

Open the eaf file with the Structure units (Step 2 codings), then proceed as follows:

Apply the function: Tier > Copy Tier.

Select a tier to copy: click on rh_Structure_R0/RX.[13]

Next.

Select the new parent tier: skip this step.

---

13 If you have conducted the automatic unit generation in the previous step, the tier name ending RX represents your initials. If you have generated the units manually and you have used the tiers that are provided in the template, the tier name ending is R0.

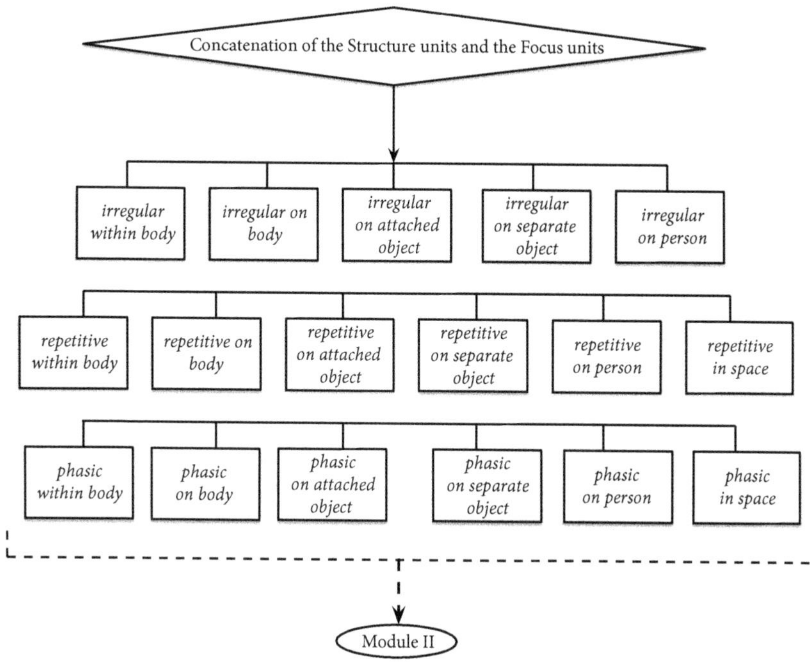

Fig. 5: Concatenation of the Structure units and the Focus units

Next.

Select another linguistic type: click on Focus.

Finish.

Apply the function: Tier > Copy Tier.

Select a tier to copy: click on lh_Structure_R0/RX.

Next.

Select the new parent tier: skip this step.

Next.

Select another linguistic type: click on Focus.

Finish.

Tab. 5: Occurrence, frequency, and duration of the StructureFocus values

StructureFocus value	Occurrence: n of individuals / sample in percentage and absolute numbers	Frequency: n of units / minute as Mean ± Standard Deviation; Median	Duration: seconds / unit as Mean ± Standard Deviation; Median
rh phasic in space	100 % (151/151)	4.23 ± 3.36; 3.24	2.34 ± 1.17; 1.93
rh phasic on body	90 % (136/151)	1.07 ± 0.95; 0.81	1.52 ± 0.94; 1.27
rh phasic on attached object	48 % (34/71)	0.19 ± 0.26; 0.00	1.45 ± 1.42; 2.15
rh phasic on separate object	21 % (22/104)	0.07 ± 0.20; 0.00	3.39 ± 5.22; 3
rh phasic within body	14 % (10/71)	0.05 ± 0.16; 0.00	1.31 ± 1.08; 1.07
lh phasic on person	no data	no data	no data
rh repetitive in space	91 % (137/151)	1.70 ± 1.56; 1.19	3.02 ± 1.56; 2.92
rh repetitive on body	74 % (111/151)	0.50 ± 0.57; 0.31	2.41 ± 1.77; 2.67
rh repetitive on attached object	8 % (6/71)	0.02 ± 0.06; 0.00	2.22 ± 2.13; 3.39
rh repetitive on separate object	3 % (3/104)	0.0 ± 0.03; 0.00	2.31 ± 1.55; 2.41
rh repetitive within body	6 % (4/71)	0.02 ± 0.06; 0.00	1.85 ± 2.36; 1.44
rh repetitive on person	no data	no data	no data
rh irregular on body	91 % (138/151)	2.46 ± 1.94; 2.28	3.23 ± 2.39; 2.72
rh irregular on attached object	13 % (9/71)	0.03 ± 0.10; 0.00	1.77 ± 1.80; 3.02
rh irregular on separate object	13 % (13/104)	0.05 ± 0.25; 0.00	5.28 ± 5.85; 4.78
rh irregular within body	40 % (47/118)	0.32 ± 1.23; 0.00	1.06 ± 0.88; 1
lh phasic in space	99 % (150/151)	3.91 ± 2.79; 3.19	2.38 ± 1.16; 1.96
lh phasic on body	93 % (140/151)	1.21 ± 1.21; 0.88	1.66 ± 1.01; 1.39
lh phasic on attached object	39 % (28/71)	0.16 ± 0.26; 0.00	1.48 ± 1.17; 1.84
lh phasic on separate object	23 % (24/104)	0.07 ± 0.18; 0.00	2.60 ± 4.39; 2.77
lh phasic within body	15 % (11/71)	0.05 ± 0.15; 0.00	1.19 ± 0.88; 1.04

lh phasic on person	no data	no data	no data
lh repetitive in space	89 % (134/151)	1.45 ± 1.41; 0.88	2.87 ± 1.43; 2.82
lh repetitive on body	72 % (108/151)	0.49 ± 0.53; 0.31	2.50 ± 1.89; 2.87
lh repetitive on attached object	7 % (5/71)	0.02 ± 0.78; 0.00	1.79 ± 1.75; 3.74
lh repetitive on separate object	4 % (4/104)	0.01 ± 0.04; 0.00	0.63 ± 0.37; 1
lh repetitive within body	6 % (4/71)	0.01 ± 0.06; 0.00	2.13 ± 2.43; 1.71
lh repetitive on person	no data	no data	no data
lh irregular on body	93 % (140/151)	2.70 ± 1.80; 2.37	3.30 ± 2.38; 2.89
lh irregular on attached object	17 % (12/71)	0.06 ± 0.20; 0.00	2.50 ± 3.86; 1.79
lh irregular on separate object	15 % (16/104)	0.09 ± 0.34; 0.00	4.03 ± 5.78; 2.43
lh irregular within body	46 % (54/118)	0.27 ± 0.44; 0.00	1.40 ± 1.72; 0.95

When the two operations are finished,

apply the function: Tier > Change Tier Attributes.

Scroll down in the list to the end:

Click on rh_Structure_R0/RX-cp.

Enter the Tier Name: rh_Focus_RX ('RX' = your initials).

Enter the Annotator: your name.

Enter the Participant: the identification of the person whom you are going to code.

Change.

Click on lh_Structure_R0/RX.

Enter the Tier Name: lh_Focus_RX ('RX' = your initials).

Enter the Annotator: your name.

Enter the Participant: the identification of the person whom you are going to code.

Change.

Close.

Now, you have the following new tiers:

rh_Focus_RX

lh_Focus_RX

If it applies, proceed analogously for the lower limbs.

5.6.2 Selecting and coding the 'to-be-coded' Focus units

The units on the tiers rh_Focus_RX and lh_Focus_RX are now taken as the basis for the coding of the Focus category (therefore, they are termed 'to-be-coded' Focus units). After the automatic generation, the units still have the copied Structure values. Depending on the Structure value, two types of 'to-be-coded' Focus units are distinguished:

(i) 'To-be-coded' Focus units with the Structure values *phasic*, *repetitive*, and *irregular* are assessed concerning the Focus. Technically, by double-clicking on the unit and clicking on the correct Focus value, the old Structure value is replaced by the Focus value:

within body
on body
on attached object
on separate object
on person
in space
Note that for irregular units the Focus value in space **cannot** be chosen.

(ii) 'To-be-coded' Focus units with the Structure values *shift* and *aborted* are not assessed. The copied value is simply kept. It is important not to delete these units on the Focus tiers, since they are needed again for the Contact category assessment.

(iii) Researchers who have also coded *rest* and *pose* units in Step 2 and kept them on the same tier as the *phasic, repetitive, irregular, shift* and *aborted* units, i.e., on the tiers rh_Structure_RX and lh_Structure_RX, delete the *r/p rest* and *r/p pose* units. (Note that if you want to conduct the R/P Contact assessment for *rest/pose* units or *r/p rest* and *r/p pose* units, you should have already saved them on separate tiers either in Step 1 (rh_Rest/Pose_RX and lh_Rest/Pose_RX) or in Step 2 (rh_R/PStructure_RX and lh_R/PStructure_RX).

In the NEUROGES® template, the values *(aborted), (shift), (rest/pose), (r/p rest),* and *(r/p pose)* are provided for occasions in which these units have to generated manually.

In addition, in the NEUROGES® -ELAN tier the value*?* is provided (see 4.5.2).

If a Focus value changes within a 'to-be-coded' Focus unit, replace the old unit by the new subunits. As an example, a 'to-be-coded' Focus unit turns out to contain two different Focus values, e.g., repetitive tapping on the table and then directly repetitive tapping on the leg. Delete the 'to-be-coded' Focus unit and replace it by two new units. In the example this is a unit with the value *repetitive on separate object* and a unit with the value *repetitive on body*. With regard to the precise segmentation of a unit into subunits, i.e., where to segment the unit, see 4.2.1).

Important: Code first all units of the tier rh_Focus_RX, then all units of the tier lh_Focus_RX. It is essential to obey this order of coding, as a simultaneous coding of the right and left hands creates the tendency to adapting the values of the two hands to each other.

5.6.3 Alternative procedure: Manual generation of 'to-be-coded' Focus units

If you start with the Focus category, i.e., you have not coded the Structure category, use the alternative procedure of manual unit generation. In this procedure, the tiers rh_Focus_R0, lh_Focus_R0, rf_Focus_R0, lf_Focus_R0 are used that are provided in the template. Directly tag and code the Focus value of the movement according to the rules described in 5.6.2.

Likewise, for short video clips you might prefer the manual unit generation, even if you have coded the Structure category before. In this procedure, the existing tiers rh_Focus_R0 and lh_Focus_R0 are used. Click on the first unit in the tier rh_Structure_R0 (or _RX, if you have used the automatic creation in Step 2). A blue vertical bar appears. Follow the bar to the level of the tier rh_Focus_R0, double click, and a tag appears. Thereby, you have copied the unit from the tier rh_Structure_R0/RX to rh_Focus_R0.

When doing so, you may choose to immediately code the Focus value and to decide whether the creation of subunits is necessary (see procedure described above).

Proceed with copying the next unit on the tier rh_Structure_R0/RX.

After having copied and re-coded all units of the tier rh_Structure_R0/RX, repeat the same procedure for the units of the tier lh_Structure_R0/RX. It is essential to obey this order of coding, as a simultaneous coding of the right and left hand creates the tendency to adapting the values of the two hands to each other.

5.6.4 Generation of the StructureFocus units by concatenating the Structure units and the Focus units

This procedure concatenates the Structure units and the Focus units and thereby generates units with StructureFocus values. Technically the fine-grained Focus units with the Focus values are taken as the basis for the concatenation and the Structure values are added.

The procedure can be conducted for multiple files at a time, e.g. for all eafs in which you have coded Structure and Focus. In order to be able to use this very time-saving Multiple files processing function in ELAN, it is absolutely **crucial that the tier names are written correctly**. Small deviations in the spelling of the tier names, e.g. gap instead of no gap, capital letter instead of small letter, entail that the Multiple files processing function becomes ineffective.

File > Multiple files processing > Annotations from Overlaps.

Step 1/4: File and Tier Selection.

Select files to use in overlaps computation:

⊙ Select files from domain. Click on the button Domain.

If you have not yet defined a domain, press the button New Domain > Specify New Domain > Add the Folder.

If you had already defined a domain > Select an existing domain > Load.

Select tiers to use for computation:

rh_Structure_RX and rh_Focus_RX.

Next.

Step 2/4: Overlaps Computation Criteria.

Create annotation when annotations overlap:

⊙ regardless of their annotation values.

Next.

Step 3/4: Destination Tier Name Specification.

Enter name for destination tier: rh_StructureFocus_RX (Cave: correct spelling).

⊙ Destination tier is a root tier.

Select a linguistic type for destination tier: click on Notes.

Next.

Step 4/4: Destination Tier Value Specification.

⊙ Concatenate the values of the annotations.

⊙ Compute values in the selected tier order:

Establish the following order by pressing ^:

first rh_Structure_RX and **second** rh_Focus_RX.

Finish.

Now you have a new tier rh_StructureFocus that contains units with the Structure and the Focus value. The result is right hand units with StructureFocus values and with the copied *aborted, shift, rest/pose, r/p rest,* and *r/p pose* values.

If you want to conduct the concatenation procedure for one file only, proceed as follows:

Apply the function: Tier > Create Annotations from Overlaps.

Step 1/4: File and Tier Selection.

Select files to use in overlaps computation:

⊙ Use currently opened file.

Proceed as described above.

Proceed analogously for the left hand, and if it applies for the right foot and the left foot.

In order to get an overview on the most frequent StructureFocus combinations, conduct descriptive statistics by applying the function:

File > Multiple file processing >Load Domain

> Select an existing domain > Load.

Tier Selection: Mark rh_StructureFocus_RX and lh_StructureFocus_RX.

Press button: Update statistics.

III. The Laterality Module (Module II)

While in Module I the right and left limbs have been assessed independently from each other, Module II focuses on the relation between the two limbs. As the limbs[14] are distally controlled by the contralateral cerebral hemispheres, Module II provides information about the role of the right and left hemispheres in the production of limb movements. For the upper limbs, the distal parts are the hands and for the lower limbs, these are the feet. In contrast to the proximal parts of the limbs that can be controlled by both hemispheres via ipsilateral and contralateral pathways, the distal parts of the limbs can only be controlled by the contralateral hemisphere. Therefore, for movements that are executed by the hands or the feet it is possible to infer the hemispheric generation. Furthermore, with regards to the cooperation between the two cerebral hemispheres, Module II provides information about the complexity of neural control in the bilateral limb movements. Thus, Module II is suited for research on hemispheric specialization as well as on executive functions, motor performance, and developmental research.

Technically, as the preparatory step in Module II (see Fig. 6), bilateral and unilateral limb units are generated from the right and left StructureFocus units and the *aborted, shift, r/p rest,* and *r/p pose* (or: *rest/pose*)[15] of Module I.

Unilateral limb *movement* units are units in which one limb moves while the other limb rests, and vice versa, unilateral limb *rest/pose* units are units in which one limb rest/poses while the other limb moves. Note that in Module I, no unilateral units had been identified, as the right limb tiers rh_Activation, rh_Structure,

14 Since most researchers analyze the upper limbs, note that hereafter the term hand will be used instead of limb but all definitions apply likewise to the lower limbs.

15 Researchers who analyze *rest/pose* units with the Contact category may either use the *rest/pose* units from the Activation category, or the *r/p rest* and *r/p pose* units from the Structure category. Because of the tier-copying process (see 5.6), these units are automatically represented on the StructureFocus tier.

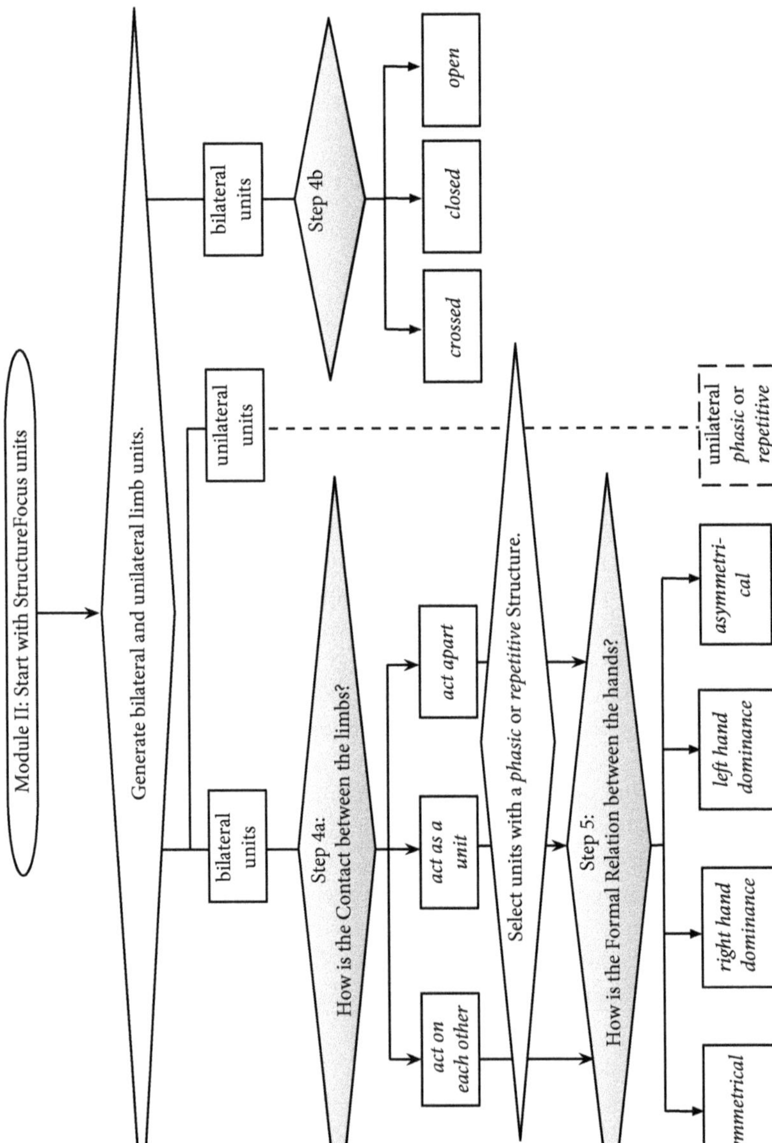

Fig. 6: The analysis algorithm of the Laterality module (Module II)

and rh_Focus tiers include **all** right hand units, i.e., those that are performed unimanually and those that are performed simultaneously with a left hand unit. Likewise, the left hand tiers include **all** left hand units. The Module II Preparation Step serves to generate unilateral StructureFocus and Rest/Pose units.

The next step in Module II is the generation of bilateral units[16]. These are units in which both limbs simultaneously move or simultaneously rest/pose. They are the temporal overlaps of the right limb and left limb StructureFocus, *aborted, shift, rest/pose, r/p rest,* and *r/p pose* units. The bilateral units are submitted to the Module II analysis. Module II comprises the Contact category and the Formal Relation category (see Fig. 6).

16 Note that throughout the coding manuals the term 'bimanual unit' will only be used for those bilateral units in which there is equal dominance of the hands (see definition of dominance in the Formal Relation manual).

6 The Contact category

6.1 Definition of the Contact category

The Contact category assesses the physical contact between the two hands (feet). Accordingly, the Contact category is applied to newly generated units in which both hands move or both hands rest/pose. The bilateral movement units are classified according to the presence/absence of physical contact and the dynamics of that contact with three Contact values: (i) *act on each other*, (ii) *act as a unit*, and (iii) *act apart* (Fig. 7, Step 4a). The bilateral Rest/Pose units are classified according to the presence/absence of physical contact and the spatial relation of that contact with three R/P Contact values: (i) *crossed*, (ii) *closed*, and (iii) *open* (Fig. 7, Step 4b).

Short definitions of the Contact values and their reliabilities as well the short definitions of the R/P Contact values are given in Tab. 6.

In the Contact category, the degree of bihemispheric sensorimotor activation (proprioceptive and tactile) decreases in the order of the three Contact values from left to right as shown in Fig. 7: *act on each other* ⇒ *act as a unit* ⇒ *act apart*. The mutual sensory stimulation of the hands stabilizes the neural control of movements and the body scheme and, with reference to psychological concepts, the body image and specifically the body boundaries. On the other hand, the expressive freedom increases from *act on each other* ⇒ *act as a unit* ⇒ *act apart*.

The aspect of body scheme and body image stabilization to some extent also applies to the three R/P Contact values *crossed* ⇒ *closed* ⇒ *open*, i.e., it decreases in the order of the three values from left to right as shown in Fig. 7 (this order between *crossed* ⇒ *closed*, however, only applies if in the *crossed rest/pose* position there is a mutual touching of the hands and arms, and it does not apply to the rare forms of a *crossed rest/pose* position without touch). Most importantly, with regards to human interaction, psychological openness and rapport increases from *crossed* ⇒ *closed* ⇒ *open*.

6.2 Generation of the 'to-be-coded' Contact and R/PContact units and selection of the unit phases submitted to Contact assessment

6.2.1 Generation of the 'to-be-coded' Contact and R/PContact units

If the right hand and the left hand simultaneously display StructureFocus units (including the copied Structure units with the values *aborted* and *shift)* a temporal overlap of the two units is generated. These temporal overlaps constitute

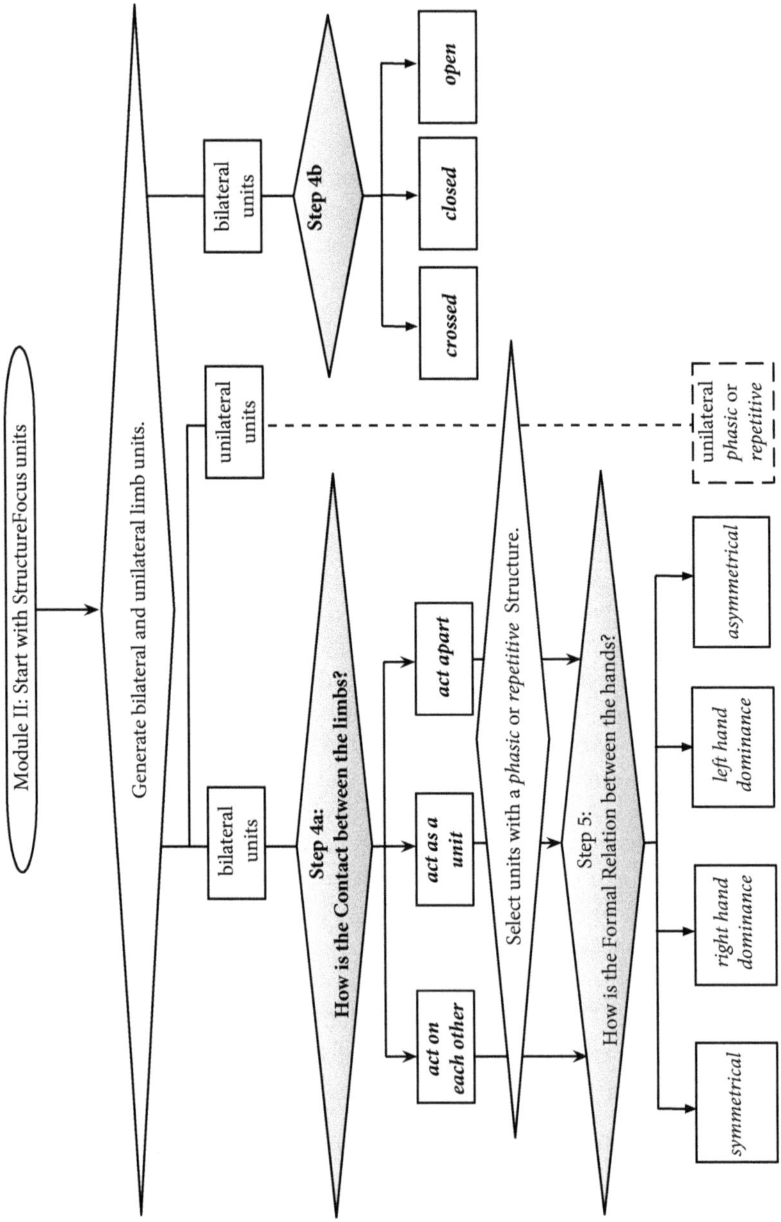

Fig. 7: The analysis algorithm for the Laterality module (Module II) with the Contact category (Step 4) in fat print

Tab. 6: Short definitions of the Contact and the R/PContact values

Contact value / R/P Contact value	Short definition	Reliability* M ± SD
act on each other	the hands dynamically touch each other	.85 ± .83
act as a unit	the two hands are in touch with a fixed configuration and take a joint action	.66 ± .16
act apart	both hands act simultaneously without touching each other	.79 ± .14
r/p crossed	in rest or pose position the knuckles of the right and left hands are crossed	no data yet available
r/p closed	in rest or pose position the right and left hands touch each other but the knuckles hands are not crossed	no data yet available
r/p open	in rest or pose position the right and left hands do not touch each other and the knuckles hands are not crossed	no data yet available

* Interrater reliability as measured with EasyDIAg (from Lausberg & Slöetjes, 2016)

the 'to-be-coded' Contact units that are characterized by the fact that both hands move simultaneously.

Likewise, if the right hand and the left hand simultaneously display Rest/Pose units (*rest/pose* units if the tiers rh_Rest/Pose_RX and lh_Rest/Pose_RX codings are used, and *r/p rest* and *r/p pose* units if the tiers rh_R/PStructure_RX and lh_R/PStructure_RX codings are used) a temporal overlap of the two units is generated. These temporal overlaps constitute the 'to-be-coded' R/PContact units that are characterized by the fact that both hands rest or pose simultaneously.

If a 'to-be-coded' Contact unit is directly followed by another 'to-be-coded' Contact unit, i.e., there is no *rest/pose* unit inbetween them, and both units get the same Contact value, do **not** fuse them (This principle applies to all following assessment steps in NEUROGES®).

If there is a change of the Contact value within a 'to-be-coded' Contact unit, create subunits. The procedure for the segmentation of a unit into subunits is the same as that for the Structure and Focus categories, i.e., the second new Contact unit starts with the second transport phase (for detailed explanation see 4.2).

It is recommended to concatenate the Contact values with the StructureFocus values after the Contact assessment and the R/PContact values with the RestPose values. The concatenation delivers StructureFocusContact and RestPoseR/PContact units, which constitute fine-grained types of kinesic behavior (see 6.6.6).

6.2.2 Selection of the unit phases submitted to Contact assessment

For the Contact assessment three types of 'to-be-coded' Contact units have to be distinguished:

(i) 'to-be-coded' Contact units that contain a complex phase of phasic or repetitive units in one hand or in both hands;
(ii) 'to-be-coded' Contact units that contain only transport or retraction phases of phasic or repetitive units in both hands;
(iii) 'to-be-coded' Contact units that contain *irregular, shift* and *aborted* movements and no complex phase

ad (i): These are 'to-be-coded' Contact units that contain a complex phase (of a *phasic* or a *repetitive* unit) in at least one hand. In this type of 'to-be-coded' Contact units, the Contact assessment refers **only** to the complex phase of the unit, for example:

- the right hand and the left hand simultaneously display Transport phase (T) – phasic or repetitive Complex phase (pC or rC) – Retraction phase (R). The Contact assessment refers to the bimanual complex phase only, i.e., the bimanual transport and retraction phases are not relevant for the Contact assessment, e.g. the two hands rise separately (T) ⇒ they come to prayer position and point (pC) ⇒ they retract separately (R). The Contact value of this bimanual unit is *act as a unit*. The fact that the two hands move separately during the transport and retraction phases is not relevant for the Contact assessment.
- the right hand displays T – pC/rC–R and the left hand simultaneously displays an *irregular, shift* or *aborted* unit. The Contact assessment refers to the right hand complex phase only, i.e., how both hands relate to each other during the right hand complex phase.

No matter if the complex phase is displayed only by one hand or by both hands, the Contact assessment only refers to the period of time during the complex phase.

ad (ii): These are 'to-be-coded' Contact units which only contain transport or retraction phases (of a *phasic* or a *repetitive* unit) in both hands. Because of algorithmic reasons, i.e., the following Formal Relation assessment, the Contact value is always *prep-retract*, for example:

- right hand performs a pointing gesture, while left hand rests (rh pC, lh *rest*) ⇒ rh retracts, while lh rises to be transported to the location where it will execute the next complex phase (rh R, lh T) ⇒ lh performs a pointing gesture, while rh rests (lh pC, rh *rest*) ⇒ lh retracts and rests (lh R). The overlap of the rh and lh sequenced StructureFocus units, only contains the retraction phase of the rh unit and the transport phase of the lh unit. Per algorithmic definition, the Contact value is *prep-retract*.

ad (iii): 'to-be-coded' Contact units that contain *irregular, shift* and *aborted* movements. They may contain a preparation or a retraction phase in one hand, but never a complex phase. The Contact assessment refers to the whole unit, for example:

- ♦ both hands rest separately (rh + lh *rest*) ⇒ both hands rise separately (rh + lh T) ⇒ left hand stops and retracts, while right hand continues to rise (lh *aborted; rh* T). The 'to-be-coded' Contact unit only contains the transport phase and an *aborted* unit.
- ♦ both hands rest folded (rh + lh *rest*) ⇒ both hands rise folded (rh + lh T), stop and retract (rh + lh complete R) (rh + lh *aborted*). The 'to-be-coded' Contact unit only contains *aborted* units.

6.2.3 Alternative generation of 'to-be-coded' Contact and R/PContact units

Researchers who start with the Contact category, i.e., who have not applied Module I before, identify all bilateral movements and optionally also all bilateral rests/poses in the ongoing flow of kinesic behavior and classify them directly with the Contact and R/PContact values according to the rules described in 6.2.4.

6.3 Criteria for the definition of the Contact and R/PContact values

The Contact values are defined according to the below listed criteria.

Presence of Physical Contact between the two hands: This criterion refers to the presence or absence of physical contact between the moving parts of the hands. The hands have...

(i) no contact: The hands are in touch.
(ii) contact: The hands are not in touch.

Dynamics of Physical Contact between the two hands: In case of the presence of physical contact, the quality of the contact is evaluated. The contact between the moving parts of the hands is...

(i) dynamic: The hands **act on** each other. The spatial relation between the hands changes, e.g. both hands rub or clap on each other. Note that during repetitive complex phases, the dynamic contact between the hands might include short phases of separation, e.g. the hands clap on each other. In rare cases, only one hand acts on the other, e.g. right hand scratches left hand, while left hand scratches leg.

(ii) static: The hand **acts with** each other. The spatial relation of the hands to each other does not change. The hands have an actively fixated relation to each other. α) The contact between the two hands has already existed during the preceding *rest* and it is maintained during the unit. β) The contact is not established until the complex phase. Then, during the complex phase the hands have an actively fixated relation to each other, e.g. the hands are brought together to form the shape of a triangle. In contrast to dynamic physical contact, the establishment of the contact before the complex phase happens without changes in the effort factors. The effort flow is bound and the effort space is direct.

StructureFocus ⇔ Contact:
The three Contact values are each associated typically with specific Module I StructureFocus values.

Contact value ⇒	**StructureFocus value**
act on each other	Focus value *on body* in at least one hand, typically in both hands
act as a unit	same StructureFocus value in both hands
act apart	all combinations are possible

The R/P Contact values that serve to classify *rest/pose* units and *r/p rest* and *r/p pose* units, respectively, are defined by two criteria:

Presence of Physical Contact between the two hands: This criterion refers to the presence or absence of physical contact between the resting/posing hands. The resting/posing hands have...

(i) no contact: The resting/posing hands do not touch each other.
(ii) contact: The resting/posing hands touch each other.

Crossing of the hands: This criterion refers to whether the knuckles of the hands are crossed (and for the lower limbs the ankles). For the upper limbs, the point of reference for the crossing are the knuckles, as they are the anatomical landmark after the crossing of which the size of the contact surface between the two hands starts diminishing again. For the lower limbs, the point of reference for the crossing is the ankles. The point of reference for assessing the crossing is a centripetal perspective, i.e., from anywhere in the body-external space to the center of the gesturer's body.

The resting/posing hands are...

(i) crossed: From a centripetal perspective, the knuckles of the hands are crossed.
(ii) uncrossed: From a centripetal perspective, the knuckles of the hands are uncrossed.

6.4 Definitions of the Contact and R/PContact values

6.4.1 *act on each other*

Short definition

THE HANDS DYNAMICALLY TOUCH EACH OTHER

Definition

The two hands act on each other. Both hands actively contribute to establishing a physical contact between them. Or, only one hand actively contributes to establishing physical contact between the hands, while the other hand acts on another focus. The spatial relation between the acting parts of the hands changes, e.g. both hands rub or clap on each other. Note that during the repetitive complex phases, the dynamic contact between the hands may include short phases of separation, e.g. when the hands clap on each other. In bi-phasic or bi-repetitive units, the *acting on each other* can result in sounds. The contact is often characterized by changes in the effort factors. Note that in units with a *phasic* or a *repetitive* Structure, the assessment refers to the complex phase only, while in units with *irregular, shift* and *aborted* Structure it refers to the whole unit.

Meeting the criteria

Presence of Physical Contact: There is physical contact between the acting parts of the two hands.

Quality of Physical Contact: The physical contact of the acting parts of the hands is dynamic.

StructureFocus: The value *act on each other* is **obligatorily** associated with the Module I Focus value *on body* in at least one hand. In few cases, only one hand acts on the other (*on body*), while the other hand has a different Focus value (e.g. *on separate object*) or performs a *shift*.

Occurrence: *Act on each other* movements were investigated in 120 individuals of the NEUROGES® archive and they were displayed by 91 % (109/120) of the individuals.

Frequency: In the NEUROGES® archive sample (n = 120), *act on each other* units were displayed with a frequency (Mean ± Standard Deviation; Median) of 3.16 ± 3.19; 2.02 units per minute.

Duration: The duration (Mean ± Standard Deviation; Median) of *act on each other* units was 2.82 ± 2.37; 2.18 seconds per unit.

Examples for *act on each other* units

To illustrate the relation between the values of the Module I and II, at the end of each example, first the Module I StructureFocus values are given, and then the Module II Contact values, and–in anticipation of the next step in Module II–the Formal Relation values. Since the principle of Concatenation is always the fusion of the right hand StructureFocus value + left hand StructureFocus value + Contact value, the Concatenation is only reported in this first example.

- i) hands rest on the thighs (*rest position*) ⇒ both hands rise to meet each other (complete T) ⇒ the hands clap once (phasic Complex phase) ⇒ move back to thigh (complete R) ⇒ rest (Module I: rh + lh *phasic on body*; Module II: Contact *act on each other*, Concatenation: *phasic on body phasic on body act on each other*, Formal Relation *symmetrical*)
- ii) the two hands rest on the lap ⇒ they start fidgeting on each other (*irregular* unit) ⇒ stop again (Module I: rh + lh *irregular on body*; Module II: *act on each other*; no Formal Relation assessment, as this is only applied to units with a *phasic* or a *repetitive* Structure).
- iii) hands rest on the thighs ⇒ both hands rise to meet each other (cT) ⇒ the index of one hand touches the fingertips of the other hand one by one (repetitive C) ⇒ move back to thigh (cR) ⇒ rest (Module I: rh + lh *repetitive on body*; Module II: *act on each other, asymmetrical*).
- iv) hands rest on the thighs ⇒ both hands rise to meet each other (cT) ⇒ clap one's hands repetitively (rC) ⇒ move back to table (cR) ⇒ rest on table (new *rest position*) (Module I: rh + lh *repetitive on body*; Module II: *act on each other, symmetrical*).
- v) hands rest on the arm rests ⇒ both hands rise to meet each other (cT) ⇒ left index points with touch on right palm (pC) ⇒ hands move back to the arm rests (cR) ⇒ rest (Module I: rh + lh *phasic on body*; Module II: *act on each other, asymmetrical*).
- vi) rest with arms crossed ⇒ hands shift along the lower arms to wrists (*shift* unit) ⇒ rest with folded hands (new *rest position*) (Module I: rh + lh *shift*; Module II: *act on each other;* no Formal Relation assessment).

Differentiate *act on each other* from ...

act as a unit: A confusion between *act on each other* and *act as a unit* may occur, if at all, only for short touches.

In an *act on each other* unit, the two hands are in dynamic contact. The dynamic contact phase typically lasts for while. If the touch is short, the presence of efforts helps to distinguish it from *act as a unit* units, as in *act on each other* units, the contact is characterized by changes in the effort factors (or in the pre-efforts or the tension flow rhythms), such as acceleration and increase of strength, e.g. a clap of the hands. A bimanual *repetitive* unit with repetitive short touches is almost always *act on each other*.

In contrast, a very short touch of the hands is an *act as a unit* unit, if the movement flow is bound and the effort space is direct. This constellation indicates that the hands create a bimanual shape and to achieve this, they *act as a unit*.

6.4.2 *act as a unit*

Short definition

THE TWO HANDS ARE IN TOUCH WITH A FIXED CONFIGURATION AND TAKE A JOINT ACTION

Definition
The term 'unit' in *act as a unit* is used here to indicate that the two hands are in touch with a fixed configuration and they take a joint action. Thus, the two hands behave as if they were one. The physical contact between the hands has typically already existed during the preceding *rest position* and it is maintained during the unit. Note that in units with a *phasic* or a *repetitive* Structure, the assessment refers to the complex phase only, while in units with an *irregular*, *shift* and *aborted* Structure it refers to the whole unit. For bimanual *phasic* and *repetitive* units, there are two subtypes:

(i) The static physical contact is first established at the beginning of the complex phase. In this case, the hands typically rest separately. During the transport phase, they approach each other (T). A contact is established without changes in the effort factors. The effort flow is bound and the effort space is direct. There may be a static phasic complex phase, e.g. both hands form a triangle and hold it for a while to present it to the addressee (static pC). The static contact between the two hands may be short, as it serves only to show a form or indicate a location (see also Training video Expert). Or, there may be a motion phasic complex phase, e.g. immediately after having established the form of a triangle the hands move while maintaining this shape (motion pC or rC). Note that if there is a long hold after the establishment of the bimanual shape before the hands start moving, this is coded as two complex phases. As an example, the hands establish a static bimanual hand shape and hold if for some time (1rst static pC), then they perform another gesture by keeping this shape (2nd motion pC), e.g. both hands form a triangle and hold it for a while to present it to the addressee (1rst static pC), and then they point while maintaining the bimanual shape of a triangle (2nd motion pC).

(ii) The static physical contact has already existed before the complex phase. The pre-existing contact is maintained during the complex phase. The fixed bimanual configuration may be taken over from the preceding *rest* or *pose position* or from the preceding complex phase. In the first case, the hands rest in a position in which they are in touch with each other, e.g. folded hands. They keep this bimanual configuration, while they rise (T) and while they perform the complex phase (C), e.g. they perform a *baton* or an *egocentric deictic* with folded hands. In the latter case, in a sequence of complex phases within the Contact unit, in the first complex phase the hands adopt a fixed bimanual shape, e.g. hands in prayer position point, and they keep this bimanual shape during the following complex phase, e.g. while maintaining the prayer position, they perform a *form presentation.*

Meeting the criteria

Presence of Physical Contact: Both hands actively contribute to establishing a physical contact between them.

Quality of Physical Contact: The physical contact between the two hands is static.

StructureFocus: The Module I right and left hand units, of which the temporal overlap constitutes the Contact unit, have the same StructureFocus value.

Exceptions from this rule are rare. As an example, the right hand repetitively opens to semicircle and closes to fist (rh rC). The left hand only joints the right hand once, i.e., it adopts the shape of a semicircle (lh pC) and together with the right hand they form a full circle. In this case, in Module I the right and left hand units have different Structure values.

Occurrence: *Act as unit* movements were investigated in 120 individuals of the NEUROGES® archive and they were displayed by 53 % (64/120) of the individuals.

Frequency: In the NEUROGES® archive sample (n = 191), *act as unit* units were displayed with a frequency (Mean ± Standard Deviation; Median) of 0.56 ± 1.20; 0.93 units per minute.

Duration: The duration (Mean ± Standard Deviation; Median) of *act as unit* units was 1.34 ± 1.01; 1.04 seconds per unit.

Examples for *act as a unit* units

- i) hands rest on the thighs (*rest position*) ⇒ both hands rise to meet each other (complete Transport) ⇒ the thumbs and indices of both hands together form a triangle, the position is a held for a moment (static phasic Complex) ⇒ the hands separate again from each other and move back to the thighs (complete Retraction) ⇒ rest (Module I: rh + lh *phasic on body*; Module II: Contact *act as a unit*, Concatenation: *phasic on body phasic on body act as a unit*, Formal Relation *symmetrical*)
- ii) hands rest separately on the thighs ⇒ rise separately (cT) ⇒ finger tips of the thumb and of the index finger of the right hand touch the palm of the left hand to form the shape of a P; the bimanual shape is held (to demonstrate the form to the addressee) (1rst C: static pC) ⇒ then the bimanual static hands shape is moved sidewards (as if the P were placed somewhere else) (2nd C: motion pC) ⇒ hands move back as a unit (cR) ⇒ rest folded (new *rest position*) (Module I: complex phase 1: rh + lh *phasic on body*, complex phase 2: rh + lh *phasic in space*!; Module II: complex phase 1: *act as a unit*, *asymmetrical*; complex phase 2: *act as a unit*, *asymmetrical*. Note that the Focus value of the complex phase 2 is *in space* and not *on body*, since the two hands do not focus on each other, but together they focus on the body-external free space.)
- iii) hands rest folded ⇒ rise as a unit (cT) ⇒ as a unit, they repetitively hit on the thigh (rC) ⇒ rest (Module I: rh + lh *repetitive on body*; Module II: *act as a unit*, *symmetrical*)
- iv) folded hands rest on lap ⇒ folded hands rise as a unit (cT) ⇒ as a unit, the hands perform a downward flick towards the left corner (motion pC) ⇒ move back as a unit to lap (cR) ⇒ rest folded (Module I: rh + lh *phasic in space*; Module II: *act as a unit*, *symmetrical*).
- v) folded hands rest on lap ⇒ folded hands shift as a unit to table (*shift* unit) ⇒ rest on table (new *rest position*) (Module I: rh + lh *shift*; Module II: *act as a unit*; no Formal Relation assessment, as this is only applied to units with a *phasic* or a *repetitive* Structure)
- vi) folded hands rest on thigh ⇒ as a unit, the folded hands start stroking on thigh in an irregular manner (*irregular* unit) ⇒ rest again (Module I: rh + lh *irregular on body*, Module II: *act as a unit*, no Formal Relation assessment.

Note the Focus value *on body* refers to the thigh, as the hands do not focus on each other but on the thigh)

Differentiate *act as a unit* from …

- *act on each other*: see above
- *act apart:* In an *act apart* unit, the hands are not in touch with each other during the complex phase. In contrast, in an *act as a unit* unit the hands are in touch during the complex phase.
- *rest* or *pose position*: In a *rest* or *pose position* with the hands being in touch, the hands are still, e.g. the hands rest folded in the lap or they are folded in a prayer position. In *act as a unit* units, the hands move or are actively held against gravity while they are 'in touch'.

6.4.3 *act apart*

Short definition

BOTH HANDS ACT SIMULTANEOUSLY WITHOUT TOUCHING EACH OTHER

General definition

The two hands move without touching each other. There is neither static nor dynamic physical contact between the hands. Note that in units with a *phasic* or a *repetitive* Structure, the assessment refers to the complex phase only, while in units with an *irregular, shift* and *aborted* Structure it refers to the whole unit.

Meeting the criteria

Presence of Physical Contact: There is no physical contact between the acting parts of the two hands.

Quality of Physical Contact: -

StructureFocus: The value *act apart* can occur with all StructureFocus values.

Occurrence: *Act apart* movements were investigated in 120 individuals of the NEUROGES® archive and they were displayed by 98 % (118/120) of the individuals.

Frequency: In the NEUROGES® archive sample (n = 120), *act apart* units were displayed with a frequency (Mean ± Standard Deviation; Median) of 7.35 ± 5.87; 5.94 units per minute.

Duration: The duration (Mean ± Standard Deviation; Median) of *act apart* units was 1.86 ± 1.52; 1.64 seconds per unit.

Examples for *act apart* units

- ♦ i) right hand rests on right arm rest, left hand rests on left arm rest (*rest position*) ⇒ both hands rise separately (rh + lh complete Transport) ⇒ the palms open (rh + lh phasic Complex) ⇒ hands move back to the arm rests (rh + lh complete Retraction) (Module I: rh + lh *phasic in space*; Module II: Contact *act apart*, Concatenation *phasic in space phasic in space act apart*, Formal Relation *symmetrical*)
- ♦ ii) right hand rests on right arm rest, left hand rests on left arm rest ⇒ both hands rise separately (rh + lh cT) ⇒ the indices happen to touch each other while each hand draws four circles one above the other (rh + lh rC) ⇒ hands move back to the arm rests (rh + lh cR) (Module I: rh + lh *repetitive in space*; Module II: Step 1 Contact *act apart*, Formal Relation *symmetrical*)
- ♦ iii) right hand and left hand rest folded ⇒ hands separate from each other and then rise simultaneously without touching each other (rh + lh cT) ⇒ left hand stops and holds (lh *aborted* unit), while right hand performs a pointing gesture (rh pC) ⇒ both hands move back to folded position (rh + lh cR) (Module I: rh *phasic in space*, lh *aborted*; Module II: *act apart*, no Formal Relation assessment because of *aborted* Structure in one hand)
- ♦ iv) hands rest folded on the right thigh ⇒ both thumbs and radial sides of palms rotate out repetitively, while ulnar fingers remain folded, i.e., the acting parts of the hands are separate (rh + lh rC) ⇒ thumbs move back to rest (rh + lh cR) (Module I: rh + lh *repetitive in space*; Module II: *act apart*, *symmetrical*)
- ♦ v) right hand rests on right arm rest, left hand rests on left arm rest ⇒ both hands start stroking the arms rests in an irregular manner and stop again (rh + lh *irregular* unit) ⇒ rest again (Module I: rh + lh *irregular on separate object*; Module II: *act apart*, no Formal Relation assessment, as this only applies to units with a *phasic* or *repetitive* Structure)
- ♦ vi) right hand rests on right arm rest, left hand rests on left arm rest ⇒ right hand shifts to right thigh, left hand shifts to left thigh (rh + lh *shift* unit) ⇒ rest on thighs (new *rest position*) (Module I: rh + lh *shift*; Module II: *act apart*, no Formal Relation assessment)
- ♦ vii) right hand and left hand rest on lap ⇒ right hand rises (rh T), while left hand remains in lap and starts with finger-to-finger movements (lh *irregular* unit) ⇒ right hand performs a pointing gesture (rh pC), while left continues with finger-to-finger movements (lh *irregular* unit) ⇒ right hand moves back to rest (rh cR), while left hand continues fidgeting (lh *irregular* unit) (Module I: rh *phasic in space*, lh *irregular on body*; Module II: *act apart*, no Formal Relation assessment)

- ◆ viii) both hands rest folded in lap ⇒ both hands separate from each other and rise (rh + lh cT) ⇒ rh performs downwards movement with hand in grip shape, lh performs downwards movement with hands in grip shape, rh performs downwards movement with hand in grip shape (alternating as if pantomiming skiing) (rh rC, lh pC) ⇒ both hands move back to folded position (rh + lh complete R) (Module I: rh *repetitive in space* + lh *phasic in space*; Module II: *act apart*, *symmetrical*)
- ◆ ix) right hand and left hand rest folded on table ⇒ right hand shifts to arm rest (rh *shift* unit), while left hand remains on table and starts with fidgeting on table (lh *irregular* unit) ⇒ right hand rests on arm rest (new *rest position*) while left hand continues fidgeting (Module I: rh *shift*, lh *irregular on separate object*; Module II: *act apart*, no Formal Relation assessment)

Differentiate *act apart* from …

act on each other: A very short touch of the hands is tolerated within an *act apart* unit, if the touch is "en passant" and seems to be accidental. The touch point represents one point on the trajectories of the two hands. Apart from that touch point, the trajectories of the two hands are separate.

However, if the touch constitutes the complex phase of a *phasic* or a *repetitive* unit, an *act on each other* unit is coded. Note that the same logic applies to short touches in the Focus value *in space* in Step 3 / Module I.

6.4.4 Special template value *prep-retract*

In bilateral units with a *phasic* or *repetitive* Structure, the Contact value refers to the complex phase. The value *prep-retract* is provided for those bilateral units with a *phasic* or *repetitive* Structure that contain only preparation or retraction phases, e.g. one hand is in the preparation phase, while the other hand is in the retraction phase. The value facilitates the preparation of the 'to-be-coded' Formal Relation units.

- ◆ i) right hand and left hand rest folded on table ⇒ right hand raises (cT), points to the right (pC), and retracts (cR). During the right hand retraction phase, the left hand raises (cT). While right hand rests again, the left hand points to the left (pC) and then retracts (cR) (Module I: rh + lh *phasic in space*; Module II: *prep-retract*, no Formal Relation assessment).

6.4.5 *r/p crossed*

Short definition

IN REST OR POSE POSITION THE KNUCKLES OF THE RIGHT AND LEFT HANDS ARE CROSSED

Definition

From a frontal perspective, the knuckles of the right and left hands and the ankles of the right and left feet, respectively, are crossed. Thus, the upper limbs and the lower limbs, respectively, form an over-closed configuration. The right and left limbs may be in touch or not.

Meeting the criteria

Crossing: From a frontal perspective, the knuckles and ankles, respectively, are crossed.

Physical Contact: In most cases the right and left limbs touch each other. In rare cases, the knuckles and ankles, respectively, are crossed but the right and left limbs do not touch each other, e.g. the sitting person has the left foot tucked back under the chair and the right leg extended, while from a frontal view the feet are crossed.

Examples for *crossed* units

- ◆ i) upper limbs *rest*: The left hands rests in the right lab and the right hand rests on the right upper thigh. From a frontal perspective, the knuckles are crossed but the hands do not touch each other.
- ◆ ii) upper limbs *pose*: a determined pose with crossed arms
- ◆ iii) lower limbs *rest*: sitting with legs crossed
- ◆ iv) lower limbs *pose*: standing in a girlish pose with legs crossed

Differentiate *crossed* from …

✐ *closed*: The *closed* position of the upper limbs closes or completes the circle formed by the right and left arms, but it does not lock the person up. The physical contact between the limbs is obligatory, but the knuckles are not crossed.

In contrast, a *crossed* position results in a closing towards the environment.

6.4.6 *r/p closed*

Short definition

IN REST OR POSE POSITION THE RIGHT AND LEFT HANDS TOUCH EACH OTHER BUT THE KNUCKLES ARE NOT CROSSED

Definition

The right and left limbs are in touch with each other but the knuckles and ankles, respectively, are not crossed. Often, the upper limbs complete a round form.

Meeting the criteria

Crossing: From a frontal perspective, the knuckles and ankles are not crossed.
Physical Contact: The right and left limbs are in touch with each other.

Examples for *closed* units

- i) upper limbs *rest*: The hands rest folded in the lab.
- ii) upper limbs *pose*: The hands are in a prayer pose.
- iii) lower limbs *rest*: relaxed standing with legs together
- iv) lower limbs *pose*: sitting upright with legs pressed together (e.g. Royal family female)

6.4.7 *r/p open*

Short definition

IN REST OR POSE POSITION THE RIGHT AND LEFT HANDS DO NOT TOUCH EACH OTHER AND THE KNUCKLES ARE NOT CROSSED

Definition

There is no touch and no crossing, i.e., the right and left limbs are not in touch with each other and the knuckles and ankles, respectively, are not crossed. From a frontal perspective, the position is open.

Meeting the criteria

Crossing: From a centripetal perspective, the knuckles and ankles, respectively, are not crossed.
Physical Contact: There is no physical contact between the right and left limbs.

Examples for *open* units

- i) upper limbs *rest*: The right hand rests on right arm rest, left hand rests on left arm rest

- ♦ ii) upper limbs *pose*: standing in a determined pose with the hands on the hips (with elbows pointed out)
- ♦ iii) lower limbs *rest*: relaxed sitting with legs open
- ♦ iv) lower limbs *pose*: standing upright with legs apart to demonstrate power (e.g. a bouncer)

Differentiate *open* from …

✐ *crossed*: Just like an *open* position, also a *crossed* position can be without mutual touching of the right and left limbs. However, in a crossed position, the knuckles and ankles, respectively, are crossed from a frontal perspective.

6.5 Generation of StructureFocusContact units and RestPoseR/PContact units

After the Contact category assessment, the StructureFocus units and the Contact units are concatenated. Researchers, who examine also Rest/Pose, concatenate these units (the *rest/pose* units from the Activation category assessment or the *rest* and *pose* units from the Structure category assessment) with R/P Contact units with the same procedure. The StructureFocusContact units and the Rest/PoseR/PContact units provide complex information about bilateral movements and rests or poses. Each Concatenation value contains the StructureFocus (and Rest/Pose) value of the right hand, the StructureFocus (and Rest/Pose) value of the left hand, and the Contact (and R/P Contact) value of both hands (see 6.6.6), e.g. right hand *irregular on body* + left hand *irregular on body* + both hands *act on each other*, or right hand *rest* + left hand *rest* + both hands *crossed*. In the examples, the corresponding Concatenation values are *irregular on body irregular on body act on each other* and *rest rest crossed*. Thereby, the interpretation of the kinesic behavior becomes even more specific.

The concatenation may theoretically result in a high number of different StructureFocusContact Concatenation values, as the 16 right hand StructureFocus values times the 16 left hand Focus values times the 3 Contact values equals 768 different Concatenation values (for the Rest/PoseR/PContact values it is only 6). However, by definition certain combinations cannot occur. As an example, the combination right hand *irregular on body* + left hand *phasic in space* + both hands *act as a unit* is not possible as the Contact value *act as a unit* can only co-occur in right and left hand units that have the same Focus value. Furthermore, several combinations are rare in naturalistic data, e.g. right hand *irregular on separate object* + left hand *repetitive on body* + both hands *act apart*. The ELAN function Annotation Statistics provides a fast overview on the most frequent bilateral combinations (see 6.6.7), e.g. an individual may display 7 *irregular on body irregular on body act on each other* units, 21 *phasic in space phasic in space act apart* units, and 3 *repetitive on body repetitive on body act as a unit* units.

6.6 Procedure for Step 4 / Module II in NEUROGES® -ELAN

6.6.1 Generation of the right hand Unilateral StructureFocus units

The tier rh_StructureFocus contains all units of the right hand, i.e., unilateral right hand units as well as right hand units that are part of bilateral units, which are accompanied by a simultaneous left hand unit. In the procedure below the right hand Unilateral StructureFocus units are generated by subtracting the left hand StructureFocus units from the right hand StructureFocus units (including units with copied *aborted* and *shift* values).

Open the eaf file with the StructureFocus units (Step 3 / Module I codings).

The subtraction procedure can be conducted for multiple eafs at a time.
File > Multiple file processing > Annotations from Subtraction.

Step 1/4: File and Tier Selection.

Select files to use for computation:

⊙ Select files from domain. Click on the button Domain.

If you have not yet defined a domain, press the button New Domain > Specify New Domain > Add the Folder.

If you had already defined a domain > Select an existing domain > Load.

Select tiers to use for computation:

rh_StructureFocus_RX and lh_StructureFocus_RX.

Next.

Step 2/4: Subtract Computation Criteria.

Create annotation based on:

⊙ Subtraction. Subtract from tier:

rh_StructureFocus_RX.

Next.

Step 3/4: Destination Tier Name Specification.

Enter name for destination tier: rh_Unilateral_StructureFocus_RX.

⊙ Destination tier is a root tier.

Select a linguistic type for destination tier (by clicking): Notes.

Next.

Step 4/4: Destination Tier Value Specification.

Specify the value for the destination tier.

⊙ Value of the annotation.

Finish.

If you want to conduct the subtraction procedure only for one eaf, proceed as follows:

Apply the function: Tier > Create Annotations from Subtraction.

Step 1/4: File and Tier Selection.

Select files to use for computation:

⊙ Use currently opened file.

Proceed as described above.

6.6.2 Generation of the left hand Unilateral StructureFocus units

The left hand Unilateral StructureFocus units are generated by subtracting the right hand StructureFocus units from the left hand StructureFocus units. The procedure is analogous to the procedure for the right hand described above.
File > Multiple file processing > Annotations from Subtraction.

Step 1/4: File and Tier Selection.

Select files to use for computation:

⊙ Select files from domain. Click on the button Domain.

Select an existing domain. Load.

Select tiers to use for computation:

lh_StructureFocus_RX and rh_StructureFocus_RX.

Next.

Step 2/4: Subtract Computation Criteria.

Create annotation based on:

⦿ Subtraction. Subtract from tier:

lh_StructureFocus_RX.

Next.

Step 3/4: Destination Tier Name Specification.

Enter name for destination tier: lh_Unilateral_StructureFocus_RX.

⦿ Destination tier is a root tier.

Select a linguistic type for destination tier (by clicking): Notes.

Next.

Step 4/4: Destination Tier Value Specification.

Specify the value for the destination tier.

⦿ Value of the annotation.

Finish.

6.6.3 Generation of Bilateral 'to-be-coded' Contact and R/PContact units

In this procedure units are generated in which both hands move simultaneously. These bilateral 'to-be-coded Contact' units are the overlaps of right hand and left hand StructureFocus and the copied *aborted* and *shift* units from the tiers rh_StructureFocus_RX and lh_StructureFocus_RX. The new tier with the overlap units is labelled bh_ Contact_RX.

Researchers who apply the R/P Contact assessment proceed analogously in order to generate the overlaps of the right hand and left hand *rest/pose* units from the tiers rh_Rest/Pose_RX and lh_Rest/Pose_RX or the overlaps of the right hand and left hand *r/p rest* and *r/p pose* units from the tiers rh_R/PStructure_RX and lh_R/PStructure_RX. The new tier with the overlap units is labelled bh_R/PContact_RX.

The overlap procedure can be conducted for multiple eafs at a time.
File > Multiple file processing > Annotations from Overlaps.

Step 1/4: File and Tier Selection.

Select files to use for computation:

⊙ Select files from domain. Click on the button Domain.

Select an existing domain. Load.

Select tiers to use for computation:

lh_StructureFocus_RX and rh_StructureFocus_RX.

Next.

Step 2/4: Overlaps Computation Criteria.

Create annotation when annotations overlap:

⊙ regardless of their annotation values.

Next.

Step 3/4: Destination Tier Name Specification.

Enter name for destination tier: bh_Contact_RX.

⊙ Destination tier is a root tier.

Select a linguistic type for destination tier: click on Contact.

Next.

Step 4/4: Destination Tier Value Specification.

⊙ Concatenate the values of the annotations.

⊙ Compute values in the selected tier order:

Establish the following order by pressing ^:

first rh_StructureFocus_RX, **second** lh_StructureFocus_RX.

Finish.

Now you have the following new tier that contains units in which both hands move simultaneously: bh_Contact_RX.

Researchers who assess the *rest/pose* units or *r/p rest* and *r/p pose* units proceed analogously. Thereby, they generate a tier that contains units in which both hands rest/pose, rest or pose simultaneously: bh_R/PContact_RX.

For some research questions it is of interest to have the Contact units and the R/PContact units on a common tier. As an example, a researcher might want to fuse the corresponding Contact and R/PContact values (*act apart* with *open, act as a unit* with *closed, act on each other* with *crossed*). In this case, the Contact and R/PContact tiers are merged (Tier > Merge Tiers… (Classic)).

6.6.4 Coding the 'to-be-coded' Contact and R/PContact units

The units on the tier bh_Contact_RX are now taken as the basis for the assessment of the Contact category. Therefore, they are termed 'to-be-coded' Contact units. Each 'to-be-coded' unit still has the copied concatenated StructureFocus values, first of the right hand and second of the left hand.

All 'to-be-coded' Contact units on the new tier bh_Contact_RX are now assessed with the four Contact values listed below. Technically, by double-clicking on the unit and clicking on the correct Contact value, the StructureFocus value is replaced by the Contact value:

act on each other
act as a unit
act apart
prep-retract

Accordingly, units on the tier bh_R/PContact_RX are taken as the basis for the assessment of the R/PContact category:

r/p crossed
r/p closed
r/p open

In addition, the value? is provided (see 4.5.2).

Reminder: When assessing the Contact category, three types of 'to-be-coded' Contact units have to be distinguished (see 6.2.2.):

(i) 'to-be-coded' Contact units that contain a phasic or repetitive complex phase (pC or rC) in at least one hand: here the Contact value refers to the complex phase only
(ii) 'to-be-coded' Contact units that contain only preparation and retraction phases: here the value is obligatorily *prep-retract*
(iii) 'to-be-coded' Contact units that contain *irregular, shift,* and *aborted* units and **no** phasic or repetitive complex phase: here the Contact value refers to the whole unit.

If the Contact value changes within a 'to-be-coded' Contact unit, replace the 'to-be-coded' unit by subunits. As an example, a 'to-be-coded' Contact unit turns out to contain different Contact values, e.g. first *act as a unit* and then *act apart.* Delete the 'to-be-coded' Contact unit and replace it by two new units, e.g. a unit with the value *act as a unit* and a unit with the value *act apart* (for the precise segmentation rules, see 4.2.1).

It might occur that the automatically generated 'to-be-coded' Contact units are very short. Automatically generated units that are shorter than 200 ms should be deleted, since they are often only artifacts of imprecise tagging (i.e., due to the fact that in Module I the beginnings and endings of the right hand and left hand units have not been tagged precisely) and since they often do not allow sufficient insight into the movement. Choose the tier bh_Contact_RX in the Grid. The last column shows the durations of the units. In the grid you can delete all to-be-coded Contact units that are shorter than 200 ms.

6.6.5 Alternative procedure: Manual generation of 'to-be-coded' Contact and R/PContact units

If you start the movement behavior analysis with the Contact category, i.e., you have not assessed Module I before, use the alternative procedure of manual unit generation. In this procedure, the tiers bh_Contact_R0 (and bf_Contact_R0) are used that are provided in the template. Directly tag all bilateral movements and optionally all bilateral rests/poses and assess the Contact and R/PContact value of the unit according to the rules described in 6.6.4.

6.6.6 Concatenation of StructureFocus values with Contact values and of Rest/Pose values with R/PContact values

This procedure concatenates the StructureFocus values and the Contact values and thereby generates units with StructureFocusContact values. Technically the fine-grained Contact units with the Contact values are taken as the basis for the concatenation and the StructureFocus values are added. Rest/PoseR/PContact values are generated analogously.

The procedure can be conducted for multiple files at a time, e.g. for all eafs in which you have coded Structure and Focus.

File > Multiple file processing > Annotations from Overlaps.

Step 1/4: File and Tier Selection.

Select files to use in overlaps computation:

⊙ Select files from domain. Click on the button Domain.

If you have not yet defined a domain, press the button New Domain > Specify New Domain > Add the Folder.

If you had already defined a domain > Select an existing domain > Load.

Select tiers to use for computation:

rh_StructureFocus_RX, lh_StructureFocus_RX, and bh_Contact_RX.

Next.

Step 2/4: Overlaps Computation Criteria.

Create annotation when annotations overlap:

⊙ regardless of their annotation values.

Next.

Step 3/4: Destination Tier Name Specification.

Enter name for destination tier: bh_StructureFocusContact_RX.

⊙ Destination tier is a root tier.

Select a linguistic type for destination tier: click on Notes.

Next.

Step 4/4: Destination Tier Value Specification.

⊙ Concatenate the values of the annotations.

⊙ Compute values in the selected tier order:

Establish the following order by pressing ^:

first rh_StructureFocus_RX, **second** lh_StructureFocus_RX, **third** bh_Contact_RX.

Finish.

Now you have a new tier that contains Contact units with the right hand StructureFocus value, the left hand StructureFocus value, and the Contact value: bh_StructureFocusContact_RX.

If you want to conduct the concatenation procedure for one file only, proceed as follows:

Apply the function: Tier > Create Annotations from Overlaps.

Step 1/4: File and Tier Selection.

Select files to use in overlaps computation:

⊙ Use currently opened file.

Proceed as described above.

6.6.7 Frequency distribution of the StructureFocusContact and the Rest/PoseR/PContact values

In order to get an overview on the most frequent StructureFocusContact (and Rest/PoseR/PContact) combinations, conduct descriptive statistics by applying the function:

File > Multiple file processing >Load Domain

> Select an existing domain > Load.

Tier Selection: Mark bh_StructureFocusContact_RX.

Press button: Update statistics.

7 The Formal Relation category

7.1 Definition of the Formal Relation category

The Formal Relation category assesses the symmetry and dominance between the two hands (two feet) in the complex phase of bilateral movement units, i.e., in bilateral units with a *phasic* or a *repetitive* Structure. Four Formal Relation values are provided: *symmetrical*, *right hand dominance*, *left hand dominance*, and *asymmetrical* (Fig. 8).

The Formal Relation assessment refers only to the complex phase, as the complex phase is the realization of a concept. Furthermore, the assessment refers to distal parts of the limbs. For the upper limbs, these are the hands and for the lower limbs, these are the feet. In contrast to the proximal parts of the limbs that can be controlled by both hemispheres via ipsilateral and contralateral pathways, the distal parts of the limbs can only be controlled by the contralateral hemisphere. Therefore, only for concepts that are executed by the hands or feet it is possible to infer the hemispheric generation.

The complexity of neural control increases in the order of the four values as shown in Fig. 8: *symmetrical* ⇒ *right hand dominance* ⇒ *left hand dominance* ⇒ *asymmetrical*. The order that *right hand dominance* is followed by *left hand dominance* applies to right-handers and it can be different for left-handers (see book I, 5.1.3.3). Furthermore, when other factors are controlled for, *right hand dominance* in bilateral complex phases suggests a left hemispheric generation, and vice versa, *left hand dominance* a right hemispheric generation (book I, 2.5).

Thus, the Formal Relation category examines the complexity of neural control in the bimanual realization of concepts. Furthermore, it provides insight into in which cerebral hemisphere the concept is primarily generated. Thus, it is suited for research on executive functions and motor performance and on hemispheric specialization as well as for developmental research.

Given that–although it is possible–only few researchers will analyze the Formal Relation category for the feet, in this chapter the terminology will refer to the hands. However, the definitions of the Formal Relation values for the feet are the same as for the hands and they apply to the sitting position in which both feet are free to move (for the assessment of the feet in a standing person in whom at least one leg is a supporting not-free leg, see 3.3). Below, for each Formal Relation values examples ◆ are given for the lower

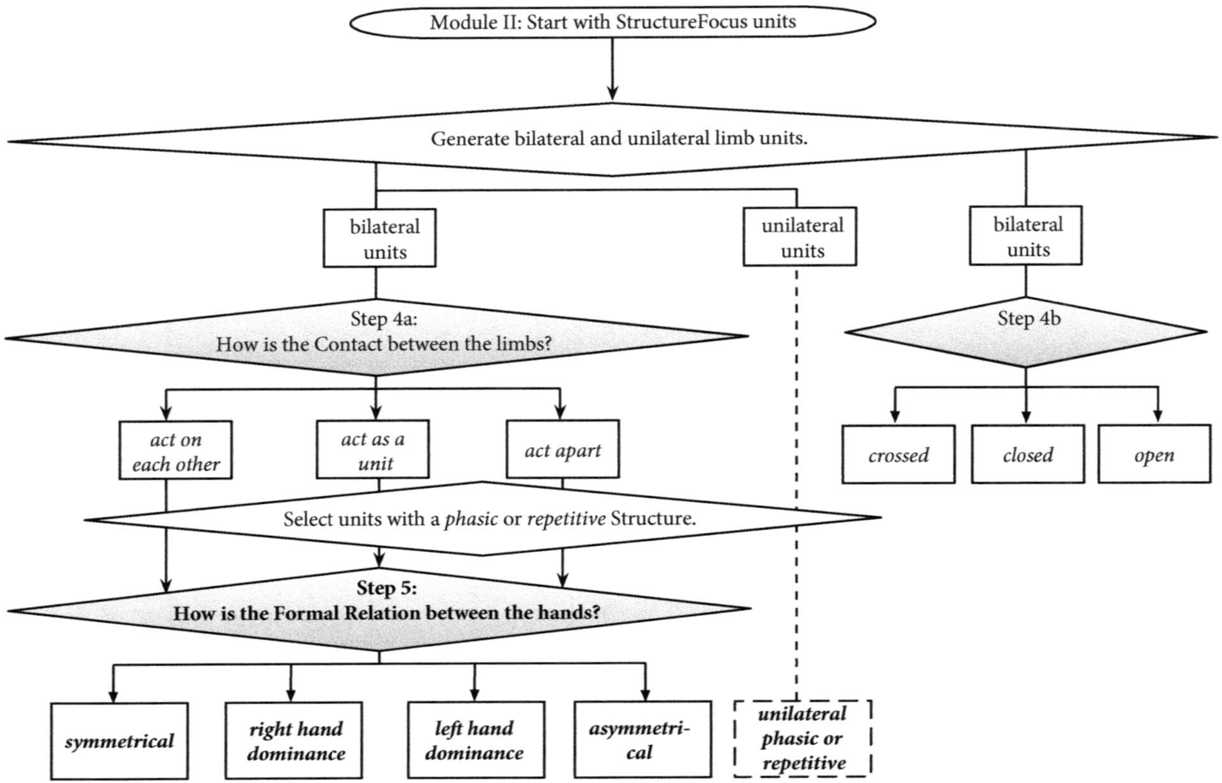

Fig. 8: The analysis algorithm for the Laterality module (Module II) with the Formal Relation category (Step 5) in fat print

Tab. 7: Short definitions and reliabilities of the Formal Relation values

Formal Relation value	Short definition	Reliability* M ± SD
symmetrical	both hands move on symmetrical trajectories	.79 ± .07
right hand dominance	the right hand displays a complex phase while the left hand displays a preparation or retraction phase or is held in partial retraction; or, both hands display complex phases but the right hand is clearly more distinct with regard to trajectory, hand orientation, and hand shape, while the left hand only crudely mirrors the right hand	.71 ± .08
left hand dominance	analogous to right hand dominance	.70 ± .11
asymmetrical	both hands move on asymmetrical trajectories are equally dominant	.68 ± .15

* Interrater reliability as measured with EasyDIAg (from Lausberg & Slöetjes, 2016)

limbs. In the NEUROGES® -ELAN template, the lower limb researchers have to create the following tiers: *bf symmetrical, rf dominance, lf dominance, bf asymmetrical.*

Function of the Formal Relation category (step 5) within the complete algorithmic analysis

Within the complete algorithmic analysis with 7 assessment steps, step 5 (Formal Relation category) marks a change in the analysis as from now on only conceptual movements, i.e., those with a *phasic* or a *repetitive* Structure, are assessed (see Fig. 8, diamond above Step 5). While steps 1 – 4 include all body movements, steps 5 – 7 focus on conceptual movements only. Thus, with regards to the content, the Formal Relation category and the subsequent Module III Function and Type categories primarily refer to the concepts that are realized in body movements.

Furthermore, the Formal Relation category serves to prepare bilateral units for the Module III Function and Type assessment. The four Formal Relation values determine whether in Module III the Function and Type is assessed only for the right hand in the bilateral movement (*right hand dominance*), only for the left hand in the bilateral movement (*left hand dominance*), for both hands together (*symmetrical* or *asymmetrical*), or separately for the right hand and for the left hand (*asymmetrical*, e.g. the left hand makes a rolling movement while the right hand points to an external location).

7.2 Generation of the 'to-be-coded' Formal Relation units and selection of the unit phases submitted to Formal Relation assessment

7.2.1 Generation of the 'to-be-coded' Formal Relation units

The 'to-be-coded' Formal Relation units are generated from the Contact units. Among the Contact units the Formal Relation units are generated only from those units that have a *phasic* or *repetitive* Structure. The exception is Contact units with a *phasic* or *repetitive* Structure that have a *prep-retract* value. These are not assessed.

7.2.2 Selection of the unit phases submitted to Formal Relation assessment

The Formal Relation assessment refers to the relation between the two hands during the complex phase. It does not matter if the complex phase is displayed by one hand alone or by both hands. The phases within the bimanual movement in which both hands perform a transport or a retraction phase (*prep-retract* value) are not assessed (same rule as for the Focus and Contact assessments for units with a *phasic* or *repetitive* Structure).

If a 'to-be-coded' Formal Relation unit is directly followed by another 'to-be-coded' Formal Relation unit and both units get the same Formal Relation value, do **not** fuse them, even if there is no gap in-between them (same rule a for the previous categories).

If there is a change of the Formal Relation value within a 'to-be-coded' unit, create subunits. Concerning the precise segmentation of a unit into subunits, i.e., where to exactly segment the unit, please see the procedure described in detail in 4.2 (same rule a for the previous categories).

7.2.3 Alternative generation of 'to-be-coded' Formal Relation units

Researchers who only analyze the Formal Relation category or the Formal Relation category and the subsequent Function or Type categories have to select all bimanual movements from the ongoing stream of kinesic behavior that show a concept realization in at least one hand according to the definitions of *phasic* and *repetitive* units (see 4.3, 4.4.2, 4.4.3). The 'to-be-coded' Formal Relation units are assessed according to the rules described in 7.2.2.

7.3 Criteria for the definition of the Formal Relation values

The Formal Relation values are defined by the two principal criteria symmetry and dominance. Furthermore, Structure, Focus, and Contact values of the 'to-be-coded' Formal Relation unit provide some hints for the Formal Relation assessment.

Concerning the two principal criteria, the simple assessment algorithm is as follows:

Is there symmetry of the trajectory of the two hands?

> If yes, the value is *symmetrical.*

> If no, …

.. is there dominance of one hand?

>> If yes, is there *right hand dominance* or *left hand dominance*?

>> If no, the value is *asymmetrical.*

The two principal criteria symmetry and dominance are defined as follows:

Symmetry (symmetry vs. asymmetry): The definition of symmetry is based on geometrical concepts. The two hands move (typically with the same effort) on symmetrical trajectories. The movement of one hand is indistinguishable from the movement of the other hand with respect to a point, an axis, or a plane of reflection, or with respect to a translation. There are different subtypes of bimanual symmetry in hand movements:

(i) body midline symmetry:
The right and left hands move synchronously and their trajectories show a reflection symmetry to the sagittal plane that goes through the body midline, e.g. when the gesturer traces the shape of a butterfly centrally in front of his/her trunk.

(ii) non-body midline symmetry:
The right and left hands move synchronously with a reflection symmetry to a point, to an axis or to a plane other than the body midline, e.g. to the right of his/her trunk, the gesturer traces the shape of a butterfly.

(iii) translational symmetry:
The right and left hands move synchronously parallel, e.g. the right hand traces in the upper right body-external free space a semi-circle that is open to the right, while the left hand traces in the lower left space a semi-circle that is open to the right.

(iv) temporally alternate symmetry:
The trajectories of the right and left hands are symmetrical as defined in (i)–(iii), but the hands move alternately, e.g. the gesturer pantomimes Nordic Walking (per definition, this subtype cannot occur in *symmetrical act as unit* movements).

Dominance (dominance of one hand vs. equal dominance of both hands): This criterion refers to the presence or absence of the dominance of one hand. Dominance is present if one hand predominantly performs the complex phase, or vice versa, if one hand is non-dominant during the complex phase. Three subtypes of non-dominance can be distinguished (it is helpful to study the video examples given below on the NEUROGES® –interactive video learning tool, section training videos):

(i) transport or retraction phase of non-dominant hand:
The non-dominant hand displays a transport phase or a retraction phase, while the dominant hand performs a complex phase, see training videos:

- Expert: *left hand dominance* 00:00:02.830
- Expert: *right hand dominance* while left hand retracts and minimally mirrors the right hand complex phase 00:00:54.790
- Beginner: *right hand dominance* during left hand retraction 00:00:31.170 und 00:00:31.760
- Advanced: *left hand dominance* during right hand transport phase 00:00:07.240

During the transport or retraction phases, the non-dominant hand might minimally mirror the dominant hand (blend with subtype iii) or there may a slight retardation at the time when the dominant hand performs a complex phase.

- Expert: *right hand dominance,* while left hand retracts and minimally mirrors the right hand complex phase 00:00:54.790

(ii) holding of non-dominant hand:
The non-dominant is held against gravity, while the dominant hand is performing the complex phase. If the non-dominant hand is held after a partial retraction, typically the hand slightly relaxes while being held.

- Expert: *right hand dominance,* while left hand is held in partial retraction 00:00:53.980

(iii) minimal mirroring of the dominant hand by the non-dominant hand:

The non-dominant hand very roughly and rudimentarily mirrors the movement of the dominant hand, while the dominant hand performs the complex phase. The non-dominant hand is indistinct with regard to trajectory, hand orientation, and hand shape. There is no precise articulation of the fingers and the hand. In anticipation of the Module III Function coding, in the non-dominant hand alone, the Function of the movement could not be assessed, because the movement is so indistinct. If at all, only by observing the dominant hand, the Function of the non-dominant hand could be guessed.

- Expert: *right hand dominance* 00:00:05.080, 00:00:51.890, 00:00:54.790; *left hand dominance* 00:00:05.560

StructureFocus: The StructureFocus values of the underlying right and left hand units are not strongly pointing the way to the Formal Relation value. Often the right and left hands have the same StructureFocus values, and this applies more or less to all four Formal Relation values.

However, vice versa, when inferring the StructureFocus values from the Formal Relation value, there is one fixed association: A ***symmetrical*** value is almost exclusively based on right and left hand StructureFocus units that are characterized by the fact that they have the **same StructureFocus** value.

Contact: There are some specific relations between the three Contact values and the four Formal Relation values:

Contact value ⇒	**Formal Relation value**
act as a unit	*asymmetrical, symmetrical*
act on each other	all Formal Relation values
act apart	all Formal Relation values

Formal Relation value ⇒	**Contact value**
right / left hand dominance	*act apart* or *act on each other*
symmetrical	all Contact values
asymmetrical	all Contact values

7.4 Definitions of the Formal Relation values

7.4.1 symmetrical

Short definition

BOTH HANDS MOVE ON SYMMETRICAL TRAJECTORIES

Definition

During the bimanual complex phase, the two hands move synchronously on symmetrical trajectories.

Meeting the criteria

Symmetry: The trajectories of the right and left hands are symmetrical.
Dominance: Symmetry implies that both hands are equally dominant.
StructureFocus: When looking at the StructureFocus values that are at the basis of the Formal Relation unit, the right and left hands **must** have the same Structure and Focus values.

The only exception to this rule can occur in *symmetrical* units with alternate movements (symmetrical subtype iv). In these units, in rare cases, the combination of a *repetitive* unit in one hand and a *phasic* unit in the other might occur (see below example ♦ iii).

Contact: *Symmetrical* units can have any Contact value, i.e., *act as a unit, act on each other*, or *act apart.*
Occurrence: *Symmetrical* movements were investigated in 80 individuals of the NEUROGES® archive and they were displayed by 96 % (77/80).
Frequency: In the NEUROGES® archive sample (n = 80), *symmetrical* units were displayed with a frequency (Mean ± Standard Deviation; Median) of 2.93 ± 2.58; 2.26 units per minute.
Duration: The duration (Mean ± Standard Deviation; Median) of *symmetrical* units was 1.90 ± 0.91; 1.76 seconds per unit.
Examples for upper limbs: *act apart–symmetrical, act as a unit–symmetrical,* and *act on each other–symmetrical*

To illustrate the relation between the values of the Modules I, II, and III, at the end of each example, first the Module I StructureFocus values are given, then the Module II Contact–Formal Relation values, and then the Module III Function–Type values. These examples also demonstrate how the Formal Relation value determines if in Module III the Function and Type is assessed for the right hand only, for the left hand only, for both hands together, or for both hands separately.

Note that the Function–Type values in the examples are only possible values and not the obligatory choice.

- i) hands rest on arm rests (*rest/pose* unit) ⇒ both hands rise (T) ⇒ repetitively perform with respect to body midline symmetrical up-down movements with downward accent (rC) ⇒ move back to thigh (complete R) ⇒ rest (*rest/pose* unit) (Module I: rh + lh *repetitive in space*; Module II: *act apart–symmetrical* subtype i body midline; Module III: bh *emphasis–batons*)
- ii) hands rest on arm rests ⇒ both hands rise (T) ⇒ right hand and left hand perform alternate up-down movements with hands in grip shape as if pantomiming Nordic walking (rC) ⇒ move back to arm rests (complete R) ⇒ rest (Module I: rh + lh *repetitive in space*; Module II: *act apart–symmetrical* subtype iv alternate; Module III: bh *pantomime–transitive*)
- iii) hands rest on arm rests ⇒ both hands rise (T) ⇒ right hand and left hand together perform alternately three beats as if drumming: right hand beat, left hand beat, right beat (rh rC, lh motion pC) ⇒ move back to arm rests (complete R) ⇒ rest (Module I: rh *repetitive in space* + lh *phasic in space*; Module II: *act apart–symmetrical* subtype iv alternate; Module III: bh *pantomime–transitive*)
- iv) hands rest on thighs ⇒ both hands rise to right upper body-external space (T) ⇒ there the right and left hands trace the upper and lower half, respectively, of a circle (motion pC) ⇒ move back to thighs (complete R) ⇒ rest (Module I: rh + lh *phasic in space*; Module II: *act apart–symmetrical* subtype ii non-body midline; Module III: bh *spatial relation presentation–position*)
- v) hands rest folded on the right thigh ⇒ both thumbs repetitively turn out while ulnar fingers remain folded, i.e., the moving parts of the fingers are separate (rC) ⇒ thumbs move back to rest (complete R) ⇒ rest (Module I: rh + lh *repetitive in space*; Module II: *act apart–symmetrical* subtype ii non-body midline; Module III: bh *emphasis–palm-out*)
- vi) both hands rest on right thigh ⇒ right hand moves to right upper body-external space and left hand to right lower space, such that the hands are in a vertical line (T) ⇒ right hand adopts an orientation with palm down, left hand adopts an orientation with palm up, both hands are held in that position (static pC) ⇒ both hands move back to right thigh (complete R) ⇒ rest (Module I: rh + lh *phasic in space*; Module II: *act apart–symmetrical* subtype ii non-body midline; Module III: bh *spatial relation presentation–position*)
- vii) hands rest on the thighs ⇒ both hands rise to meet each other in front of body midline (T) ⇒ the thumbs and indices of both hands together form a triangle (static pC) ⇒ move back to thigh (complete R) ⇒ rest (Module I: rh + lh *phasic in space*–Reminder: The two hands act **with** each other and

not **on** each other. Therefore, the Focus is *in space* and not *on body*; Module II: *act as a unit–symmetrical* subtype i body midline; Module III: bh *form presentation–shape*)

- ♦ viii) hands rest separately on the thighs ⇒ both hands rise towards left to meet each other in the left body-external space (T) ⇒ both hands form a bimanual prayer shape, short hold (static pC) ⇒ while keeping this bimanual shape, both hands move further to the left space to point (motion pC) ⇒ hands move back as a unit to thigh (complete R) ⇒ rest (Module I: rh + lh *phasic in space*; Module II: *act as a unit–symmetrical* subtype ii non-body midline; Module III: bh *egocentric deictic–external target*)
- ♦ ix) hands rest separately on the thighs ⇒ rise separately (T) ⇒ finger tips of the two thumbs and finger tips of the two indices touch each other to form a circle and hold to demonstrate the form (static pC) ⇒ then the bimanual static hands shape is moved sidewards, as if placed somewhere else (motion pC) ⇒ hands move back as a unit to thigh (complete R) ⇒ rest (Module I: rh + lh *phasic in space*; Module II: *act as a unit–symmetrical*: 1^{rst} pC: subtype i body midline, 2nd pC: subtype ii non-body midline; Module III: bh 1^{rst} pC: *form presentation–shape*, 2nd pC: *spatial relation presentation–position*)
- ♦ x) hands rest folded in lap ⇒ fingers rise folded (T) ⇒ folded fingers repetitively hit on the thigh (rC) ⇒ rest (Module I: rh + lh *repetitive on body*; Module II: *act as a unit–symmetrical* subtype i body midline; Module III: bh *subject-oriented action*)
- ♦ xi) folded hands rest on lap ⇒ folded hands rise as a unit towards left upper body-external space (T) ⇒ as a unit, the hands perform a upward flick towards the left corner (motion pC) ⇒ move back to lap as a unit (complete R) ⇒ rest (Module I: rh + lh *phasic in space*; Module II: *act as a unit–symmetrical* subtype ii non-body midline; Module III: bh *egocentric deictic–external target*).
- ♦ xii) hands rest on the thighs ⇒ both hands rise to meet each other in front of body midline (T) ⇒ the hands clap repetitively (rC) ⇒ move back to thigh (complete R) ⇒ rest (Module I: rh + lh *repetitive on body*; Module II: *act on each other–symmetrical* subtype i body midline; Module III: bh *emotion/attitude–clap/beat*)

Examples for lower limbs: *act apart–symmetrical, act as a unit–symmetrical,* and *act on each other–symmetrical*

- ♦ xiii) sitting person with both feet standing on the ground (*rest/pose* unit) ⇒ both forefeet raise while heals remain on the floor (T) ⇒ both forefeet symmetrically and alternatingly tap on the floor (rC) ⇒ rest again (*rest/pose* unit) (Module

I: rf + lf *repetitive on separate object*; Module II: *act apart–symmetrical* subtype iv temporally alternate symmetry; Module III: bf *subject-oriented action*)

- ♦ xiv) child sitting of a high chair with lower legs hanging down ⇒ presses both lower legs together and raises them (T) ⇒ starts rocking with the lower legs as one unit (rC) ⇒ rest again (Module I: rf + lf *repetitive within body*; Module II: *act as a unit–symmetrical* subtype i body midline; Module III: bf *subject-oriented action*)
- ♦ xv) freezing person sitting with feet together ⇒ moves the right feet on the left one (T) ⇒ starts rubbing the feet on each other (rC) ⇒ rest again (Module I: rf + lf *repetitive on body*; Module II: *act on each other–symmetrical* subtype iv temporally alternate symmetry; Module III: bf *subject-oriented action*)

Differentiate *symmetrical* from…
✐ *right / left hand dominance*: see below

7.4.2 *right hand dominance*

Short definition

THE RIGHT HAND IS DOMINANT

Definition

In *right hand dominance* units, the right hand displays a complex phase in a distinct manner with regard to trajectory, hand orientation, and hand shape. There is a precise articulation of the fingers and the hand. At the same time, the left hand either displays a transport phase or a retraction phase, or it is held against gravity (often with some relaxation), or it rudely mirrors the right hand. In the latter case, the articulation of the fingers and hand is so crude that no clear trajectory, hand orientation, and hand shape emerge.

Meeting the criteria

Symmetry: There is no symmetry.
Dominance: The right hand is dominant and the left hand is non-dominant.
StructureFocus: When looking at the StructureFocus values that are at the basis of the Formal Relation unit, the right and left hands often have the same StructureFocus value.
Contact: When looking at the Contact value that is at the basis of the Formal Relation unit, the Contact value is either *act apart* or *act on each other*. Per definition, it cannot be *act as a unit* movement.

Note that in *act on each other–right hand dominance* units, as a rule, the Contact is established primarily by the right hand, i.e., the right hand acts on the left hand (compare Contact category criterion Presence of Physical Contact subtype β).

Occurrence: *Right hand dominance* movements were investigated in 80 individuals of the NEUROGES® archive and they were displayed by 83 % (66/80) of the individuals.

Frequency: In the NEUROGES® archive sample (n = 80), *right hand dominance* units were displayed with a frequency (Mean ± Standard Deviation; Median) of 0.96 ± 1.14; 0.56 units per minute.

Duration: The duration (Mean ± Standard Deviation; Median) of *right hand dominance* units was 1.67 ± 1.26; 1.35 seconds per unit.

Examples for upper limbs: *act apart–right hand dominance* and *act on each other–right hand dominance*

- i) hands rest in lap (*rest/pose* unit) ⇒ right hand rises (T), left hand remains in lap ⇒ right hand repetitively performs up-down movements with downward accent (rC), left hand in lap displays small mirror movements ⇒ move back to thigh (complete R) ⇒ rest (*rest/pose* unit) (Module I: rh *repetitive in space*; Module II: *act apart–right hand dominance* (subtype iii: minimal mirroring); Module III: bh *emphasis–batons*)
- ii) hands rest folded in lap ⇒ right thumb turns out with supination while ulnar fingers remain folded (pC), left thumb minimally mirrors right thumb with a small movement (pC) ⇒ fingers close again (complete R) ⇒ rest (Module I: rh *phasic in space*; Module II: *act apart–right hand dominance* (subtype iii: minimal mirroring); Module III: bh *emphasis–palm-out*)
- iii) hands rest on arm rests ⇒ both hands rise separately (T) ⇒ both hands rotate outwards (lh pC, rh rC subphase 1) ⇒ right hand performs another outward rotation (rh rC subphase 2), while left hand moves back to arm rest (lh complete R) ⇒ rh moves back to arm rest (rh complete R) ⇒ rest (during the first rC subphase the Formal Relation is *symmetrical*, and during the second rC subphase there is a *right hand dominance* of the subtype i) (Module I: rh *repetitive in space*, lh *phasic in space*; Module II: *act apart–symmetrical* subunit and *right hand dominance* (subtype i retraction) subunit; Module III: subunit 1: bh *emphasis–palm-out*; subunit 2: bh *emphasis–palm-out*)
- iv) hands rest on table ⇒ both hands perform a toss with upward and outward accent (lh pC, rh rC subphase 1) ⇒ right hand performs another toss (rh rC subphase 2), while left hand is held against gravity ⇒ both hands retract separately (bh complete R) ⇒ rest (during the first rC subphase the Formal

Relation is *symmetrical*, and during the second rC subphase there is a *right hand dominance* of the subtype ii) (Module I: rh *repetitive in space*, lh *phasic in space*; Module II: *act apart–symmetrical* subunit and *right hand dominance* (subtype ii holding) subunit; Module III: subunit 1: bh *emphasis–back-toss*; unit 2: bh *emphasis–back-toss*)

- ♦ v) hands rest in lap ⇒ right hand rises (T), left hand remains in lap ⇒ right hand performs repetitive beats on the left hand (rC), while left hand resting in lap displays small mirror movements (rC) ⇒ rh moves back to thigh (complete R) ⇒ rest (Module I: rh *repetitive on body*; Module II: *act on each other–right hand dominance* (subtype iii minimal mirroring); Module III: bh *emphasis–batons*)

Examples for lower limbs: *act apart–right foot dominance* and *act on each other–right foot dominance*

- ♦ vi) sitting person with feet standing apart on the floor (*rest/pose* unit) ⇒ both lower limbs rise a bit (T) ⇒ both feet performs a pointing gesture (lh pC, rf rC subunit 1) ⇒ then right foot performs a pointing gesture (rf rC sub-unit 2) while left foot is held against gravity ⇒ both feet move back to floor (complete R) ⇒ rest (*rest/pose* unit) (Module I: rf *repetitive in space*, lf *phasic in space*; Module II: subunit 1: *act apart – symmetrical*, subunit 2: *right foot dominance* (subtype ii holding); Module III: subunit 1: bh *egocentric deictic-external target*; subunit 2: bf *egocentric deictic–external target*)
- ♦ vii) freezing person sitting with feet together ⇒ moves the right feet on the left one (T) ⇒ right foot starts rubbing on the left one (rC) with left foot only performs minimal movements (rC) ⇒ rest again (Module I: rf + lf *repetitive on body*; Module II: *act on each other–right foot dominance*; Module III: bf *subject-oriented action*)

Differentiate *right hand dominance* from...

✐ *symmetrical*: In *right hand dominance* units, only the subtype in which the non-dominant hand rudely mirrors the dominant hand may be confused with *symmetrical* units.

In *right hand dominance* units of the subtype minimal mirroring of the dominant hand by the non-dominant hand, there is often some kind of symmetry, as the non-dominant hand roughly and rudimentarily mirrors the movement of the dominant hand, while the dominant hand performs the complex phase. However, the non-dominant hand is indistinct with regard to trajectory, hand orientation, and hand shape. There is no precise articulation of the fingers and the hand. In anticipation of the Module III Function coding, in the non-dominant hand alone, the Function could not be assessed, because the movement is so indistinct. As a tip, one could imagine how the bimanual movement would be like if the non-dominant hand would be mirrored. In this case, a highly indistinct movement would result.

In contrast, in *symmetrical* movements both hands are equally dominant. Even if one hand performs the movement somewhat smaller, the trajectory, the hand orientation, and the hand shape could still be identified.

🖉 *asymmetrical*: In *right hand dominance* units, only the subtype in which the non-dominant hand is held against gravity may be confused with *asymmetrical* units.

In *right hand dominance* units, the non-dominant is held against gravity while the dominant hand is performing the complex phase. If the non-dominant hand is held after a partial retraction, the hand slightly relaxes while being held.

In contrast, if in an *asymmetrical* unit the hand is held, the hand is never retracted and never relaxed, but it has a distinct hand orientation and hand shape and it is held a specific position in the body-external free space. As an example, the left hand pantomimes holding a nail while the right hand pantomimes hammering. Or, the left hand marks a position in space while the right hand traces a path. The motionlessness of the left hand is not be confused with indistinctness, as the left hand perfectly fulfils its function of representing something static.

7.4.3 *left hand dominance*

Short definition

THE LEFT HAND IS DOMINANT
analogous to *right hand dominance*

Occurrence: *Left hand dominance* movements were investigated in 80 individuals of the NEUROGES® archive and they were displayed by 71 % (57/80) of the individuals.

Frequency: In the NEUROGES® archive sample (n = 80), *left hand dominance* units were displayed with a frequency (Mean ± Standard Deviation; Median) of 0.64 ± 0.95; 0.24 units per minute.

Duration: The duration (Mean ± Standard Deviation; Median) of *left hand dominance* units was 1.50 ± 0.98; 1.24 seconds per unit.

7.4.4 *asymmetrical*

Short definition

BOTH HANDS MOVE ON ASYMMETRICAL TRAJECTORIES AND ARE EQUALLY DOMINANT

Definition

During the bimanual complex phase, the two hands move on asymmetrical trajectories.

(In anticipation of the Module III Function coding, it shall be noted that the two hands are often complementary in fulfilling a common function).

Meeting the criteria

Symmetry: The trajectories of the right and left hands are asymmetrical.
Dominance: Both hands are equally dominant.
StructureFocus: The Module I units of both hands often have the same Structure and Focus values.

However, sometimes, the Structure or Focus values of the units of the right and left hands differ, e.g. when left hand pantomimes 'nail holding' (*phasic*) and right hand pantomimes 'hammering' (*repetitive*).

Contact: *Asymmetrical* units can have any Contact value, i.e., *act as a unit*, *act on each other*, and *act apart*.
Occurrence: *Asymmetrical* movements were investigated in 80 individuals of the NEUROGES® archive and they were displayed by 59 % (47/80) of the individuals.
Frequency: In the NEUROGES® archive sample (n = 80), *asymmetrical* units were displayed with a frequency (Mean ± Standard Deviation; Median) of 0.41 ± 0.68; 0.13 units per minute.
Duration: The duration (Mean ± Standard Deviation; Median) of *asymmetrical* units was 2.36 ± 2.02; 1.83 seconds per unit.
Examples for upper limbs: *act apart–asymmetrical, act as a unit–asymmetrical,* and *act on each other–asymmetrical*

- ◆ i) hands rest on the arm rests (*rest position*) ⇒ both hands rise (T) ⇒ the left hand adopts a shape with the finger tips of the thumb and index touching each other, left hand is held in the tweezers grip (as if holding a nail), and the right hand adopts a grip shape as if shaping around an imaginary handle, right hand performs repetitive up-and-down movements directed towards the left hand finger tips (as if hammering with a hammer) (rh rC, lh static pC) ⇒ both hands move back to arms rests (complete R) ⇒ rest (Module

I: lh: *phasic in space*; rh: *repetitive in space*; Module II: *act apart–asymmetrical*; Module III: bh *pantomime–transitive*)

- ◆ ii) hands rest on the arm rests ⇒ both hands rise (T) ⇒ with finger tips oriented downwards, the left hand is positioned and held in left body-external space, while the right hand moves with small bounces repetitively around the left hand (e.g. as if someone is jumping around something) (rh rC, lh static pC) ⇒ both hands move back to arms rests (complete R) ⇒ rest (Module I: lh: *phasic in space*; rh: *repetitive in space*; Module II: *act apart–asymmetrical*; Module III: bh different functions (rh: *motion quality presentation–manner*, lh *spatial relation presentation–position*)
- ◆ iii) hands rest on the thighs ⇒ both hands rise to meet each other (T) ⇒ finger tips of the thumb and the index finger of the right hand touch the palm of the left hand to form the shape of a P, the hands are held in this shape (P is presented to the addressee) (static pC) ⇒ hands move back to the thighs (complete R) ⇒ rest (Module I: rh + lh *phasic in space*–Reminder: The two hands act **with** each other and not **on** each other. Therefore, the Focus is *in space* and not *on body*; Module II: *act as a unit–asymmetrical*; Module III: bh *form presentation–shape*)
- ◆ iv) hands rest on the thighs ⇒ both hands rise to meet each other (T) ⇒ finger tips of the thumb and the index finger of the right hand touch the palm of the left hand to form the shape of a P, the hands are held in this shape (P is presented to the addressee) (1rst C: static pC) ⇒ the bimanual static hand shape is moved sidewards (as if the P is placed somewhere else) (2nd C: motion pC) ⇒ hands move back to the thighs (complete R) ⇒ rest (Module I: rh + lh *phasic in space*; Module II: *act as a unit–asymmetrical*; Module III: 1rst C bh *form presentation–shape*; 2nd C bh *spatial relation presentation–position*)
- ◆ v) hands rest on the thighs ⇒ both hands rise to meet each other (T) ⇒ the index of one hand touches the fingertips of the hand one by one (rC) ⇒ hands move back to the thighs (complete R) ⇒ rest (Module I: rh + lh *repetitive on body*; Module II: *act on each other–asymmetrical*; Module III: bh *spatial relation presentation–position*).
- ◆ vi) hands rest on the arm rests ⇒ both hands rise to meet each other (T) ⇒ left index points with touch on right palm, hands are held in this bimanual shape (static pC) ⇒ hands move back to the arm rests (complete R) ⇒ rest (Module I: rh + lh *phasic on body*; Module II: *act on each other–asymmetrical*; Module III: bh *egocentric deictic–body*)

Examples for lower limbs: *act apart–asymmetrical, act as a unit–asymmetrical,* and *act on each other–asymmetrical*

- ◆ vii) sitting person with both feet standing apart on the floor (*rest/pose* position) ⇒ right foot moves forward (T), left foot moves to the left (T) ⇒ right foot kicks something away (pC), while left foot brings something (pC) ⇒ rest (*rest/pose* position) (Module I: rf + lf: *phasic on separate object*; Module II: *act apart–asymmetrical*; Module III: bf: *object-oriented action*)
- ◆ viii) sitting person with feet standing apart on the floor ⇒ left foot moves under a piece of paper on the floor (T), right foot moves on the piece of paper on the floor (T) ⇒ moving the piece of paper away (lf: pC; rf: pC) ⇒ moving back to rest position (cR) (Module I: lf *phasic on separate object*, rf: *phasic on separate object*; Module II: *act as a unit–asymmetrical*; Module III: bf *object-oriented action*)
- ◆ ix) sitting person with feet standing apart on the floor ⇒ right foot moves to left calf (T) ⇒ right foot moves up and down on left calf (rC), while left lower leg moves down and up (rC) ⇒ rest (Module I: rf *repetitive on body*, lf *repetitive on body*; Module II: *act on each other–asymmetrical*; Module III: bf *subject-oriented action*)

Differentiate *asymmetrical* from…

✐ *right / left hand dominance*: see above

7.5 Procedure for Step 5 / Module II in NEUROGES® -ELAN

7.5.1 Generation of the 'to-be-coded' Formal Relation units

The 'to-be-coded' Formal Relation units are generated in two steps:

First, the bh_StructureFocusContact units are copied.

Second, among these units only those are selected that have a *phasic* or *repetitive* Structure in both hands. Only if the Contact value of this unit is *prep-retract*, the unit is not selected.

7.5.1.1 Copying the bh_StructureFocusContact units

The 'to-be-coded' Formal Relation units are first generated by copying the StructureFocusContact units.

Open the eaf file with the Contact units, then proceed as follows:

Apply the function: Tier > Copy Tier.

Select a tier to copy: click on bh_StructureFocusContact_RX.

Next.

Select the new parent tier: skip this step.

Next.

Select another linguistic type: click on Formal Relation.

Finish.

Apply the function: Tier > Copy Tier.

When the operation is finished,

apply the function: Tier > Change Tier Attributes.

Scroll down in the list to the end:

Click on bh_StructureFocusContact_RX-cp.

Enter the Tier Name: bh_FormalRelation_RX ('RX' = your initials).

Enter the Annotator: your name.

Enter the Participant: the identification of the person whom you are going to code.

Change.

Close.

Now, you have the following new tier:

bh_FormalRelation_RX

7.5.1.2 Selecting units with a phasic *or* repetitive *Structure value in both hands*

The 'to-be-coded' Formal Relation units still have the concatenated StructureFocusContact values. For the Formal Relation category assessment, among the 'to-be-coded' Formal Relation units only those units are selected that have the following Structure:

- *phasic–phasic*
- *repetitive–repetitive*
- *phasic–repetitive*
- *repetitive–phasic*

The exception is units have a *prep-retract* Contact value. They are deleted, unless for your research you need complete units with preparation and retraction phases and not only the complex phases. In this case, the *prep-retract* units are kept but they are NOT coded with the Formal Relation category.

All other units are deleted.

Proceed as follows:

In the grid, choose the tier bh_FormalRelation_RX.

In the column Annotation, click on the first 'to-be-coded' Contact unit.

If the unit does not fulfill the above listed selection criteria go to Annotation > Delete Annotation.

7.5.2 Assessing the 'to-be-coded' Formal Relation units

The 'to-be-coded' units are evaluated with the Formal Relation values listed below.

symmetrical

rh dominance

lh dominance

asymmetrical

(prep-retract)

? (see 4.5.2).

If the Formal Relation value changes within a 'to-be-coded' Formal Relation unit, replace the 'to-be-coded' unit by the new subunits. As an example, a 'to-be-coded' Formal Relation unit turns out to contain different Formal Relation values, e.g. first *symmetrical* and then *right hand dominance.* Delete the 'to-be-coded' unit and replace it by two subunits, i.e., a unit with the value *symmetrical* and a unit with the value *right hand dominance* (see Intermediate 00:00:06.320 and compare the unit on the Contact tier and the corresponding units on the Formal Relation tier: the Contact unit is split up into two Formal Relation units).

With regard to the rules for the precise segmentation of a unit into subunits, see 4.2.

7.5.3 Alternative procedure: Manual generation of 'to-be-coded' Formal Relation units

If you start with the Formal Relation category, i.e., you have not assessed Module I and the Contact category before, use the alternative procedure of manual unit generation. In this procedure, the tiers bh_Formal Relation_R0 (and bf_Formal Relation_R0) are used that are provided in the template. Directly tag all bilateral movements that show a concept realization in at least one hand (foot) according to the definitions of *phasic* and *repetitive* units (see 4.3, 4.4.2, 4.4.3) and assess the Formal Relation value of the unit according to the rules described in 7.5.2.

7.5.4 Optional: Concatenation of the Formal Relation values with the StructureFocusContact values

In order to achieve complex values the tiers bh_FormalRelation_RX can be concatenated with the StructueFocusContact tiers. The most fine-grained unit segmentation of the Formal Relation tier is automatically adopted.

This procedure can be conducted for multiple files at a time.

In order to be able to use the time-saving Multiple files processing function in ELAN, it is absolutely **crucial that the tier names are written correctly in all eafs**. Small deviations in the spelling of the tier names, e.g. gap instead of no gap, capital letter instead of small letter, entail that the Multiple files processing function becomes ineffective.
File > Multiple files processing > Annotations from Overlaps.

Step 1/4: File and Tier Selection.

Select files to use in overlaps computation:

⊙ Select files from domain. Click on the button Domain.

If you have not yet defined a domain, press the button New Domain > Specify New Domain > Add the Folder.

If you had already defined a domain > Select an existing domain > Load.

Select tiers to use for computation:

bh_StructureFocusContact_RX and bh_FormalRelation_RX.

Next.

Step 2/4: Overlaps Computation Criteria.

Create annotation when annotations overlap:

⊙ regardless of their annotation values.

Next.

Step 3/4: Destination Tier Name Specification.

Enter name for destination tier: bh_StructureFocusContactFormalRelation_RX (Cave: correct spelling).

⊙ Destination tier is a root tier.

Select a linguistic type for destination tier: click on Notes.

Next.

Step 4/4: Destination Tier Value Specification.

⊙ Concatenate the values of the annotations.

⊙ Compute values in the selected tier order:

Establish the following order by pressing ^:

first bh_StructureFocusContact_RX and **second** bh_FormalRelation_RX.

Finish.

Now you have a new tier bh_StructureFocusContactFormalRelation_RX that contains bimanual units with the Structure, Focus, Contact, and Formal Relation values.

If you want to conduct the concatenation procedure for one file only, proceed as follows:

Apply the function: Tier > Create Annotations from Overlaps.

Step 1/4: File and Tier Selection.

Select files to use in overlaps computation:

⊙ Use currently opened file.
Proceed as described above.

IV The Gesture and Action Module (Module III)

The Gesture and Action module (Module III) offers an analysis of conceptual body movements, i.e., gestures and actions, regarding their emotional, cognitive, physical, or practical functions. Thus, just as in the preceding Formal Relation category only body movement units with a complex phase, which implies the presence of a concept, are analyzed–in contrast to Module I and the Contact category, in which all body movements are analyzed.

The NEUROGES® definition of a function is first based on the proposition that any body movement has a function and that–with the exception of some hyperkinetic syndromes in neuropsychiatric diseases–body movements are not displayed accidentally or randomly. Second, it grounds on the empirical evidence that body movements do not only reflect emotional, cognitive, and interactive processes but that they, likewise, affect these processes (see book I, sections I and II). The function of a body movement can be to regulate and process emotional experience, to facilitate speech outflow, to promote cognitive processing, to change the external physical world or the mover's psychosomatic state, etc. It is evident that a body movement not only affects the mover her-/himself but likewise, has an effect on the interactive partner. While Module III refers to the within-subject functions, the between-subjects effects of body movements can be examined with NEUROGES® evaluation procedures for interaction (book I, chapter 18).

All parts of the body, i.e., the upper limbs, the lower limbs, the head, and the trunk can be analyzed with Module III.

The function of a body movement determines its form. The form is defined by a cluster of movement features, for example a combination of a one-dimensional path, a hand shape with index pointing, a use of far kinesphere, a bound movement flow, etc. In order to fulfil a specific function, a movement has to have specific features. As an example, if somebody wants to point to something, certain aspects in his movement can be varied, e.g. the dynamics, but other features are essential. For instance, in order to indicate a precise location in space it is most effective to bring the longitudinal hand axis (wrist to finger tips) in line with a vector that leads to the target and to shape the hand in such a way that a tip is created, e.g. the tip of the index finger, which results in a precision of the course of the vector. The imaginary prolongation of this vector leads to the intended target in space. Floppy hand movements with a relaxed hand, for example, would not be effective for pointing out precise locations in space. Or, if both hands create the shape of a triangle, this gesture could refer to all concrete and abstract entities that share aspects of a triangle. However, it would not, for instance, serve to refer to round entities. Thus, there is a bidirectional form to function link: The function requires essential features of movement form and vice versa, the form of a movement allows only for a limited set of functions or meanings. The Module III values refer to these essential features, i.e., those features without which the movement could not fulfil the function.

The two categories of Module III, the Function category and the Type category, offer a course and a fine-grained classification, respectively. In the Function category, based on the movement form eleven groups of body movements that share form and function are provided (Function values). In the Type category, nine of these groups, namely those that classify gestures, can be further specified with 24 Type values. Researchers can apply either category alone, i.e., conduct a Function category analysis or a Type category analysis, or they can analyze both categories (Fig. 9).

The NEUROGES® Gesture and Action module shows similarities with traditional gesture coding systems. However, in contrast to these systems, which often classify the body movements by the verbal context that accompanies the body movement or other non-movement criteria, in NEUROGES® Module III the function is inferred from the form of the movement. Since neuropsychological research provides ample evidence that some gesture types are generated in the right hemisphere independent from left-hemispheric speech production, and phenomenologically, the existence of gesture–speech mismatches has been demonstrated, it is methodologically indicated to investigate gesture as a phenomenon per se, i.e., independent of other modes of expression such as language, prosody, etc. If gesture-speech or multi-modal research is intended, then in a second analysis step the relation between gesture and speech or other cognitive, emotional, and interactive functions is explored. This two-step approach ensures that the gesture analysis is not biased by the verbal context and consequently, that the information that is specific to the gesture and not to be found in language is discovered (for the detailed theoretical background see book I and Lausberg & Slöetjes, 2016).

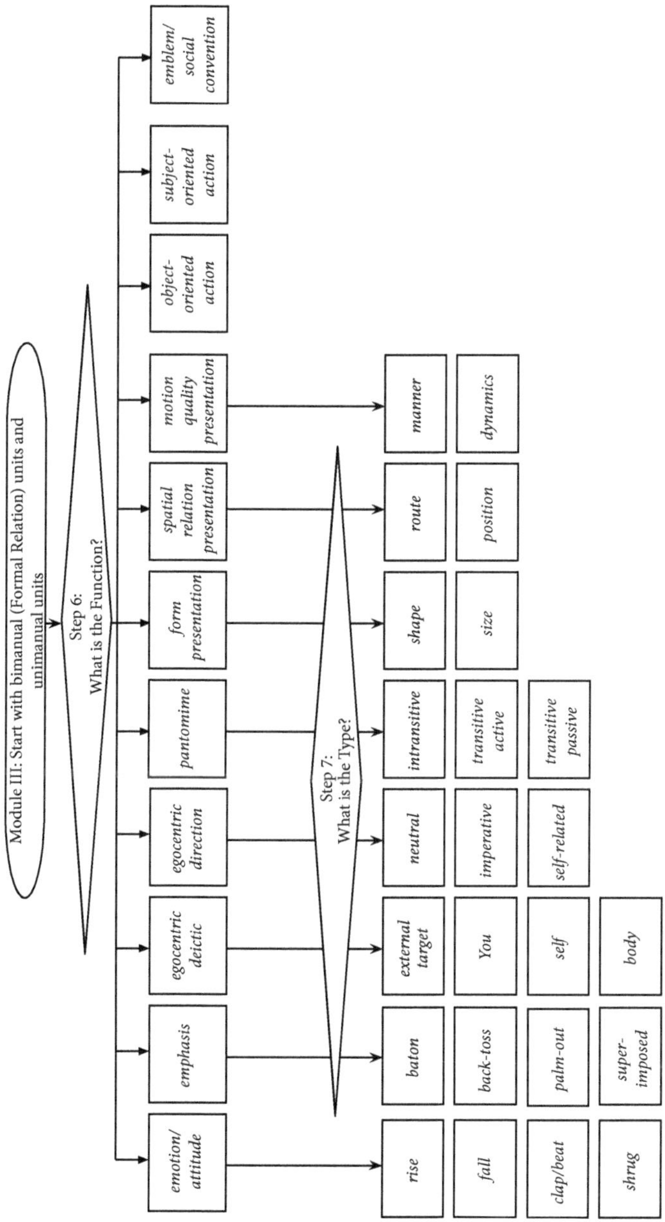

Fig. 9: The analysis algorithm for the Gesture and Action module (Module III)

8 The Function category

8.1 Definition of the Function category

The Function category registers groups of body movements that share specific movement features that are associated with emotional, cognitive, physical, or practical functions. In order to describe the essential movement form of a group of body movements that have the same function, a high number of movement parameters is needed. Thus, the Function values are operationalized by several movement criteria: gesture/action space, path during complex phase, orientation, hand shape, efforts, body involvement, and gaze. In addition, the assessments of all preceding categories, the Structure, Focus, Contact and Formal Relation values, are (re-)used. Based on the combinations of functionally essential movement features, eleven Function values are defined: *emotion/attitude, emphasis, egocentric deictic, egocentric direction, pantomime, form presentation, spatial relation presentation, motion quality presentation, object-oriented action, subject-oriented action*, and *emblem/social convention*.

Tab. 8 provides the short definitions and reliabilities of the Function values. Note that these short definitions only contain the most typical or specific movement features. Since gestures and actions are performed most often with the upper limbs and rarely with the lower limbs, the head, and the trunk, and since most researchers focus on the upper limbs, the definitions of the Function and Type values are formulated for the hands. However, the value definitions likewise apply to the other parts of the body.

In the algorithm (Fig. 10) the horizontal order of the eleven Function values from left to right reflects a development from emotional motions via gestures via actions to conventionalized gestures/actions.

The Function value *emotion/attitude* registers genuine and learned expressions of emotions and attitudes. Genuine emotional expressions are motor components of an emotional experience. Since they are not based on cognitive planning processes, they are movements without a transport phase.

The Function values *emphasis, egocentric deictic, egocentric direction, pantomime, form presentation, spatial relation presentation, motion quality presentation* register movements that are classically defined as gestures. A gesture is a *phasic* or *repetitive* movement with a transport phase, typically with the Focus *in space*. It serves to promote cognitive processing and to communicate information. The horizontal order of these seven gesture values in Fig. 10 reflects a

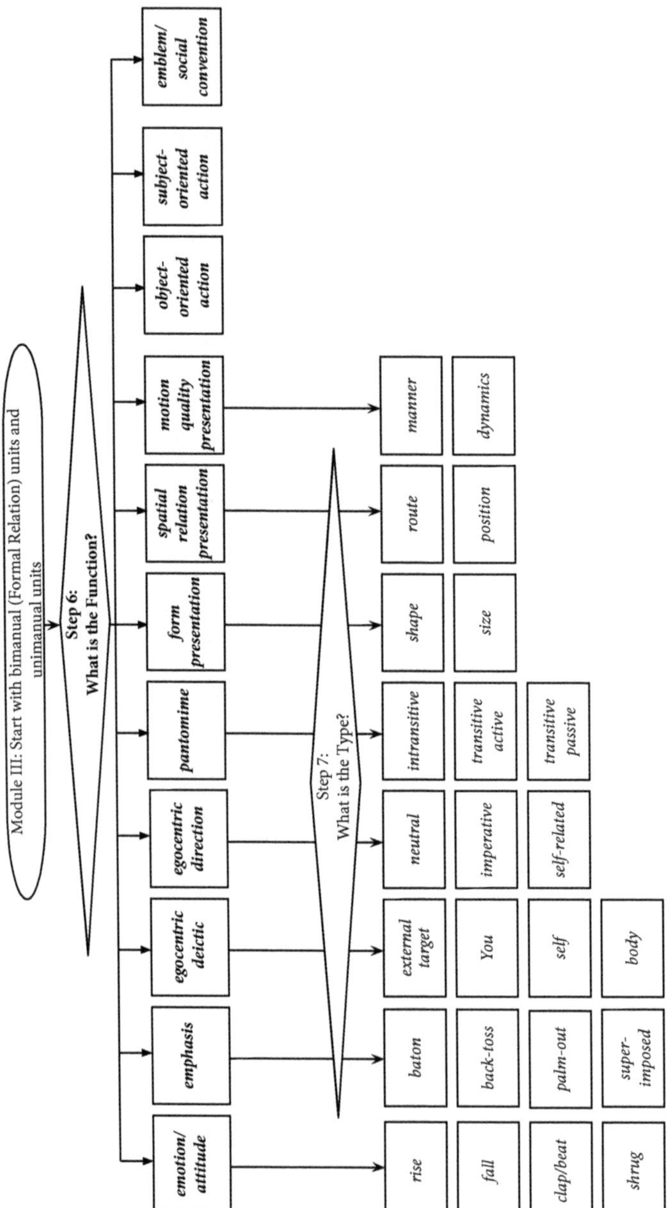

Fig. 10: The analysis algorithm for the Gesture and Action module (Module III) with the Function category in fat print

Tab. 8: Short definitions of the form and the function of the Function values and reliabilities

Function value	**Short definitions of form and function**	**Reliability* M ± SD**
emotion / attitude	Form: *phasic in space or within body, bilateral symmetrical;* one- or two-dimensional path; dynamic display of efforts, in particular of the effort factor weight, distinct from the individual's baseline; ipsilateral neutral gesture hemi-space; proximally initiated movement, obligatorily accompanied by a postural-facial expression; Function: displaying exclusively an emotion or an attitude	.66 ± .21
emphasis	Form: *repetitive in space;* one- or two-dimensional up-down or supination-pronation path with end point accent; ipsilateral neutral gesture hemi-space; synchronized with mouth and head movements; Function: setting accents on speech	.75 ± .07
egocentric deictic	Form: *phasic in space unilateral,* spoke- or arch-like path, direct space, bound flow; distinct use of gesture space, determined by the designated location; longitudinal hand axis in line with the vector to designated target, tip of fingers oriented toward to a specific location; gesturer typically looks at the designated location he/she is pointing at Function: indicating a location by using an egocentric frame of reference	.56 ± .41
egocentric direction	Form: *phasic in space unilateral,* arch-like movement path, most often free flow, relaxed hand; longitudinal hand axis in line with the designated direction line; distinct use of gesture space, determined by the designated direction; gesturer looks into the designated direction Function: indicating a direction or a route by using an egocentric frame of reference	.62 ± .26
pantomime	Form: *phasic / repetitive in space,* sometimes *act apart asymmetrical;* the hand keeps its natural orientation as a part of gesturer's body, involvement of head and trunk or even whole body, the gaze is typically on the hands; variable use of gesture space, determined by the action space of the action of reference Function: pretending to perform an action	.74 ± .06
form presentation	Form: *phasic in space,* often *symmetrical;* distinct hand shape in static Techniques of Presentation; invariant use of efforts: bound flow, direct space, no time, no weight; central gesture space, in front of body midline, middle kinesphere Function: creating a form	.57 ± .16

(*continued on next page*)

Tab. 8: Continued

Function value	Short definitions of form and function	Reliability* M ± SD
spatial relation presentation	Form: *phasic in space*, often *act apart asymmetrical*, in unilateral presentations also *repetitive;* distinct and creative use of gesture space, complex phases are displayed at specific non-central locations in the gesture space; often longitudinal hand axis in line with the vertical space axis; invariant use of efforts: bound flow, direct space, no time, no weight Function: creating a spatial relation	.43 ± .29
motion quality presentation	Form: *repetitive in space unilateral;* variation of effort factors, use of efforts distinctly different from the gesturer's base line; never a static complex phase Function: showing a specific quality of movement	.59 ± .16
object-oriented action	Form: *phasic or repetitive, on separate object, unilateral or act apart asymmetrical*; often involvement of other parts of the body; gaze at hand (in order to control the execution of the action) Function: changing the external physical world	.71 (only one study)
subject-oriented action	Form: *phasic or repetitive, on body* or *within body,* often unilateral Function: changing the own physical (and secondarily mental) state	.71 ±.14; .87 ± .00
emblem / social convention	Form: distinct StructureFocusContactFormalRelation combination, specific path, hand shape, and hand orientation; the identification has to be learned for each single emblem / social convention Function (*emblem*): using culture-specific hand signs with conventionalized arbitrary meanings Function (*social convention*): conventionalized actions in specific social contexts	.79 ± .06

* Interrater reliability as measured with EasyDIAg (from Lausberg & Slöetjes, 2016)

development from more emotional to more cognitive with an increase in creative complexity and abstraction. *Emphasis* gestures serve to tone the message, they show the importance that the gesturer lends to certain aspects. *Emphasis* gestures are a proxy to *emotion/attitude* motions as they often – in line with prosody–have an emotional connotation. They do not provide pictorial information, such as gestural images. *Egocentric deictic* gestures refer to something from an egocentric perspective and do not create a gestural image. *Egocentric direction* gestures indicate a direction from an egocentric perspective. *Pantomime gestures* depict an action from an egocentric perspective – the gesturer acts as if s/he would perform an action. While the *pantomime* gestures can be very creative gestural depictions, they are still based on an egocentric perspective. Therefore, *egocentric deictic, egocentric direction*, and *pantomime* form the main group of egocentric gestures. In the horizontal order of the Function values, they are followed by the main group of *presentation* gestures in which gestural images are created. *Form presentation* gestures are gestural creations of forms. *Spatial relation presentation* gestures create spatial relations, potentially including *form presentations. Motion quality presentation* gestures present the dynamics or manner of movement. They may include *form* and *spatial relation presentation.* As such they are highly creative and potentially the most complex *presentation* gestures.

The Function values *object-oriented action* and *subject-oriented action* constitute the main group of actions. They register movements that are classically defined as actions. In NEUROGES®, an action is defined as a *phasic* or *repetitive* movement, typically with the Focus *on separate object, on attached object,* or *on body* movement that directly changes the physical world, i.e., the gesturer's environment or his/her physical state.

Finally, the Function value *emblem / social convention* registers conventionalized gestures and actions with a culturally defined fixed form – meaning link.

8.2 Generation of the 'to-be-coded' Function units

8.2.1 Selection of units for the generation of 'to-be-coded' Function units

The Function assessment refers only to the complex phase, which is the realization of a concept. Accordingly, only units are assessed that have *phasic* or *repetitive* Structure and a complex phase.

In order to generate the 'to-be-coded' Function units, units from the following preceding tiers are used:

'to-be-coded' Function units for the tier ...	**adopted from the preceding tier ...**
rh_Function_R0 (right hand)	rh_Unilateral_StructureFocus_R0
lh_Function_R0 (left hand)	lh_Unilateral_StructureFocus_R0
bh_Function_R0 (both hands)	bh_Formal Relation_R0
rf_Function_R0 (right foot)	rf_Unilateral_StructureFocus_R0
lf_Function_R0 (left foot)	lf_Unilateral_StructureFocus_R0

bf_Function_R0 (both feet)	bf_Formal Relation_R0
head_Function_R0	head_Structure_R0
trunk_Function_R0	trunk_Structure_R0

Among the units that have been adopted from StructureFocus and Structure tiers, all those are deleted that have the Structure values *irregular, shift,* and *aborted.*

The remaining units as well as the units that have been adopted from Formal Relation tiers are the 'to-be-coded' Function units.

8.2.2 The Formal Relation values as an orientation for the assessment of bilateral 'to-be-coded' Function units

In the both hands (both feet) Function tier, the value of the copied Formal Relation unit determines whether the Function is assessed for both hands together or whether it is assessed separately for the right hand and left hand.

(i) *symmetrical:* This Formal Relation value implies that both hands together contribute to one form, and thus, to the same function. Therefore, the Function is evaluated for both hands together.

(ii) *right hand dominance:* Since a complex phase is displayed distinctly only by the right hand, the Function is assessed only for the right hand.

(iii) *left hand dominance:* The Function is assessed only for the left hand. Note that for the investigation of hemispheric specialization in the production of a Function value it is useful to investigate unilateral right hand units and *right hand dominance* units as one group, and accordingly unilateral left hand units and *left hand dominance* units as one group (Lausberg et al., 2000).

(iv) *asymmetrical:* The two hands may either fulfil the same function or they may have different complementary functions.

  (α) If both hands have the same Function value, they are assessed together.

  (β) If the two hands have different Function values, they are given the special template value *different functions.*

8.2.3 The chronology of coding the 'to-be-coded' Function units

In Module III as compared to Module I, the chronology of the unit coding changes. In Module I, first the right hand and then the left hand was coded. The independent coding of the right and left hands prevents an interpretation of their functional relation and promotes an objective coding based on the Movement form of the movement alone.

In contrast to Module I, in Module III the right hand, left hand, and bimanual 'to-be-coded' Function units are coded in the chronological order of their occurrence, e.g. rh unit, lh unit, rh unit, bh unit, etc. This procedure enables to use the information provided by how the units are sequenced in time to better understand their function.

In hand movements, the change of function is typically associated with a change in Structure, Focus, Contact, and Formal Relation. Therefore, the 'to-be coded' Function units, which result from the fine-grained segmentation processes in the Modules I and II, are likely to represent functional units. If, however, there is a change of the Function value within a 'to-be-coded' Function unit, then the change demarcates subunits. With regard to the precise segmentation of a unit into subunits (where to segment the unit), the procedure is described in detail in 4.2).

8.2.4 Alternative generation of 'to-be-coded' Function units

Researchers who only apply the Function category (and/or the Type category) select from the ongoing stream of kinesic behavior all conceptual body movements according to the definitions of *phasic* and *repetitive* units (see 4.3, 4.4.2, 4.4.3). For the limbs, the units have to be differentiated as unilateral right, unilateral left, and bilateral in order to use the existing Function tiers in the NEUROGES® -ELAN template. Concerning the bilateral units, it is helpful to classify them first with the Formal Relation values, since this pre-assessment facilitates the analysis of the bilateral 'to-be-coded' Function units. The 'to-be-coded' Function units are assessed according to the rules described in 8.2.2 and 8.2.3.

8.3 Criteria for the definition of the Function values

The Function values are defined according to the following criteria:

Structure: Specific Function values are obligatorily or typically associated with either a *phasic* or a *repetitive* Structure value. As an example, an *egocentric deictic* unit typically has a *phasic* Structure. Tab. 9 gives an overview on the most frequent combinations of Structure values with Function values. Therefore, the table can be used for a first orientation when assessing the Function, as it allows the researcher to narrow down the choice of Function values.

Tab. 9: The most frequent associations of StructureFocus values and Function values.

StructureFocus value	**Function value**
phasic within body	*emotion/attitude*
	subject-oriented action
phasic or *repetitive on body*	*emotion*
	egocentric deictic
	pantomime
	subject-oriented action
	emotion/attitude
phasic or *repetitive on attached object*	*object-oriented action*
	subject-oriented action
phasic or *repetitive on separate object*	*object-oriented action*
	subject-oriented action
phasic or *repetitive on person*	*egocentric deictic*
	egocentric direction
	object-oriented action
phasic or *repetitive in space*	*emotion/attitude*
	emphasis
	egocentric deictic
	egocentric direction
	pantomime
	form presentation
	spatial relation presentation
	motion quality presentation
	emblem

Rarely occurring combinations are not listed in the table, e.g. an *emblem* unit with the StructureFocus value *repetitive on attached object* (tapping on the watch to indicate that the time has to be kept in mind), or an *egocentric deictic* unit that emerges from a *repetitive* Structure unit that in the Function assessment is split up into an *egocentric deictic* unit and a *superimposed emphasis* unit.

Focus: Likewise, a specific Function value can be obligatorily or typically associated with a specific Focus value (see Tab. 4).

Gesture/action space: In the Focus category coding manual the criterion location was defined. Six locations were differentiated: body-internal space, body-surface, attached object, separate object, person, and body-external space.

The body-external space is the space within the personal reach space of the fingers tips, when the arms are extended (accordingly for the lower limbs). The body-external space matches the gesture/action space. However, while the criterion body-external space applied also to *irregular* units, the criterion gesture/action space refers to the complex phase, i.e., it specifies where the complex phase is displayed. The gesture/action space can defined by:

(i) neutral versus distinct: A neutral position in the gesture/action space is the position of the hand when it is moved up from the neutral anatomical position without a further transport to a specific position in the gesture/action space, e.g. left arm is hanging in its natural anatomical position besides the trunk and then the lower arm is directly raised up and performs baton gestures. Accordingly, a distinct position in the gesture/action space is a position to which the hand is explicitly transported in order to perform a gesture.

(ii) planes: The three anatomical planes, the horizontal plane (table plane, divides the body-external space into upper and lower parts), the sagittal plane (divides the body-external space into the left and right parts), and the frontal plane (divides the body-external space in front and back parts) enable to describe hand position in the gesture/action space.
horizontal plane: To specify the horizontal plane in which the complex phase is displayed, body parts are used as the frame of reference, e.g. plane of the shoulders, plane of the head.
sagittal plane: The sagittal plane that is in line with the body midline (hereafter referred to as 'body midline sagittal plane') is used as a frame of reference. A hemi-space is defined as the gesture/action space that is to the left or to the right of the body midline sagittal plane. Four Execution Hemi-Space values are defined: (α) ipsilateral: the laterality of the hand that displays the complex phase matches the laterality of the hemi-space, e.g. right hand in right hemi-space, (β) contralateral: the laterality of the hand that displays the complex phase contrasts the laterality of the hemi-space, e.g. right hand in left hemi-space, (γ) body midline: the hand displays the complex phase in the sagittal plane that is in line with the body midline, and (δ) ipsi-contra: within the given unit, the hand displays one or more complex phases in both hemi-spaces, e.g. right hand uses both hemi-spaces. If of interest for the research question, the use of the hemi-spaces can be coded with the Supplementary category Execution Hemi-Space.
frontal plane: The frontal plane is specified by the same values as the kinesphere (see below).

(iii) kinesphere: With regard to the distance of the hands from the trunk, with reference to Laban's concept of kinesphere (1988), three values are distinguished: (α) near: the hands move on the body surface or within a distance from the trunk that is less than a length of a hand, (β) middle: the hands move in a space that is further away than a length of a hand and closer than a length of a lower arm plus hand, (γ) far: the hands move in the space that is further away from the trunk than a length of a lower arm plus hand, i.e., close to the periphery of the kinesphere.

(iv) central versus peripheral: As defined by McNeill (1992, p. 89), the center of the gesture space is in front of the chest, the periphery reaches from the eyes down to the pelvis and extends the position of the hanging arms, and the extreme periphery is beyond the periphery.

Path: In the Structure category coding manual the criterion trajectory has been defined. The trajectory refers to the path the hand takes between two *rest/pose* positions, i.e., while executing the transport phase, the complex phase, and the retraction phase. The criterion path differs from the criterion trajectory as it refers only to the complex phase (just as all other Function criteria, e.g. gesture/action space). The path, the hand takes during the complex phase may be straight, angular, or curved, or one-, two-, or three-dimensional, respectively (Laban, 1988). The point of reference for the evaluation of the criterion path is the part of hand/arm that displays the most complex spatial and dynamic movement. Two values are distinguished: (α) path during complex phase (with qualitative description, e.g. straight, angular, or curved, or one-, two-, or three-dimensional), and (β) no path, i.e., static complex phase. In the latter case, the hand is stationary during the complex phase, i.e., there is no displacement.

Hand orientation: The hand adopts a specific orientation relative to the body and to the gesture/action space. The orientation is maintained for a moment during the complex phase (compare Ochipa et al., 1994 "external configuration orientation"; Haaland & Flaherty, 1984 "orientation"; Hermsdörfer, Mai, Spatt, Marquardt, Veltkamp, & Goldenberg, 1996 "final position"). The point of reference for defining the orientation is the position of the palm or the back of the hand, respectively, or the orientation of the finger tips. The sagittal, horizontal, and frontal planes are used to describe the orientation of the hand, e.g. flat hand in frontal plane, finger tips pointing upward, palm facing the body. Alternatively, the orientations of the longitudinal and sagittal hand axes are defined relative to the vertical, sagittal, and horizontal axes in the objective space. The longitudinal hand axis runs from the middle of the wrist to the middle finger tip. The sagittal hand axis runs from the middle of the palm through the hand to the middle of the back.

Two values are distinguished: (α) distinct orientation (with qualitative description), and (β) no distinct orientation. In the latter case, the hand has an anatomically neutral orientation, e.g. up-down movements of the lower arm with a relaxed hand. A neutral orientation is typically combined with a relaxed hand (no distinct hand shape).

Hand shape: The hand adopts a distinct shape that is maintained for a moment during the complex phase such that a static picture of the hand shape emerges (compare McNeill, 1992; Ochipa, Rothi, & Heilman, 1994 "internal configuration"; Bressem, 2006). The configuration of the fingers substantially contributes to the shape. Thus, the hand shape is often described by the configuration of the fingers, e.g. index and thumb form a ring, a hand with an extended index. Two values are distinguished: (α) distinct shape (with qualitative description), and (β) no distinct hand shape, i.e., relaxed hand. In the latter case, there is no active shaping of the hand and the hand often remains relaxed (flat hand with slightly flexed fingers).

Efforts: See detailed description of the criterion efforts (Laban, 1988; Dell, 1979; North, 1990) in Structure category (4.3) and the Supplementary category Effort coding manuals. Two values are distinguished: (α) variation in the effort factors (with qualitative description), and (β) no variation in the effort factors. If of interest for the research question, the use of the effort qualities can be coded with the Supplementary category Efforts.

Body involvement: The hand movement is accompanied by the movement of another part of the body, e.g. the trunk, the head.

Gaze: The hand movement is accompanied by a specific gaze focus, e.g. the gaze may be directed at the hand, at the addressee, at the imaginary form that is presented by the gesture, at an external object, etc. The gaze does not need to be focused on the target all the time during the complex phase, a short glance at that target is sufficient.

Other criteria: This criterion refers to any other feature that regularly accompanies a hand movement of the specific Function value.

8.4 Definitions of the Function values

The following definitions of the Function values are structured as follows:

First, a **Short definition** of the Function is given.

Second, if the Function value belongs to a main group of Function values, this is reported in the section **Main group.**

A more detailed **Definition** follows that starts with the Function and then reports the Movement form. As the definitions are formulated for the upper limbs, additional examples ♦ are given for lower limbs, head, and trunk. If the Function value can be further specified with Type values (Type category assessment), for a better overview a list of the corresponding Type values is provided. Furthermore, the Supplementary categories that may be used to specify the Function value are listed (see book section V).

The section **Meeting the criteria** provides a quick overview on the movement features as well as on the occurrence, frequency and duration of the value. It is necessary to read the above section (8.3.) to profit from this section.

Finally, having been most appreciated by many researchers, in the section **Differentiate...** it is reported how to distinguish the given Function value from other Function values. Criteria are provided here that help to distinguish Function values that share certain movement features and that, therefore, may be mixed up.

8.4.1 *emotion/attitude*

Short definition

DISPLAYING EXCLUSIVELY AN EMOTION OR AN ATTITUDE

Definition

Function:
Emotions are congenital stimulus-response patterns that enable to react to environmental stimuli and to regulate interaction. They are defined by a subjective experience, a physiological response, and a motor or vocal/verbal response. Basic emotions that different researchers agree on are happiness, sadness, fear, anger, surprise, and disgust. As compared to the cognitive system, the emotion system is the onto- and phylogenetically older system. It responds rapidly with a limited number of partially innate operative schemata including motor plans to relevant stimuli for the basic needs of the individual.

The motor component of a genuine emotion is characterized by a muscle innervation pattern specifically including the postural muscles and the face. It is accompanied by a specific vegetative activation pattern and, unless the individual has a deficit in recognizing her/his emotions, by an explicit emotional experience. There are direct neural pathways from the emotional system in the brain to the facial muscles. Furthermore, the pathways for the control of the axial and proximal muscles differ from those for the muscles of the distal limbs and there is evidence that they are linked more to the emotional system than those of the distal limbs. Thus, genuine emotions involve directly the face and the head (neck), trunk and the proximal limbs. The learned and socially motivated display of emotions is controlled by different neural systems and it differs in movement form from the genuine emotions.

In experimental settings and videotaped natural social encounters genuine *emotions* are displayed rarely or only in very subtle manner. Special methods such as the microanalysis of facial expression are needed to register these fine motions. Rather, there is a display of learned emotional expressions for social purposes. Furthermore, *attitudes* such as resignation, pride, or firmness can be observed. These are longer-lasting states that are regularly evident in *rest* and *pose* positions as well as in posture, but sometimes also single motions may reflect a basic attitude such as shrugging of the shoulders in resignation.

The NEUROGES® Function value *emotion/attitude* refers to genuine emotions or attitudes as well as to the display of learned emotional expressions. Note that while any gesture can be performed with an emotional connotation, e.g. a *deictic* with firmness or an *emblem* with anger, the NEUROGES® Function value *emotion/attitude* refers to body movements that **only** express an emotion and that convey **no** other meaning. Thus, didactically the Function value *emotion/attitude* can be identified through a process of elimination.

Movement form: *Emotion/attitude* limb movements are initiated proximally and always co-occur with a facial-postural expression. Therefore, also the researcher who only investigates the upper limbs should check the synchronously occurring head and trunk movements. *Emotion/attitude* movements are characterized by a clear change in the effort factors, the quality of which depends on the type of emotion. During the emotional experience, the use of the effort factors differs from that of the individual's baseline. Since genuine *emotion/attitude* movements are motor correlates of an emotional experience and not based on cognitive planning processes, they are motorically simple with a one-dimensional path. Accordingly, also their learned counter-parts are motorically simple.

Researchers who want to explore if an emotional expression is of genuine origin or a learned display should consider the following movement criteria:

(i) The genuine *emotion/attitude* movement is the intrinsic motor component of an emotional experience. It is obligatorily accompanied by a specific vegetative activation pattern, a specific facial expression (even if only recognizable in micro-analysis), and postural innervation. Genuine *emotion/attitude* limb movements are initiated in the trunk. They are typically executed bilaterally and symmetrically. If there is a shaping of the hand, it is part of the general body tension, e.g. clenching the hand to a fist while the muscle tension in the whole body rises. Thus, isolated movements of the hands are not compatible with a genuine emotional expression. Furthermore, the genuine *emotion/attitude* movements have no transport phase, since they are not based on cognitive planning processes.

(ii) The learned *emotion/attitude* movement is typically displayed for social purposes or as part of cognitive processing of the emotional experience. As the expression of the emotion is based on a planning process, learned *emotion/attitude* limb movements have a transport phase. They are more often displayed unilaterally than the genuine expressions. The degree of the facial-postural involvement and of the vegetative arousal depends on the degree of the true emotional engagement, unless there is perfect simulation.

Technically, the researcher notes her/his observation genuine vs. learned in the tier Notes.

Types: The four Type values that are subordinated to the Function value *emotion/attitude* reflect the most frequent gestural expressions of emotions and attitudes that have been observed in the NEUROGES® archive. These are (formulated for the upper limbs): *rise* (dynamic fast raising up of the arms), *fall* (letting the arms fall down heavily), *clap/beat* (clapping, beating, or punching with the hands resulting in contact), and the postural gesture *shrug* (raising and falling of the shoulders). In order to enable researchers to note other emotional expressions that they observe and that – most importantly–fulfil the criteria of the Function value *emotion/attitude,* in the NEUROGES®-ELAN template a special template value (*other e-motion)* is provided.

Meeting the criteria

Structure	*phasic*
Focus	*in space, within body*
Gesture/action space	**ipsilateral neutral** hemi-space
Path	**one- or two-dimensional**
Hand orientation	the hand orientation is coordinated with the direction of the hand/arm and trunk movement, e.g. when opening the arms the palms are oriented toward the addressee, i.e., the hand does not adopt an orientation independently from the rest of the body

Hand shape	the hand shaping is coordinated with the whole body shaping
Efforts	**dynamic display of efforts, in particular of the effort factor weight, distinct from the individual's baseline**
Body involvement	**obligatorily accompanied by a postural-facial expression**; proximal initiation of limb movements; strong involvement of the trunk, head, and face; in learned gestures the postural involvement depends on the degree of "true" emotional engagement
Gaze	not at hands

Occurrence: *Emotion/attitude* units were investigated in 91 individuals of the NEUROGES® archive. Right hand *emotion/attitude* units were displayed by 48 % (44/91), left hand *emotion/attitude* units by 45 % (41/191), and bimanual *emotion/attitude* units by 74 % (67/91).

Frequency: In the NEUROGES® archive sample (n = 91), right hand *emotion/attitude* units were displayed with a frequency (Mean ± Standard Deviation; Median) of 0.31 ± 1.07; 0.00 units per minute, left hand *emotion/attitude* units with a frequency of 0.20 ± 0.35; 0.00, and bimanual *emotion/attitude* units with a frequency of 0.52 ± 0.83; 0.35.

Duration: The duration (Mean ± Standard Deviation; Median) of right hand *emotion/attitude* units was 2.45 ± 2.80; 1.83 seconds per unit, of left hand *emotion/attitude* units 2.02 ± 1.50; 1.42, and of bimanual *emotion/attitude* units 1.18 ± 0.54; 1.21.

Differentiate *emotion/attitude* from...

✎ *subject-oriented action*: *Emotion/attitude* movements reflect or show specific emotions such as happiness, sadness, fear, anger, surprise, or disgust. In contrast, *subject-oriented actions* serve the regulation of the individual's physical needs, the improvement of her/his visual appearance, or the regulation of mental processes.

Difficulties in distinguishing between the Function value *emotion/attitude* and the Function value *subject-oriented action* apply primarily to *phasic within body* units, as otherwise *emotion/attitude phasic* units are most often *in space,* whereas *subject-oriented action* units are *on body, on attached object,* or more rarely, *on separate object. Within body subject-oriented actions* more often have a *repetitive* Structure, since they typically serve the regulation of physical needs, e.g. rolling the shoulders because of muscle tension or to exercise. *Within body emotion/attitude* movements more often have a *phasic* Structure and a one-dimensional path, e.g. shrugging the shoulders in resignation.

- *emphasis*: *Emphasis* gestures that accompany the speech process may have an emotional connotation. However, while the *emotion/attitude* movements are exclusively expressions or reflections of emotion or attitudes, *emphasis* gestures serve the accentuation of certain segments of speech of the word retrieval. They set accents and may create rhythms.

Emotion/attitude movements are *phasic* units, while *emphasis* gestures are often *repetitive.* In *emotion/attitude* movements the movements are proximal, bilateral, and accompanied by a facial-postural expression, and the arm embodies the (emotional) direction. In *emphasis* gestures, the hand or arm is used as a baton to set accents in specific directions. The movements are peripheral, unilateral, and accompany speech (see also Type category: Differentiations of *emotion–clap/beat* from *emphasis–baton* and *emphasis–superimposed).*

- *emblem: Emblems* are hand signs that fulfil the criteria conventionality, isolation / distal distinction, explicitness, and novel meaning. Some *emblems* are conventionalized signs for specific emotions, e.g. a fist as a symbol for aggression. These *emblems* may be displayed without experiencing the emotion.

In an *emblem*, the hand sign alone is sufficient to convey the information about the designated emotion. There is always a transport phase. In *emotion/attitude* movements the hand movement is embedded in a postural-facial emotional expression. The hand movement per se can be quite unspecific, and only the whole body movement and facial expression that accompany the limb movement clarify the underlying emotional state or attitude.

8.4.2 *emphasis*

Short definition

SETTING ACCENTS ON SPEECH

Definition

Function: Emphasis is defined as force or intensity of expression that gives impressiveness or importance to something. In gesture, emphasis can be produced by strong, direct, and quick movements that thereby set dynamic accents. These movement accents point out short segments of the speech. In synchrony with prosody, they emphasize certain aspects of the verbal statement. As such, *emphasis* gestures can be regarded as manual equivalents of prosody. Rarely, they are displayed in speech pauses. Obviously, a sequence of accents creates a meter or a rhythm and therefore, *emphasis* gestures convey rhythmical and potentially acoustical information (if the Focus value is *on body* or *on separate object*). In the latter case, their effect is less dependent on a well visible location of the hand in the gesture/action space.

Furthermore, emphasis can be put on the process of bringing out in speech a concept and presenting it. By rotating the palm out, these *emphasis* gestures accompany and thereby enforce the process of quasi rotating out words (thoughts) and then presenting them.

Emphasis gestures do not only set accents on speech but they can also superimpose emphasis on gestures: *emotion/attitude* (primarily the learned display), *egocentric deictic, egocentric direction, form presentation, spatial relation presentation,* and *emblem* gestures. Kinesically, in order to place an accent on a gesture, the gesture has to have a static complex phase.

As there are only few movement forms that are effective for setting accents, *emphasis* gestures are performed inter-individually and also intra-individually in stereotypic manners. Thus, if in a video sample, an individual repeatedly displays of a certain gesture form that fulfils the criteria of the Function value *emphasis*, the repeated display supports the assessment.

Movement form: *Emphasis* gestures are *repetitive* or *phasic in space* (rarely *on body* or *on separate object*) movements. They are spatially simple seesaw movements, either up-down, in-out (supination-pronation), or rarely, if superimposed, forth-back. All *emphasis* gestures have an endpoint accent. The up-down movements can have a downward accent or an upward accent. The supination-pronation movements have an outward accent. All *emphasis* gestures are synchronized with mouth and head movements (unless they accompany internal speech, which is not accompanied by mouth movements but often by head movements).

If *emphasis* gestures follow the static complex phase of *emotion/attitude* (mainly the learned display), *egocentric deictic, egocentric direction, form presentation, spatial relation presentation,* or *emblem* gestures (*superimposed emphasis*), they have up-down or forth-back path with a downward or forward accent. Once the primary gesture has come to the static complex phase, *the superimposed emphasis* gesture follows. The hand shape, the hand orientation, and the position in gesture/action space of the primary gesture are preserved during the display of the *superimposed emphasis* gesture. As an example, the fingers are shaped to V-sign and a *repetitive* forth-back movement is superimposed (*emblem + superimposed emphasis*), or hand points and up-down movements are added (*egocentric deictic + superimposed emphasis).* Technically in *superimposed emphasis*, the unit adopted from Module I or II, which typically has the Structure value *repetitive*, is split into a subunit with the primary Function value and a subunit with the Function value *emphasis*.

Types: As outlined above, the movement forms used to create emphasis differ with regards to the path during complex phase and to the direction towards end point. Accordingly, four Type values are distinguished: *baton* (up-down movements of lower arm with downward accent), *back-toss* (small up-down movements with wrist of hand resting and upward accent), *palm-out* (small supination-pronation movements with outward accent), *superimposed* (up-down or back-forth movements with downward or forward accent that directly follow the static complex phase of another gesture type).

Specifications: *Emphasis* gestures can be further specified with the Supplementary category Temporal Structure, which enables to register the temporal structure that is created by the *emphasis* gesture.

Meeting the criteria

Structure	***repetitive*** > *phasic*
Focus	*in space*, in exceptional cases *on body* or *on separate object*
Gesture/action space	**ipsilateral neutral** hemi-space, level of trunk, middle kinesphere (only *superimposed emphasis* gesture may adopt the distinct position from the primary gesture)
Path	**one-dimensional up-down** or **two-dimensional archlike supination – pronation**
Hand orientation	no distinct orientation; if superimposed to other gesture types, hand orientation of primary gesture is maintained
Hand shape	relaxed open hand; if superimposed to other gesture types, hand shape of primary gesture is maintained
Efforts	acceleration (quick) with change from free to bound flow to generate **end point accent**
Body involvement	*emphasis* gestures are **synchronized with mouth and head** movements
Gaze	not at hands
Other criteria	in line with prosody

Occurrence: *Emphasis* units were investigated in 91 individuals of the NEUROGES® archive. Right hand *emphasis* units were displayed by 78 % (71/91), left hand *emphasis* units by 76 % (69/91), and bimanual *emphasis* units by 93 % (85/91).

Frequency: In the NEUROGES® archive sample (n = 91), right hand *emphasis* units were displayed with a frequency (Mean ± Standard Deviation; Median) of 0.98 ± 1-47; 0.40 units per minute, left hand *emphasis* units with a frequency of 1.15 ± 2.79; 0.38, and bimanual *emphasis* units with a frequency of 1.69 ± 1.78; 1.01.

Duration: The duration (Mean ± Standard Deviation; Median) of right hand *emphasis* units was 1.54 ± 0.76; 1.40 seconds per unit, of left hand *emphasis* units 1.73 ± 1.18; 1.49, and of bimanual *emphasis* units 1.72 ± 0.80; 1.65.

Differentiate *emphasis* gestures from…

- *emotion*: see *emotion*
- *egocentric direction: Egocentric direction* gestures are used explicitly to convey the message concerning a designated direction. The information about the designated direction can be conveyed independently from the verbal utterance. As specific directions are indicated, there is a great variety in spatial direction, e.g. from down left to up right. The Structure is *phasic.*

In contrast, *emphasis* gestures are typically performed implicitly and they accompany the speech (or inner speech) process. The spatial directions of the path during the complex phase are stereotypical, i.e., up-down, in-out. The Structure is typically *repetitive.*

- *pantomime*: In *pantomime* gestures with a *repetitive* Structure the meaning is conveyed by the repetition per se, e.g. when pantomiming tooth brushing or hammering. In these cases, one up-down brush movement in front of the mouth or one downward hammering movement would not unambiguously convey the meaning of tooth brushing or hammering, respectively. In *repetitive pantomimes* there is often a displacement of the hand, e.g. the hand moves in front of the mouth from the left side to the right side while executing the up-down movements. Furthermore, there is a distinct hand shape or hand orientation and the gaze is at the hand.

In contrast, in *emphasis* gestures there is no displacement of the hand during the forth-back movement, there is no distinct hand shape or hand orientation, and the gaze is not at the hand.

- *form presentation:* In *form presentation* gestures with a *repetitive* Structure the repetition serves to create a repetitive pattern, e.g. to depict a star with six sharps. The repetition of one segment of the form is necessary to create the whole form, e.g. six identical sharps are needed to create a star. There is a displacement of the hand, there is a distinct hand shape or hand orientation and the gaze is at the presented form.

In contrast, as the *repetitive* movements of *emphasis* gestures are back and forth, they cannot create a form. There is no distinct hand shape or hand orientation, and the gaze is not at the hand.

- *spatial relation presentation: Spatial relation presentation* gestures with a *repetitive* Structure may serve to present several independent locations or to create a route with a repetitive pattern, e.g. a zig-zag path.

In *spatial relation presentation* gestures there is always a distinct use of gesture/action space reflecting the mento-heliocentric perspective and thus, a displacement of the hand. The hand is typically shaped, with a distinct orientation, and the gaze is typically at the presented path. This is not the case in *emphasis* gestures.

- *motion quality presentation*: *Motion quality presentation* gestures and *emphasis* gesture share the *repetitive* Structure. However, *motion quality presentation* gestures typically have a complex dynamics, and a shaped hand to present the object that is moving, and a displacement of the hand to represent locomotion. The gaze is typically at the presented motion.

In contrast, *repetitive emphasis* gestures are spatially simple back-forth movements, with an endpoint accent and they are synchronized with the mouth and head movements.

- *emblems:* In *emblems* with a *repetitive* Structure the repetition is part of the conventionalization, e.g. waving the hand to say good-bye or tapping on the temple to indicate that someone is crazy. In this case, a one-way wave or one tap would not unambiguously constitute the sign and the repetition helps to clarify the message. Note, however, that *emblems* with a *phasic* Structure and a static complex phase may be combined with a superimposed *emphasis* gestures, e.g. adopting the shape of the victory sign and then moving the V-shaped hand repetitively back and forth. In this case, the unit is split up into an *emblem* and a *superimposed emphasis* gesture.

In contrast to *emphasis* gestures, *emblems* are not a complement to a verbal utterance, but they constitute the message itself. Furthermore, *emblems* are displayed explicitly, i.e., within the gesturer's awareness, while *emphasis* gestures are not.

8.4.3 *egocentric deictic*

Short definition

INDICATING A LOCATION BY USING AN EGOCENTRIC FRAME OF REFERENCE

Main group
The values *egocentric deictic, egocentric direction,* and *pantomime* share the characteristic that an egocentric frame of reference is adopted as cognitive perspective.

Cognitive perspective: A gesturer who provides information about space or motion may choose (i) an egocentric or (ii) an allocentric perspective (e.g. Klatzky, 1998; Meilinger and Vosgerau, 2010).

(i) egocentric: In the egocentric perspective, the gesturer is the point of reference.

(α) If the gesturer displays spatial information from an egocentric perspective, she/he constitutes the point of spatial reference which the other points in space are related to: "I am here and it is there." (*egocentric deictic)* or "I am here and it is in that direction." (*egocentric direction*). More precisely, the body midline is taken as the point of spatial reference. Therefore, if the target is not in front of the gesturer, (s)he typically rotates the trunk and head to be vis-à-vis with the target. Furthermore, the hand axis (from middle of wrist to middle finger) is oriented centrifugally from the body midline. As an example, if the target is on the gesturer's right, (s)he rotates the head and upper trunk to the right and then points to the target. Note that the gesturer may project him-/herself into an imaginary space while keeping the egocentric frame of reference, e.g. "In my old apartment, if I entered it, the bathroom was on my right." Here, the egocentric frame is projected into a mental imagery space. Further, there can be an egocentric reference to a location in the abstract mental space, e.g. where relevant are emotionally located relative to the gesturer.

(β) If the gesturer displays a movement from an egocentric perspective. Thus, the gesturer is the actor: "I move, I act" (*pantomime*). In the gestural display,–in contrast to the mento-heliocentric perspective–the hands keep their natural orientation as parts of the gesturer's body relative to the other parts of the body, i.e., in order to successfully perform actions, the hand and head positions are coordinated such that the actions of the hands can be visually controlled. Therefore, in *pantomime*, there is typically an involvement of the head and upper trunk in coordination with the hand/arm movement. As an example, in the *pantomime* of hammering the hand, the arm, the head, and the trunk are spatially and dynamically coordinated.

(ii) allocentric / mento-heliocentric: In gesture, allocentric perspectives are most often "mento-heliocentric" (heliocentric = the sun is at the center of the solar system). The term "mento-heliocentric" is introduced here to convey the concept that the gesturer mentally takes the perspective of the sun. Thus, his/her view on spatial relations, motions, and actions differs from the view that is obtained from an egocentric perspective.

(α) The gesturer displays a spatial relation from a mento-heliocentric perspective, i.e., (s)he mentally takes the perspective of the sun and looks on the imaginary spatial scenery: "In the presented environment, it would be over there." (*spatial relation presentation*). In the gestural display, the mental image that is generated with a mento-heliocentric perspective is projected onto the horizontal or frontal plane. Within the frame of this map, the gesturer may show a position or a route. If the imaginary map is projected to the horizontal plane, the hand axis is in line with the vertical space axis. If the imaginary map is projected to the frontal plane, e.g. an imaginary map of the city of Cologne, the hand axis is in line with a sagittal axis. In this case, it is more difficult to use the hand orientation as a movement indicator of the cognitive perspective, as it is the same for the mento-heliocentric and egocentric perspectives. Here, the gesturer's gaze focus helps to identify the cognitive perspective: In the mento-heliocentric perspective the visual focus is on the imaginary map, which is projected within reach/kinesphere onto the frontal plane. In contrast, in the egocentric perspective the visual focus is on the target (or, if it is invisible, on its assumed position) that is typically beyond the reach/kinesphere.

A special case is experimental settings in which animations are presented to the gesturer on a screen in front of her/him. In this case, based on the gestural behavior alone it is difficult to say if the gesturer employs an egocentric or a mento-heliocentric perspective. S/he might really consider objects on the right side of the screen as being on her/his right and objects on the left side of the screen as being on her/his left, i.e., relate these objects to her/himself. Or, alternatively, s/he might adopt a mento-heliocentric perspective on the scene on the screen.

(β) The gesturer may display a motion from a mento-heliocentric perspective, i.e., the gesturer's hand–instead of the gesturer her-/

himself–represents an agent that moves or acts and the gesturer looks at this presentation mentally taking the perspective of the sun (*motion quality presentation*). The hands are used as if they were marionettes and **not** as if they were the gesturer's hands that relate to the gesturer's body. In most cases, there is an indirect reference to the ground on which the motion or action takes place. This ground is typically projected to the horizontal plane. The gesturer's body is not involved in the presentation. The hands are functionally separated from the gesturer's body. The wrist is often flexed such that the hand axis is in line with the vertical space axis and the hand is displaced on the horizontal plane, e.g. the index and middle finger represent two legs (pars pro toto for a human being) walking on a ground.

However, while *egocentric deictic, egocentric direction* and *pantomime* obligatorily have an egocentric perspective in a concrete or mental imagery space, *spatial relation presentation* often and *motion quality presentation* sometimes have a mento-heliocentric perspective. However, in special experimental settings, e.g. in which animations are presented to the gesturer on a screen, it is difficult to determine whether or not the gesturer keeps the egocentric perspective (on the screen) when re-presenting the spatial relations of the animation. Thus, the relevant difference between *egocentric deictic* and *egocentric direction* on the one hand and *spatial relation presentation* on the other is that the latter Function value space is **created** while in the first two values space is **referred to**. Thus, the creative performance is higher in *spatial relation presentation* than in *egocentric deictic* or *direction.*

Definition

Function: An *egocentric deictic* indicates where something is located, by using an egocentric frame of reference. The gesturer's body midline is the spatial point of reference for defining the location. Thus, from his/her actual location in space, the gesturer indicates another location in the space by pointing to it. The indication of a location is direct reference to a locus in space, and furthermore, it may be an indirect reference to an object/subject. As an example, the gesturer points to the location of the chair in order to designate the chair. The target may be visible ("There is the table") or invisible ("The basket is behind the door"). However, for targets that are invisible because they are far away, *egocentric direction* gestures are preferred.

The gesturer may project him-/herself into a mental space while keeping the egocentric frame of reference, e.g.: "In my old apartment, if I entered it, the bathroom was on my right." Thus, the egocentric frame is maintained in an imagery space. The mental space can also be an abstract space, e.g. a reflection of emotional relations to other persons.

Egocentric deictics with reference to concrete locations are typically displayed explicitly, i.e., the gesturer is aware of displaying the gesture.

Movement form: The longitudinal hand axis (wrist–finger tips) is typically oriented centrifugally from the body midline. The target is located in the estimated prolongation of this vector. Only if the gesturer points to him/herself, the body midline can no longer function as the spatial point of reference. In this case, the vector of the pointing hand adopts a centripetal orientation, as if pointing from an external point of reference to the body midline. There is a distinct hand shape with a flat hand, an extended index or an extended thumb. The tips of fingers are oriented toward the designated location. The path during complex phase is one-dimensional spoke-like or two-dimensional arch-like. The effort qualities are direct space and bound movement flow, as a precise localization of the target is intended. The gesturer looks at the designated location he/she is pointing at, except for when he/she is referring to him/herself. Often a trunk rotation can be observed, in which the body midline is oriented towards the target. As an example, the gesturer rotates the trunk to the right and performs an *egocentric deictic* to a target on his/her right side.

Types: The four Type values of the Function value *egocentric deictic* specify the target: *external target* (indicating a target in the external space), *You* (referring to the addressee as a person or to a part of her/his body), *body* (referring to parts of the own body), and *self* (referring to oneself as a person).

Specifications: *Egocentric deictics* can be further assessed with the Supplementary categories Target Location, Execution Hemi-Space, and Referent.

Target Location: The category specifies the location the hand points to.

Execution Hemi-Space: The category specifies the location where the hand displays the complex phase.

Referent: This category enables the rater to code whether (s)he assumes that the Referent of the *egocentric deictic* gesture is

(i) *material:* e.g. referring to the chair in the room
(ii) *non-material:* e.g. referring to angels in heaven, a point in time.

Meeting the criteria

Structure	***phasic***
Focus	*in space > on body > on attached object, on separate object, on person*

Gesture/action space	**distinct use, determined by the designated location**
Path	one- or two-dimensional, **spoke-** or **arch-like** path
Hand orientation	**tip of fingers oriented toward designated location;** hand axis is oriented centrifugally from the body midline; **longitudinal hand axis in line with the vector to designated target**
Hand shape	distinct hand shape: flat hand, or extended index or thumb (if referring to something behind).
Effort	**direct space**, often end point accent; rather bound flow
Body involvement	If the hand is inhibited, the pointing might also be executed with the elbow or the shoulder, or the head.
Gaze	The gesturer looks at the designated location he/she is pointing at, except for when he/she is referring to him/herself (*self-deictic*).
Other criteria	The pointing gesture can be accompanied by words "here", "there", "I", etc.

Occurrence: *Egocentric deictic* units were investigated in 91 individuals of the NEUROGES® archive. Right hand *egocentric deictic* units were displayed by 36 % (33/91), left hand *egocentric deictic* units by 26 % (24/91), and bimanual *egocentric deictic* units by 26 % (24/91).

Frequency: In the NEUROGES® archive sample (n = 91), right hand *egocentric deictic* units were displayed with a frequency (Mean ± Standard Deviation; Median) of 0.23 ± 0.52; 0.00 units per minute, left hand *egocentric deictic* units with a frequency of 0.12 ± 0.30; 0.00, and bimanual *egocentric deictic* units with a frequency of 0.10 ± 0.39; 0.00.

Duration: The duration (Mean ± Standard Deviation; Median) of right hand *egocentric deictic* units was 1.75 ± 0.83; 1.59 seconds per unit, of left hand *egocentric deictic* units 1.77 ± 0.90; 1.65, and of bimanual *egocentric deictic* units 2.12 ± 1.27; 1.77.

Differentiate *egocentric deictic* from…

✎ *egocentric direction*: The *egocentric direction* gesture indicates a direction towards a location with no distance information, or a route. An *egocentric direction* gesture that indicates a route is easy to differentiate from an *egocentric deictic*, as it marks a line and does not indicate a point. In an *egocentric direction* gesture that indicates a direction with no distance information, the hand is quasi 'thrown' into the designated direction. The hand is relaxed. There is a free flow and acceleration with an end point accent, the path is arch-like.

In contrast, the *egocentric deictic* directly designates a specific location with distance information. The target is located in the estimated prolongation of the pointing hand or finger. The hand has a distinct shape, the path during complex phase is spoke- or arch-like, and the movement flow is bound. Often only the index is extended to indicate the localization of the target. Thereby, a precise localization can be realized.

spatial relation presentation: The *egocentric deictic* might be confused with the Type *position* of the *spatial relation presentation* gesture. However, the *spatial relation presentation* gesture creates a position in an imaginary space by positioning or placing the hand in the gesture space. In contrast, in *egocentric deictics* a location is not created but it is only referred to. Thus, there is reference to a location in the gesturer's real or imaginary environment.

A related aspect regarding the difference between *spatial relation presentations* and *egocentric deictics* concerns the cognitive perspective. In *egocentric deictics* the gesturer obligatorily applies an egocentric frame of reference by using her/himself as the point of spatial reference. In contrast, in *spatial relation presentations*, there is often a mento-heliocentric perspective. The gesturer adopts the cognitive perspective of looking down on an imaginary map that s/he creates by setting positions and routes. As the imaginary map is often projected to the horizontal plane, the fingertips are oriented downwards to the horizontal plane, i.e., the longitudinal hand axis (wrist – finger tips) is in line with the vertical space axis. If the imaginary map is projected to the frontal plane, e.g. a mental map of the city of Cologne, the hand axis is in line with the sagittal space axis. The gaze is at the target on the imaginary map. In contrast, in an *egocentric deictic*, the gesturer indicates a location with spatial reference to her/his body midline. The vector of the pointing hand is in centrifugal orientation (with the exception of pointing to the oneself). The gaze is at the target in the real or imaginary environment.

In rare cases, the gesturer creates an imaginary spatial map and then refers to a specific location by pointing on this map by keeping the mentio-heliocentric perspectives. While these pointing gestures share many features of movement form with *egocentric deictics*, they are coded as *spatial relation presentations* because they are based on a mento-heliocentric cognitive perspective.

emblem: *Emblems* that include pointing have a novel meaning that differs from the meaning of the gesture that they (hypothetically) originate from, e.g. tapping with the index at the temple may have originally been a *deictic* to the temple and then in the process of conventionalization has been linked with the meaning "You are crazy / That is crazy!". In contrast, *egocentric deictics* do not have a novel meaning, they are one-to-one indications of a location of a material or non-material referent.

Emblems are not variable with regard to the hand shape, hand orientation, and the position of the hand in the gesture/action space, e.g. tapping with the index at the temple. In contrast, for *egocentric deictics* the position and orientation of the hand in the gesture/action space is determined by the designated location.

8.4.4 *egocentric direction*

Short definition

INDICATING A DIRECTION OR A ROUTE BY USING AN EGOCENTRIC FRAME OF REFERENCE

Main group

see *egocentric deictic*

Definition

Function: The *egocentric direction* gesture indicates a direction or a route[17] by using an egocentric frame of reference. The gesturer's body midline is the spatial point of reference for defining the direction or the route.

(i) direction: "Direction is the information contained in the relative position of one point with respect to another without the distance information" (Wikipedia). In accordance with this definition, the *egocentric direction* gesture indicates a direction (towards where) without distance information, e.g. heavenwards, northwards, etc. Theoretically, the distance can be infinite. As the frame of reference is egocentric, the point of reference is the gesturer's body midline. As a direction does not contain distance information, *egocentric directions* are preferred to *egocentric deictics* for indicating locations that are far away and invisible.

(ii) route: A route is defined as "a way or course taken in getting from a starting point to a destination" (Oxford Dictionaries). In contrast to a direction, the depiction of a route implies the indication of a start point and an end point.

In an *egocentric direction* gesture, the emphasis may be on the change of position with an accent on the start point and the end point (from where to where) or on

17 Since in the egocentric perspective, there are more often indications of directions than of routes, the Function value was termed *egocentric direction*.

the path between the start and end positions (where along). *Egocentric direction* gestures may not only indicate the path from the gesturer to an external location ("...from me to there"), or the path from an external location to the gesturer ("...from there to me"), but also the route between two or more locations in the external space ("... from there to over there"). Especially in the latter case, for coding the value *egocentric direction* rather than *spatial relation presentation* the criterion is that the egocentric frame of reference is maintained ("[I am here and] it is from there to there").

The *egocentric direction* gestures indicating a direction or a route may be used in a transitive context: the hand indicates the direction towards where an entity is moved or should be moved. The (to be) moved entity may be an object, the addressee, parts of his /her body, or his/her mental state, or in mental training conditions or self-suggestion, the gesturer's own body or mental state. As an agent is required to execute the movement of an entity in a specific direction, these *egocentric direction* gestures also imply information about the agent.

Just like *egocentric deictics, egocentric direction* gestures may be based on the gesturer's mental rotation into an imaginary space. Here, the gesturer projects him-/herself into an imaginary space while keeping the egocentric frame of reference, e.g.: "If I stood in front of the Eiffel Tower, it would be in that direction". Thus, the egocentric frame is projected into the imagery space and then the *egocentric direction* gesture is performed.

Just like *egocentric deictics, egocentric direction* gestures for concrete spatial directions or routes are typically displayed explicitly, i.e., the gesturer is aware of displaying the gesture.

Movement form: The movement form is described separately for the direction and route subtypes:

(i) direction: In *egocentric direction* gestures that indicate a direction, the hand is quasi 'thrown' in the designated direction. Thereby, the impression of a far or even infinite distance is conveyed. The gesturer's body midline is the point of reference from where the direction starts and the longitudinal hand axis (from wrist to finger tips) embodies the designated direction. The hand is relaxed. The path during complex phase is two-dimensional arch-like. There is a free flow and acceleration with an end point accent. At the end of the complex phase, the longitudinal hand axis is in line with the designated direction.

(ii) route: In *egocentric direction* gestures that indicate a route, the hand marks the complete line of the route from the start point to the endpoint. The trace between the start position and the end position may be direct or indirect. If a change of position is emphasized (from where to where), e.g. in a gesture accompanying the phrase "The bird flew from the high tree to the smaller one", the trace between the start position and the end position is straight. If the path per se is emphasized (where along), e.g. the finger follows the visible skyline of a city, the trace can be spatially complex. As the emphasis is not on the precise depiction of a route (and not on the motion on that route as in *motion quality presentation* gestures), there is no variation in the effort qualities. The movement flow is bound and there is a direct use of space in order to deliver a precise depiction of the route.

The orientation of the hand depends on the transitivity versus intransitivity of the *egocentric direction* gesture. In intransitive gestures, the longitudinal hand axis is in line with the direction. In transitive gestures, the sagittal hand axis (from back to palm of hand) is in line with the designated direction line, as if moving something with the palm/back of the hand into the designated direction.

Types: For *egocentric direction* gestures, the Type values specify the absence or presence of an agent who executes the direction. There are three Type values: *neutral* (indication of a direction without information about an agent), *imperative* (the addressee is the agent), and *self-related* (the gesturer is the agent).

Specifications: *Egocentric direction* gestures can be further assessed with the Supplementary categories Target Location, Execution Hemi-Space, and Referent.

Target Location: The category registers the location the hand directs at or the endpoint of the route.

Execution Hemi-Space: The category registers the location where the hand displays the complex phase.

Referent: This category enables the rater to code whether (s)he assumes that the Referent of the *egocentric direction* gesture is

(i) *material:* e.g. towards Paris;
(ii) *non-material:* e.g. an idea that is moved down such as "Forget it!".

Meeting the criteria

Structure	*phasic*
Focus	*in space,* rarely: *on separate object*
Gesture/action space	**distinct use, determined by the designated direction**
Path	one- or two-dimensional; in egocentric route depictions (where along) also three-dimensional

Hand orientation	(i) direction: **in line with the designated direction line:** in intransitive gestures, the longitudinal hand axis in line with the designated direction line; in transitive gestures, the sagittal hand axis in line with the designated direction line; (ii) route: fingers tips trace route
Hand shape	**relaxed hand;** in route indications, the index may be extended
Effort	(i) direction: **free flow, hand is often "thrown" in the direction,** emphasis on end-point of gesture; (ii) route: bound flow
Body involvement	proximal arm muscles are often involved
Gaze	gesturer **looks into the designated direction**
Other criteria	*egocentric direction* gestures can be accompanied by words such as "northwards", "upwards", "backwards", "forwards", "sidewards", "to the right", etc.

Occurrence: *Egocentric direction* units were investigated in 91 individuals of the NEUROGES® archive. Right hand *egocentric direction* units were displayed by 33 % (30/91), left hand *egocentric direction* units by 30 % (27/91), and bimanual *egocentric direction* units by 36 % (33/91).

Frequency: In the NEUROGES® archive sample (n = 91), right hand *egocentric direction* units were displayed with a frequency (Mean ± Standard Deviation; Median) of 0.16 ± 0.39; 0.00 units per minute, left hand *egocentric direction* units with a frequency of 0.11 ± 0.30; 0.00, and bimanual *egocentric direction* units with a frequency of 0.14 ± 0.40; 0.00.

Duration: The duration (Mean ± Standard Deviation; Median) of right hand *egocentric direction* units was 2.56 ± 1.53; 2.20 seconds per unit, of left hand *egocentric direction* units 2.18 ± 1.18; 2.01, and of bimanual *egocentric direction* units 2.59 ± 1.63; 2.29.

Differentiate *egocentric direction* from…

- *emphasis:* see there
- *pantomime: Pantomime* gestures depict a complex action. The path during complex phase is spatially complex and the use of efforts distinct. Often, an imaginary object is manipulated. The *pantomime* gestures of throwing something or of pushing away something share dynamic features with *egocentric*

direction gestures. In *pantomimes*, however, there is a distinct hand shape in adaptation to the imaginary object, which is thrown or pushed away.

In contrast, *egocentric directions* that are transitive and show only the direction to which something is moved or shall be moved (move it to the right, away) and the focus is not on the action of moving. The spatial path is one-way two-dimensional. The hand is relaxed, as no information about the object is provided.

spatial relation presentation: The *egocentric direction* of the subtype (ii) route might be confused with the Type *route* of a *spatial relation presentation* gesture. However, the *spatial relation presentation* gesture creates a route in an imaginary space by tracing a path in the gesture space. In contrast, in *egocentric directions* a route is not created but it is only referred to.

Another aspect regarding the difference between *spatial relation presentations* and *egocentric deictics* concerns the cognitive perspective. In *egocentric directions* the gesturer obligatorily applies an egocentric frame of reference by using her-/himself as the point of spatial reference. In contrast, in *spatial relation presentations* with a material referent, there is often a mento-heliocentric perspective. The gesturer adopts the cognitive perspective of looking down on an imaginary map that s/he creates by setting positions and routes. As the imaginary map is often projected to the horizontal plane, the fingertips are oriented downwards to the horizontal plane, i.e., the longitudinal hand axis (wrist – finger tips) is in line with the vertical space axis. If the imaginary map is projected to the frontal plane, e.g. a mental map of the city of Cologne, the hand axis is in line with the sagittal space axis. The gaze is at the target on the imaginary map. In contrast, in *egocentric directions*, the gesturer indicates a direction or a route with spatial reference to her/his body midline. The gaze is in the direction or at the route in the real or imaginary environment.

In rare cases, the gesturer creates an imaginary spatial map and then refers to a route on this map by keeping the mentio-heliocentric perspectives. While these tracing gestures share many features of movement form with *egocentric directions* subtype route, they are coded as *spatial relation presentations* because they are based on a mento-heliocentric cognitive perspective.

motion quality presentation: A *motion quality presentation* gesture presents a specific kind or quality of movement, e.g. rolling or exploding. It may include information about spatial relations, e.g. representing something rolling from one point to another. In contrast to *egocentric direction* gestures, the manner or the quality of movement is superimposed to the direction or route trajectory. Thus, there is always a specific within hand movement trajectory (e.g. circulating the hand to demonstrate rolling) or specific effort qualities (e.g. sudden, strong, and direct to demonstrate something exploding). Furthermore, just like in *spatial relation presentation* gestures, the cognitive perspective is mento-heliocentric, i.e. as if looking on something that is moving without any spatial reference to the own body.

8.4.5 *pantomime*

Short definition

PRETENDING TO PERFORM AN ACTION

Main group

see *egocentric deictic*

Definition

Function: The gesturer pretends ("as if") to perform a motor action her-/himself.

"Action is defined as an intentional (wilful) human body movement, a behavior caused by an agent in a particular situation" (Oxford Dictionary), "something done" (Webster's Dictionary). In NEUROGES®, actions are defined as all hand movements that effect changes in the external physical world that surrounds the gesturer's body or in the gesturer's state (see Function values *object-oriented action* and *subject-oriented action*).

The Function value *pantomime* refers to the "**as if**" demonstration of an action but **not** to the actual execution. Examples for *pantomime* gestures are pretending to brush the teeth with an imaginary toothbrush, pretending to climb up a mountain, moving the arms as if marching, or pretending that an external object hits the gesturer. It is an essential criterion for the Function value *pantomime* that the cognitive perspective is egocentric. The gesturer is the actor in the pretended action. Even in the latter example (being hit by an object), the egocentric cognitive perspective is maintained: The gesturer is the actor with whom something happens.

Not coded with the value *pantomime* are "as if" demonstrations of non-action movements such as pretending to show an emotion, pretending to perform a deictic, etc. As an example, the gesturer, who narrates a movie in which the main character performs an *egocentric deictic*, may behave as if s/he were the main character and perform an *egocentric deictic*. In this case, the Function value *egocentric deictic* is given. The same applies to imitations of all other types of gestures, notably *emotion, egocentric direction,* or *emblem*.

In special experimental settings, an actual tool may held in the hand and an actual counter-part may be present but the action is only pantomimed, e.g. holding an actual hammer in the hand and pretending to hammer (but not really doing it) on an actual nail. In the neuropsychological literature, this condition is termed tool use demonstration but in NEUROGES® it is coded as *pantomime*.

Movement form: The *pantomime* gesture is executed as similar to the actual action of reference as possible. As the gesturer is the actor, potentially her/his whole body is involved. If the gesturer displays the *pantomime* while sitting, there is regularly an involvement of other parts of the body, such as the head and the trunk. While in *presentation* gestures (9.4.5 – 9.4.8), the hand represents something else, e.g. a running dog, in *pantomime* the gesturer's hand is the actor's hand. Thus, the hands adopt a specific orientation, in which they keep their natural orientation as a part of the gesturer's body, e.g. when pretending to climb up a mountain the hands have to be moved to a position in which they could potentially drag the body upward. The longitudinal hand axis (wrist to finger tips) is often oriented centrifugally from the body-midline. The use of the gesture space is determined by the action space of the action of reference. As an example, when pretending to march there is use of the lateral gesture space, as in actual marching the arms move on the right and left sides of the trunk.

There are few exceptions to the rule that the gesturer's hand is the actor's hand. Occasionally, the hands may be used as if they were the feet. Furthermore, the hand may embody the tool, e.g. the index embodies the toothbrush, or a separate object, e.g. the hand represents a ball that hits the gesturer. In this case, the hand does not function as a part of the gesturer's body but it represents an object. The Supplementary category Technique of Presentation enables to register this information with the value *hand-as-object*. In any case, the egocentric perspective is maintained: The gesturer is the actor. The hand representing the object relates to the gesturer's body as the actor's body.

Types: For the Function value *pantomime,* the Type values register (in)transitivity. There are three Type values: *intransitive* (acting "as if" without any imaginary object or counter-part, e.g. pretending to walk), *transitive-active* (acting "as if" with an imaginary object or counterpart, e.g. pretending to hammer a nail into the wall), and *transitive-passive* (acting "as if" with a separate object or agent acting on oneself, e.g. pretending being hit by a ball).

Specifications: *Pantomime* gestures can be further assessed with the Supplementary categories Technique of Presentation, Effort, and Referent.

Technique of (Form) Presentation: This category registers which technique is used to represent the imaginary object or counterpart the gesturer-actor acts with/on:

(i) *enclosure*: The hand adopts a specific shape, which is defined by the form of the imaginary tool / imaginary counterpart. The hand embraces the imaginary tool, e.g. grasping and holding the handle of an imaginary toothbrush; or the hand embraces an imaginary rope that the gesturer-actor pretends to climb up;
(ii) *hand-as-object*: The hand is shaped as if it were the tool or the counterpart, e.g. the index representing a tooth brush, the hand with index and middle finger extended embodies scissors, or the flat hand represents a cake that is thrown into the gesturer' face;

Efforts: This category enables to code the dynamics of the *pantomime*, e.g. the *pantomime* of hammering may be performed with the Effort quality *strong*.

Referent: This category enables the rater to code whether (s)he assumes that the Referent of the pretended action is

(i) *material:* Most *pantomime* gestures are *material*, i.e., they refer to concrete actions, such as actually brushing the teeth, swimming in the ocean, getting hit by something, etc.;
(ii) *non-material*: However, the *pantomime* gesture may refer to *non-material* phenomena, e.g. the gesture pretends to weigh two ideas with his/her hands when considering the pros and cons for the two ideas.

Note: The pantomimed action can be typically clearly be recognized by the rater. Thus, the action may be noted, e.g. cutting with a knife, throwing a ball.

Meeting the criteria

Structure	*phasic, repetitive*
Focus	*in space >> on body > on separate object, on attached object*
Gesture/action space	variable use, **determined by the action space of the action of reference**
Path	distinct, depends on the pantomimed action
Hand orientation	The hand adopts a specific orientation, which enables to execute the action and in which **the hand keeps its natural orientation as a part of gesturer's body.** The exception is the *hand-as-object* Technique of Presentation, in which the hand itself becomes the imaginary object.

Hand shape	distinct, depends on the shape of the imaginary counterpart or the shape of the imaginary tool
Effort	distinct, variation in the Effort qualities, depends on the pantomimed action
Body involvement	**involvement of head and trunk or even whole body**
Gaze	on the hands (exception: Referent *non-material*)

Occurrence: *Pantomime* units were investigated in 91 individuals of the NEUROGES® archive. Right hand *pantomime* units were displayed by 47 % (43/91), left hand *pantomime* units by 36 % (33/91), and bimanual *pantomime* units by 44 % (40/91).

Frequency: In the NEUROGES® archive sample (n = 91), right hand *pantomime* units were displayed with a frequency (Mean ± Standard Deviation; Median) of 1.01 ± 2.80; 0.00 units per minute, left hand *pantomime* units with a frequency of 0.29 ± 0.60; 0.00, and bimanual *pantomime* units with a frequency of 0.58 ± 1.41; 0.00.

Duration: The duration (Mean ± Standard Deviation; Median) of right hand *pantomime* units was 2.57 ± 1.86; 2.25 seconds per unit, of left hand *pantomime* units 2.13 ± 0.64; 2.25, and of bimanual *pantomime* units 2.33 ± 0.99; 2.20.

Differentiate *pantomime* from...

- *egocentric directions:* see there
- *motion quality presentation*: The same actions that is presented in *pantomime* gestures may, likewise, be demonstrated as a *motion quality* gesture. In the latter Type value the gesturer uses his/her hands to present someone/something moving ("It is moving."), while in *pantomime* gestures the gesturer is the actor and pretends to move him-/herself ("I am moving."). In *motion quality presentation* gestures, the gesturer's hand presents a quality of motion, e.g. it moves heavily or it contracts and expands repetitively. The hand serves to embody the motion quality. Often, the hand represents an agent/object who/that moves with that quality. In contrast, in *pantomime* the hand is the actor's hand (see exceptions above).

  In some *motion quality presentation* gestures a mento-heliocentric perspective is adopted. Then there is an indirect reference to the ground on which the motion or action takes place. This ground is typically projected to the horizontal plane. Accordingly, the longitudinal hand axis is in line with the vertical axis. The gesturer's body is not involved in the presentation.

Expressively isolated from the gesturer's body, the hands present the motion quality. In contrast, in *pantomimes*, the hand is oriented just like the actor's hand in the action would be and at least the upper body, head and trunk, is involved in the demonstration. Even if only the hand acts, e.g. pantomiming sewing, the orientation of the head towards the hand reveals the egocentric perspective.

- *form presentation*: *Form presentation* gestures focus on the form of the object of reference. *Pantomimes* may also include information about the form of the imaginary counter-part or the imaginary tool, e.g. the hand shapes around an imaginary object which is round. However, the *form presentation* gesture emphasizes the static features of an object, while the *pantomime* focuses on how an object is used. As an example, a *form presentation* gesture may depict how long a hammer is by enclosing the imaginary form, whereas in *pantomime*, the tool use is demonstrated, such as holding the imaginary hammer and hammering with it. *Form presentation* gestures are characterized by a bound flow without variation in the effort qualities. The imaginary object is presented in the central gesture space. In contrast, *pantomimes* are characterized by a variation in the effort elements and by a distinct use of gesture space.
- Techniques of Presentation (Supplementary category): To present forms or spatial relations, there are Techniques of Presentation such as *tracing, palpating,* or *marking a position*. The motion image of a form is created by tracing or stroking along an imaginary object, or the image of a position is presented by marking it on an imaginary map. In these *form presentation* and *spatial relation presentation* gestures, tracing, palpating, and marking a position are used as techniques to present a form or a position. The gestural message is "This is a square" or "Here is the location". In this case, the gestures are coded with the Function values *form presentation* or *spatial relation presentation,* and the Supplementary category Technique of Presentation is applied to register whether *tracing, palpating,* or *marking a position* was used to create the motion image or the motion image. These gestures do **not** have the Function of a *pantomime*, i.e., the gestural message is **not** "I am tracing/drawing", "I am palpating/sculpturing", or "I am marking a position".

  If, however, the gesturer intends to *pantomime* the actions of tracing, palpating, or marking a position, the tracing, palpating, or marking a position are displayed with dynamics. There is a variation in the effort qualities, because the emphasis is on the action per se, i.e., **how** it is performed. As an example, the *pantomime* of palpating could be performed lightly, sustained, indirectly as if stroking alone on something precious. Or, it could be performed with strength as if working with plastic modelling material. In contrast, if tracing, palpating, or marking a position are used merely as Techniques of Presentation, the focus is on the end product, i.e., the image of form or a location on an imaginary map, and there is no variation in the effort qualities.

emblems: Emblems share with *pantomimes* that they can be used to communicate without words.

However, *emblems* differ in several aspects from *pantomimes:*

(i) conventionality: *Emblems* are conventionalized gestures with a specific meaning that could be translated into language. The movement form and meaning of the gesture is familiar to most members of a given culture or subculture. The specific meaning is fully conveyed without words. In contrast, *pantomimes* are understood without words by the addressee, because they precisely imitate an action that is known to the addressee, e.g. preparing coffee with a coffee machine. In other words, the addressee has to know the original action to understand the *pantomime* (unless the addressee is in a natural surroundings with real objects for which instructions are given by pantomiming, e.g. on a sailing boat the instructor pantomimes how to move the rope). *Emblem* gestures that may be confused with *pantomimes* are especially those that are conventionalized signs for specific actions, e.g. using the telephone. However, these 'action' *emblems* have a strongly conventionalized movement form, e.g. in the telephone-emblem there is a *hand-as-object* use with thumb and little finger extended, while in the original *pantomimes* a broad spectrum of movement forms can be observed to present the same action, e.g. picking up the receiver, dialling, and then moving the receiver to the ear.

(ii) isolation: The *emblem* can be identified by the movement of the hand alone. A facial expression or an involvement of other parts of the body is not necessary to understand the meaning of the hand movement. In contrast, in *pantomimes* the head and often the trunk or even the whole body is involved in the gestural demonstration.

(iii) distal distinction: In *emblems*, the isolated hand movement is distally distinct, i.e., typically the fingers adopt a specific form or are moved on a specific path. Depending on the original action that is pantomimed, in *pantomimes*, the movement may be proximal, e.g. pantomiming swimming.

(vi) novel meaning: *Emblems* that are not arbitrary (see below Function value *emblem*) but that share the movement form with the action of reference have to be differentiated from *pantomime* gestures that show a similar movement form. As an example, a gesture that demonstrates the action of sweeping away dirt from the clothes (*pantomime*) has to be differentiated from an *emblem* gesture that sweeps away imaginary dirt from the shoulder (this location is part of the conventionalization) and that indicates contempt. While *pantomimes* demonstrate almost exclusively concrete actions (e.g. acting as if brushing the teeth), action *emblems* often are signs for symbolic actions, e.g. throwing a kiss (sympathy, affection), tearing the hair out (desperation), cutting the throat (anger, hate, the end), throw up (strong dislike), my hands are tied (helplessness), firing at someone (anger, hate). In all these examples for action *emblems*, the movement form is highly conventionalized and the meaning is novel, i.e., it differs from the meaning that a simple *egocentric deictic, egocentric direction, pantomime, form presentation,* or *motion quality presentation* gesture would have. There are, however, few *emblems* in which only the movement form is conventionalized, e.g. the telephone-sign, but the meaning is that of the concrete action, i.e., the meaning does not differ from that of an equivalent *pantomime* gesture.

8.4.6 *form presentation*

Short definition

CREATING A FORM

Main group

The three Function values *form presentation, spatial relation presentation,* and *motion quality presentation* have in common that they present something: a form, a spatial relation, or a motion quality.

The term ***presentation***, which is shared by the three values, is used in delimitation to the term re-presentation as defined by Freedman (1972, p. 159): "… a *representational hand movement* in which either an abstract idea, or an image having clearly definable space and time referents, is given motor expression." (see also book I, chapter 3.4). In contrast to Freedman's conceptualization, the term *presentation* focuses on the creative act of the gestural expression and it implies that the gesture is not a mere reflection of a cognitive concept but that the formation of the gesture is a creative process that, in turn, can also affect the cognitive concept (book I, chapter 2.1). The term *presentation* also lends emphasis to on what can actually be seen in the hand movement rather than on assumptions about the underlying cognitive concept. As examples, the hand is formed to a round shape and thereby presents a round shape, the two hands are placed at different positions in the gesture/action space and thereby a spatial relation emerges between the two hands, or the hand opens and closes with strength and thereby a motion quality is presented. In contrast, the term re-presentation refers to the assumed referent, e.g. the hand re-presents a ball, the two hands show the distance between two churches in a city, or the hand re-presents the movement of hand-bellows.

In *form presentation* and *spatial relation presentation* gestures, the form or the spatial relation may be presented in a static complex phase (see definition in 4.3). As examples, the hand adopts a certain shape that is held for a while or the two hands present a spatial relation by adopting static positions. Thus, the information is conveyed by a **still image**, i.e., a photo could capture the relevant information. However, likewise, in *form presentation, spatial relation presentation,* and *motion quality presentation* gestures, the information can be conveyed in a motion complex phase (see 4.3). As examples, the image of a form is created by tracing the shape of the imaginary object (Technique of Presentation value *tracing)* or by stroking along the imaginary object (Technique of Presentation value *palpating),* or a spatial relation is presented by two sequential gestures (here… and there), or a motion quality is depicted. These kinds of gestures create a **motion image** (in delimitation to a still image). The creation of still and motion images is based on mental images that are grounded in multi-modally stored mental representations in memory structures (e.g. Kosslyn, 1980). In turn, the addressee recognizes the still and motion images, which the gesturer presents, based on her/his own stored mental representations. In case of motion images, the addressee has to follow the gesturer's hand movements and to memorize the path of the movements in order to recognize the final form or spatial relation. This may imply that the addressee mentally tunes into the gesturer's creative movement and that (s)he uses his/her own sensori-motor experience to comprehend the motion image. The mental recording of the movement path (as if the path were materialized) results in the motion image.

The NEUROGES® definitions of the three *presentation* values imply a **hierarchy** between them: *motion quality presentation* > *spatial relation presentation* > *form presentation.* A *motion quality presentation* gesture may include information about a form and a spatial relation (how what moves where). A *spatial relation presentation* may include information about a form (what is where). A *form presentation* is the most basic *presentation* value as it only includes information about the form.

Definition

Function: The *form presentation* gesture creates a form.

"Form refers to the shape, visual appearance, and configuration of an object." (Wikipedia). "The shape and structure of anything, as distinguished from the material of which it is composed." (Webster's Dictionary).

The *form presentation* gesture presents (only) a form. The *form presentation* gesture includes **no** information, where the form is situated or what is done with the form.

Movement form: There are different techniques to create the still or motion image of a form: (i) *hand-as-object:* the hand creates a still image of a form by embodying the form, e.g. it is formed to a fist (and thereby embodies a round object); (ii) *enclosure:* the hand creates a still image of a form by enclosing an empty space; thus, the configuration and width of the hand aperture provides information about the form, e.g. the hands shape a triangle (enclose an imaginary triangle); (iii) *tracing*: the hand creates a motion image of a form by tracing a closed contour, e.g. it traces a square; (iv) *palpating*: the hand creates a motion image of a form by palpating an empty space; thus, the configuration and width of the hand aperture and the movement path provides information about the form, e.g. the hands palpates a three-dimensional sculpture.

Independent of the technique that is chosen to create the form, *form presentation* gestures in general are characterized by the fact that gesture is displayed in the central gesture space right in front the body midline. The central position is a spatially quasi neutral position, as no specific spatial position is taken. Only in exceptional cases, pure *form presentations*, i.e., those that are not embedded in a *spatial relation presentation* (see below), are **not** executed in the body midline gesture space. For example, because of obvious external circumstances the gesturer chooses another location in the gesture space, such as orientation to the interactive partner or lack of space. As an example, the gesturer addresses a person who sits behind him and performs a *form presentation* gesture above his right shoulder (under normal circumstances, s/he would have displayed this gesture in the central body midline gesture space). Furthermore, in *form presentation* gestures there is often bilateral hand use, as the use of both hands facilitates the creation of complex forms. There is an invariant effort quality use, as information about a static form and **not** about dynamic processes shall be conveyed. Most often, the *form presentation* gesture is performed with a constantly bound flow and direct use of space, in order to provide a precise delineation of the form.

Hierarchy: A *form presentation* (what) may be embedded in a *spatial relation presentation* (where) or in a *motion quality presentation* (how) (see 8.4.7 and 8.4.8). If it is embedded in a *spatial relation presentation* (what is where), the unit is coded as *spatial relation presentation.* If it is embedded in a *motion quality presentation* (what is moving how), the unit is coded as *motion quality presentation.*

Types: For *form presentation* gestures, two Type values classify the geometric aspect presented: *size* (presenting a length) and *shape* (presenting a shape).

Specifications: *Form presentation* gestures can be further assessed with the Supplementary categories Technique of Presentation and Referent.

Technique of Presentation: The category serves to register the technique that is applied to create a form: (i) *hand-as-object,* (ii) *enclosure,* (iii) *tracing*, (iv) *palpating* (see above).

Referent: This category enables the rater to register whether (s)he assumes that the Referent of the *form presentation* gesture is

(i) *material:* e.g. a ball, the height of a child;
(ii) *non-material:* e.g. a perfect concept, a big profit, a super event.

Meeting the criteria

Structure	*phasic*
Focus	*in space*; only in exceptional cases, *on body* or *on separate object*, e.g. the form of an object is traced on the thigh or on a table
Gesture/action space	**central gesture space, in front of body midline, middle kinesphere**
Path	depends on the Technique of Presentation: in *hand-as-object* and *enclosure* Techniques, there is a static complex phase, i.e., no path; in *tracing*, the path is often closed with the start point and end point matching each other, e.g. to establish the contour of a circle; in *palpating* often three-dimensional path
Hand orientation	in bimanual *form presentation* gestures with *enclosure* and *palpating*, the palms of the hands are typically oriented to each other, i.e., towards the center of the imaginary form
Hand shape	**distinct hand shape**, depends on the form to be created and on the Technique of Presentation

Effort	**invariant use of efforts:** typically bound flow, direct space, no time, no weight
Body involvement	isolated use of hands/arms
Gaze	When referring to concrete objects (Referent: *material*), the gesturer often looks at the hand or at the imaginary object, respectively.

Occurrence: *Form presentation* units were investigated in 91 individuals of the NEUROGES® archive. Right hand *form presentation* units were displayed by 21 % (19/91), left hand *form presentation* units by 20 % (18/91), and bimanual *form presentation* units by 43 % (39/91).

Frequency: In the NEUROGES® archive sample (n = 91), right hand *form presentation* units were displayed with a frequency (Mean ± Standard Deviation; Median) of 0.10 ± 0.38; 0.00 units per minute, left hand *form presentation* units with a frequency of 0.06 ± 0.17; 0.00, and bimanual *form presentation* units with a frequency of 0.29 ± 0.54; 0.00.

Duration: The duration (Mean ± Standard Deviation; Median) of right hand *form presentation* units was 1.59 ± 0.81; 1.55 seconds per unit, of left hand *form presentation* units 1.58 ± 0.59; 1.69, and of bimanual *form presentation* units 1.62 ± 0.67; 1.58.

Differentiate *form presentation* from…

- *pantomime*: see there
- *spatial relation presentation*: In a *spatial relation presentation*, a specific position in an imaginary space is indicated. In order to express this, the complex phase is displayed at a specific location in the gesture space, i.e., other than in front of the body midline, e.g. in the right upper gesture space. In the rare cases in which a position is set in front of the body midline, it is relative to another position in the gesture space, i.e., it is one of two positions. In contrast, *form presentation* gestures provide no information about the spatial position of the form. Thus, the complex phase is displayed at spatially quasi neutral position, i.e., in front of the body midline in the central gesture space in the middle kinesphere. Therefore, if a form is not presented in front of the body midline but at another specific location in the gesture space, the Function value *spatial relation presentation* has to be coded, unless an obvious reason can be identified that forces for

the gesturer to display the *form presentation* gesture at an unusual location in the gesture space.

In a *spatial relation presentation*, **two** points (exceptions see 8.4.7) are presented and the focus is on the relation **between** these two points. In *form presentation*, **one** form is presented. Confusion is most likely to arise, when the two hands are used to present a form. Here, the two values can best be distinguished by the hand orientation. In a bimanual *form presentation* unit, both hands are oriented towards the center of the imaginary object, i.e., the palms are oriented **towards each other**. In contrast, in a bimanual *spatial relation* unit, in which the spatial relation is created by the position of the two hands, both hands orient **towards the same plane**, in most cases the fingertips of both hands are oriented downwards.

Note that the Technique of Presentation *tracing* can be used for *spatial relation presentation* as well as for *form presentation*. In *form presentations*, the start- and end-points of the trace overlap such that a closed contour is created. In *spatial relation presentations*, the trace is typically open, e.g. representing a way in an imaginary landscape.

✐ *motion quality presentation*: A *motion quality presentation* is characterized by a variation in the effort factors, since information about dynamic processes shall be provided. Only in special cases, e.g. when representing the monotonous movement of a machine, a *motion quality presentation* might be performed without the use of efforts. In this case, however, special emphasis will be put on demonstrating the monotony by performing a strictly invariant repetition. In contrast, *form presentation* gestures only show a static form and hence, there is no elaboration of dynamics.

Furthermore, a *motion quality presentation* has obligatorily a path during complex phase, while *form presentations* only have a path during complex phase, i.e., a motion complex phase, when the Technique of Presentation is *tracing* or *palpating*. *Motion quality presentations* often have a *repetitive* Structure in order to demonstrate the manner of a movement, while *form presentation* gestures are typically *phasic*.

Note that a *motion quality presentation* (how something moves) may include information on a form (how what moves), whereas a *form presentation* per definition does not include information about a motion quality. Thus, the combination of form and motion is always coded as *motion quality presentation*.

✐ *emblems*: *Emblems* that show forms (e.g. the Peace-sign, crossed fingers, T-sign) have to be distinguished from *form presentations*. These *emblems* have a highly conventionalized movement form, e.g. the Peace-sign is defined by extended index and middle fingers. The fixed meaning is linked to a fixed form. In contrast, in *form presentation* gestures, information about a specific form can be conveyed with many different movement forms, e.g. four different Techniques of Presentation may be used to present a round form. While *form presentations* inform primarily about a form, *emblems* that show forms have a meaning that is beyond the mere form information, e.g. the T-sign does not mean T but it means Time out.

Furthermore, *emblems* are always executed explicitly, i.e., intentionally, while *form presentations*, especially with the Referent value *non-material*, may be executed implicitly. As an example, the gesturer may, without being aware of it, show a *form presentation* with a big size, e.g. reflecting his/her impression of a big problem.

8.4.7 *spatial relation presentation*

Short definition

CREATING A SPATIAL RELATION

Main group

see *form presentation*

Definition

Function: *Spatial relation presentation* gestures create a spatial relation.

Space is defined as "Extension, considered independently of anything which it may contain", "the unlimited expanse in which everything is located (Webster's Dictionary); "Space is the boundless, three-dimensional extent in which objects and events (motions) occur and have relative position and direction." (Wikipedia). "... space was a collection of relations between objects, given by their distance and direction from one another..." (Wikipedia). The latter definitions underline the importance of spatial relations to define space. Accordingly, if a gesturer provides spatial information, (s)he needs to establish in gesture a spatial relation. As a location in space can only be defined relative to another, in gesture at least two points have to be created. Thus, the *spatial relation presentation* gesture creates an imaginary spatial map by setting positions or outlining routes. A *spatial relation presentation* gesture may include forms (what is where on the imaginary map).

The *spatial relation presentation* gesture differs from *egocentric deictics* and *egocentric directions* in which a location or a direction is not created but only referred to. Thus, if the gesturer refers to her/his actual (or imaginary) surroundings, s/he does not need to create locations, but can simply refer to them by using *egocentric deictics* and *egocentric directions.*

Another aspect regarding the difference between *spatial relation presentations* and *egocentric deictics / directions* concerns the cognitive perspective. In *egocentric deictics / directions* the gesturer obligatorily applies an egocentric frame of reference by using her/himself as the point of spatial reference (see 8.4.3 and 8.4.4). In contrast, in *spatial relation presentations*, especially those with a material Referent, there is often a mento-heliocentric perspective (see 8.3, paragraph Cognitive Perspective). The gesturer adopts the cognitive perspective of looking down on an imaginary map that s/he creates by setting positions and routes.

In rare cases, the gesturer creates an imaginary spatial map and then refers to specific locations by pointing or indicating a direction on this map by keeping the mentio-heliocentric perspectives. While these gestures share many features of movement form with *egocentric deictics / directions* (see below Differentiate…), they are coded as *spatial relation presentations* because they are based on a mento-heliocentric cognitive perspective.

Movement form: A *spatial relation presentation* gesture is characterized by a distinct use of gesture space, i.e., the complex phase is displayed at a specific location in the gesture space, e.g. right upper gesture space. As stated above, at least two points in the gesture space need to be presented to establish a spatial relation. There are different creative techniques to present a static spatial relation in gesture, which can be identified by considering the Structure, Contact, and Formal Relation values:

(α) bimanual unit, Contact value *act apart,* Formal Relation values *symmetrical* or *asymmetrical*: The two hands act simultaneously to present the spatial relation. As an example, one hand is placed on the right of the gesturer's body midline and the other hand on the left.

(β) unimanual unit, Structure value *repetitive:* One hand acts sequentially to present the spatial relation. The hand is first positioned on the gesturer's right and then on her/his left. The addressee recognizes the spatial relation as (s)he memorizes the first positions of the hand in the gesture space and relates it–as if it were materialized – to the second position.

(γ) unimanual unit, Structure value *phasic:* The gesturer's body midline is used as an implicit point of reference (Lausberg et al., 2003). The hand only presents one position in the gesture space. The addressee recognizes the spatial relation as (s)he relates the position of the gesturer's hand to the her/his body midline. However, in this technique the positioning of the one hand has to be spatially very distinct such that it becomes clear that the position of the hand is not incidentally.

While the above techniques refer to points in space, lines in space are presented by a steady displacement of the hand in the gesture space, e.g. when representing a route in a landscape.

The points and lines establish spatial relations and thereby create two- or three-dimensional spaces. Two-dimensional spaces (maps) are often projected onto the horizontal plane. In that case, the longitudinal hand axis (wrist to fingertips) is in line with the vertical axis, if the imaginary map is projected to the horizontal plane. If the imaginary map is projected to the frontal plane, the longitudinal hand axis is in line with the sagittal axis.

Hierarchy: A spatial relation presentation may be embedded in a motion quality presentation, but it may include a form presentation.

Spatial relation presentation > *form presentation*: Per definition, a *form presentation* does not include spatial information, but a *spatial relation presentation* gesture (where) may include information on a form (what is where). If a *spatial relation presentation* includes a *form presentation*, the form is presented at a specific location in the gesture space. As an example, at a location in right gesture space the right hand adopts the shape of a reversed V (e.g. representing a house with a pointed roof on the right in the imaginary spatial map). Thus, the combination of a form and a spatial relation is always coded as *spatial relation presentation*. The included form information can be coded with the Supplementary category Technique of Presentation.

If the *spatial relation presentation* is embedded in a *motion quality presentation* (where [along] something is moving how), the unit is coded as *motion quality presentation*.

Types: For *spatial relation presentation* gestures, the Type category classifies the geometric configuration, i.e., line versus point. There are two *spatial relation* Type values: *route* (creating a route in an imaginary space), and *position* (creating a position relative to another one in an imaginary space).

Specifications: *Spatial relation presentation* gestures can be further assessed with the Supplementary categories Execution Hemi-Space, Target Location, Referent, and if it applies Technique of Presentation.

Execution Hemi-Space: The Supplementary category specifies in which hemi-space the complex phase is displayed.

Target Location: The Supplementary category Target Location specifies in which hemi-space the spatial target is located.

Referent: This category enables the rater to register whether (s)he assumes that the referent of the *spatial relation presentation* is

(i) *material*: referring to concrete spatial relations, e.g. to places or ways in a landscape;

(ii) *non-material*: referring to abstract entities, e.g. a point in time, a theoretical position or a direction of thinking; arithmetics. As examples for calculation, in bimanual counting on the fingers, the index of the dominant hand touches one after the other the fingertips of the non-dominant hand. In unimanual counting, the one finger after the other is extended and the fingers embody positions. In the 'opposing' gesture a palm-out with complex phase hold of one hand is followed by a palm-out with a complex phase hold by the other hand. The meaning emerges: "On one hand… on the other…". Thereby, the two thoughts are spatially opposed to another. –

Technique of Presentation: If the *spatial relation presentation* includes a *form presentation*, the Technique of Presentation can be assessed.

Meeting the criteria

Structure	*phasic*, typically only in bimanual units; *repetitive*, in unimanual but also in bimanual units. In unimanual *position* presentations, there is a sequential presentation of the two locations ("here … and there")
Focus	*in space*; only in exceptional cases *on body* or *on separate object*, e.g. the position is marked on the thigh or on the table
Gesture/action space	**distinct and creative use of gesture space**, i.e., the complex phases are displayed at specific locations in the gesture space, e.g. right upper gesture space
Path	depends on the Type value of the *spatial relation presentation:* in *spatial relation–position*, there is a static complex (sub)phase; in *spatial relation–route*, there is a path during complex phase
Hand orientation	The hand orientation reflects the mento-heliocentric perspective. As a two-dimensional map is typically projected to the horizontal plane, the **longitudinal hand axis** (wrist–finger tips) is **in line with the vertical space axis**, i.e., the fingertips are oriented downwards. Only if the map is projected to the frontal plane, the longitudinal hand axis is in line with the sagittal space axis, i.e., the fingertips are oriented forward.

Hand shape	depends on the Technique of Presentation
Effort	invariant use of efforts: bound flow, direct space, no time, no weight, no variation in the effort factors
Body involvement	-
Gaze	When referring to concrete spatial locations (Referent: *material*), the gesturer looks at the hand(s), i.e., more specifically, at the designated position or route on the imaginary spatial map.
Other criteria	Cognitive perspective often mento-heliocentric; in very special settings ambiguous (see 8.4.3)

Occurrence: *Spatial relation presentation* units were investigated in 91 individuals of the NEUROGES® archive. Right hand *spatial relation presentation* units were displayed by 30 % (27/91), left hand *spatial relation presentation* units by 30 % (27/91), and bimanual *spatial relation presentation* units by 33 % (30/91).

Frequency: In the NEUROGES® archive sample (n = 91), right hand *spatial relation presentation* units were displayed with a frequency (Mean ± Standard Deviation; Median) of 0.10 ± 0.24; 0.00 units per minute, left hand *spatial relation presentation* units with a frequency of 0.07 ± 0.15; 0.00, and bimanual *spatial relation presentation* units with a frequency of 0.08 ± 0.16; 0.00.

Duration: The duration (Mean ± Standard Deviation; Median) of right hand *spatial relation presentation* units was 2.43 ± 1.26; 1.20 seconds per unit, of left hand *spatial relation presentation* units 3.10 ± 3.42; 2.04, and of bimanual *spatial relation presentation* units 1.78 ± 1.18; 1.51.

Differentiate *spatial relation presentation* from…

- *egocentric deictic* or *egocentric direction*: see there
- *form presentation*: see there
- *motion quality presentation*: A *motion quality presentation* focuses on 'how' something/-one moves. The manner and dynamics of a motion are presented. In contrast, a *spatial relation presentation* provides spatial information (where, where along). A *spatial relation presentation* of the Type route may be confused with a *motion quality presentation* that includes a *spatial relation presentation* (loco-motion).

As the *motion quality presentation* presents the manner and dynamics of a motion, there is obligatorily a variation in the effort factors and/or a *repetitive* Structure. Thus, the displacement of the hand in the gesture space (in order to depict the path) is obligatorily combined with a variation in the effort factors, e.g. the gestural depiction of the explosion of a volcano, or with a repetitive movement. In the latter case the repetitive trajectory is superimposed to the displacement trajectory, e.g. opening and closing the hand while moving sidewards.

Only if the displacement of the hand is performed without variation in the effort factors and without a superimposed repetitive trajectory, it is a mere *spatial relation presentation*. The movement flow is bound such that a precise presentation of spatial relations can be given, e.g. moving the hand from right upper to left lower gesture space, or a moving the hand on a curved path.

8.4.8 *motion quality presentation*

Short definition

SHOWING A SPECIFIC QUALITY OF MOVEMENT

Main group

see *form presentation*

Definition

Function: *Motion quality presentation* gestures show a manner or a dynamics of moving. In contrast to *pantomime* gestures, in which the gesturer her-/himself acts "as if", in *motion quality presentation* gestures the hand presents how something/-one moves, e.g. circulating, contracting-expanding, quick, tense, strong, light, or heavy. Motion quality presentations not only show how something moves but indirectly also how something feels like. In gesture, tactile sensations or sensory impressions can only be conveyed by showing the motion in response to it, e.g. motorically exploring a soft surface.

Movement form: The most essential movement features of *motion quality presentation* gestures are a distinct use of effort qualities and a path during the complex phase with or without a repetitive trajectory.

(i) The effort factors are described in detail in the chapters 4.3 and 11. The distinct presentation of a movement dynamics in a *motion quality presentation* gesture is characterized by the fact that it differs from the gesturer's baseline movement dynamics. Each gesturer has his/her personal style of effort quality use, e.g. one gesturer may have a rather free movement flow in his/her gestures, while the gestural behavior of another gesturer is characterized by directness. Thus, only the distinct presentation of a specific movement dynamics in gesture that differs from the gesturer's habitual gestural pattern constitutes a *motion quality presentation*. Only in exceptional cases, when a monotonous, non-biological movement shall be re-presented such the rotation of gears, a *motion quality presentation* gesture is performed without changes in the effort factors. However, in this case, the monotony and invariance of the movement is explicit.

(ii) In *motion quality presentation* gestures, there is always a path during the complex phase, i.e., there is a motion complex phase and never a static complex phase. Often, there is a repetitive trajectory. The repetitive trajectory is either produced by a within-hand movement that is displayed at one location in the gesture space, e.g. re-presenting jumping at a place, or as a superimposition to a displacement trajectory, re-presenting jumping forward. Obviously, the repetitive trajectory may be performed with a certain dynamics, e.g. jumping forward faster and faster. In contrast, a mere displacement trajectory without a superimposed repetitive trajectory and without efforts constitutes a mere presentation of a route in space, i.e., *spatial relation presentation,* e.g. re-presenting a winding road in the mountains.

Hierarchy: A *motion quality presentation* may include a *form presentation* and/or a *spatial relation presentation.*

Motion quality presentation > form presentation: A *motion quality presentation* gesture (how something moves) may include information on a form (how what moves), i.e., presenting a specific form in motion. As an example, the hand forms a round shape and then moves up and down, e.g. representing a ball that is bouncing.

Motion quality presentation > spatial relation presentation: A *motion quality presentation* may include a *spatial relation presentation.* The gesture presents a motion quality that takes place at a specific location or on a specific route in an imaginary space. As examples, the gesture shows a circular motion from left upper to right lower gesture space (e.g. representing something rolling down a hill), or a bimanual symmetrical quick and strong movement upward and outward (e.g. representing an explosion).

Motion quality presentation > spatial relation presentation + form presentation: A *motion quality presentation* may include a *spatial relation presentation* and a *form presentation.* As an example, the index and middle finger (*form presentation* representing legs of a human being) move alternately (*motion quality presentation* representing walking) on a path from the lower left to the upper right gesture space (*spatial relation presentation* representing a path in the mountains).

While these combinations are coded as *motion quality presentation*, the included form information can be coded with the Supplementary category Technique of Presentation and the included spatial relation information with the Supplementary categories Target Location and Execution Hemi-Space.

Types: For *motion quality presentation* gestures, the Type category classifies the quality presented. There are two *motion quality* Type values: *manner* (presenting a specific manner of movement) and *dynamics* (presenting a specific dynamics of movement).

Specifications: *Motion quality presentation* gestures can be further assessed with the Supplementary categories Efforts, Execution Hemi-Space, Target Location, and Referent. If additional *form* information is included in the *motion quality presentation* gesture, the Supplementary category Technique of Presentation can be coded as well.

Efforts: This category enables to code the dynamics of the *motion quality presentation,* e.g. *sudden.*

Referent: This category enables the rater to register whether (s)he assumes that the referent of the *motion quality presentation* gesture is

(i) *material*: e.g. a ball rolling, a volcano exploding;

(ii) *non-material*: e.g. a revolution starts to get rolling, an explosive dispute, an instable situation or an insecure statement. As an example, in a waggling gesture there is fast supination–pronation shaking of the flat hand indicating that something is instable or insecure. It can also present the gesturer's judgement about his own thoughts, i.e. indicating that s/he is insecure about s/he states.

Technique of Presentation: If the *motion quality presentation* includes a *form presentation*, the Technique of Presentation can be assessed.

Note: The *quality of motion* can be noted.

Meeting the criteria

Structure	*phasic, repetitive.* A *repetitive* Structure is present when a manner of movement is represented.
Focus	*in space*; only in exceptional cases *on body* or *on separate object*
Gesture/action space	If the *motion quality presentation* includes a *spatial relation presentation* (where to or where along the object/subject moves), there is a distinct and creative use of gesture space.

Path	A path during complex phase is an obligatory feature of *motion quality presentations*. There is **never a static complex phase**.
Hand orientation	If the gesture includes a *form* or *spatial relation presentation,* a specific hand orientation is adopted.
Hand shape	If the *motion quality* gesture includes a *form presentation* (the shape and size of what moves), a specific hand shape is adopted.
Effort	The **variation of effort factors**, which distinctly differs from the gesturer's base line, is the most prominent movement feature of *motion quality presentation*. The only exception is the intentional representation of monotonous motion, e.g. when re-presenting gear transmission. In this case, special emphasis is put on the monotony and the invariance of the effort factors.
Body involvement	-
Gaze	If representing an actual motion quality, i.e., a concrete object displaying a concrete motion (Referent: *material*), the gaze is directed at the hand.

Occurrence: *Motion quality presentation* units were investigated in 91 individuals of the NEUROGES® archive. Right hand *motion quality presentation* units were displayed by 47 % (43/91), left hand *motion quality presentation* units by 41 % (37/91), and bimanual *motion quality presentation* units by 58 % (53/91).

Frequency: In the NEUROGES® archive sample (n = 91), right hand *motion quality presentation* units were displayed with a frequency (Mean ± Standard Deviation; Median) of 0.47 ± 1.28; 0.00 units per minute, left hand *motion quality presentation* units with a frequency of 0.25 ± 0.56; 0.00, and bimanual *motion quality presentation* units with a frequency of 0.50 ± 0.93; 0.10.

Duration: The duration (Mean ± Standard Deviation; Median) of right hand *motion quality presentation* units was 2.28 ± 0.86; 2.05 seconds per unit, of left hand *motion quality presentation* units 2.45 ± 1.40; 2.16, and of bimanual *motion quality presentation* units 2.41 ± 1.25; 2.08.

Differentiate *motion quality presentation* from…

- *emphasis*: see there
- *pantomime*: see there
- *form presentation*: see there
- *spatial relation presentation*: see there
- *emblems: Emblems* that include the depiction of motion qualities have to be distinguished from the *motion quality presentations*. An example for such an *emblem* is a gesture in which the hand is formed as if it were a mouth with the thumb being the lower jaw and the other four fingers being the upper jaw and which opens and closes to indicate that a person is a blabbermouth. The movement form is highly conventionalized. *Emblems* are always executed explicitly.

In contrast, in *motion quality presentation* gestures many different movement forms can be used to present a certain motion quality. In addition, the gesture may be executed implicitly, e.g. the gesturer without intention, displays a waggling gesture reflecting that s/he is not sure about what (s)he is saying.

8.4.9 *object-oriented action*

Short definition

CHANGING THE EXTERNAL PHYSICAL WORLD

Main group

The two Function values *object-oriented action* and *subject-oriented action* have in common that they register actions.

Action is defined as "… exertion of power or force, as when one body acts on another" (Webster's dictionary). The exertion of power on something results in a change of that thing. Given this definition, *phasic* and *repetitive* units may be actions as the complex phase can serve to change something. In contrast to gestures, which are classified with the Function values *emphasis, egocentric deictic, egocentric direction, pantomime, form presentation, spatial relation presentation, motion quality presentation, emblem,* and *emotion/attitude* (learned display) and which are merely expressions, actions result in changes in the physical world. The Focus value helps to differentiate between gestures and actions, since there is a high likelihood that units with the Focus value *in space* are gestures and those with the Focus values *within body, on body, on attached object, on separate object,* and *on person* are actions. The exceptions are *shrugs* (per definition: *within body),* and *on body body-deictics* and *emblems*, which include touching the body. These are gestures although they are not *in space*.

Definition

Function: The term *object-oriented* refers to all material things that are outside the gesturer's body.
Typical hand movements that cause changes in the external physical world are **tool-specific** manipulation of tools (praxis), e.g. winding up a watch results in a change of the state of the watch, writing results in a written text on a piece of paper, hammering results in a change of the position of a nail, taking a pen out of the pocket and putting it on the table results in a change in the position of a pen, or combing another person's hair results in a different order of the hair. **Tool-unspecific** manipulations, e.g. hammering with scissors, however, are only in rare cases *object-oriented actions*. Mostly, tool-unspecific actions, such as tapping with a pen (when stressed), are *subject-oriented actions*.
It is obvious that *object-oriented actions* often have the Focus values *on separate object, on attached object,* or *on person. Object-oriented actions* with the Focus value *in space* are an absolute rarity. In this case, the air or the water is the physical substrate that is manipulated, e.g. fanning air with the hand or swimming in the water.
Non-material changes in the external world such as changes in social relations are **not** given the value *object-oriented action*.

Movement form: *Object-oriented actions* are *phasic* or *repetitive* movements that result in a material change of the external world. Each action has a highly specific movement form that is tailored to achieving the desired material change. Movement groups can be formed based on the StructureFocus values: *on person*, e.g. helping another person in the jacket; *on attached object*, e.g. winding up a watch or looking at the watch (both examples are tool use); *on separate object*, e.g. writing on a piece of paper, hammering; *in space* (rarity), e.g. fanning air with the hand to the embers (as the hand is in primary dynamic contact with the air, the Focus is *in space* and not *on separate object*).

Types: No Type values are defined for the Function value *object-oriented action*.

Specifications: *Object-oriented action*s can be further assessed with the Supplementary category Target Location.

Target Location: This category registers the location of the target. For *object-oriented actions*, the target is defined as the material subject/object in the external world that the hand acts on.

Note: the action

Meeting the criteria

Structure	*phasic, repetitive*
Focus	***on separate object,*** *on attached object, on person,* rarely *in space*
Gesture/action space	mobile target objects are typically manipulated in front of the body midline; otherwise, the use of the action space is determined by the location of the target object
Path	distinct path during complex phase, specified for each action
Hand orientation	depends on the object and the action
Hand shape	depends on the object that is manipulated
Effort	variation of the effort factors
Body involvement	**often involvement of other parts of the body**
Gaze	**typically at the hand**, in order to control the execution of the action

Occurrence: As *object-oriented actions* were rarely elicited or investigated in the experimental studies included in the NEUROGES® archive, data on *object-oriented action* units are available only for 53 individuals. Right hand *object-oriented action* units were displayed by 0 % (0/53), left hand *object-oriented action* units by 15 % (8/53), and bimanual *object-oriented action* units by 0 % (0/53).

Frequency: In the NEUROGES® archive sample (n = 53), right hand *object-oriented action* units were displayed with a frequency (Mean ± Standard Deviation; Median) of 0.00 ± 0.00; 0.00 units per minute, left hand *object-oriented action* units with a frequency of 0.05 ± 0.00; 0.15, and bimanual *object-oriented action* units with a frequency of 0.00 ± 0.00; 0.00.

Duration: The duration (Mean ± Standard Deviation; Median) of right hand *object-oriented action* units was 2.05 ± 0.00; 2.05 seconds per unit, of left hand *object-oriented action* units 1.93 ± 0.76; 1.69, and of bimanual *object-oriented action* units 4.92 ± 3.62; 4.92.

Differentiate *object-oriented action* from…

✎ *subject-oriented action*: *Object-oriented actions* may be difficult to distinguish from those *subject-oriented actions* that were originally object-oriented and in the individual development have become subject-oriented (compare Darwin, 1872, 2009, p. 38: "The principle of serviceable associated Habits"). In this case, the action no longer serves its original function, e.g. shifting a chair to improve vision on the scene, but it becomes a habit that is triggered by certain mental states, e.g. shifting a chair to deal with embarrassment.

As a general orientation, in *subject-oriented action* the gaze is not at the hand, whereas in *object-oriented actions* it is. Furthermore, the inappropriate, tool-unspecific use of an (attached or separate) object is typically indicative of a *subject-oriented action*, while the appropriate, tool-specific use indicates an *object-oriented action*. *Subject-oriented actions* are displayed repeatedly (and seemingly unmotivated) by an individual, whereas *object-oriented actions* are displayed only if the situation requires them. More specific criteria to distinguish between *subject-oriented actions* and *object-oriented actions* are reported separately for the different StructureFocus values:

(i) Actions with the Focus values *within body* and *on body* are per definition *subject-oriented actions*.
(ii) *On attached object* actions are most often *subject-oriented actions*. They result in a change of the gesturer's physical state, his/her visual appearance, or his/her mental state. Examples are pulling the zipper of a jacket when getting cold (physical state), correcting the tie if it is twisted to look appropriate in a given social context or putting on sunglasses[18] to look more attractive (visual appearance), or playing with the necklace when embarrassed (mental state). In rare cases, *on attached object* actions may be *object-oriented action*. In this case, the attached object itself is subject to a change, e.g. winding up a watch results in a change of the state of the watch.
(iii) *On separate object* actions are most often *object-oriented actions*. They are practical tool-use actions and they result in a change in the external physical world, e.g. writing results in a written text on a piece of paper, shifting a computer mouse results in a new position of the mouse on the table, taking a pen out of the pocket and putting it on the table results in a change in the position of a pen. If, however, the manipulation of the separate object primarily aims at changing the state of the gesturer him/herself, e.g. tapping with a pen on the table to get rid of nervousness, the action is coded as *subject-oriented*. The inappropriate use of a tool, e.g. tapping a pen instead of writing with it, is typically indicative of a *subject-oriented action*. Furthermore, *subject-oriented actions on separate object* can serve physical

18 In the Focus coding, putting on glasses is coded as *on object attached*, as the goal of the action is to attach the object to the body, while taking off glasses is coded as *on object separate*, as the goal of the action is to separate the object from the body.

needs, e.g. taking off glasses to read a text in small print, or they can serve to change the visual appearance, e.g. taking off glasses to look more attractive.

(iv) *On person* actions are almost exclusively *object-oriented actions.* (As a psychologically special condition, the exception is symbiotic relationships. In this case, the physical manipulation of the other person may be *subject-oriented*, e.g. playing with other person's hair to calm oneself down.)

(v) *In space object-oriented* or *subject-oriented actions* are an absolute rarity. In this case, the air (or the water) is the physical substrate that is manipulated. An example for an *in space object-oriented action* is to fan the embers with the hand. In contrast, fanning fresh air to the face is an *in space subject-oriented action.*

social convention: An action that causes a change in the external physical world, is only coded as a *social convention* if the only recognizable reason for its performance is a specific social context that requires the action, e.g. shaking the other person's hand to greet her/him.

8.4.10 *subject-oriented action*

Short definition

CHANGING THE OWN PHYSICAL (AND SECONDARILY MENTAL) STATE

Main group

see *object-oriented action*

Definition

Function: The term *subject-oriented* refers to the gesturer's psychosomatic state that is defined by his/her physical state, visual appearance, and mental state. A *subject-oriented action* can directly aim at (i) changing the body state, (ii) changing the visual appearance, or, (iii) indirectly via the body, changing the mental state.

(i) *Subject-oriented actions* that aim at changing body states give relief from unpleasant physical states or produce pleasant states. They are reactions to somatosensory perceptions. Perceiving pain, being cold, being hot, etc. triggers actions to regulate the body state. Thus, the action has a clearly identifiable effect on the body, e.g. getting warm, improving vision.

(ii) *Subject-oriented actions* may change the gesturer's visual appearance. As a matter of fact, this subfunction is primarily social. However, as it reflects the gesturer's subjective desire to look more attractive, it is coded as *subject-oriented action*. In general, the gesturer intends to improve his/her appearance in order to look more attractive (only occasionally, in shy individuals or in specific situations these actions may serve to look less attractive). Thus, most often these *subject-oriented actions* are preening behavior and they have a social effect. They may be reactions to deviations in the visual appearance, e.g. if the tie is not straight or if the hair is not in place. However, these *subject-oriented actions* may also be displayed if no corrections of the visual appearance are necessary. In this case, they are rather displayed as an appeasement behavior indicating to the addressee that the gesturer wants to please him/her. These appeasement actions are often stereotypical, e.g. repeatedly stroking the hair behind the ear even if actually the hair is in place.

(iii) *Subject-oriented actions* may serve to regulate the gesturer's mental state. As compared to *irregular* movements that serve arousal regulation on a non-conceptual level (e.g. to work off energy or to stimulate her-/himself), the *subject-oriented actions* are conceptual movements that promote emotional and cognitive processing.

Movement form: A *subject-oriented action* is a *phasic* or *repetitive* movement that results in a change of the gesturer's psychosomatic state. Each action has a highly specific movement form that is tailored to achieving the desired change in the gesturer's psychosomatic state. Movement groups can be formulated based on the StructureFocus values: *on body,* e.g. scratching because there is an itching; *within body*, e.g. rolling the shoulders because of muscle tension or to exercise; *on attached object*, e.g. pulling the zipper of a jacket when getting cold, correcting the tie if it is twisted to look appropriate in a given social context or putting on sunglasses to look more attractive, playing with the necklace when embarrassed; *on separate object,* e.g. taking off glasses to read a text in small print, taking off glasses to look more attractive, tapping with a pen on the table when impatient; i*n space*, e.g. fanning with the hand to get fresh air (compare also *object-oriented action*).

Types: No Type values are defined for the Function value *subject-oriented action*.

Specifications: *Subject-oriented action* movements can be further assessed with the Supplementary categories Target Location and Trigger/Motive.

Target Location: This category enables to localize the target that is affected by the *subject-oriented action*.

Trigger/Motive: The category enables the rater to code if (s)he assumes that the trigger or motive of the *subject-oriented action* is to regulate the physical state, the visual appearance, or the mental state.

Note: Note the type of action, e.g. scratching.

Meeting the criteria

Structure	*phasic, repetitive*
Focus	***on body, within body***, *on attached object*, rarely: *on separate object, in space*
Gesture/action space	variable, determined by the action
Path	distinct path during complex phase, depends on the action
Hand orientation	depends on the action and on the target
Hand shape	depends on the action and on the target
Effort	variation of the effort factors
Body involvement	possible
Gaze	depends on the trigger or motive; often gaze at hand, if action serves to regulate physical needs; no gaze at hand, if the action serves to regulate the mental state

Occurrence: *Subject-oriented action* units were investigated in 91 individuals of the NEUROGES® archive. Right hand *subject-oriented action* units were displayed by 89 % (81/91), left hand *subject-oriented action* units by 97 % (88/91), and bimanual *subject-oriented action* units by 86 % (78/91).

Frequency: In the NEUROGES® archive sample (n = 91), right hand *subject-oriented action* units were displayed with a frequency (Mean ± Standard Deviation; Median) of 1.03 ± 1.40; 0.62 units per minute, left hand *subject-oriented action* units with a frequency of 1.47 ± 2.26; 0.73, and bimanual *subject-oriented action* units with a frequency of 1.24 ± 2.05; 0.51.

Duration: The duration (Mean ± Standard Deviation; Median) of right hand *subject-oriented action* units was 2.50 ± 1.86; 1.96 seconds per unit, of left hand *subject-oriented action* units 2.76 ± 1.86; 2.30, and of bimanual *subject-oriented action* units 2.57 ± 1.62; 2.05.

Differentiate *subject-oriented action* from...

- *emotion:* see there
- *object-oriented action*: see there
- *social convention:* An action that causes a change in the gesturer's physical state, is only coded as a *social convention* if the only recognizable reason for its performance is the social convention, e.g. lifting the head to greet another person.

8.4.11 *emblem/social convention*

The NEUROGES® values are proven to represent universal kinesic and gestural phenomena. All NEUROGES® values occur in all cultures[19] of five continents (Germans, British, US Americans, francophone and anglophone Canadians, Suisse, Koreans, Kenyans, and Papua) that have been investigated so far in the NEUROGES® archive. Thus, all cultures also show the Function value *emblem / social convention*, but this is the only NEUROGES® value that requires knowledge of the culture.

Emblems and *social conventions* have fixed form – meaning links that are based on cultural conventions. Therefore, the Function value *emblem / social convention* can only be assessed reliably by a rater who is familiar with the gesturer's (sub-)culture, as the rater has to know the gesturer's cultural repertoire of *emblems* and *social conventions* in order to identify these gestures and actions. Therefore, observers who are not familiar with the gesturer's cultural repertoire of *emblems* and *social conventions* proceed by applying the other Function values, as any *emblem* or *social convention* can be described with one of the other Function values. Only the information is lost that the gesture or action is conventionalized and that it has a fixed meaning and/or a specific social context.

8.4.11.1 emblem

Short definition

USING CULTURE-SPECIFIC HAND SIGNS WITH CONVENTIONALIZED ARBITRARY MEANINGS

Definition

Function: The Function value *emblem / social convention* differs from the other Function values for gestures, as it provides no information about the content of the gestural depiction but only the formal information that form and meaning of the gesture are conventionalized. The Function values *egocentric deictic, egocentric direction, pantomime, form presentation, spatial relation presentation,* and *motion quality presentation* provide information on **what**

---

19 While all NEUROGES® values occur in all cultures, the cultures differ concerning the frequency of the display of the NEUROGES® values, e.g. in response to the same stimulus, Koreans display more *egocentric deictics* (number/minute) than Germans (Kim & Lausberg, 2017).

is displayed, indicated, pantomimed, or presented (an emotion, an accent, a location, a direction, an action, a form, a spatial relation, or a motion quality). In contrast, the Function value *emblem / social convention* only refers to the aspect of conventionalization. Therefore, any gesture that is coded as an *emblem / social convention* can likewise be classified with one of the other Function values according to its content.

In NEUROGES®, at least the first three criteria have to be fulfilled to classify a gesture as an *emblem*:

(i) conventionality: The movement form and meaning of the *emblem* gesture is familiar to most members of a specific culture or subculture. Thus, *emblems* are conventionalized hand (or head) movements with a fixed form – meaning link. The movement form is invariant with regard to gesture space, path during complex phase, hand orientation, and hand shape. If one criterion would be changed, the *emblem* could possibly no longer be reliably recognized. The meaning is fully conveyed by the emblematic gesture alone. Thus, it can be understood without words and it could be translated into language.

(ii) isolation / distal distinction: An *emblem* can often solely be identified by the hand shape, the hand orientation, and the movement path executed by the hand. Facial expression and trunk involvement, as in *emotion* movements, are not necessary to understand the meaning of the *emblem*. Because the full meaning can be conveyed by the isolated hand, e.g. the Peace sign is sufficiently defined by the hand shape, *emblems* can be easily depicted with icons showing hand shapes. As complex information is conveyed by the hand alone (or/and its relation to another part of the body), the isolated hand movement is often distally very distinct, e.g. the 'Keep one's fingers crossed' gesture.

(iii) explicitness: The gesturer is aware of displaying the gesture.[20]

(iv) relating to the addressee: As *emblems* are conventionalized in movement form and meaning, they are perfectly suited to interact with the addressee. Many *emblems* are instructions for the addressee or show the gesturer's opinion about the addressee. Thus, a translation of such an *emblem* into language often contains the word "You".

20 As an exception, in certain mental states the gesturer may not be aware of (or at least, pretend to not be so) the display of the *emblem*. This applies typically to obscene or insulting *emblems*.

(v) novel / arbitrary meaning: *Emblems* that contain pointing or directing, pantomiming, depicting of a form, or a motion quality have to be differentiated from *egocentric deictic, egocentric direction, pantomime, form presentation,* or *motion quality presentation* gestures that show a similar movement form. In the respective *emblems,* the movement form is highly conventionalized and the meaning is novel, i.e., it differs from the meaning that a genuine *egocentric deictic, egocentric direction, pantomime, form presentation,* or *motion quality presentation* gesture would have. Examples:

A gesture that presents the form of a T (*form presentation*) has to be differentiated from an *emblem* gesture that shows the form of a T in a highly conventionalized form and that has the novel meaning 'Time out'. The criterion iv relating to the addressee is also fulfilled and the hand is typically moved into the direction of the addressee or in the upper gesture space to be visible for the addressee, whereas for the mere depiction of a T-shape in a *form presentation* gesture the hand typically remains in the central gesture space in front of the body midline.

A gesture that points to the temple in order to indicate the temple (*egocentric deictic*) has to be differentiated from an *emblem* gesture that points to the temple in a highly conventionalized repetitive manner and that has the novel meaning 'somebody is nuts'.

A gesture that presents the action of sweeping away dirt from the clothes (*pantomime*) has to be differentiated from an *emblem* gesture that sweeps away imaginary dirt from the shoulder (this location is part of the conventionalization) and that conveys the novel meaning of contempt.

A gesture that presents a quality of motion (*motion quality)* has to be differentiated from an *emblem* gesture that has the conventionalized movement form in which the hand is formed as if it were a mouth with the thumb being the lower jaw and the other four fingers being the upper jaw and which it opens and closes with the novel meaning '... is a blabbermouth'.

Movement form: Each *emblem* has its specific movement form (see 9.4.9). However, most *emblems* share the following features: The hand movement is distally distinct. There is a specific hand shape, a specific hand orientation, and a specific location in the gesture space. With regard to the movement form, *emblems* can be grouped according to their StructureFocus values, e.g. *phasic in space emblems* (e.g. Victory sign), *phasic on body emblem* (e.g. Blockhead), *repetitive in space emblems* (e.g. wagging), *repetitive on body emblems* (e.g. tapping on the temple to indicate that somebody is nuts), or *repetitive on attached object emblems* (e.g. tapping repetitively on the watch to indicate that you want to know what time it is or to indicate that the time has to be kept in mind).

Types / Notes: Since there is a large number of different *emblems* within one culture and even more so across all cultures, it is not possible to list the single *emblems* in the NEUROGES®-template. In chapter 9.4.9, a list of *emblem* gestures for the Western part of Germany is provided. However, given the (sub)cultural differences in the use of *emblems*, it is recommended that based on the above defined criteria each research group sets up its own list of *emblem* gestures.

Meeting the criteria

Structure	*phasic, repetitive*
Focus	*in space, on body, on attached object, on person*
Gesture space	**distinct** and specific for many *emblems*
Path	in case of motion complex phase, **distinct** and specific for each *emblem*
Hand orientation	**distinct orientation**, specific for each *emblem*
Hand shape	**distinct shape**, specific for each *emblem*
Effort	if it applies, **specific** for each *emblem*
Body involvement	-
Gaze	often to addressee

Occurrence: *Emblem* units were investigated in 91 individuals of the NEUROGES® archive. Right hand *emblem* units were displayed by 11 % (10/91), left hand *emblem* units by 13 % (12/91), and bimanual *emblem* units by 13 % (12/91).

Frequency: In the NEUROGES® archive sample (n = 91), right hand *emblem* units were displayed with a frequency (Mean ± Standard Deviation; Median) of 0.03 ± 0.16; 0.00 units per minute, left hand *emblem* units with a frequency of 0.03 ± 0.13; 0.00, and bimanual *emblem* units with a frequency of 0.07 ± 0.25; 0.00.

Duration: The duration (Mean ± Standard Deviation; Median) of right hand *emblem* units was 1.65 ± 0.85; 2.05 seconds per unit, of left hand *emblem* units 1.40 ± 1.13; 1.28, and of bimanual *emblem* units 1.22 ± 0.47; 1.10.

Differentiate *emblems* from…

- *emotion:* see there
- *egocentric deictics:* see there
- *egocentric direction:* see there
- *pantomime:* see there
- *emphasis*: see there

- *form presentation:* see there
- *motion quality presentation:* see there
- other Function values in general: *Emblems* that contain pointing, directing, pantomiming, depicting of a form or a motion (and which hypothetically originate from Function values such as *egocentric deictic, egocentric direction, pantomime, form presentation,* or *motion quality presentation)* may be difficult to distinguish from these Function values. In general, *emblems* differ from the hypothetically original gestures by the facts that their meaning differs from that of the original gesture and/or that their movement form has become more sophisticated and conventionalized. Furthermore, *emblems* are displayed explicitly while *motion quality presentation* and *form presentation* gestures may be displayed beyond the gesturer's awareness.

8.4.11.2 social convention

Short definition

CONVENTIONALIZED ACTIONS IN SPECIFIC SOCIAL CONTEXTS

Definition

Function: Social conventions are actions or gestures that displayed in a conventionalized manner in a specific recurrent social context, such as in a greeting situation. The movement form and the social context of the *social convention* is familiar to most members in a specific culture or subculture. The movement form is invariant. If one movement feature would be changed, the *social convention* could possibly no longer be reliably recognized.

Movement form: Each *social convention* has its specific movement form (see 9.4.9). With regard to the movement form, *social conventions* can be grouped according to their StructureFocus values, e.g. *phasic on body social convention* (e.g. Military salute), *phasic on person social convention* (e.g. "High five"), *repetitive in space social convention* (e.g. waving good bye), *repetitive on body social convention* (e.g. clapping one' hands to applaud), *repetitive on separate object* (e.g. applauding in a university context, knocking on the table).

Types / Notes: Since there is a large number of different *social conventions* within one culture and even more so across all cultures, it is not possible to list the single *social conventions* in the NEUROGES®-template. In chapter 9.4.9, a list of *social convention* for the Western part of Germany is provided. However, given the (sub)cultural differences in the use of *social conventions*, it is recommended that based on the above defined criteria each research group sets up its own list of *social conventions.*

Meeting the criteria

Structure	*phasic, repetitive*
Focus	*on person, on body, on separate object, on attached object, in space*
Gesture/action space	specific for each *social convention*
Path	specific for each *social convention*
Hand orientation	specific for each *social convention*
Hand shape	specific for each *social convention*
Effort	specific for each *social convention action*
Body involvement	specific for each *social convention action*
Gaze	often to the addressee

Occurrence, frequency and duration: *Social convention* behaviors were not investigated in the empirical studies that build the NEUROGES® archive.

Differentiate *social conventions* from…

✐ *object-oriented action:* see there
✐ *subject-oriented action:* see there

8.4.12 Special template value *different functions*

This value can only be used for *asymmetrical* bimanual 'to-be-coded' Function units in which the right and left hands display different Function values, e.g. the right hand a *form presentation* and the left hand a *motion quality presentation.* The value *different functions* reveals that the individual shows complex bimanual performances with independent acting of the right and left hands.

For some research questions, for example if the distinct functions of the right and left hands in unimanual and bimanual performances shall be examined, it is recommended to double-code in order to not lose information: In the example, in addition to the value *different functions* on the tier bh_Function, the value *form presentation* is coded on the tier rh_Function and the value *motion quality presentation* on the tier lh_Function.

8.5 Procedure for Step 6 / Module III in NEUROGES®-ELAN

8.5.1 Copying units from preceding tiers

In order to generate the 'to-be-coded' Function units for the Function analysis, the units from the following previously created tiers are copied:

'to-be-coded' Function units for the tier …	…are adopted from the preceding tier
rh_Function_R0 (right hand)	rh_Unilateral_StructureFocus_R0
lh_Function_R0 (left hand)	lh_Unilateral_StructureFocus_R0
bh_Function_R0 (both hands)	bh_Formal Relation_R0
rf_Function_R0 (right foot)	rf_Unilateral_StructureFocus_R0
lf_Function_R0 (left foot)	lf_Unilateral_StructureFocus_R0
bf_Function_R0 (both feet)	bf_Formal Relation_R0
head_Function_R0	head_Structure_R0
trunk_Function_R0	trunk_Structure_R0

As an example, the generation of the tier bh_Function_R0 by copying the units from the tier bh_Formal Relation_R0 is described here:

Open the eaf file, which contains the Formal Relation units, then proceed as follows:

Apply the function: Tier > Copy tier.

Select a tier to copy: bh_Formal Relation_RX.

Next.

Select a new parent tier: skip this step.

Next.

Select another linguistic type: click on Function.

Finish.

Apply the function: Tier > Change Tier Attributes.

Scroll down in the list to the end:

Click on bh_FormalRelation_R0-cp.

In the field Tier Name change the tier name to: bh_Function_RX ('RX' = your initials).

(In the field Participant enter the identification of the videotaped person whose behavior you are going to code.)

(In the field Annotator enter your name.)

Press the button Change.
Close.

Proceed analogously for all other Function tiers–as listed in the table above–that you intend to analyze.

8.5.2 Selecting the copied units with a *phasic* or *repetitive* Structure

The following procedure applies to the newly created tiers rh_Function_RX, lh_Function_RX, rf_Function_RX, lf_Function_RX, head_Function_RX, and trunk_Function_RX.

Among the copied units, all those are deleted that have the Structure values *irregular, shift,* and *aborted*. Since the newly created 'to-be-coded' Function units still have the concatenated StructureFocus values, you have the information necessary to delete all units with an *irregular, shift,* or *aborted* Structure.

As an example, the procedure of deletion is described here for the tier rh_Function_RX:

In the grid, choose the tier rh_Function_RX.

In the column Annotation, click on the first 'to-be-coded' Function unit.

If the unit has an *irregular, shift,* or *aborted* Structure go to Annotation

> Delete Annotation.

In the grid, choose the tier lh_Function_RX.

In the column Annotation, click on the first 'to-be-coded' Function unit.

If the unit has an *irregular, shift,* or *aborted* Structure go to Annotation

> Delete Annotation.

Proceed analogously for all other Function tiers–as listed above–that you intend to analyze (for bh_Function_RX and bf_Function_RX that are based on Formal Relation units, the deletion procedure is not necessary, since it has already been conducted during the generation of the Formal Relation units, see. 7.5.1.2).

8.5.3 Assessing the 'to-be-coded' Function units

While in Module I, first all right hand units were coded, and then all left hand units, in Module III the coding procedure follows the chronology of the units on the three tiers. Thus, in the order of their occurrence, the units on the three Function tiers are coded one after the other, e.g. rh unit, lh unit, bh unit, bh unit, rh unit etc.

The new units of the tiers bh_Function_RX, rh_Function_RX, and lh_Function_RX, bf_Function_RX, rf_Function_RX, lf_Function_RX, head_Function_RX, and trunk_Function_RX are now coded with the following values:

emotion/attitude

emphasis

egocentric deictic

egocentric direction

pantomime

form presentation

spatial relation presentation

motion quality presentation

subject-oriented action

object-oriented action

emblem / social convention

different functions

(prep-retract)
? (see 4.5.2)

Note the special rules for bilateral Function units. The 'to-be-coded' units on the tier bh_Function_RX still have the Formal Relation values. The Formal Relation value determines the Function assessment:

symmetrical ⇒ The Function value refers to the joint performance of both hands.

rh dominance ⇒ The Function value is determined by the performance of the right hand.

lh dominance ⇒ The Function value is determined by the performance of the left hand.
asymmetrical ⇒ The Function value refers to the joint performance of both hands. If, however, the two hands have different Function values, use the template value (*different functions)* and note in the tier Notes what the two Functions are.

If a Function value changes within a 'to-be-coded' Function unit, replace the old unit by the new subunits (see 4.2).

8.5.4 Alternative procedure: Manual generation of 'to-be-coded' Function units

If you start with the Function category, i.e., you have not assessed Modules I and II before, use the alternative procedure of manual unit generation. In this procedure, the tiers bh_Function_R0, rh_Function_R0, lh_Function_R0, bf_Function_R0, rf_Function_R0, lf_Function_R0, head_Function_R0, and trunk_Function_R0 are used that are provided in the template. Directly tag all body movements that show a concept realization according to the definitions of *phasic* and *repetitive* units (see 4.3, 4.4.2, 4.4.3). For the limbs, the units have to be differentiated as unilateral right, unilateral left, and bilateral. Unimanual limb units are units in which one limb moves while the other limb rests. Bimanual units are units in which both limbs move simultaneously (compare the definitions given in III). The bilateral units should first be classified with the Formal Relation values (see 8.5.3). The 'to-be-coded' Function units are assessed according to the rules described in 8.5.3.

8.5.5 Optional: Concatenation of the Function values with the values of the preceding categories

In order to achieve complex values that include the assessments of the previous categories, concatenation procedures can be conducted. The most fine-grained unit segmentation of the Function tier is automatically adopted.

The units of the tiers rh_Function_RX, lh_Function_RX, rf_Function_RX, lf_Function_RX can be concatenated with the corresponding units of the Unilateral_StructureFocus_RX tiers.

The units of the tiers head_Function_RX and trunk_Function_RX can be concatenated with the corresponding units of the Structure_RX tiers.

The units of the tiers bh_Function_RX and bh_Function_RX can be concatenated with the corresponding units of the StructureFocusContactFormalRelation tiers.

As an example, the procedure is described here for the latter concatenation.
This procedure can be conducted for multiple files at a time.

In order to be able to use the time-saving Multiple files processing function in ELAN, it is absolutely **crucial that the tier names are written correctly in all eafs**. Small deviations in the spelling of the tier names, such as capital letter instead of small letter, entail that the Multiple files processing function becomes ineffective.
File > Multiple files processing > Annotations from Overlaps.

Step 1/4: File and Tier Selection.

Select files to use in overlaps computation:

⊙ Select files from domain. Click on the button Domain.

If you have not yet defined a domain, press the button New Domain > Specify New Domain > Add the Folder.

If you had already defined a domain > Select an existing domain > Load.

Select tiers to use for computation:

bh_StructureFocusContactFormalRelation_RX and bh_Function_RX.
Next.

Step 2/4: Overlaps Computation Criteria.

Create annotation when annotations overlap:

⊙ regardless of their annotation values.
Next.

Step 3/4: Destination Tier Name Specification.

Enter name for destination tier: bh_StructureFocusContactFormalRelationFunction_RX (Cave: correct spelling, or choose another term).

⊙ Destination tier is a root tier.

Select a linguistic type for destination tier: click on Notes.
Next.

Step 4/4: Destination Tier Value Specification.

⊙ Concatenate the values of the annotations.

⊙ Compute values in the selected tier order:

Establish the following order by pressing ^:

first bh_StructureFocusContactFormalRelation_RX and **second** bh_Function_RX.

Finish.

Now you have a new tier bh_StructureFocusContactFormalRelationFunction_RX that contains bimanual units with the Structure, Focus, Contact, Formal Relation and Function values.

If you want to conduct the concatenation procedure for one file only, proceed as follows:

Apply the function: Tier > Create Annotations from Overlaps.

Step 1/4: File and Tier Selection.

Select files to use in overlaps computation:

⊙ Use currently opened file.
Proceed as described above.

9 The Type category

9.1 Definition of the Type category

The Type category classifies gestures according to their overall function, as defined in the Function category, and to certain aspects of form and meaning.

Emotion/attitude expressions are classified according to direction and weight, and *emphasis* gestures according to formal aspects concerning how the dynamic accent is created. *Egocentric deictics* are specified according to the target and *egocentric direction* gestures according to the absence or presence of an agent who executes the direction. *Pantomime* gestures are classified according to transitivity versus intransitivity. For *form presentation* gestures, shape versus size is specified, for *spatial relation presentation* gestures, route versus position, and for *motion quality presentation* gestures, manner versus dynamics.

The 24 Type values (see Fig. 11) are operationalized by several movement criteria: gesture/action space, path during complex phase, orientation, hand shape, efforts, body involvement, gaze, Structure, Focus, Contact, Formal Relation, and Function (the latter criteria refer to the preceding categories).

For researchers who aim at naming single *emblems*, a list of *emblems* used in West Germany is provided at the end of this chapter.

Tab. 10 provides the short definitions and reliabilities of the Type values. Since gestures are performed most often with the upper limbs and rarely with the lower limbs, the head, and the trunk, and since most researchers focus on the upper limbs, the definitions of the Type values are formulated for the hands. However, the value definitions likewise apply to the other parts of the body.

Researchers who conduct the complete NEUROGES® analysis should note that within the algorithmic structure of NEUROGES®, the Type category differs from the previous categories as it is a dependent category. While the relation between the previous categories is primarily independent, i.e., in principle any value of the previous category can be combined with any value of the following category, the choice of Type values is determined by the Function value. Thus, as the Type values are typifications of the Function values, the label of a Type value includes the parent Function value, e.g. *emphasis–baton*. Furthermore, as the Type values describe smaller groups of gestures than the Function values, the definition of the movement features of the Type values is more precise and less general than that of the Function values. Therefore, the Type category coding can be used as a control for the Function coding. The precise definitions of the movement

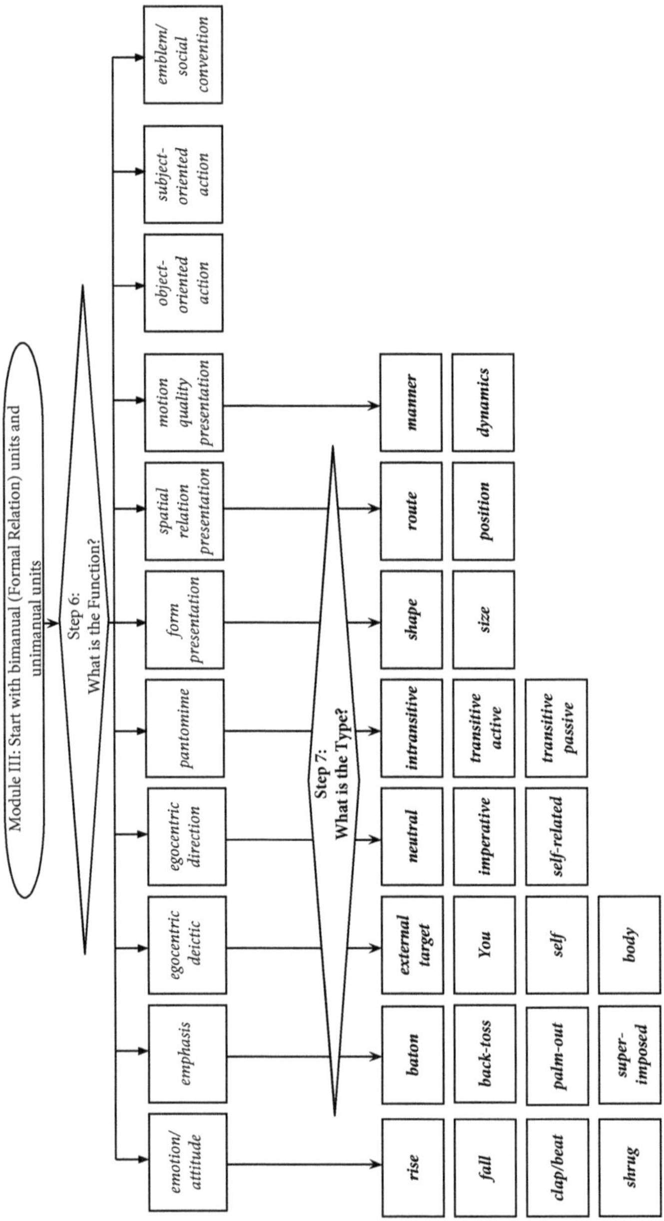

Fig. 11: The analysis algorithm for the Gesture and Action module (Module III) with the Type category in fat print

features of the Type values enable to determine the Type value and thereby, to verify if the correct Function value was chosen.

9.2 Generation of the 'to-be-coded' Type units

9.2.1 Selection of units for the generation of 'to-be-coded' Type units

The Function units that result from the Step 6 / Module III analysis are adopted for the Type evaluation.

The exception is Function units with the values *object-oriented action, subject-oriented action,* and *emblem/social convention*. These are not assessed with the Type category.

The copied Function units are termed 'to-be-coded' Type units and they are further classified with the Type values. As stated above, the Type category is a dependent category. The Function value determines which Type values can be coded.

If there is a change of the Type value within a 'to-be-coded' Type unit, then the change demarcates subunits. With regard to the precise segmentation of a unit into subunits (where to segment the unit), the procedure is described in detail in the Structure Coding Manual.

Researchers who only apply the Type category select all movements that they identify as gestures from the ongoing stream of behavior and thereby generate 'to-be-coded' units.

9.2.2 Alternative generation of 'to-be-coded' Type units

Researchers who only apply the Type category, i.e., who have not assessed the Function category before, select from the ongoing stream of kinesic behavior all gestures. With very few exceptions, *in space* movements are functionally gestures. Therefore, it is recommended to follow the definitions of *in space* units (see 5.4.6, on the basis of *phasic* and *repetitive* units see 4.3, 4.4.2, 4.4.3). Only rarely, *on body* (or *on attached object* and *on separate object*) movements are functionally gestures, e.g. a self-deictic that includes touching of the sternum.

For the limbs, the units have to be differentiated as unilateral right, unilateral left, and bilateral in order to use the existing Type tiers in the NEUROGES®-ELAN template. Concerning the bilateral units, it is helpful to classify them first with the Formal Relation values, since this pre-assessment facilitates the analysis of the bilateral 'to-be-coded' Types units (see 8.2.2). The 'to-be-coded' Type units are assessed according to the rules described in 9.2.1.

Tab. 10: Short definitions of the Type values and their reliabilities

Type value	**Short definition**	**Reliability*** M ± SD
emotion/attitude–rise	dynamic fast raising up of the arms (against gravity)	.74 ± .04
emotion/attitude–fall	letting the arms fall down heavily (giving in to gravity)	.74 ± .08
emotion/attitude–clap/ beat	dynamic fast strong movement of the arms	-
emotion/attitude–shrug	shrug of the shoulders	.78 ± .04
emphasis – baton	up-down movements with downward accent	.86 ± .08
emphasis–back-toss	small up-down movements with upward accent	.73 ± .09
emphasis–palm out	small supination-pronation movements with outward accent	.88 ± .00
emphasis–super-imposed	up-down or back-forth movements with downward or forward accent that directly follow the static complex phase of another gesture type	.69 ± .04
deictic–external target	indicating a target in the external space by using an egocentric frame of reference	.19 ± .27
deictic – You	referring to the addressee as a person or to a part of her/his body	.60 ± .01
deictic – self	referring to oneself as a person	.78
deictic – body	referring to parts of the own body or to objects attached to the body	-
direction – neutral	indicating a direction without specifying an agent	.76 ± .10
direction–imperative	indicating to the addressee to move (something) in a specific direction	.79 ± .02
direction- self-related	showing the direction of oneself's (bodily or mental) movement	.88 ± .02
pantomime–intransitive	acting as if without an imaginary object or counterpart	.67 ± .00
pantomime – transitive-active	acting as if with an imaginary (or real) object or counterpart	.18
pantomime – transitive-passive	acting as if an imaginary agent/object acts on oneself	-
form[21]*–shape*	creating a shape	.90 ± .14

21 For convenience, in the *egocentric* Function values the term '*egocentric*' is dropped, e.g. *deictic- body*, and in the *presentation* Function values the term '*presentation*', e.g. *form–shape* instead of *form presentation – shape.*

Tab. 10: Continued

Type value	Short definition	Reliability* M ± SD
form – size	creating a length	.66 ± .13
spatial relation–route	creating a spatial route by producing a line	.82 ± .07
spatial relation–position	creating a spatial position by setting a point relative to another one	.86 ± .06
motion quality–manner	presenting a specific type of movement	.82 ± .04
motion quality–dynamics	presenting a specific dynamics of movement	.84 ± .03

* Interrater reliability as measured with EasyDIAg (from Lausberg & Slöetjes, 2016)

9.3 Criteria for the definition of the Type values

The Type values are defined according the same criteria as the Function values: Structure, Focus, Contact, Formal Relation, gesture/action space, path, hand orientation, hand shape, efforts, body involvement, and gaze. The most frequent associations of specific StructureFocus values with Function and Type values are given in Tab. 11.

9.4 Definitions of the Type values

The definitions of the Type values build up on the definitions of the corresponding Function values. Thus, it is necessary to first read the Function value definitions. The following definitions of the Type values are structured as follows:

First, a **Short definition** is given. A more detailed **Definition** follows that first defines the criterion for the typification and then describes the movement form. In Notes recommendations are given to note certain qualitative observations.

In **Meeting the criteria** the movement features are listed in note form. The lecture of section 8.3 in the Function category chapter is necessary to understand this paragraph.

Finally, having been most appreciated by many raters, in **Differentiate**... criteria are provided that help to distinguish Type values that share certain movement features and that, therefore, may be mixed up.

9.4.1 Types of the Function value *emotion/attitude*

Given that there is a controversial scientific discussion about the definition and the number of distinct emotions, the NEUROGES® Type category does not aim at describing movements associated with distinct emotions. Rather, the

Tab. 11: The most frequent associations of StructureFocus values with Function and Type values

StructureFocus value	Function value	Type value
phasic **or** ***repetitive within body***	*emotion/attitude*	*shrug*
phasic **or** ***repetitive on body***	*emotion/attitude*	*fall*
		clap/beat
	egocentric deictic	*body*
		self
	pantomime	*transitive*
phasic **or** ***repetitive on person***	*egocentric deictic*	*You*
	egocentric direction	*imperative*
phasic **or** ***repetitive in space***	*emotion/attitude*	*rise*
		fall
		clap/beat
		shrug
	emphasis	*baton*
		superimposed
		back-toss
		palm-out
	egocentric deictic	*external target*
		You
		self
		body
	egocentric direction	*neutral*
		imperative
		self-related
	pantomime	*transitive*
		intransitive
		passive
	form presentation	*shape*
		size
	spatial relation presentation	*route*
		position
	motion quality presentation	*manner*
		dynamics

Type category classifies basic movement forms associated with emotional experience. The four *emotion/attitude* Type values register the four most frequent expressions of emotions and attitudes in the upper limbs, as identified with the Function value *emotion/attitude*, that have been observed in the NEUROGES® archive. Other emotional expressions can be coded with the special template value *other e-motion*. These four values are characterized by a specific direction in space (here: up, down) and a specific attitude towards weight, according to Laban's effort factor weight: It can be light (overcoming the body weight, e.g. as in happiness), heavy (passive giving in to gravity, e.g. as in sadness), or strong (getting behind the body weight, e.g. as in anger).

9.4.1.1 emotion/attitude–rise

Short definition

DYNAMIC FAST RAISING UP OF THE ARMS

Definition

Direction and weight: The arms are raised up against the gravity. The direction implies that the body weight overcomes gravity.

Movement form (features other than direction and weight):

The emphasis is on the act of moving up. The fast upward movement of the arms typically involves the whole arm rather than only the lower arm. In case of a genuine emotional expression, the movement is typically *phasic*, bilateral and it is accompanied by a postural stretching up, e.g. a little child throwing up the arms with joy.

Note: underlying emotion or attitude.

Meeting the criteria

Structure	*phasic*
Focus	*in space*
Gesture/action space	upper peripheral space
Path	spoke-like or arch-like upwards
Hand orientation	variable
Hand shape	variable

Effort	sudden, often free flow and strong, as if throwing up the arms in the air, sometimes with accent at endpoint
Body involvement	There is a stretching up of the trunk and a facial expression, e.g. happiness, surprise, pride.
Gaze	looks at addressee or up in space, not at hand

Differentiate *emotion/attitude-rise* from...

- *direction-neutral:* A *direction-neutral* gesture may indicate the direction upwards. In the *direction* gestures the hand leads the movement. In case of a concrete referent the gaze is oriented in the intended direction. In contrast, *emotion/attitude-rise* movements are initiated in trunk and proximal muscles, there is a specific facial expression, and the gaze is not in line with direction indicated by the hand.
- *direction-imperative:* In *direction – imperative* gestures with the direction 'up', e.g. meaning 'Rise' or 'Cheer up', the hand and arm is extended into the direction of the addressee and the palm is oriented upwards. In *emotion/attitude-rise,* the gesturer raises the whole arm quickly and dynamically with endpoint accent. There is only a movement in the vertical axis and no hand displacement in direction of the addressee.
- *direction-self-related:* In *direction-self-related* gestures with the direction 'up', the hand is moved upward in front of the gesturer's body, most often with the palm oriented upwards. The gesturer may perform the gesture as a self-suggestion: "Cheer up!". In contrast, *emotion/attitude-rise,* the gesturer raises the whole arm quick and dynamically with endpoint accent. There is only movement in the vertical axis.
- *spatial relation-route:* A *spatial relation-route* gesture may show a route in the vertical axis that runs up. This gesture is performed with the effort quality bound flow in order to provide a precise depiction of the route per se, and **not** with the effort qualities sudden or strong. The *spatial relation-route* gesture is restricted to the arm and in case of a concrete referent the gaze is at the imaginary route.
- *motion quality- dynamics:* A *motion quality-dynamics* gesture may picture something that is rising, e.g. a balloon rising. In this case, the movement is restricted to the arm and in case of a concrete referent the gaze is at least for short moment at the imaginary object. In contrast, the *emotion/attitude-rise* movement is accompanied by a corresponding facial-postural expression.

9.4.1.2 emotion/attitude–fall

Short definition

LETTING THE ARMS FALL DOWN HEAVILY

Definition

Direction and weight: The gesturer lets the (lower) arm fall down heavily. The heavy fall implies giving in to gravity, i.e., no effort is undertaken to resist the force of gravity on the body weight.

Movement form:

The emphasis is on the act of falling. The movement involves the lower arm or the whole arm, rarely only the hand. The heavy fall typically expresses resignation or helplessness. In learned emotional expressions that serve to demonstrate resignation or helplessness, in order to be able to let the arm fall (complex phase), it has to be raised first (transport phase), unless the arm happens to be in a raised position before.

(Only for researchers who have not coded the Focus category before: If the *fall* gesture co-occurs with a *shrug* (see 9.4.1.4), the *fall* is coded.)

Meeting the criteria

Structure	*phasic*
Focus	*in space, on body* or *on separate object* (if there is a heavy landing on a surface)
Gesture/action space	in the middle kinesphere, not extended extra into the gesture/action space
Path	one-dimensional in the vertical axis
Hand orientation	no active orientation
Hand shape	hand is relaxed
Effort	heavy
Body involvement	The *fall* gesture may be accompanied by a shrug. The gesture is accompanied by a facial expression, most likely that of resignation or helplessness.
Gaze	looks at addressee or down

Differentiate *emotion/attitude–fall* from…

✐ *direction–neutral:* A *direction–neutral* gesture may indicate the direction downwards. In the *direction* gesture the hand leads the movement. The gaze is oriented in the intended direction. *Direction* gestures have a free flow and an endpoint accent (to emphasize the direction), while in *emotion/attitude–fall* the weight is heavy and there is never an endpoint accent. Furthermore, in *emotion/attitude–fall*, there is a specific facial expression.

- *direction–imperative:* In *direction–imperative* indicating the direction 'down', e.g. meaning 'Sit down' or 'Calm down', the hand and arm is extended into the direction of the addressee and the palm is oriented towards the floor. In *emotion/attitude–fall,* the gesturer lets the (lower) arm fall heavily. There is only a movement in the vertical axis and no hand displacement in direction of the addressee.
- *direction–self-related:* In *direction – self* gestures with the direction 'down' the hand is moved downward in front of the gesturer's body with the palm oriented to the ground. The gesture may be displayed in a context in which the gesturer self-suggests: Calm down! or I move down. In contrast, in *emotion/attitude–fall,* the gesturer lets the arm fall heavily. The hand is not shaped. The gesture typically reflects an emotional state of resignation.
- *spatial relation–route:* A *spatial relation–route* gesture may depict a route in the vertical axis that runs down. The gesture is performed with the effort quality bound flow to provide a precise depiction of the route per se, and **not** with the effort quality heavy.
- *motion quality–dynamics:* A *motion quality–dynamics* gesture may depict something falling heavily, e.g. representing an apple falling from the tree. The movement is restricted to the arm, the gesturer's hand embodies or encloses an imaginary object that falls, and in case of a concrete referent the gaze is at least for a moment at the imaginary object and hand, respectively. In contrast, the *emotion/attitude–fall* is accompanied by a corresponding facial-postural expression and the gaze is not directed at the hand.

9.4.1.3 emotion/attitude–clap/beat

Short definition

DYNAMIC FAST STRONG MOVEMENT OF ARMS

Definition

Direction and weight: These are arm movements that are displayed with strength and that end by contacting a counter-part, e.g. a piece of furniture, the other hand, another part of the body, or another person. The contact can result in a sound. It implies that strength is put behind the body weight.

Movement form:

The emphasis is on the act of clapping, beating, and punching. The movement is accompanied by a postural-facial expression such as in clapping the hands with joy, slapping on the thigh with joy, or punching on the table with anger (the latter is akin to the leg movement of stamping on the ground in anger).

Note: underlying emotion or attitude

Meeting the criteria

Structure	*phasic*
Focus	*on body, on separate object, on person*
Gesture/action space	depends on the Focus
Path	one-dimensional, straight
Hand orientation	contact surface of the hand towards the contact surface of the counter-part
Hand shape	defined shape, often flat or fist
Effort	sudden, strong
Body involvement	There is a postural-facial expression, e.g of joy, or anger.
Gaze	often at addressee

Differentiate *emotion/attitude–clap/beat* from ...

✎ *emphasis–baton* and *emphasis–superimposed*: The *emphasis – baton* and *emphasis–superimposed* gestures are akin to the *emotion/attitude–clap/beat* gestures insofar as these Type values are strong gestures that set accents. Furthermore, they may also have an emotional tone.

However, the *emphasis–baton* and *emphasis–superimposed* gestures are primarily rhythmical gestures that accompany prosody. They are most often *in space*, i.e., there is no counter-part, and they are more often displayed unimanually. In rare cases, in which *emphasis–baton* and *emphasis–superimposed* are executed on a separate object, there is, however, a clear coordination with the speech output. Especially *superimposed* gestures are more often *repetitive*.

In contrast, the *clap/beat* is primarily a motor outflow of an emotion or its learned equivalent for social display. The hand acts on a counter-part, i.e., something/-one is clapped or hit on. The Structure is *phasic.*

✐ *emblem/social convention:* There is a *social convention* of clapping both palms repeatedly onto each other in order to applaud somebody in a defined social context. The Structure is obligatorily *repetitive* and of a particularly long duration. Since the purpose is not primarily to express an emotion but to honor somebody, the facial-postural involvement is less pronounced than in *emotion/attitude–clap/beat.* In the latter case, especially in genuine emotional expressions, in contrast, the Structure is rather *phasic.*

9.4.1.4 emotion/attitude–shrug

Short definition

SHRUG OF THE SHOULDERS

Definition

Direction and weight: There is an up-down movement of the shoulders.

Movement form:
In the NEUROGES® archive different subtypes of *shrugs* were observed that slightly differ in form:

(i) shrugging of the shoulders that accompanies laughing, crying and other emotional expressions.
(ii) shrug with palming: There is a sustained pulling up of the shoulder that is accompanied by a bilateral and symmetrical palming of the hands. The shoulders are raised and moved forward and the shoulder movement initiates the arm and hand movement. There is a turning inward of the elbows, i.e., bending and adducting the elbows to the waist. Thereby, the lower arms are supinated and palms become visible. Often, the head is tilted to one side and the facial expression is frowning. To render the palms visible to the addressee, the wrist is flexed, i.e., the back of the hand towards lower arm, and the palms are tilted down to a plane that is between the horizontal and the frontal levels. The full visibility of the palms indicates to the addressee that the gesturer has nothing to hide, that (s)he is not guilty, in a broader sense. Palming demonstrates defenceless and serves appeasement.
(iii) shrug with a heavy fall of the shoulders: The accent is on the fall of the shoulders. It is accompanied by a specific facial expression that conveys the attitude of resignation. (Only for researchers who have not coded the Focus category before: If the *fall* gesture co-occurs with a *shrug*, the *fall* is coded.)
(iv) short shrug. The shrug is displayed at the start or at the end of a speech turn or a gesture sequence. It typically indicates that the gesturer is not confident

about her/his gestural or verbal statement. In contrast to the *emblem* shrug, it is displayed beyond the gesturer's awareness and is not primarily produced for the addressee.

Meeting the criteria

Structure	*phasic*
Focus	*within body*
Gesture/action space	in shrug with palming, ipsilateral gesture space, middle kinesphere with hands at the level of the navel
Path	one-dimensional in vertical axis; in *shrug* with palming static complex phase
Hand orientation	In *shrug* with palming, palms in a medium level between horizontal and frontal such that they are fully visible to the addressee; finger tips pointing downwards
Efforts	heavy (falling of shoulders)
Body involvement	accompanied by facial expression, may co-occur with palming
Gaze	looks at addressee or looks down
Frequency	mean number of *shrugs* per minute (± SD; Median) = 0.22 ± 0.19; 0.16; Cronbach´s Alpha: 0.8 (Lausberg); 2.41 ± 3.24; 1.41 (Sassenberg)
Duration	mean number of seconds per *shrug* (± SD): 0.75 ± 0.23 (Sassenberg)

Differentiate *emotion/attitude-shrug* from…

- *deictic-external target*: A *deictic-external target* may be performed with the shoulder. Only one shoulder moves forward-upward to designate a location. The shoulder *deictic* is unilateral, with an upward accent, no emphasis on falling, often accompanied by a turning of the head to the same direction. It never co-occurs with a *fall* gesture, a *palming* gesture, or with a specific facial expression such as frowning. The shoulder *deictic* is typically performed if the hands or elbows are inhibited from moving. Furthermore, while for a *unilateral emotion/attitude-shrug* the left shoulder may be preferred, this left side preference is not found for the shoulder *deictic*.
- *deictic-body:* A subtype of *deictic-body* is hand-showing. The hand may be designated by showing it to the addressee, e.g. a child demonstrating to the

parent that its hands are clean. ThE showing of one hand may be accompanied by a pointing gesture of the other hand, e.g. the other hand points to the palm. The gaze is at the hand.

In contrast, in a *shrug* with palming the gaze is at the addressee and the hand/arm movement is initiated in the shoulders and it co-occurs with a specific facial expression. The palming is typically displayed bimanually.

✐ *emblem*: The isolated *shrug* is an *emblem* and then used explicitly to communicate to the addressee "I do not know" or "I do not care". In this case, the *shrug* is displayed as an isolated shoulder gesture, not accompanied by a facial expression. It may be used independent from speech as an autonomous sign, i.e., the *shrug* may constitute a complete response to a question and no verbal statement is needed.

9.4.1.5 Special template value other e-motion

As indicated above, the four Type values are **not** intended to represent the complete spectrum of *emotion/attitude* expressions as registered with the Function value. Rather, they are the most frequent types of *emotion/attitude* expressions observed in the NEUROGES® archive. Therefore, in the NEUROGES®-ELAN template the value *other e-motion* is provided in order to offer researchers the option to note other types of *emotion/attitude* expressions, e.g. fist clenching.

9.4.2 Types of the Function value *emphasis*

The Type values of the Function value *emphasis* refer among others to the direction towards the end point as the dynamic accent.

9.4.2.1 emphasis–baton

Short definition

UP-DOWN MOVEMENTS WITH DOWNWARD ACCENT

Definition

Direction: up-down movements with a downward accent

Movement form: *Batons* are up-down movements with a downward accent. They are most often conducted with the lower arm and performed in synchrony with head and mouth movements. They are often displayed *repetitive*ly and then create a meter or a rhythm. In *phasic batons*, the single accent emphasizes a certain aspect of the verbal message.

Meeting the criteria

Structure	***repetitive > phasic***
Focus	*in space >> on body, on separate object*
Gesture/action space	ipsilateral neutral gesture/action space, middle kinesphere, no distinct creative use of gesture/action space
Path	**up-down** movements in the vertical axis
Hand orientation	often ulnar side of hand oriented downwards
Hand shape	the hand muscles are often tensioned so that the **hand** can function **as a 'baton'**
Effort	acceleration (quick) with change from free to bound flow to generate **downward accent**
Body involvement	**synchronized with mouth and head movements**
Gaze	not at hand

Differentiate *emphasis-batons* from...

- *emotion/attitude-clap/beat*: see there Differentiate...
- *pantomime-transitive*: A *pantomime-transitive* gesture may present the action of beating or drumming. The hand adopts a specific shape to present the object that is used for beating or the imaginary counter-part, i.e., the object that is beaten. In the first case, the hand is either shaped as if holding the object (Supplementary category Technique of Presentation value *enclosure*) or as if embodying the object (Technique of Presentation value *hand-as-object*). There is a distinct use of gesture/action space. In addition, the gesturer looks at the imagined object that is beaten or drummed on, whereas during *batons* the gaze is not directed at the hand but rather at the addressee. Furthermore, in *pantomime-transitive* here is no synchronization with mouth movements.
- *motion quality-manner*: A *motion quality-manner* gesture may present something that is bouncing up and down. However, in contrast to the *emphasis-baton* gesture, the hand is often shaped to present the object that is moving. Furthermore, there is often a displacement of the hand to represent locomotion. The gaze is typically at the presented motion.

9.4.2.2 emphasis–back-toss

Short definition

SMALL UP-DOWN MOVEMENTS WITH UPWARD ACCENT

Definition

Direction: up-down movements with an upward accent

Movement form: *Back-tosses* are short up-down movements with a downward or upward accent. The movement is typically restricted to the wrist, occasionally even only to the knuckles (metacarpophalangeal joints). The upward movement of the hand is often performed while the wrist remains resting on a support. The back or the radial side of the hand is leading the upward movement. *Back-tosses* are often displayed as a series, i.e., *repetitive* rather than *phasic*, and their performance is synchronized with head and mouth movements while speaking.

Meeting the criteria

Structure	***repetitive* > *phasic***
Focus	***in space***
Gesture/action space	most often ipsilateral space
Path	**short** one-dimensional **up-down** movement, often limited to **wrist movement starting from rest position**
Hand orientation	**back or radial side of hand** oriented **upwards**
Hand shape	relaxed hand
Effort	**upward accent**
Body involvement	**synchronized with mouth and head movements**
Gaze	not at hand

Differentiate *back-tosses* from...

- Only for researchers who have not coded the Structure category before, as in the complete algorithmic analysis by the time of Module III coding, *irregular within body* movements have been excluded from the evaluation: *irregular within body* movements: While *back-tosses* have a stereotypical movement form with an upward accent *in space* and they are synchronized with the mouth and head movements, this is not the case for *irregular within body* movements, which have no structured form and no accents.

9.4.2.3 emphasis–palm-out

Short definition

SMALL SUPINATION-PRONATION MOVEMENTS WITH OUTWARD ACCENT

Definition

Direction: in-out movements with an outward accent

Movement form: *Emphasis–palm-out* gestures are supination–pronation movements, i.e., an outward – inward rotation of the hand or lower arm. The accent is outwards, i.e., on the supination phase. The supination has to reach an extent between 10° and 90° (in the neutral position 0° the flat hand is line with the sagittal plane). Thereby, the palm becomes visible. *Emphasis–palm-out* gestures are often displayed a *repetitive*ly and they are synchronized with the head and mouth movements.

There are two subtypes of *emphasis–palm-out* gestures:

(i) palm-toss: There is a supination–pronation alternating movement with an outward accent. This subtype serves to set accents or to create a meter or a rhythm in line with prosody.
(ii) palm-presenting: There is a static complex phase in the supination end position. This subtype is a hybrid as it is also an *egocentric direction–self-related* gesture of bringing / rotating a thought out and presenting it. The palm may be presented as long as the idea is presented. However, since it is displayed inter- and intra-individually stereotypically and frequently, it is coded as an *emphasis* gesture. Palm-presenting may be followed by an *emphasis–superimposed* gesture. In this case, the static complex phase in the supination end position is followed by *repetitive* up-down movements with downward accent (*emphasis–palm-out* + *emphasis–superimposed*).

Meeting the criteria

Structure	*repetitive > phasic*
Focus	*in space*
Gesture/action space	ipsilateral neutral gesture space, middle kinesphere, no distinct creative use of space
Path	two-dimensional, arch-like path, **supination-pronation**
Hand orientation	hand/lower arm in supination position, palm upward

Hand shape	relaxed open hand
Effort	**outward accent towards supination**
Body involvement	**synchronized with mouth and head movements**
Gaze	not at hand

Differentiate *emphasis–palm-out* from…

- *emotion/attitude–shrug* with palming: The *shrug* with palming has a defensive connotation. The bilateral hand/arm movements are initiated by the shoulders, the lower arms are rotated outward and the palms are held in a level between the horizontal and the frontal levels to demonstrate to the addressee that the hands are empty. There is a defensive facial expression. In the *emphasis–palm-out*, the supination of the lower arm and hand and the presentation of the palm(s) accompanies the speech process of bringing out and presenting the idea. The palms are held in line with the horizontal level as if to present an idea on the flat hand. *Emphasis–palm-out* gestures are characterized by an accentuated supination movement and there is no specific facial-postural involvement.
- *direction–self-related:* A *direction–self-related* gesture with a wrist circulation of the hand may seem similar to an *emphasis–palm-out* gesture with a supination – pronation but it differs among others by path (circular rather than back-forth). The *direction–self-related* 'rotating out' gesture reflects a (repeated) attempt to bring out an idea by (repetitively) rotating the hand. It seems as if the gesturer tries to rotate a word out of his/her brain. Thus, the gesture is displayed to promote cognitive processes, e.g. if the gesturer is desperately searching for a word. In contrast, the *emphasis–palm-out* gestures reflects the successful process of bringing out the idea and presenting it.

The *direction–self-related* 'rotating out' gesture is characterized by a (repetitive) rotation in the wrist. The Structure is often *repetitive*, the Focus *in space*, and the gesture is performed unimanually. The hand is relaxed rather than actively opened. The hand orientation is in the horizontal plane with the palm oriented toward body. The path during complex phase is circular. The effort quality is sudden time, i.e., as if the gesturer tries to accelerate the thinking process. The *direction–self-related* rotating gesture may be performed at the level of the head, or they may even be localized precisely at the level of the temple. The head might be bowed and the gaze might be casted down (to improve concentration). In case of a right hand movement, there is a clockwise rotation, in case of the left hand a counter-clockwise one.

In contrast, in the *emphasis-palm-out gesture,* there is a simple back-forth movement (supination–pronation) with no variation. Or, there is a supination movement with a static complex phase. *Emphasis palm-out* gestures are typically performed in the lower gesture space, i.e., below or at the level of the ribcage.

✐ *pantomime-transitive:* A *pantomime-transitive* gesture may present carrying something on the flat hand, e.g. a tray. The hand is carefully moved to a precisely horizontal level and stretched to a perfectly flat shape. The gaze is directed at the imaginary object that is carried on the flat hand.–Furthermore, a *pantomime-transitive* may present the action of shovelling, e.g. pretending to take something and present it with a supination movement. There is a clear grasping of the imaginary object and then an outward rotation.

In contrast, in *emphasis-palm-out*, the accent is on the outward rotation of the palm and the hand is open but relaxed. The movement is synchronized with head and mouth movements and the gaze is not at hand.

✐ *motion quality-manner*: The *repetitive emphasis-palm-out* turning gesture may be confused with the *motion quality-manner* 'waggling' gesture which serves to depict something which is shaky, unclear, ambivalent etc. The hand is flat and oriented in the sagittal plane and the emphasis is on the fast alternating movement. In contrast, in the *emphasis-palm-out* turning gesture there is an outward accent and the emphasis is on the presentation of the palm.

9.4.2.4 emphasis–superimposed

Short definition

UP-DOWN OR BACK-FORTH MOVEMENTS WITH DOWNWARD OR FORWARD ACCENT THAT DIRECTLY FOLLOW THE STATIC COMPLEX PHASE OF ANOTHER GESTURE TYPE

Definition

Direction: up-down or forth-back movements with a downward or forward accent, respectively, which is determined by hand orientation in the primary gesture

Movement form: *Emphasis–superimposed* gestures are up-down or forth-back movements, often *repetitive*, with downward or forward accent that directly follow an *emphasis–palm-out, emphasis–baton, egocentric deictic, egocentric direction, form presentation, spatial relation presentation*, or *emblem* gesture. In *repetitive emotion/attitude* movements, *superimposed emphasis* can follow the learned display of an emotion but not a genuine emotional expression, since the latter is the direct motor correlate of an emotional experience. Setting *emphasis* is a cognitive process that is not compatible with an immediate emotional expression.

Once the primary gesture has come to the static complex phase, the *superimposed* gesture follows while preserving the hand shape, the hand orientation, and the position in gesture/action space of the primary gesture. Notably, there is no transport phase like the one for the primary gesture but the hand performs the *superimposed emphasis* at the place where the hand happens to be for the primary gesture. Examples are a pointing gesture to which up-down movements are added (*deictic–external target + emphasis–superimposed*), or a gesture marking in an imaginary landscape a position that is underlined *(spatial relation–position + emphasis–superimposed)*, or an *emphasis–palm-out* gesture that is re-enforced by short up-down movements with a downward accent *(emphasis – palm-out + emphasis–superimposed)*.

Meeting the criteria

Structure	***repetitive* > *phasic***
Focus	*in space*, rarely *on body* or *on separate object*
Gesture/action space	**kept from primary gesture**
Path	one-dimensional, **up-down** or **forth-back** movements
Hand orientation	**kept from primary gesture**
Hand shape	**kept from primary gesture**
Effort	acceleration (quick) with change from free to bound flow to generate **downward** or **forward accent**
Body involvement	**synchronized with mouth and head movements**
Gaze	not at hand

Differentiate *emphasis–superimposed* from…

🖉 Only for researchers who have not coded the Function category before: While the differentiation between a primary gesture followed by an *emphasis* gesture versus a primary *repetitive pantomime* or *presentation* gesture should have already been made in the Function category coding, for researchers who only apply the Type category, the criteria for this distinction are repeated here: *Emphasis–superimposed* gestures can only follow a primary gesture with a static complex phase. *Emphasis–superimposed* gestures are **not** to be confused with a gesture in which the repetition is an intrinsic component of the meaning. As an example, the repetitions in a *pantomime–transitive* gesture presenting tooth brushing or in a *form–shape* gesture presenting a star by tracing several sharp points are **not** superimposed *emphasis* as the repetition does **not** serve to reinforce a primary gesture but the repetition per se constitutes the meaning. One up-down movement in front of the mouth does not convey the meaning of tooth brushing nor does one sharp point not make up a star. In these *repetitive pantomimes* and *presentation* gestures, there is often a locomotive component in the repetition, e.g. the hand moves sideward during the up-down movements. In contrast, in *emphasis–superimposed* there is no displacement of the hand during the up-down or forth-back movement. Furthermore, a movement of the other hand in-between the sub-complex phases of a *repetitive* unit basically excludes *emphasis–superimposed.*

emotion/attitude–clap/beat: see there Differentiate...

emphasis – baton or emphasis–palm-out: In a *repetitive emphasis – baton*, the hand is moved several times up and down again with a downward accent (the up phase is the transport phase, the down phase the complex phase). In contrast, in a *phasic baton* with *superimposed emphasis*, the hand is moved once down with a downward accent, is a held in that position, and then small up-down movements are added in that position. Likewise, in a *repetitive emphasis – palm-out*, the hand is moved several times in and out again with an outward accent (the in phase is the transport phase, the out phase the complex phase). In contrast, in a *phasic palm-out* with *superimposed emphasis*, the hand is moved once out with an outward accent, is a held in that position, and then small up-down movements are added in that position.

pantomime – transitive, – intransitive, or *– passive*: In *pantomime* gestures with a *repetitive* Structure the meaning is conveyed by the repetition per se, e.g. when pantomiming tooth brushing or hammering. In these cases, one up-down movement in front of the mouth or one downward movement would not unambiguously convey the meaning of tooth brushing or hammering, respectively. In *repetitive pantomimes* there is often a displacement of the hand, e.g. the hand moves in front of the mouth from the left side to the right side while executing the up-down movements. Furthermore, there is a distinct hand shape or hand orientation and the gaze is at the hand. In contrast, in *superimposed emphasis* gestures there is no displacement of the hand during the forth-back movement, there is no distinct hand shape or hand orientation, and the gaze is not at the hand.

- *form–shape:* In *form–shape* gestures with a *repetitive* Structure the repetition serves to create the repetitive pattern of the shape, e.g. to depict a staircase with several steps. The repetition of one segment of the form is necessary to create the whole form, e.g. several steps are needed to create a staircase. There is a displacement of the hand, there is a distinct hand shape or hand orientation and the gaze is at the presented form. In contrast, as the repetitive movements of *emphasis–superimposed* gestures are back and forth, they cannot create a form. There is no distinct hand shape or hand orientation, and the gaze is not at the hand.
- *spatial relation–position* or*–route: Spatial relation presentation* gestures with a *repetitive* Structure may serve to present several independent locations or to create a route with a repetitive pattern, e.g. a zig-zag path. There is always a distinct use of gesture / action space reflecting the mento-heliocentric perspective and thus, a displacement of the hand. The hand is typically shaped, with a distinct orientation, and the gaze is typically at the presented path.
- *motion quality–manner*: *Motion quality–manner* gestures, which always have a *repetitive* Structure, have a complex trajectory, complex dynamics, and often the hand is shaped to present the object that is moving. Furthermore, there is often a displacement of the hand to represent locomotion. The gaze is typically at the presented motion. In contrast, *repetitive emphasis–superimposed* gestures are spatially simple back-forth movements, with an endpoint accent and they are synchronized with the mouth and head movements.

9.4.3 Types of the Function value *egocentric deictic*

The Type values of the Function value *egocentric deictic* specify the target.

9.4.3.1 deictic – external target

Short definition

INDICATING A TARGET IN THE EXTERNAL SPACE BY USING AN EGOCENTRIC FRAME OF REFERENCE

Definition

Target: The gesturer points to a target in the body-external space (with the exception of pointing to the addressee, which is coded as *You–deictic*). The *deictic–external target* is based on an obligatorily egocentric frame of reference, in which the gesturer relates from an egocentric point of view to another actual location in the external space. The gesturer can also project him/herself into an imaginary space and point there, e.g. "In my old apartment, if I entered it, the bathroom was on my right." Here, the egocentric frame is kept in mental spatial imagery.

Movement form: The hand is extended and the finger tips are oriented towards the target. Alternatively, only the index is extended, or if the target is behind the gesturer, s/he might use the thumb. The target is located in the estimated line that is the prolongation of the longitudinal hand axis (wrist–finger tips). The hand axis is centrifugal from the body midline. If the target is not in front of the gesturer, it is typical for the egocentric perspective that the gesturer rotates the trunk to be vis-à-vis with the target. As an example, if the target is on the gesturer's right, (s) he turns the trunk to the right.

Meeting the criteria

Structure	*phasic*
Focus	*in space > on separate object*
Gesture/action space	use of gesture/action space determined by the location of the target
Path	most often **one-dimensional spoke-like** or **two-dimensional arch-like**
Hand orientation	**tips of fingers are oriented toward designated object/subject**
Hand shape	**flat hand with fingers** or **only index** or **thumb extended**; the thumb can be preferred when pointing to a location behind the speaker's back
Effort	**direct space, emphasis on end-point of gesture, bound flow**
Gaze	gesturer tends to fixate the designated object/subject he/she is pointing at
Other criteria	The pointing gesture can be accompanied by words "here", "there".

Differentiate *deictic-external target* from…

- *direction-neutral:* The *direction-neutral* indicates a potentially infinite direction ("upwards, northwards") or the relative position of an external target without the distance information, while *deictic-external target* indicates the relative position and distance. In fact, for targets that are far away and therefore invisible, *direction-neutral* gestures are preferred.

In the *direction–neutral* gesture, the path during complex phase is two-dimensional and arch-like. The hand is relaxed. There is a free flow and acceleration with an end point accent, as if throwing something. Thereby, the image is generated of something moving towards a specific direction. Furthermore, the loose hand shape conveys the impression that the target cannot be located precisely.

In contrast, in *deictic–external space* gestures the hand has a distinct shape often with the index extended, the path during complex phase is one-dimensional and spoke-like and the movement flow is bound. This movement combination enables to precisely indicate a location (which is to be found at the end of the estimated prolongation of the index).

spatial relation–position: In *spatial relation–position* gestures the location is indicated from a mento-heliocentric perspective, i.e., a position is indicated on an imaginary map which is the projection of a mental map into the body-external space ("Imagine a map and on this map, it is there."). In contrast, in *deictic–external target* the location is indicated from an egocentric perspective ("Relative to me, it is there.").

The cognitive perspectives are typically revealed by the hand orientation: In *deictic–external target*, the hand axis, more specifically the index, is oriented sagittal centrifugally from the gesturer's body midline. In *spatial relation–position* gestures if the imaginary map is projected to the horizontal level, the hand axis, more specifically the index, is in line with the vertical axis. If the imaginary map is projected to the frontal level (especially if the gesturer refers to animations presented on a screen as a typical experimental setting), it is more difficult to identify the mento-heliocentric perspective as compared to a projection to the horizontal level, as the hand axis may be the same as for *egocentric deictics* and *directions*. In this case, the gesturers gaze directed to the imaginary map, which is not further away than the length of the arms, helps to identify the target and thereby, the cognitive perspective.

9.4.3.2 deictic–You

Short definition

REFERRING TO THE ADDRESSEE AS A PERSON OR TO A PART OF HER/HIS BODY

Definition

Target: The gesturer points to the addressee to designate him/her as a person (2nd person: You) or to designate a part of the addressee's body.

Movement form: If the gesturer points to the addressee to designate him/her as a person, the finger tips are oriented towards the addressee's sternum or, in a more offensive context, towards the addressee's face. Furthermore, pointing with the index as compared to pointing with all fingers as well as a very direct spoke-like path seem to be more offensive. Pointing with the palm up appears to be more polite, possibly in contexts of offering something. If the gesturer points to a part of the addressee's body, the finger tips are oriented towards that part. The *deictic–You* gesture may include touching the other.

Meeting the criteria

Structure	*phasic*
Focus	*in space, on person*
Gesture/action space	the position of the hand in the gesture space is determined by the addressee's position in the body-external space
Path	one-dimensional spoke-like or two-dimensional arch-like
Hand orientation	**tip of fingers oriented towards the addressee's sternum or body midline or to a part of her/his body**
Hand shape	**flat hand** or **only index extended**
Effort	direct space, emphasis on end-point of gesture
Gaze	gesturer looks at addressee, no fixation of hand
Other criteria	The pointing gesture may be accompanied by the word "You".

9.4.3.3 deictic–self

Short definition

REFERRING TO ONESELF AS A PERSON

Definition

Target: The gesturer refers to her-/himself as a person (1^{rst} person: I).

Movement form: The gesturer points to the sternum without looking at it. In some Asian cultures, there is also pointing to the nose. The pointing may include touching the body. In contrast to other Types of *egocentric deictics*, the gesturer does **not** look at the target (s)he is pointing at, i.e., at the sternum.

Meeting the criteria

Structure	*phasic*
Focus	*in space, on body*
Gesture/action space	hand at level of sternum (or nose)
Path	one-dimensional spoke-like
Hand orientation	**tip of fingers point towards sternum;** longitudinal hand axis (wrist – finger tips) in centripetal orientation to body midline
Hand shape	**flat hand or only index extended**
Effort	direct space, emphasis on end-point of gesture
Gaze	**gesturer does not look at the target (own sternum) but at the addressee**
Other criteria	The pointing gesture may be accompanied by the words "myself", "I", especially when talking about one's personal opinion, feelings, etc. In symbiotic relationships, the linguistic analysis might reveal that the gesturer refers to a person (s)he has a very close relation to.

9.4.3.4 deictic–body

Short definition

REFERRING TO PARTS OF THE OWN BODY OR TO OBJECTS ATTACHED TO THE BODY

Definition

Target: The gesturer designates a part of the own body by pointing to it or by showing it. Or, the gesturer points to or shows an object that is attached to the body, e.g. the finger ring that (s)he is wearing.

Movement form: The hand is extended and the finger tips are oriented toward the designated part of the body (or attached object). The gesturer looks at the designated part of the body. The pointing may include touching the part of the body.

Alternatively, the part of the body is moved into the gesture space in order to designate it, e.g. moving the hand into the gesture space to show the hand or to show a finger ring. The showing of a part of the body is often complemented by a pointing gesture of the other hand, e.g. left hand is presented to the partner and the right hand points at left hand (in that case, one Type unit is coded: *asymmetrical body-deictic*).

Note: laterality and part of the body or attached object that the gesturer points at

Meeting the criteria

Structure	*phasic*
Focus	*on body, on attached object*
Gesture/action space	**near kinesphere**
Path	one-dimensional spoke-like
Hand orientation	**tip of index oriented towards designated part of the body**
Hand shape	**index extended**
Effort	direct space, emphasis on end-point of gesture
Gaze	gesturer looks at the designated part of the body

Differentiate *deictic–body* from…

✐ *deictic–self*: In the *egocentric deictic–self* gesture, the gesturer points to the sternum but does not look at the sternum. In contrast, in a *deictic–body* gesture designating her/his sternum, the gesturer looks at the sternum.

9.4.4 Types of the Function value *egocentric direction*

For egocentric direction gestures, the Type values specify the absence or presence of an agent who executes the direction.9.4.4.1 direction–neutral

Short definition

INDICATING A DIRECTION WITHOUT SPECIFYING AN AGENT

Definition

Agent: The *direction – neutral* gesture contains no information about an agent who would execute the direction or route. Thus, the direction or route is indicated in an agent-neutral manner.

As in all *egocentric direction* gestures, the gesturer is the point of spatial reference for indicating the direction ("[I am here and] it is in that direction") or the route ("[I am here and] it is from there to over there"). (The direction from somewhere towards the gesturer is most often to be found in the Type value *direction – imperative.*)

Movement form: *Direction – neutral* gestures are one- or two-dimensional gestures with a clear direction. They often involve the lower arm or even the whole arm.

(i) a direction from the gesturer towards somewhere: As the gesturer's body is the point of spatial reference for the direction, the gesturing hand is oriented centrifugally from the gesturer's body. The hand embodies the designated direction in the way that at the end of the complex phase, the longitudinal hand axis (from wrist to finger tips) is in line with the designated direction. The impression that there is no precise distance information is generated by the movement dynamics, the gesture space use, and the relaxed hand. The quasi throwing of the relaxed hand in the upper gesture space creates the impression of something far away or open-ended.

(ii) a route from an external target to another external target: The longitudinal hand axis (from wrist to finger tips) runs centrifugally from the gesturer's body. The hand traces the route and the movement flow is bound in order to provide precise information about the route. In case of spatially complex routes, the path during the complex phase can be three-dimensional.

Note: the indicated direction, e.g. backwards

Meeting the criteria

Structure	*phasic*
Focus	*in space*
Gesture/action space	**distinct use of gesture space determined by the designated direction;** often use of the upper gesture at shoulder level or higher
Path	one- or two- dimensional; in depictions of complex routes (where along) also three-dimensional
Hand orientation	longitudinal hand axis in line with **the designated direction;** in route indications hand axis typically orthogonal to traced route
Hand shape	**relaxed flat hand;** in route indications often index extended
Effort	**free flow, hand is often "thrown" in the direction**; in route indications bound flow
Body involvement	**often lower arm or even whole arm**

Gaze	gesturer looks to into the designated direction or at route
Other criteria	The *egocentric direction* gesture can be accompanied by words such as "towards", "upwards", "backwards", "forwards", "sidewards", "to the right", "to the left", "there along" etc.

Differentiate *direction-neutral* from...

- *deictic-external target*: see there
- *spatial relation-route*: In *spatial relation - route* gestures, the route is depicted from a mento-heliocentric perspective, i.e., an imaginary map is projected into the gesture space. In *direction-neutral* gestures, the direction is indicated from an egocentric perspective, i.e., the gesturer him/herself constitutes the point of spatial reference and no imaginary map is created.

The perspectives are typically revealed by the hand orientation: In *direction - neutral* gestures that show a route, the longitudinal hand axis is oriented centrifugally from the gesturer's body midline. In *spatial relation-route,* the longitudinal hand axis is in line with the vertical space axis. If the imaginary map, on which the gesturer looks, is projected to the frontal level (especially if the gesturer refers to animations presented on a screen as a typical experimental setting), it is more difficult to identify the mento-heliocentric perspective as compared to a projection to the horizontal level, as the hand axis may be the same as for *egocentric directions*. In this case, the gesturer's gaze helps to identify the Type: In *spatial relation - route* gestures, the gesturer looks at the imaginary map, which is not further away than the length of the arms, while in *direction - neutral* gestures that show a route, the gaze is typically directed far away.

9.4.4.2 direction-imperative

Short definition

INDICATING TO THE ADDRESSEE TO MOVE (SOMETHING) IN A SPECIFIC DIRECTION

Definition

Agent: The agent is the addressee. S/he is asked to execute the direction. As these gestures often have a suggestive or an imperative tone (e.g. "Move to the left!"), this *egocentric direction* Type value was labelled "imperative". *Direction-imperative* gestures may ask the addressee to move to the respective direction him-/

herself, a part of his/her body, her/his mental state (e.g. to calm down, to cheer up), or something (e.g. to move an object into a specific direction). Coded here are also those gestures that indicate to the addressee not to move in a certain direction, i.e., to stop.

The direction, to which the addressee shall move (something), is indicated from the gesturer's egocentric perspective.

Movement form: *Direction – imperative* gestures are one- or two-dimensional gestures with a clear direction. They often involve the lower arm or even the whole arm. The gesture is conducted in the gesturer's far kinesphere, the arm is extended into the direction of the addressee. The palm (or more rarely the back) of the hand is oriented in the designated direction as if shifting the entity (the addressee, a part of his/her body, her/his mental state, or an object that s/he shall move) with the palm in the direction. The gesturer may display them repeatedly to emphasize his/her demand. Thus, the Structure may be *repetitive.*

Note: the direction or the message of the gesture: [Come] here! [Sit] down! [Calm] down! [Put] it down! [Get] up! [Cheer] up! [Turn] around! [Bring] it out! Stop! No–No! [Go] away! [Move it] away!

Meeting the criteria

Structure	*phasic, repetitive*
Focus	*in space*; only in rare occasions *on person*, if the gesturer actually moves the other into a direction
Gesture/action space	the **arm is extended towards the addressee**; the gesture is conducted in the gesturer's far kinesphere
Path	one- or two-dimensional
Hand orientation	the flat hand is typically orthogonal to the path during complex phase, as if the hand would shift an entity
Hand shape	**relaxed flat hand**
Effort	direct space
Body involvement	often lower arm or even whole arm
Gaze	directed at the addressee or at the object that the addressee shall move

Differentiate *direction–imperative* from…

- *emotion/attitude–rise:* see there
- *emotion/attitude–fall:* see there

- ✎ *direction-self-related:* In *direction-imperative* gestures the hand is extended towards the addressee (far kinesphere), whereas in *direction-self-related* gestures the hand remains close to the gesturer's body (near-middle kinesphere).
- ✎ *pantomime-transitive*: The *direction-imperative* gesture refers to a direction, while the *pantomime-transitive* gesture refers to an action.

The *pantomime-transitive* gesture of throwing something away "I throw something away" may be confused with *direction-imperative* gesture "[Put it] down / Forget it". However, the *pantomime-transitive* gesture is conducted in the middle kinesphere of the gesture space, with a distinct hand shape (e.g. first holding the imaginary object, then letting go), a distinct path during complex phase (spoke- or arch-like), and efforts (strong and quick). The gaze is directed at the imaginary object that is thrown down.

In contrast, the *direction-imperative* 'down' gesture is conducted in the far kinesphere and the arm is extended in the direction of the addressee. The hand is relaxed and there is no distinct hand shape, as the hand does not handle an imaginary object. The movement flow is free, and the gaze is **not** directed at the hand.

- ✎ *emblem*: The *direction-imperative* gesture may be confused with *emblems* that include commands to move to a certain direction. However, *direction-imperative* gesture and *emblem* differ in movement form. As an example, in the *emblem* "Come here!" there is an isolated repetitive flexion of the index. The movement form is distinct, distal, invariable, and conventionalized. In contrast, the *direction-imperative* gesture "Come here!" is a motorically simple, proximally controlled gesture with no hand shaping. Accordingly, the *emblem* 'Come here!' is a more controlled movement, while the *direction-imperative* 'Come here!' is more impulsive.

9.4.4.3 direction-self-related

Short definition

SHOWING THE DIRECTION OF ONESELF'S (BODILY OR MENTAL) MOVEMENT

Definition

Agent: The agent is the gesturer her-/himself. S/he shows the direction that s/he takes or intends to take. The direction can refer to the gesturer's body or mental state.

As an example, a ballet dancer rehearses the directions in her/his choreography by moving the hands (up, to right, forward, etc). Furthermore, the *direction – self-related* gesture may present the directions of bodily processes, e.g. swallowing (down). Or, the gesturer directs the mental state or cognitive processes by performing a self-suggestive gesture, e.g. to calm down, to forget an idea, to bring out an idea. Thus, the *direction – self-related* gesture presents the (intended) direction of the own mental or cognitive processes.

Movement form: *Direction–self-related* gestures are one- or two-dimensional gestures in which the flat hand is moved in a specific direction. The hand is oriented orthogonal to the path during complex phase, i.e., the palm of hand is oriented in the designated direction. The hand acts in the near to middle kinesphere gesture space, i.e., close to the trunk. For mental or cognitive processes the hand may move close to the head. As *direction – self-related* gestures are often autosuggestive, i.e., requiring repeated self-related interventions, the Structure may be *repetitive.*

Note: the direction or the message of the *direction–self-related* gesture, e.g. [I calm] down; [I put] it down (I forget it); [I cheer] up; [I bring] it out!

Meeting the criteria

Structure	*phasic, repetitive*
Focus	*in space >> on body*
Gesture/action space	**hand acts in the near to middle kinesphere, close to the gesturer' trunk, or head.**
Path	one- or two-dimensional, straight or curved, even rotating
Hand orientation	the **flat hand is typically orthogonal to the path during complex phase**
Hand shape	**relaxed flat hand**
Effort	direct space

Differentiate *direction–self-related* from …

- *emotion/attitude–rise:* see there
- *emotion/attitude–fall:* see there
- *emphasis–palm-out:* see there
- *direction–imperative:* see there
- *pantomime–transitive*: The *pantomime–transitive* gesture refers to an action, while the *direction–self-related* gesture refers to a direction.

The *pantomime-transitive* gesture of throwing something away "I throw something away" may be confused with *direction-self-related* gesture "[I put it] down / [I] forget it". The *pantomime-transitive* gesture is presented precisely with regard to hand shape (first holding the imaginary object, then letting go) and efforts (strong and quick). The gaze is directed at the imaginary object that is thrown down. In contrast, in the *direction-self-related* 'down' gesture (e.g. in self-talk: Forget it!) the hand is relaxed and there is no distinct hand shape, as no imaginary object is handled. The gesture is executed with rather free flow, and the gaze is typically **not** directed at the hands.

motion quality-manner: A *motion quality-manner* gesture presents a specific kind of movement which is characterized by a complex within hand repetitive trajectory. It often contains spatial information about a route. The *motion quality-manner* gesture that depicts something rolling may be confused with the *direction-self-related gesture* indicating a circular route (e.g. a circulating hand movement close to the temple to indicate that the gesturer is thinking about something).

However, the *motion quality-manner* gesture is conducted in the central gesture space. Often the manner is presented with a locomotion (e.g. rolling downward), the within hand or wrist trajectory (manner) is superimposed to a displacement of the hand – trajectory (path). In contrast, the *direction-self-related* gesture is performed close to the body and there is no combination of two trajectories.

emblems: *Emblems* have specific hand shapes and they are performed for the addressee. As an example, an *emblem* with a rotation movement is "Let me think about it." It indicates to the addressee that one has to think about something. The gaze is at the addressee. The hand has a distinct shape, often the index and middle finger are extended. It is held at the plane of the temple in the frontal plane, as if the gesturer rotates the thought out of his/her head. In contrast, the *direction-self-related* gesture is a simple movement with a relaxed hand indicating one direction or a rotation. The movement is mainly a wrist movement and the hand is not shaped. The gesturer performs the gesture for him-/herself. The gaze might be casted down.

9.4.5 Types of the Function value *pantomime*

The Type values of the Function value *pantomime* register transitivity versus intransitivity. Transitivity is "characterized by having or containing a direct object < a transitive verb >"; "being or relating to a relation with the property that if the relation holds between a first element and a second and between a second and a third, it holds between the first and third elements < equality is a transitive relation > " (Webster's dictionary). "In syntax, a transitive verb is a verb that requires both a subject and one or more objects. The term is used to contrast intransitive verbs, which do not have objects." (Wikipedia). Accordingly, in NEUROGES® those *pantomimes* are classified as transitive in which the gesturer pretends to either directly act **on** something or **with** something **on** something. The rare cases, in which the gesturer pretends to act **with** something but not **on** something, e.g. waving with a stick, are also coded as transitive.

9.4.5.1 pantomime–intransitive

Short definition

ACTING AS IF WITHOUT AN IMAGINARY OBJECT OR COUNTERPART

Definition

Transitivity: The *pantomime–intransitive* gesture includes no imaginary or real object and counter-part that the gesturer pretends to act with or on, respectively. In NEUROGES®, air and water are not considered as counterparts. Thus, *pantomimes* such as pretending to swim or to fly (like a bird) are coded as *intransitive.* As an example, gesturer moves the arms as if doing a physical exercise such as marching, swimming, sit-ups, etc. The pantomimed action is executed as similar to the actual action as possible.

Movement form: see Function value

Note: Note the type of action that is pantomimed, e.g. flying.

Meeting the criteria

Structure	*phasic, repetitive*
Focus	*in space*
Gesture/action space	**the use of gesture space is typically equivalent to the use of the action space in the action of reference**, e.g. when pretending to march there is use of the lateral gesture space, as in actual marching the arms move on the right and left sides of the trunk
Path	distinct, depends on the action of reference

Hand orientation	The hand adopts the same orientation as in the action of reference. The **hand keeps its natural orientation as a part of gesturer's body**. In rare cases, the hands may be used as if they were the gesturer's feet.
Hand shape	distinct, depends on the action of reference
Effort	distinct, variation in the Effort qualities, depends on the action of reference
Body involvement	involvement of head and trunk or even whole body
Gaze	distinct, depends on the action of reference, typically directed toward the surrounding

Differentiate *pantomime-intransitive* from…

✐ *motion quality-manner*: In *motion quality-manner* gestures the gesturer's hand may represent an object/agent that/who moves, e.g. the index and middle fingers represent two legs (pars pro toto for a human being) walking on a ground. The hands are used as if they were marionettes, i.e., they adopt a function other than being the gesturer's hand. The gesturer's body is not involved in the presentation. In most cases, there is an indirect reference to the ground on which the motion takes place. This ground is typically projected to the horizontal plane.

In contrast, in *pantomime-intransitive* gestures, given the egocentric perspective, the hand remains its function as the gesturer's hand, e.g. in the pantomime of swimming, the arms are extended to the far kinesphere and describe a half circle in the horizontal plane. The whole body, or at least the trunk and head are involved in the demonstration of the movement.

9.4.5.2 pantomime-transitive-active

Short definition

ACTING AS IF WITH AN IMAGINARY (OR REAL) OBJECT OR COUNTERPART

Definition

Transitivity: A *pantomime-transitive* gesture includes an imaginary (or real) object or counterpart that the gesturer pretends to act with/on. The pantomimed action is executed as similar to the actual action as possible. Often, in these *pantomimes*, imaginary tools are used to act on an imaginary counterpart, e.g. the gesturer pretends to act **with** imaginary drumsticks **on** imaginary drums. However, the gesturer can also pretend to act directly, i.e., without an imaginary object, on something, e.g. climbing up a stony mountain.

In special experimental settings, an actual tool may held in the hand or an actual counterpart may be present but the action is only pantomimed, e.g. holding an actual hammer in the hand and pretending to hammer (but not really doing it) on an actual nail. In NEUROGES®, this condition is also coded as *pantomime – transitive.*

Movement form: If the gesturer pretends to act **with** something **on** something, the hand adopts a distinct shape that reveals the form of the object/tool. If the gesturer pretends to act directly with bare hands on something, the hand adopts a distinct shape that reveals the form of the counterpart. In order to represent the imaginary tool or counterpart two Techniques of Presentation (see Supplemetary category) can be used: *enclosure* and *hand-as-object.*

For general information on the movement form of *pantomime* gestures see Function value *pantomime.*

Note: Note the type of action that is demonstrated, e.g. combing the hair.

Meeting the criteria

Structure	*phasic, repetitive*
Focus	*in space > on body*, e.g. pantomiming combing hair
Gesture/action space	**use of gesture space is typically equivalent to the use of the action space in the action of reference**, e.g. when pantomiming brushing teeth, the hand is moved in front of the teeth
Path	distinct, depends on the action of reference
Hand orientation	The hand adopts the same orientation as in the action of reference. The **hand keeps its natural orientation as a part of gesturer's body**. The exception is the *hand-as-object* Technique of Presentation, in which the hand itself becomes the imaginary object.
Hand shape	distinct, depends on the shape of the imaginary object of counterpart; *enclosure* or *hand-as-object*
Body involvement	**involvement of head and trunk or even whole body**
Gaze	often on the hands

Differentiate *pantomime–transitive-active* from…

- ✎ *direction–self-related*: see there
- ✎ *form–shape*: *Form–shape* gestures depict only the form of the object of reference, e.g. what form the hammer has, but **not** on what is done with the object.

In contrast, *pantomime – transitive-active* gestures provide information about the form of the object/counterpart that is acted with/on, but the essential message is how the object is used, e.g. holding the imaginary hammer and hammering with it.

Form–shape gestures are displayed in the central gesture space. There is no variation in the effort qualities, and a variety of Techniques of Presentation can be used to create the image of the form. The body involvement is limited to the hands and arms. In contrast, *pantomime – transitive-active* gestures are characterized a distinct use of gesture space reflecting the action space of the action of reference, by a variation in the Effort factors and by a large body involvement. The Techniques of Form Presentation are limited to *hand-as-object* and *enclosure.*

motion quality–manner: In *motion quality–manner* gestures, the gesturer's hand may represent an object/agent that/who moves, e.g. the index and middle fingers represent two legs (pars pro toto for a human being) walking on a ground. The hands are used as if they were marionettes, i.e., they adopt a function other than being the gesturer's hand. The gesturer's body is not involved in the presentation. In most cases, there is an indirect reference to the ground on which the motion takes place. This ground is typically projected to the horizontal plane.

In contrast, in *pantomime – transitive-active* gestures, given the egocentric perspective, the hand keeps its function as the gesturer's hand and encloses an imaginary object or environment (Technique of Presentation: *enclosure*). The exception is the *hand-as-object* Technique of Presentation, in which the hand itself becomes the imaginary object.

Techniques of Presentation (Supplementary category): see section *Differentiate...* for the Function value *pantomime*

9.4.5.3 pantomime–transitive-passive

Short definition

ACTING AS IF AN IMAGINARY AGENT/OBJECT ACTS ON ONESELF

Definition

Transitivity: The *pantomime – transitive-passive* gesture includes an imaginary agent/object that acts on the gesturer. The gesturer pretends to react to the imaginary agent/object that affects him, e.g. pretending reacting to a pancake flying

into the gesturer's face or being moved away by a gust of wind. As in all *pantomime* Type values, the perspective is egocentric, i.e., the relation between the gesturer and the separate agent/object is presented from an egocentric perspective.
Movement form: Often, the body adopts a distinct shape that reveals the form or quality of the agent/object that is acting on the gesturer. If the hand is used to represent the agent/object, it loses its natural orientation as a part of gesturer's body. Typically the Technique of Presentation *hand-as-object* is chosen.

For general information on the movement form of *pantomime* gestures see Function value *pantomime*.

Note: Note the type of action that is pantomimed, e.g. being hit by something.

Meeting the criteria

Structure	*phasic, repetitive*
Focus	*in space > on body*, e.g. hand representing a stick that hits the body
Gesture/action space	**the use of gesture space is typically equivalent to the use of the action space in the reaction of reference,** e.g. being moved away by a high wave
Path	distinct, depends on the reaction of reference
Hand orientation	The **hand keeps its natural orientation as a part of gesturer's body.** The exception is when the hand is used to represent the agent/object (Technique of Presentation *hand-as-object*.)
Hand shape	see hand orientation
Efforts	distinct, variation in the Effort qualities, depends on the reaction of reference
Body involvement	involvement of head and trunk or even whole body
Gaze	depends on the reaction or reference, typically directed toward the surrounding

Differentiate *pantomime–transitive-passive* from…

- *form–shape*: *Form–shape* gestures depict only the form of the object of reference, e.g. what form the hammer has, but **not** how one is affected by the object. In contrast, *pantomime – transitive-passive* gestures may provide information about the form of the agent/object who/that acts on the gesturer, but the essential message is how the gesturer reacts to the agent/object.

Form–shape gestures are displayed in the central gesture space. There is no variation in the effort qualities, and a variety of Techniques of Presentation can be used to create the image of the form. The body involvement is limited to the hands and arms. In contrast, *pantomime – transitive-passive* gestures are characterized a distinct use of gesture space reflecting the action space of the reaction of reference, by a variation in the Effort factores and by a large body involvement.

9.4.6 Types of the Function value *form presentation*

For *form presentation* gestures, the Type category classifies the geometric aspect of the form that is presented: shape and size.

9.4.6.1 form–shape

Short definition

CREATING A SHAPE

Definition

Geometric aspect: Shape is defined as "any spatial attributes as defined by outline" (Webster's Dictionary). "The shape of an object located in some space is a geometrical description of the part of that space occupied by the object, as determined by its external boundary – abstracting from location and orientation in space, size, and other properties such as color, content, and material composition." (Wikipedia).

In NEUROGES®, gestural shape information is coded with the value *form – shape.* Since size information can be abstracted from shape information, pure gestural size information is coded with the value *form – size*. Information about location and orientation in space is coded with the *spatial relation presentation* values. Some information about content and material (how something feels like, how heavy it is) can be expressed with the *motion quality presentation* values.

Movement form: see Function value *form presentation*; independently of the Technique of Presentation *hand-as-object, enclosure, tracing,* and *palpating,* the resulting still or motion image of a shape is a 2- or 3-dimensional form.

Hierarchy: A *form–shape* gesture may include a *form–size* gesture.

Form–shape > form–size: As defined above for the geometric aspect, the shape is – in the first line – abstracted from the actual size, i.e., the correct shape information does not automatically include the correct size information. As an example, in gesture the sun may depicted by a round shape or a pitched rool by a triangle shape, but the size information would not be correct. However, the *form–shape presentation* **can** include information about the correct size of the object of reference, especially if the size of the object of reference does not extend that of the gesturer's kinesphere, i.e., the reach of his/her arms. In other words, it is likely that for the presentation of the shape of an apple, the shape and the size may match that of a real apple, whereas it is unlikely that a *shape presentation* referring to a roof matches the size of an actual roof. The combination of *form–shape* + *form–size* is coded as *form–shape.*

Specifications: *Form presentation* gestures can be further assessed with the Supplementary categories Technique of Presentation and Referent.

The referent of a *form–shape* gesture may be

(i) *material*: the shape of a concrete object / subject, e.g. a car
(ii) *non-material:* the shape-like quality of an abstract entity, e.g. a perfect round concept

Note: Note or draw the shape.

Meeting the criteria

Structure	*phasic*
Focus	*in space*; only in exceptional cases *on body* or *on separate object*, e.g. the shape is traced on a table or on the leg
Gesture/action space	there is no distinct/creative use of gesture space; a *form–shape* gesture is typically displayed in the quasi "neutral" central gesture space, in front of body midline, middle kinesphere
Path	depends on the Technique of Presentation: in *hand-as-object* and *enclosure* Techniques, there is a static complex phase, i.e., no path; in *tracing*, the path is closed with the start point and end point matching each other in order to establish a contour; in *palpating* often three-dimensional path

Hand orientation	in bimanual *form presentation* gestures with *enclosure* and *palpating*, the palms of the hands are oriented to each other, i.e., towards the center of the imaginary shape
Hand shape	depends on the Technique of Presentation
Efforts	**bound flow, direct space**, no time, no weight, **no variation in the effort factors**
Body involvement	-
Gaze	When referring to concrete objects (Referent: *material*), the gesturer often looks at the hand or at the imaginary shape, respectively.

Differentiate *form-shape* from…

- *form-size*: A *size* gesture only provides information about the size but not about the shape. In contrast, a *shape* gesture may or may not include information about the size. Since for *form – size* gestures only the Techniques of Presentation (ToP) *tracing* and *enclosure* are suitable, difficulties in differentiating between *form – shape* and *form – size* may only arise when these two techniques are used.

If the ToP *tracing* is chosen, in a *form – size* presentation the trace indicating a length is always straight, whereas in a *form – shape* presentation, the trace indicating the contour of a *shape* is often closed. Thus, a one-dimensional path is indicative of a *form-size* gesture, while a two- or three-dimensional path characterizes a *form-shape* gesture.

If the ToP *enclosure* is chosen, the *form-shape* presentation is characterized by a two- dimensional hand shape, e.g. the two- or three-dimensional shape of a form is shown by the empty space between two rounded hands, the palms of which face each other and may or may not touch each other. In contrast, in the *form-size* presentation with *enclosure*, there may some indirect rough reference to the form of an object by the hand shape. If the *size* of broad objects shall be presented, the flat hands may be held straight and parallel to each other. If the size of thin objects shall be presented, only the indices show the size. However, the hands are never rounded nor adopt another complex shape.

9.4.6.2 form–size

Short definition

CREATING A LENGTH

Definition

Geometric aspect: Size is defined as "physical magnitude of something (how big it is)" (Webster's Dictionary). Size does not include information about the shape. **Movement form:** In gesture, a size is indicated by the depiction of a length by a *phasic* one-dimensional gesture. This can be either the height, the width, or the depth of one object. Thus, if the presentation of the size of an area (height and width) is intended, two sequential *phasic* one-dimensional gestures are needed. If the representation of the size of a volume (height, width, depth) is intended, three sequential *phasic* one-dimensional gestures are needed, i.e., representing the height, the width, and the depth of the volume. Depending on whether the height, the width, or the depth shall be presented, the depiction is strictly in the vertical, the horizontal, or the sagittal space axis, i.e., it is not depicted on a cross axis.

In order to create a length, the two Techniques of Presentation (ToP) *enclosure* and *tracing* are suitable.

(i) *enclosure*: In bimanual gestures with the ToP *enclosure*, simultaneously one hand is at one end of the length and the other hand at the other end. If the length refers to an object, as a reflection of the gesturer's mental imagery it might seem as if the object is held between the two hands and the size of the object becomes evident as the two hands mark the two endpoints of the object. Alternatively in unimanual gestures, a length may be presented by using an external point of reference as one end of the length, e.g. the table or the floor, and the hand as the other end. Furthermore, as indicated above, the *form–size* gesture provides no information about the shape of the object but it may include indirect rough information about the second dimension of the object of reference. If the *size* of broad objects shall be presented, the flat hands may be held straight and parallel to each other. If the size of thin objects shall be presented, only the indices show the size. In case of small objects, the size may be indicated by the distance between the index and the thumb of the same hand. Thus, the size presentation may include information about a second dimension of the object of reference.

(ii) *tracing*: In order to emphasize the aspect of the extension of a length, a line may be drawn from one end to the other. The trace is straight (thus, open) and strictly one-dimensional in either the sagittal, or the horizontal, or the vertical dimension.

Specifications: *Form presentation* gestures can be further assessed with the Supplementary categories Technique of Presentation (see 8.4.6) and Referent.

The referent of a *form–size* gesture may be

(i) *material*: the actual size of a concrete subject/object, e.g. indicating the height of a child;
(ii) *non-material*: the size-like quality of an abstract entity, e.g. a great event.

Note: Note the size.

Meeting the criteria

Structure	*phasic*
Focus	*in space*; only in exceptional cases *on body* or *on separate object*, e.g. a length is depicted on a table or on the thigh
Gesture/action space	The length is depicted in the central gesture space, middle kinesphere. In case of a presentation in the vertical or sagittal axis, the presentation is strictly in front of the body midline. In case of a presentation in the horizontal axis, the middle of the length is in front of the body midline. However, if there is reference to the size of a concrete object/subject that normally stands on the ground, e.g. a child, the height may be depicted to the right or left of the gesturer.
Path	depends on the Technique of Presentation: *enclosure*: static complex phase; *tracing*: **one-dimensional** path during complex phase, the one-dimensional path is always **in line with the vertical, the horizontal, or the sagittal axis**, i.e., it is not displayed on a cross axis
Hand orientation	In bimanual gestures, the palms are oriented towards each other, i.e., toward the center of imaginary object. As an exception, when demonstrating a length in the vertical dimension, the lower hand may be with the palm down to present the ground on which the object of reference stands.

Hand shape	When referring to thin objects, the tips of the indices might be used to indicate the size, i.e., the imaginary object is held between the tips of the two indices, whereas for larger objects the extended fingers or straight hand are used.
Efforts	**no variation in the effort factors,** bound flow, direct space, no time, no weight
Body involvement	-
Gaze	When referring to the size of concrete objects (Referent: *material*), the gesturer often looks at the hand(s) or at the presented length, respectively.

Differentiate *form–size* from…

- *form–shape*: see there
- *spatial relation–position*: *Spatial relation–position* gestures in which the spatial relation between **two** different points is presented, have to be differentiated from *form–size* gestures in which the size of **one** object is presented. The difficulty in differentiation can only arise when the ToP *enclosure* is used for the *form – size* gesture. In *spatial relation–position* gestures each hand orients to each position on the mental map. As an example, if the mental map is projected to the horizontal plane, the fingertips are oriented downwards to show the two positions on the map. In contrast, in the *form–size* gesture, the presentation refers only to one object. Therefore, the palms are oriented towards each other in order to enclose the imaginary object.
- *spatial relation–route: Spatial relation–route* gestures in which a route is depicted by tracing have to be differentiated from *form–size* gestures in which a length is depicted by tracing it. *Spatial relation–route* gestures show the spatial relation between to endpoints (from there to there) on an imaginary map, while *form–size* gestures focus on the length of one object, i.e., the space between the endpoints. In *form – size* gestures the path is obligatorily straight and one-dimensional and the length is depicted strictly in either the sagittal, the horizontal, or the vertical axis, which are quasi "neutral" with regards to specific spatial information. In contrast, in *spatial relation–route* gestures the path is often two- or three-dimensional, and there is a distinct use of gesture space with the trace often running in a cross axis.

9.4.7 Types of the Function value *Spatial relation presentation*

For *spatial relation presentation* gestures, the Type category classifies the geometric configuration that is presented: line/curve (*route*) versus point (*position*).

9.4.7.1 spatial relation–route

Short definition

CREATING A SPATIAL ROUTE BY PRODUCING A LINE

Definition

Geometric configuration: A route is defined as "a way or course taken in getting from a starting point to a destination" (Oxford Dictionaries). A route can be depicted as a line or a curve. A line is "a concept which includes, but is not limited to, an infinitely-extended one-dimensional figure with no curvature" and a curve is "an object similar to a line but that need not to be straight" (Wikipedia).

Movement form: In order to create a line or a curve, there is a displacement of the hand in the gesture space. Thus, the most prominent movement feature of *spatial relation–route* gestures is the distinct use of gesture space.

The hand creates a line or a curve with a start point and an endpoint. If a *spatial relation–route* gesture focuses on the change of position, i.e., the end position as being spatially different from the starting position (from where to where), the trace between the start position and the end position is straight. If it focuses on the path between the start and end position (where along), the trace is often curved and spatially complex. As *spatial relation – route* gestures provide no information about motion, there is no variation in the effort qualities. Rather, in order to create a precise outline of the route, the movement flow is bound, there is a direct use of space, and often the index is used to trace the route. The hand can trace with the index a route in an imaginary space or the hand can shift the hand from one position to another in an imaginary space. The shifting can be done by placing the flat hand or the fingertips on the position and then moving the hand.

A direction gesture that is displayed with a mento-heliocentric perspective is also coded as *spatial relation–route*. The gesturer creates an imaginary space with a mento-heliocentric perspective and in this space s/he indicates a direction. As an example, the gesturer creates a map of Cologne, which s/he projects on the horizontal plane, and on this imaginary map s/he shows the direction northwards. The movement form of the (mento-heliocentric) direction gesture is similar to that of an *egocentric direction*, but the body involvement and hand orientation differs. The movement is conducted with the hand only and the finger tips are oriented to the imaginary map, i.e., if the map is projected to the horizontal plane, the finger tips are oriented downwards.

Hierarchy: A *spatial relation–route* gesture may include a *form – shape*, a *form – size*, or/and a *spatial relation – position* presentation, and it may be embedded in a *motion quality – manner* or a *motion quality – dynamics presentation.*

spatial relation–route > form–shape: *Spatial relation–route* gestures, especially those with the Referent *material*, may include information about the form of a route, e.g. the right hand adopts a round shape with fingertips pointing down and then moves up from the right lower to the left upper gesture space without variation in the effort factors (e.g. in order to represent the course of the tunnel in the mountains). Or, the gesture includes information about an object that is displaced in space, e.g. the flat hand is displaced from the left half to the right half of the gesture space (e.g. in order to represent a board that is shifted from the left to the right). The combination of *spatial relation–route* and *form–shape* is coded as *spatial relation–route.*

spatial relation–route > form–size: A *spatial relation–route* gesture may include information about the size of a route, e.g. the tips of index and thumb are held with a distance of 1 cm, oriented downwards like an inverted U, and then the hand is moved in curves (e.g. in order to represent the course of a narrow path in a landscape). The combination of *spatial relation–route* and *form–size* is coded as *spatial relation–route.*

Specifications: *Spatial relation–route* gestures can be further assessed with the Supplementary categories Technique of Presentation, Execution Hemi-Space, Target Location (see all 8.4.7), and Referent.

The Referent of the *spatial relation–route* gesture may be

(i) *material*: route: a concrete trace in space, e.g. a highway in a landscape; a concrete change in position, e.g. the chess figure moving from field a2 to b3; direction: a concrete direction on an imaginary map of Cologne, e.g. northwards, towards the next city Düsseldorf
(ii) *non-material*: route: a temporal course, e.g. a development of person's body weight or the decline of reading abilities in pupils over the years; an ideographic course, e.g. the path to a solution; direction: e.g. the direction of an economic development.

Meeting the criteria

Structure	*phasic*
Focus	*in space*; only in exceptional cases, *on body* or *on separate object*, e.g. the path is traced on a table or on the thigh.
Gesture/action space	**distinct use of gesture space**, i.e., the motion complex phase shows a distinct use of the gesture space, e.g. from frontal near kinesphere to left far kinesphere
Path	**straight or curved path during complex phase**
Hand orientation	The hand orientation reflects the mento-heliocentric perspective. As the imaginary map is typically projected to the horizontal plane, the fingertips are oriented downwards, i.e., the longitudinal **hand axis is line with the vertical space axis**. Only if the map is projected to the frontal plane, the fingertips are oriented forward and the hand axis is in line with the sagittal space axis.
Hand shape	depends on Technique of Presentation
Efforts	bound flow, direct space, no time, no weight, no variation in the effort factors
Body involvement	-
Gaze	Especially if referring to concrete spatial routes, the gesturer looks at the imaginary path or object displacement.

Differentiate *spatial relation-route* from…

- *direction-neutral:* see there
- *form-shape*: see there
- *form-size*: see there
- *motion quality-manner*: In *motion quality-manner* gestures, the manner of motion as evidenced by a repetitive pattern is relevant. Thus, in *motion quality-manner* gestures, there is a repetitive trajectory with or without an additional displacement of the hand, e.g. representing rolling at a place or in locomotion. Furthermore, in *motion quality-manner* gestures with a few exceptions (see 9.4.8.1) there are typically changes in the effort factors.

In contrast, *spatial relation–route* gestures focus on the spatial information about the change of position and the course of a path. The distinct use of gesture space is prominent. Thus, in *spatial relation–route* there is only displacement of the hand, without any repetitive trajectory that is superimposed to the trajectory and without any change in the effort factors.

- *motion quality–dynamics*: In *motion quality–dynamics*, the emphasis of the presentation is on the dynamics. Thus, there is a distinct variation of the effort factors. If there is a direction of the motion, it is always intrinsic to the dynamics, e.g. the presentation of heaviness is associated with a downward motion. In contrast, in *spatial relation–route* only the spatial information is relevant and there is a distinct use of gesture space with a straight or a curved path.
- *spatial relation–position*: A *spatial relation – route* gesture may be confused with a *spatial relation–position* gesture in which two different positions are presented. However, in *spatial relation–position* there is a partial retraction between the creations of the two positions, e.g. hand moves to the left gesture space (preparation 1), indicates a position there (complex phase 1), partially retracts (partial retraction 1), and then moves to the right gesture space (preparation 2) and indicates a position there (complex phase 2). Thus, the creations of the two positions constitute two complex phases and the Structure value is *repetitive.* In contrast, in *spatial relation–route* gestures, there is direct trajectory between the two positions. This trajectory constitutes the complex phase.

9.4.7.2 spatial relation–position

Short definition

CREATING A SPATIAL POSITION BY SETTING A POINT RELATIVE TO ANOTHER ONE

Definition

Geometric configuration: A position "… represents the position of a point … in space in relation to an arbitrary reference origin". A point is "an entity that has a location in space or on a plane, but has no extent" (Wikipedia). As a spatial position is defined by its relation to another one, at least two points in space need to be presented in gesture. Therefore, the *spatial relation–position* gesture presents two or more points relative to each other.

Movement form: The most prominent movement feature of *position* gestures is the distinct use of gesture space. In order to create a spatial position, the hand can mark a position on an imaginary map or in an imaginary space, which is created into the gesture space. The marking can be done by placing the flat hand or the fingertips on the position or by making an imaginary sign (dot or cross) at that position. Alternatively, the hand points to a specific position on the imaginary map (*mento-heliocentric deictic*).

Hierarchy: A *spatial relation–position* gesture may include a *form – shape* or a *form – size* presentation, and it may be embedded in a *motion quality – manner* or a *motion quality – dynamics presentation.*

spatial relation–position > form–shape: A *spatial relation–position* gesture, especially those with the Supplementary category Referent value *material*, may include information about the form of an object, e.g. in the right gesture space the right hand adopts the shape of a reversed V (e.g. to represent a house with a pointed roof located in the east of the city) and in the left gesture space the left flat hand is held parallel to the floor (e.g. to represent a supermarket with a flat roof located in the west of the city). The combination of *spatial relation–position* and *form–shape* is always coded as *spatial relation–position.*

spatial relation–position > form–size: A *spatial relation–position* gesture may include information about the size of an object. As an example, in the right gesture space the flat right hand is held with palm down 10 cm above the table and in the left gesture space further away from the body the flat left hand is held palm down 30 cm above the table (e.g. to present the different heights of two buildings in different parts of the city). The combination of *spatial relation–position* and *form–size* is always coded as *spatial relation–position.*

Specifications: *Spatial relation–position* gestures can be further assessed with the Supplementary categories Technique of Presentation, Execution Hemi-Space, Target Location (see all 8.4.7), and Referent.

The Referent of a *spatial relation–position* gesture may be

(i) *material:* e.g. the position of a church… and that of a supermarket;
(ii) *non-material:* e.g. temporal positions, such as in the past… and in the future; political positions, such as the right-wing political party…. and the left-wing political party; positions reflecting the sequence of thoughts, e.g. “You start with the vocabulary (position gesture 1), then you learn the grammar (position gesture 2), then you translate (position gesture 3) “. In the ‘turning’ gesture, a palm-out with a complex phase hold is followed by a pronation with a complex phase hold. In the supination complex phase

hold, there is a presentation of a thought as/on the palm, while in the pronation complex phase hold there is a presentation of the other side of a thought by showing the back of the hand. The meaning emerges: "So–so". Thus, two positions and aspects, respectively, are opposed to each other.

Meeting the criteria

Structure	*phasic*, typically only in bimanual units; *repetitive*, in bimanual but also in unimanual units. In the latter case, there is a sequential presentation of the two locations ("here….and there")
Focus	*in space*; only in exceptional cases, *on body* or *on separate object*, e.g. the position is marked on a table or on the thigh
Gesture/action space	**distinct use of the gesture space**, i.e., the complex phases are displayed at specific locations in the gesture space, e.g. right upper gesture space and right lower space
Path	static complex phase
Hand orientation	The hand orientation reflects the mento-heliocentric perspective. If an imaginary map is projected to the horizontal plane, the fingertips are oriented downward, the **longitudinal hand axis is line with the vertical space axis**. Only if the map is projected to the frontal plane, the fingertips are oriented forward and the hand axis is in line with the sagittal axis.
Hand shape	depends on Technique of Presentation
Efforts	end-point accent to emphasize the position, otherwise no variation in the effort factors
Body involvement	-
Gaze	When referring to concrete spatial locations (Referent: *material*), the gesturer looks at the hand(s), i.e., more specifically, at the designated position(s) on the imaginary spatial map.

Differentiate *spatial relation–position* from…

✎ *deictic–external target*: see there
✎ *form–shape*: see there

✐ *form–size:* see there
✐ *spatial relation–route:* see there

9.4.8 Types of the Function value *Motion Quality Presentation*

For *motion quality presentation* gestures, the Type category classifies the quality that is presented: *manner* or *dynamics.*

9.4.8.1 motion quality–manner

Short definition

PRESENTING A SPECIFIC TYPE OF MOVEMENT

Definition

Quality: The hand presents a specific type of movement, e.g. displaying a pulsating or rotating movement. The manner of movement can be typically defined by a verb, e.g. to roll, to jump, etc.

Movement form: The Structure of a *motion quality–manner presentation* is obligatorily *repetitive.* The movement type is presented by a specific within-hand/wrist trajectory, e.g. the hand repetitively opens and closes or the hand repetitively rotates in the wrist. The repetitive trajectory is often accompanied by a parallel variation in the effort factors, e.g. accelerating in the down-phase of the circle and decelerating in the up-phase of the circle. The only exception in which there is no variation in the effort factors is the intentional representation of monotonous motion, e.g. representing gear transmission. In this case, special emphasis in gestural expression is put on the invariance of the effort factors.

In case of the representation of a stationary movement, there is no displacement of the hand in the gesture space. As an example, the hand remains at the same place in the gesture space while opening and closing repetitively. In case of the representation of loco-motion, the repetitive within-hand/wrist trajectory is superimposed to a displacement trajectory, e.g. the hand is displaced in the gesture space while opening and closing repetitively.

Hierarchy: A *motion quality – manner presentation* may include *form – shape, form – size, spatial relation – route, spatial relation – position* and *motion quality–dynamics presentations,* or combinations of these presentations.

motion quality–manner > form–shape: A *motion quality–manner presentation* may include *form–shape* information about the object/subject that/who moves, e.g. the hand represents a jellyfish (Technique of Presentation ToP: *hand-as-object)* that contracts and expands, or the index and middle finger represent two legs (ToP: *hand-as-object*) that walk, or the two hands shape around an imaginary ball (ToP: *enclosure)* that bumps up and down.

motion quality–manner > form–size: A *motion quality–manner presentation* may include *form–size* information about the object/subject that/who moves, e.g. the hand depicts a size by the distance between thumb and index and moves up and down to represent an object of a certain size (ToP: *enclosure*) that is bouncing.

motion quality–manner > spatial relation–route: A *motion quality–manner presentation* often includes route information, e.g. a manner of movement is depicted on a path from the upper right to the lower left gesture space representing something rolling down a hill.

(If the **mere** presentation of locomotion is intended, the direction that the presented object takes relative to itself (forward, sideward, backward) is depicted. The spatial relation of the object to other positions is not relevant, i.e., the gesturer does not create spatial surroundings when presenting the manner of movement. In this case, the movement is typically depicted on a one-dimensional path on a main space axis, i.e., in the sagittal space axis in front of the body midline (to represent the general concept of forward and backward), in the horizontal space axis (to represent the general concept of sideward), or on the vertical space axis (to represent the concept of up and down).

motion quality–manner > spatial relation–position: A *motion quality–manner presentation* may include position information, e.g. the *manner* gesture is displayed at a specific position in the gesture space in order to represent a stationary movement at a specific location in an imaginary space, e.g. something bouncing on a roof.

motion quality–manner > motion quality–dynamics: A *motion quality–manner presentation* often includes dynamics, e.g. rolling fast, jumping heavily.

motion quality–manner > form – shape or *size + spatial relation – route or position + motion quality–dynamics:* A *motion quality–manner presentation* may include *form–shape* or *size, spatial relation–route* or *position,* and *motion quality–dynamics* information.

While these combinations are all coded as *motion quality – manner*, the included *form* information can be coded with the Supplementary category Technique of Presentation, the included *spatial relation* information with the Supplementary categories Target Location and Execution Hemi-Space, and the included dynamics information with the Supplementary category Efforts.

Referent: The Referent of the *motion quality–manner* gesture may be

(i) *material*: a concrete physical movement, e.g. rolling;

(ii) *non-material*: an abstract movement, i.e., more precisely, the translation of a manner of movement that is originally displayed by a physical object/subject onto an abstract entity, e.g. a revolution starts to get rolling.

Note: Note the manner of movement that is represented, e.g. rolling.

Meeting the criteria

Structure	***repetitive* only**
Focus	*in space*; only in exceptional cases *on body* or *on separate object*
Gesture/action space	If a *manner* of loco-motion is represented, there is a distinct use of gesture space.
Path	A *manner* of movement is characterized by a specific repetitive trajectory during complex phase, e.g. a circular trajectory to depict rolling, an up-down trajectory to depict jumping. If the manner is presented as locomotion, e.g. rolling forward, there is an additional displacement trajectory of the hand.
Hand orientation	If the *motion quality-manner* gesture includes form or spatial relation information on what moves where, a specific hand orientation is adopted.
Hand shape	If the *motion quality-manner* gesture includes form information, a specific hand shape is adopted.
Efforts	The repetitive trajectory is often accompanied by a parallel variation in the effort factors, e.g. an up-down trajectory to depict bouncing with a heavy down phase and a light up-phase.
Body involvement	-
Gaze	If the manner of movement of a concrete object (Referent: *material*) is presented, the gaze is directed at the hand.

Differentiate *motion quality-manner* from…

✐ *direction-self-related*: see there
✐ *pantomime-transitive*: see there
✐ *spatial relation-route*: see there

✎ *motion quality–dynamics:* A *motion quality–manner presentation* typically has a *repetitive* Structure, whereas a *motion quality–dynamics presentation* has a *phasic* Structure. In *motion quality – dynamics* the variation in effort qualities is essential and in *motion quality – manner* the repetitive trajectory.

9.4.8.2 motion quality–dynamics

Short definition

PRESENTING A SPECIFIC DYNAMICS OF MOVEMENT

Definition

Quality: Dynamics is defined by a variation in the Effort factors (see 4.3 and 11). The depiction of a dynamic quality is the primary function of *motion quality–dynamics* gestures. The dynamics of movement can be typically defined by an adverb, e.g. light, free, sustained, rigid etc. The *motion quality–dynamics* gesture can also refer to tactile or sensory experiences, e.g. how something feels like. In this case, the gesturer transforms tactile and sensory impressions into movement dynamics, e.g. the tactile experience of a soft surface is presented by the movement dynamics when stroking along it. These impressions can be typically defined by an adjective.

Movement form: The variation of the Effort qualities is the core movement feature of the value *motion quality–dynamics*. The distinct gestural depiction of dynamics in a *motion quality–dynamics presentation* is characterized by the fact that the gestural dynamics differ from the gesturer's baseline movement dynamics. Each gesturer has his/her personal style, e.g. one gesturer may have a rather free movement flow in his/her gestures, while the gestural behavior of another gesturer is characterized by directness. As a rule, the distinct presentation of a specific movement dynamics, which is registered by the value *motion quality–dynamics*, differs from the gesturer's personal pattern of effort quality use.

To some kinds of dynamics a specific direction of the movement is intrinsic, e.g. the dynamics of exploding (effort qualities: strong, sudden, direct) is associated with an outward motion. Or, the depiction of heaviness is associated with a downward motion, while the depiction of lightness implies an upward motion.

Hierarchy: A *motion quality – dynamics presentation* may include *form – shape, form – size, spatial relation – route, spatial relation – position,* or combinations of these presentations.

motion quality-dynamics > form-shape: A *motion quality-dynamics presentation* may include *form-shape* information about the object/subject that/who moves or that is touched, e.g. the hand is formed to a fist and moves downward heavily to represent a ball (ToP: *hand-as-object*) falling down heavily, or the hand strokes tenderly along an imaginary flat object (ToP: palpating) to represent the softness of a fur.

motion quality-dynamics > form-size: A *motion quality-dynamics presentation* may include *form-size* information about the object/subject that/who moves, e.g. the hand shows a size by the distance between thumb and index and is moved up and out with strong, quick, and direct dynamics to represent an object of a certain size (ToP: *enclosure*) that is part of an explosion.

motion quality-dynamics > spatial relation-route: A *motion quality-dynamics* presentation often includes route information, e.g. a quick strong movement is depicted on a path from the upper right to the lower left gesture space representing something crashing down a hill. Given physical laws, a specific direction or route may imply a dynamics, i.e., the dynamics are induced by the route itself, e.g. getting faster on downward routes. On the other hand, the depiction of a specific dynamics may imply a direction in space, e.g. the depiction of heaviness implies a downward direction.

motion quality-dynamics > spatial relation-position: A *motion quality-dynamics presentation* may include position information, e.g. the *manner* gesture is displayed at specific position in the gesture space to represent how something feels like that is at a specific location in an imaginary space.

motion quality-dynamics > form – shape or *size + spatial relation – route or position:* A *motion quality-dynamics presentation* may include *form-shape* or *size* and *spatial relation-route* or *position* information.

While these combinations are all coded as *motion quality – dynamics*, the included form information can be coded with the Supplementary category Technique of Presentation and the included spatial relation information with the Supplementary categories Target Location and Execution Hemi-Space.

Referent: The Referent of the *motion quality-dynamics* gesture may be

(i) *material*: a concrete physical movement, e.g. an explosion of a volcano, a feather in the air; a concrete somatosensory quality, e.g. how a rough or gravely surface feels like
(ii) *non-material*: an abstract movement, i.e., more precisely, the translation of a quality of movement that is originally displayed by a physical object/subject onto an abstract entity, e.g. an explosive dispute.

Meeting the criteria

Structure	*phasic*
Focus	*in space;* only in exceptional cases *on body* or *on separate object*
Gesture/action space	If the dynamics takes a certain direction or occurs on a route, e.g. rushing down, or at a certain position in an imaginary space, there is a distinct use of gesture space.
Path	There is a path during the complex phase.
Hand orientation	If the *motion quality–dynamics* gesture includes form or spatial relation information, there is a specific hand orientation.
Hand shape	If the *motion quality–dynamics* gesture includes form information, a specific hand shape is adopted.
Efforts	The variation of the effort factors is the core movement feature of *motion quality–dynamics.*
Body involvement	-
Gaze	If the dynamics refer to a concrete object (Referent: *material*), the gaze is directed at the hand.

Differentiate *motion quality–dynamics* from…

✎ *spatial relation–route*: see there
✎ *motion quality–manner*: see there

9.4.9 Specific emblems and social conventions

Since there is a large number of *emblems* and *social conventions,* which furthermore differ between cultures and sub-cultures, it is not possible to list them in the NEUROGES®-template. Given the (sub)cultural differences in the use of *emblems,* it is recommended that based on the criteria defined for the Function value *emblem / social convention* (8.4.11) each research group sets up its own list of *emblems* and *social conventions*. Technically, when coding with the NEUROGES®-template, based on this list the name of the specific *emblem* or *social convention* is noted in the tier Notes.

Tab. 12: Specific *emblems* used in a population in the Western part of Germany

Proposed Name	Movement form	Meaning
Crazy	Tapping or rotating the finger on the temple	To indicate that someone is crazy / nuts
Wagging	Wagging one's finger at the addressee	"Be careful!" (angrily)
Throwing a kiss	Kissing the palmar fingers of one hand and then blowing the kiss towards the conversational partner	Showing sympathy, fondness or affection for someone
Hitchhiking	Extending the thumb from the fist and pointing it up or away from the body	Signing that you want to hitchhike
Peace- or Victory-sign	Forming a V-shape with the middle- and the index-finger with the palm oriented towards the addressee	Signing Victory or Peace
OK-sign	Forming a ring with the thumb and the index-finger	Indicating that something is alright, understood, good, or accepted
Keep one's fingers crossed	Crossing the index- and the middle finger of the same hand	To wish someone good luck
Crossed fingers	Crossing the index- and the middle finger of the same hand (unseen by the conversational partner)	Cancel a promise or statement
The fingers' cross	Forming a cross with the index-fingers of both hands	Indicating refusal
The eyelid pull	Pulling down the eyelid with the index-finger	Indicating to the addressee that you do not believe him (lack of credibility)
The forearm jerk	Clenching a fist, knocking the other fist into the crook of the arm and lifting the clenched fist upwards	"Fuck you!"
Thumbs up	Forming a fist with the thumb raised upwards (also possible with both hands)	Indicating that something is good
Thumbs down	Forming a fist with the thumb pointing downwards (also possible with both hands)	Indicating that something is bad

(*continued on next page*)

Tab. 12: Continued

Proposed Name	Movement form	Meaning
Showing the watch	Tapping on (or only looking at) the plantar side wrist, where a wristwatch is usually worn	Indicating that someone should hurry up "You are late!" "Keep track of the time!"
Shrug	Isolated shrugging of the shoulders, no accompanying facial or postural movement	I do not know
Counting with one's fingers	The emblem is typically performed unimanually.), in Germany by stretching out one after the other the thumb, index, middle, ring, and little finger. In Anglophone countries the index is extended, then the middle, ring, little finger, and finally the thumb In contrast, counting on the fingers of the other hand is used more ideographically.	Signs for the numbers 1-10
Loser-sign	Forming an L with the right hand and placing it in front of the forehead	Showing someone that (s)he is a loser
To press one's thumbs	Forming a fist (with the thumb inside or outside) in front of the chest and pressing the fingers together	To wish someone good luck
The silent fox	Pressing thumb, middle and ring finger on each other while extending the index and little finger upwards	Keep your mouth shut and your ears perked
To give someone the finger	Raising the middle finger out of the fist with the back of the hand facing the conversational partner (also possible with the little finger)	"Fuck you!"
Silence sign	Placing the index-finger vertically on the (open) lips	Indicate to keep the mouth shut / to be silent
The swear	Raise the index and middle finger / the palm of the hand closed together above shoulder height (often combined with placing the right hand on the heart / the bible)	To swear

Time-out sign	Forming a T with both flat hands	To ask for a break
Malice	Brushing the right index-finger along the extended left index finger	To be malicious Shame on you! So there!
Stop sign	Extending the palm of the hand in front of the body	Stop!
The fingers hook	Hooking the index fingers of both hands into each other and pulling in opposite directions	Indicating a strong bond / relationship
Showing a fool's nose	Placing the thumb of one hand at the nose and wagging the fingers / With both hands	To tease someone; Showing someone a fool's nose
Raising the index	Raising the index above the head	Indicating that one wants to say something
Showing fool's ears / elephant ears	Placing the thumbs at the temples / the ears and wagging the fingers	To tease someone, Showing someone is a fool
Pulling the earlobe	Pulling down the earlobe with the thumb and the index-finger towards the conversational partner	"What did you say?" "Speak louder!"
Strain one's ears	Cupping one ear in one hand towards the addressee	To strain ones ears "Tell me!" "Speak louder!" "What did you say?"
Expensive!	Rubbing thumb, index and middle finger	Indicating that something is expensive
Craziness	Waving the hand with spread fingers and the palm in front of the face	Indicating that a person is crazy
Snobbishness	Lifting the nose with the plantar side of the index finger	Indicating that a person is a snob
Gossip	Making the shape and motion of a talking mouth	Indicating that a person is a blabber mouth / gossiping Not believing what a person says
Sneaking	Making a small circular motion with the wrist next to the hip	Sign for sneaking / stealing

(*continued on next page*)

Tab. 12: Continued

Proposed Name	Movement form	Meaning
Long beard	Imitating to complex phase a very long beard underneath the chin	"I do not believe you"
Talking to the hand	Extending the palm of the hand in front of the body and averting one's face away from the conversational partner	"Do not talk to me!"
Exploding throat	Placing the cupped hand in front of the throat and making a rocking motion with the hand	"I could explode with anger!" "I am sick and tired of it!"
Getting the idea	Tapping the tip of the index finger on the forehead and then into the air	I have an idea! Now I understood!
Requital	Curling the index finger repeatedly towards oneself (the arm is extended forward) Not be confused with the *direction–imperative*, a rough proximal gesture.	Come here! (angrily)
Twiddle one's thumbs	Folding the hands and circling the thumbs around each other	Indicating boredom Waiting for something
To the heart	Putting the fist on one's chest	"Upon my honour"
Watch out!	Raising the extended index finger up to the level of the head	"Attention, please"
Blockhead	Knocking the palm at the forehead	"I am / You are a blockhead
Pride	Knocking the fist at the chest	Indicating that one is proud of himself
Quotation marks	A word or a short phrase is accompanied by gestural quotation marks	Citing someone and giving an ironical connotation to the verbal statement

Tab. 13: Specific *social conventions* used in a population in the Western part of Germany

Proposed Name	**Movement form**	**Meaning**
Military salute	Placing the radial side of the index finger of the extended hand at the temple	Military greeting
High five	Two persons batter their right hands at the level of their heads	Greeting; Indicating that something went well
Shake hands	Interactive: The conversational partners grab each others right hand and shake it	Greeting; Confirming a contract
Lift the hat	To lift the hat from the head with one hand	Greeting
Clapping one's hands	Clapping both (flat) palms repeatedly onto each other	Applauding
Salute	Raising two fingers at the temples and then away from the forehead	Indicating that a command is understood
Knocking on wood	Knocking three times on wood or the head	Wishing someone good luck
University applause	Knocking on the table	Applauding

The tables below provide the most common *emblems* and *social conventions* in the Western part of Germany. The compilation is based on a pilot study by Michaela Klüh from 2011.

9.5 Procedure for Step 7 / Module III in NEUROGES®-ELAN

The 'to-be-coded' Type units are simply generated by copying the Function units.

9.5.1 Generation of the 'to-be-coded' Type units

Open the eaf file with the Function units (Step 6 / Module III), then proceed as follows:

Apply the function: Tier > Copy Tier.

Select a tier to copy: click on bh_Function_RX.

Next.

Select the new parent tier: skip this step.

Next.

Select another linguistic type: click on Type.

Finish.

Apply the function: Tier > Copy Tier.

Select a tier to copy: click on rh_Function_RX.

Next.

Select the new parent tier: skip this step.

Next.

Select another linguistic type: click on Type.

Finish.

Apply the function: Tier > Copy Tier.

Select a tier to copy: click on lh_Function_RX.

Next.

Select the new parent tier: skip this step.

Next.

Select another linguistic type: click on Type.

Finish.

When the three operations are finished,

apply the function: Tier > Change Tier Attributes.

Scroll down in the list to the end:

Click on bh_Function_R0-cp.

Enter the Tier Name: bh_Type_RX ('RX' = your initials).

Enter the Annotator: your name.

Enter the Participant: the identification of the person whom you are going to code.

Change.

Click on rh_Function_R0-cp.

Enter the Tier Name: rh_Type_RX.

Enter the Annotator: your name.

Enter the Participant: the identification of the person whom you are going to code.

Change.

Click on lh_Function_R0-cp.

Enter the Tier Name: lh_Type_RX.

Enter the Annotator: your name.

Enter the Participant: the identification of the person whom you are going to code.

Change.

Close.

Now, you have the following new tiers:

bh_Type_RX

rh_Type_RX

lh_Type_RX.

9.5.2 Coding the 'to-be-coded' Type units

The units on the tiers bh_Type_RX, rh_Type_RX, lh_Type_RX are now taken as the basis for the coding of the Type category (therefore, they are termed 'to-be-coded' Type units). The units still have the copied Function values. The Function value determines the choice of Type values (see Fig. 11).

When coding the units of the tiers bh_Type_RX, rh_Type_RX, and lh_Type_RX, proceed chronologically, i.e., code the units in the order of their occurrence, e.g. rh unit, lh unit, bh unit, bh unit, rh unit, etc.

If a Type value changes within a 'to-be-coded' Type unit, replace the old unit by the new subunits (compare 4.2).

The Type assessment is not conducted for 'to-be-coded' Type units with the Function values *object-oriented action, subject-oriented action,* and *emblem/social convention.* Thus, these units are not re-coded with Type values but they are kept as they are in order to potentially serve as a basis for the generation of the 'to-be-coded' units for the Supplementary category assessment.

9.5.3 Alternative procedure: Manual generation of 'to-be-coded' Type units

If you start with the Type category, i.e., you have not assessed Modules I and II and the Function category before, use the alternative procedure of manual unit generation. In this procedure, the tiers bh_Type_R0, rh_Type_R0, and lh_Type_R0 are used that are provided in the template. If you intend to analyze foot gestures, head gestures, and trunk gestures as well, please generate the tiers yourself. Then directly tag all gestures according to the definition given in 9.2.2. For the limbs, the units have to be differentiated as unilateral right, unilateral left, and bilateral. Unimanual limb units are units in which one limb moves while the other limb rests. Bimanual units are units in which both limbs move simultaneously (compare the definitions given in III). The bilateral units should first be classified with the Formal Relation values (see 8.5.3). The 'to-be-coded' Type units are assessed according to the rules described in 9.5.2.

V Supplementary categories

The Supplementary categories offer an advanced examination of specific topics: Technique of Presentation, Efforts, Temporal Structure, Target Hemi-Space, Execution Hemi-Space, Referent, and Trigger/Motive. These categories differ from the main categories Activation, Structure, Focus, Contact, Formal Relation, Function and Type, as they are not part of the proper assessment algorithm but they constitute an additional assessment for specific main values. Furthermore, since the Supplementary categories deal with highly specific topics, thus far, they have only been employed in few empirical studies (e.g. Lausberg & Kita, 2002; Lausberg & Kita, 2003; Lausberg et al., 2003; Densing et al., 2017) and therefore,–in contrast to the main categories–no substantial data on reliability and validity are yet available. Thus, researchers who apply these categories have to thoroughly test the interrater agreement.

The Supplementary categories serve to specify certain main values. For some main values several Supplementary categories can be applied, e.g. for the Function value *motion presentation* the categories Technique of Presentation, Target Hemi-Space, Execution Hemi-Space, Techniques of Presentation, and Referent. Obviously, the choice of a Supplementary category depends on the research question. Technically in NEUROGES®-ELAN, the units of the main values that shall be submitted to the supplementary assessment are copied to the new tier that is linked with the Linguistic Type of the Supplementary category (same procedure as for the main categories, see the sections Procedures in NEUROGES®-ELAN in the chapters on the main categories).

10 Supplementary category Technique of Presentation

10.1 Definition of the category Technique of Presentation

The Supplementary category Technique of Presentation refers to the gestural techniques that are used to present information about a form: *tracing, palpating, enclosure,* or *hand-as-object.*

10.2 Selection of units for the Technique of Presentation assessment

The category Techniques of Presentation is applied to the Function value *form presentation* and the Type values *form–shape* and *form–size,* respectively (primary form values).

If the Function values *pantomime, spatial relation presentation, motion quality presentation,* or the respective Type values *pantomime–transitive-active, pantomime–transitive-passive, spatial relation–position, spatial relation–route motion quality–manner,* and *motion quality–dynamics* contain information about the shape or the size of an object (secondary form values), the Techniques of Presentation can be applied also to these Function and Type values. However, only the Techniques of Presentation *hand-as-object* and *enclosure,* in which information about a shape or a size is conveyed by a static technique, i.e., a static hand shape, can be used for the presentation of form information in *pantomime–transitive-active, pantomime–transitive-passive, motion quality–manner,* and *motion quality–dynamics presentations.* In other words, if the Technique of Presentation per se is already dynamic as in *tracing* and *palpating,* it cannot be combined with a (dynamic) *pantomime* or *motion quality presentation,* e.g. if the hand is *tracing* the shape of an object it cannot – at the same time – present a manner of motion. In contrast, if the hand embodies an object (*hand-as-object*) it can, in addition, present a manner of motion. Tab. 14 shows the Techniques of Presentation for primary and secondary form values.

If there is a change of the Technique of Presentation within a unit, which had been adopted from the Function or Type category coding, then the Technique of Presentation change demarcates subunits.

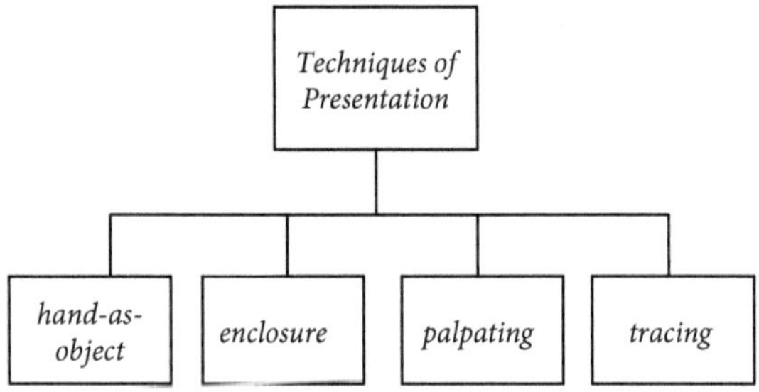

Fig. 12: Values of the category Technique of Presentation

Differentiate the Supplementary category Techniques of Presentation from…

- Type value *pantomime–transitive*: Techniques of Presentation serve to present a form, i.e., the gestural message is "This is a square" or "Here is round shape". They do **not** have a pantomiming function, i.e., the gestural message is **not** "I am tracing" or "I am palpating". Techniques of Presentation are **not** displayed with dynamics (variations in the effort factors), as the emphasis is on the presented image. In contrast, the corresponding *pantomime–transitive* gestures such palpating, embracing, or positioning are displayed with dynamics as the emphasis is on the action per se. As an example, the *pantomime–transitive* positioning could be performed with light and sustained effort qualities as if placing something precious on a table. Or, it could be performed with strong and direct effort qualities as if throwing something on the floor (The differentiation should have already been made in the Function or Type category assessment. However, for didactical purposes the differentiation is reported here again).

10.3 Definitions of the Techniques of Presentation values

10.3.1 *hand-as-object*

Short definition

EMBODIMENT OF AN IMAGINARY OBJECT

Definition

The shape of the imaginary object is embodied by the hand. Therefore, this technique is characterized by a very distinct hand shape. The hand adopts the shape of the object of reference. The hand may not only provide information about the shape but also on a very basic level about the content of the object (solid versus

Tab. 14: Techniques of Presentation used to present a form in different Type values

Type value	Techniques of Presentation
form–size	*enclosure* of an imaginary object by indicating the endpoints in one dimension
	tracing the length of an imaginary object
form–shape	*hand-as-object* embodiment of the imaginary object (and thereby revealing the shape)
	enclosure of an imaginary object
	tracing the contour of an imaginary object
	palpating an imaginary object
*pantomime – transitive-active**	manipulating an imaginary object embodied by the hand (*hand-as-object)*
	manipulating an imaginary object presented by *enclosure*
*pantomime – transitive-passive**	reacting to an imaginary object embodied by the hand (*hand-as-object)*
	reacting to an imaginary object presented by *enclosure*
*motion quality – manner**	*hand-as-object* moves in a specific manner
	imaginary object presented by *enclosure* moves in a specific manner
*motion quality–dynamics**	*hand-as-object* moves with a specific dynamics
	imaginary object presented by *enclosure* moves with a specific dynamics
*spatial relation – position**	*hand-as-object* at a specific position
	enclosure of an imaginary object at a specific position
	tracing a contour of an imaginary object at a specific position
	palpating an imaginary object at a specific position
*spatial relation – route**	*hand-as-object* moves on an imaginary route
	enclosure of an imaginary object that moves on an imaginary route
	palpating an imaginary route

* The Technique of Presentation is assessed if the value in includes size or shape information.

vacuum), e.g. making a fist to present a round, solid object or forming a whole to present a round object with a vacuum. Furthermore, the hand may not only represent the shape of an object but also of an agent, e.g. index and middle finger with tips down re-present legs (the legs being a pars pro toto for a human being). In the rare case of the hand embodying an agent make a note: hand-as-agent.

Hand-as-object is a static Technique of Presentation, i.e., the hand becomes a static sculpture in order and presents a still image of a form (see 8.4.6). Thus, the complex phase is a static complex phase. As *hand-as-object* is a static Technique of Presentation, it can be combined with all Function and Type values that include primary and secondary form information.

Function values

primary: *form presentation*

secondary (i.e., that include a *form presentation*): *pantomime, spatial relation presentation*, and *motion quality presentation*

Type values

primary: *form-shape*

secondary: *pantomime–transitive-active, pantomime–transitive-passive, spatial relation–position, spatial relation–route, motion quality–manner*, and *motion quality–dynamics presentations*

Examples for *hand-as-object* in primary and secondary form values

- *form-shape:* The hand adopts the shape of the object of reference, e.g. index and middle finger are extended and spread out to present the shape of a V, or thumb and index form the shape of a ring.
- *motion quality–manner:* In *motion quality – manner,* the hand may embody either an object or an agent. The hand may embody a passive object in motion, e.g. a ball that bumps up down (hand adopts a round shape and displays the up-down movement). Or, the hand embodies an agent who acts, e.g. a frog that jumps or legs that walk (index and middle finger with tips down move alternatingly re-presenting legs that walk). Both subtypes are coded as *hand-as-object,* but in the latter case, the researcher can make an additional note: hand-as-agent.
- *motion quality–dynamics:* In *motion quality – dynamics,* the hand may embody a passive object in motion, e.g. a stone that is catapulted out of a volcano with high speed and force (hand adopts a round shape). In rare cases, the hand embodies an agent who acts with a certain dynamics, e.g. somebody falling heavily.
- *pantomime – transitive-active:* In *pantomime – transitive-active,* the hand embodies an object that is acted with, e.g. the hand represents the scissors that the gesturer pretends to cut with.
- *pantomime – transitive-passive:* In *pantomime – transitive-passive,* the hand represents a separate object or an agent that the gesturer re-acts to, e.g. a pancake flying into the gesturer's face.

10.3.2 *enclosure*

Short definition

ENCLOSURE OF AN IMAGINARY OBJECT

Definition
The hand(s) encloses the imaginary object. The shape of the imaginary object is presented by a hand grip. Thus, there is a distinct shape that enables to infer the specific shape of the represented object.

Enclosure is a static Technique of Presentation, i.e., the hand adopts a static shape (grip) and presents a still image of a form. Thus, the complex phase is a static complex phase. As *enclosure* is a static Technique of Presentation, it can be combined with all Function and Type values that include primary and secondary form information.

Function / Type values

primary: *form–shape, form–size*

secondary: *pantomime–transitive-active, pantomime–transitive-passive, spatial relation–position, spatial relation–route, motion quality–manner*, and *motion quality–dynamics presentations*

Examples for *enclosure* in primary and secondary Type values

- *form–shape:* There are two forms of *enclosure* that depend on the shape of the imaginary object: the hand completely encloses the imaginary object, or the hand holds the imaginary object, i.e., there is no complete enclosure but the extent of the hand grip aperture provides information about the shape, e.g. a pincer grip, fist grip, cup-shaped grip.
- *form–size:* The hand(s) indicate the endpoints of the imaginary object. The length may be presented
  - (i) unimanually by showing the distance between the thumb and the index of one hand;
  - (ii) bimanually showing the distance between the two flat hands with the palms (at least one of them) oriented to the center of the imaginary object, i.e. the palms are oriented to each other;
  - (iii) unimanually showing the distance between the hand in space (palm oriented to the center of the imaginary object) and an external surface such as the floor or the table.

- *pantomime – transitive-active:* In *pantomime – transitive-active,* the hand encloses an imaginary object and acts with it, e.g. pretending to hold a glass in the hand and drink.
- *pantomime – transitive-passive:* In *pantomime – transitive-passive,* the hand encloses an imaginary separate object or agent that the gesturer-actor re-acts to, e.g. a stone (presented by *enclosure*) flying into the gesturer's face.
- *spatial relation–position:* In *spatial relation – position,* the hand encloses an object that is placed at a certain position on an imaginary spatial map.
- *spatial relation–route:* In *spatial relation – route,* the hand encloses an object that is shifted from one position to another (without manner and dynamics).
- *motion quality–manner:* In *motion quality–manner presentations,* the hand holds an imaginary object that moves in a certain manner, e.g. the hand encloses an imaginary ball that bumps.
- *motion quality–dynamics:* In *motion quality–dynamics presentations,* the hand holds an imaginary object that moves with a certain dynamics, e.g. the hand encloses an imaginary stone that is catapulted out of a volcano with high speed.

Differentiate *enclosure* from…

- *palpating*: *Enclosure* is a static Technique of Presentation. The shape of the imaginary object is presented by a fixed hand grip. The complex phase is a static complex phase. In contrast, *palpating* is a dynamic Technique of Presentation. The shape is presented by stroking along the imaginary object. The complex phase is a motion complex phase.

10.3.3 *palpating*

Short definition

PALPATING AN IMAGINARY OBJECT

Definition

The hand palpates, feels, or strokes along an imaginary object. The sensitive palms are fully used to feel the imaginary object and they dynamically adapt to the shape of the imaginary object. The palms are oriented toward the center of the imaginary object. *Palpating* enables to present 2- and 3-dimensional shapes. Thus, is refers to *shape* presentation and per definition not to *size* presentation, which presents only one dimension.

Palpating is a dynamic Technique of Presentation. Via the process of palpating a motion image (see 8.4.6) of the shape is created. Thus, there is a motion complex phase.

Function / Type values

primary: *form–shape*

secondary: *spatial relation–route, spatial relation–position*
Examples for *palpating* in primary and secondary form values

- *form–shape:* The hand creates a motion image of a round object which represents a melon by palpating it.
- *spatial relation–route: Palpating* may be used for *spatial relation–route* gestures that include form information, e.g. the course of a broad street is presented by palpating with the flat hand along the imaginary broad street.
- *spatial relation–position: Palpating* may be used to present a shape at a certain position, e.g. the hand creates a motion image of an object that is placed at a certain position, e.g. the hands stroke along an imaginary pointed roof in the right gesture space and then they stroke along an imaginary skyscraper in the left gesture space.

Differentiate *palpating* from…
The following differentiation should have already been made in the Function or Type category coding. However, for didactical purposes the differentiation is reported here again:

- *pantomime–transitive* of palpating an object: Gestures in which *palpating* is used as a Technique of Presentation lack movement dynamics because the message focuses on the motion image of the shape that is created, e.g. "This is a ball". In contrast, *pantomime – transitive* gestures of palpating an object focus on the action of palpating from an egocentric perspective, e.g. "I am palpating".

10.3.4 *tracing*

Short definition

TRACING THE CONTOUR OR THE EXTENT OF AN IMAGINARY OBJECT

Definition
The hand traces or draws with the fingertips, often only with that of the index, the contour of an object (*shape*) or the line of an extent (*size*).

Tracing is a dynamic Technique of Presentation. Via the process of tracing a motion image of the shape or the size is created. Thus, there is a motion complex phase.

Function / Type values

primary: *form–shape*, *form–size*

secondary: *spatial relation–position*

Examples for *tracing* in primary and secondary form values

- *form–shape*: The Technique of Presentation *tracing* is used primarily to present 2-dimensional *shapes*. The trace is closed, i.e., the end point of the line matches the starting point. Thereby, a contour is created. The fingertips are oriented to the frontal or horizontal planes as if they would trace on an imaginary board.
- *form–size: Tracing* can be used to present only the *size* of something. The trace is always straight and is in line with one of the main space axes, i.e., the vertical, sagittal, or horizontal space axis. In contrast to showing a *size* by *enclosure*, i.e., by indicating the two endpoints, *tracing* emphasizes the extent of the *size* ("soo big"). One hand may be held at the starting point from where the extension starts.
- *spatial relation–position:* Tracing can serve to create a motion image of the *shape* or *size* of an imaginary object that is located at a distinct position in an imaginary space.

Differentiate *tracing* from…

- *palpating:* In *tracing* a fine imaginary line is created by the using the fingertips. In *palpating* the full palm of the hand moves along the imaginary object. In *tracing* the hand keeps a fixed shape, whereas in *palpating* the hand is flexible within itself.
- *enclosure*: While in *tracing* a motion image is created in a dynamic process, *enclosure* is a static presentation creating a still image.

The following differentiations should have already been made in the Function or Type category coding. However, for didactical purposes they are reported here:

- *tracing* a shape from *tracing* a size: When *tracing* a shape, the contour is closed, i.e., the starting point of the trace matches the endpoint of the trace. When *tracing* an extent, the trace is open, i.e., the starting point of the trace does not match the endpoint of the trace, and the path is strictly one-dimensional.
- *tracing* a shape from *tracing* a route: When *tracing* a shape, the contour is closed, i.e., the starting point of the trace matches the endpoint of the trace. The fingertips are oriented to the frontal or horizontal planes as if there would be an imaginary board. The shape is presented in the neutral central

gesture space. When *tracing a* route, the trace is open, i.e., the starting point of the trace does not match the endpoint of the trace. The fingertips are oriented towards the imaginary spatial map, which is most often projected to the horizontal plane. There is a distinct use of gesture space.

tracing a size from *tracing* a route: The *size* trace is always a straight and in line with one of the main space axes, i.e., vertical, sagittal, horizontal. In contrast, in *tracing* a route the trace is typically open and, spatially distinct with a complex course, i.e., **not** straight and **not** in line with one of the complex axes. The fingertips are oriented towards the imaginary spatial map, which is most often projected to the horizontal plane.

pantomime of *tracing*: Gestures in which *tracing* is used as a Technique of Presentation lack movement dynamics because the message focuses on the line or the contour which is created, e.g. "This is a rectangle". In contrast, *pantomime–transitive* gestures of tracing focus on the action of tracing from an egocentric perspective, e.g. "I am tracing".

11 Supplementary category Efforts

11.1 Definition of the category Efforts

The Supplementary category Efforts enables to assess the dynamics of movement units, i.e., how a movement is performed. The category is directly adopted from the Laban movement analysis (see also 4.3). Laban (1988) defined Efforts as the inner impulses from which movement originates. He distinguished the four factors flow, weight, time, and space. Each factor comprises a continuum of qualities with 2 polarities, i.e., flow changes between *free* and *bound*, weight between *strong* and *light*, time between *sustained* and *sudden*, and space between *direct* and *indirect*. These effort qualities result from the inner attitude (conscious or unconscious) towards the four Effort factors. The definitions and examples in this chapter are adopted from Robyn Cruz's lecture material (1995) and from Dell (1979). The only modification of the original Laban Effort analysis is that in NEUROGES®, because of clinical relevance, the value *heavy* has been added in the factor weight.

11.2 Selection of units for the Effort assessment

Variations in the Effort factors, i.e., dynamics, are components of many gesture types and actions. They are conceptually intrinsic to *pantomime* and *motion quality* gestures, to *object-oriented* and *subject-oriented actions*, and to *emotion/attitude* movements. As an example, if the gesturer presents a *motion quality – dynamics* gesture in which something is crashing *suddenly* or falling *heavily*, the dynamic quality is part of the creative depiction. Or, if the gesturer pretends to hammer (*pantomime*) or actually hammers (*object-oriented action*), the effort qualities *strong* and *direct* are intrinsic components of the *pantomime* and *action*, respectively. *Subject-oriented actions* such as *lightly* stroking the face can also include dynamics. Likewise, effort qualities are intrinsic to *emotion/attitude* movements (genuine and learned emotional expressions), e.g. the expression of sadness implies *heaviness*.

Effort qualities might also serve to lend an emotional connotation or a certain dynamics to other Function values. Effort qualities often occur in *emphasis* gestures, e.g. to perform a baton *strongly* and *directly*. *Egocentric deictics, directions,* and *emblems* may also be performed with effort dynamics, too, e.g. an insulting emblem. Thus, the Supplementary category Effort can be applied to all Function and Type values with the exception of *form presentation* and *spatial*

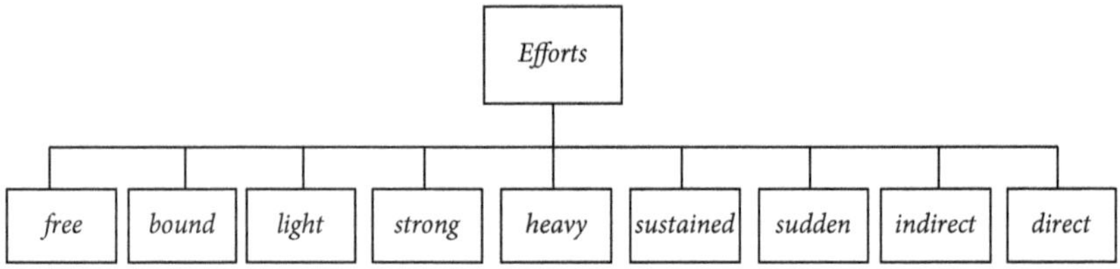

Fig. 13: Values of the category Efforts

relation presentation, which focus on providing information about forms and spatial relations but not about dynamics.

Furthermore, the Supplementary category Effort can be further applied to all other NEUROGES® main categories and values, e.g. a *sudden shift* to a closed position, a *light on body* movement, or *strong act on each other* movements. However, it should be noted that especially for non-conceptual movements Laban-based analyses offer more fine-grained differentiations, e.g. precursors of efforts as described by Kestenberg (1965a,b; 1967) with tension flow rhythms (sucking, snapping/biting, twisting, strain/release, running/drifting, starting/stopping, swaying, surging/birthing, jumping, spurting/ramming) and tension flow attributes (flow adjustment/even flow, low intensity/high intensity, graduality/abruptness) and possibly pre-efforts (flexibility/channeling, gentleness/vehemence-straining, hesitation/suddenness) (Eberhard, personal communication, 2012). However, for most research questions, the Supplementary category Efforts will be sufficient to describe the observed phenomenon.

If there is a change of the Effort quality within a unit, which had been adopted from the main categories, then the Effort quality change demarcates subunits.

11.3 Definition of the Effort values

11.3.1 *free flow*

A variation in body tension representing ease: going with, allowing energy to go through and beyond the body boundaries; indulgent / expansive use of flow

11.3.2 *bound flow*

a variation in body tension representing restraint of movement: restricted, controlled, keeping energy flow within body boundaries; fighting / condensing use of flow, e.g. in the *pantomime – transitive-active* threading a needle, carrying a pot of hot coffee. "Examples of changing between *free* and *bound* flow might be found in: 1) a free sweep of your arm during a conversation, in which you knock something over, and then freeze; 2) carrying a full pan of water over a distance, setting it down and then shaking yourself for relief." (Dell, 1979, p. 15)

11.3.3 *light weight*

force or pressure exerted in movement holding body weight: rarefied, delicate, fine touch, overcoming the body weight; indulgent / expansive intention in weight, e.g. *pantomime–intransitive* walking on ice, *motion quality–dynamics* representing a feather that is gliding to the ground, *pantomime–transitive* carrying a delicate porcelain figure

11.3.4 *strong weight*

force or pressure exerted in movement using body weight: having impact, penetrating, getting behind the body weight; fighting / condensing intention in weight, e.g. *pantomime–transitive* hammering a nail into a wall

11.3.5 *heavy weight*

no force or pressure exerted in movement: passive giving of body weight into gravity, e.g. *motion quality–dynamics* presenting the falling of a heavy stone

11.3.6 *sustained time*

compensation to outward time demands, or attitude toward duration of action: stretching out time, leisurely, actively indulging in time; indulgent / expansive decision in time (distinguish from slow motion or evenness of bound flow), e.g. *pantomime – transitive-active* taking all the time in the world to get up

11.3.7 *sudden time*

compensation to outward time demands, or attitude toward duration of action: urgent, instantaneous, a sense of urgency recreated each time; fighting / condensing decision in time (distinguish from fast or tempo increase), e.g. *pantomime–intransitive* runner making a quick start

11.3.8 *indirect space*

attention or orientation to space, how energy is focused in action, free-floating attention: multi-overlapping foci, multi-faceted attention, active meandering;

indulgent / expansive attention in space, e.g. *pantomime–intransitive* of trying to orientate blind-folded

11.3.9 *direct space*

attention or orientation to space, how energy is focused in action, selective attention: channeled, pin-pointing; fighting / condensing attention in space, e.g. *deictic–external target* to a tiny target

12 Supplementary category Temporal Structure

12.1 Definition of the category Temporal Structure

The Supplementary category Temporal Structure enables to register temporal aspects of a movement unit. The Temporal Structure is defined by the equality versus inequality of the durations between the subphases [22] in units with a *repetitive* Structure (see 4.4.2). Thus, it determines whether the durations between the subphases vary or not. At least three subphases are needed in order to identify the temporal pattern of a *repetitive* unit, as this enables to compare the duration between subphase 1 and subphase 2 with the duration between subphase 2 and subphase 3.

Technically, in NEUROGES®-ELAN the durations between the subphases are compared by noting the instants of the turn-points of the subphases. A turn-point is a change of direction, e.g. back – forth.

12.2 Selection of units for the Temporal Structure assessment

The Temporal Structure assessment is applied to units with a *repetitive* Structure. In the Function analysis, these units often turn out to be *emphasis* gestures[23]. Furthermore, *irregular* units, which may include transient repetitive phases, may be assessed regarding the Temporal Structure.

As a rhythm may contain metric phases and furthermore, as rhythm and meter contain single accents, it is important to stick to the rule that the Temporal Structure value always refers to the complete *repetitive* unit. This implies that in the Temporal Structure assessment per definition no subunits are created. As an example, a *repetitive* unit with the temporal pattern _ …_ … would not be segmented into *single accent – metrical – single accent – metrical* subunits, but be coded as a whole unit with the value *rhythmical.*

---

22 As an example, a *repetitive* unit in which the same direction – with or without displacement in one dimension–is taken three times, e.g. back – forth – back – forth – back – forth, consists of three subphases.

23 However, *superimposed emphasis* units cannot be used as to-be-coded units for the Temporal Structure assessment, since they are often a subunit of the original *repetitive* unit. As stated above, the Temporal Structure assessment refers to the complete *repetitive* unit.

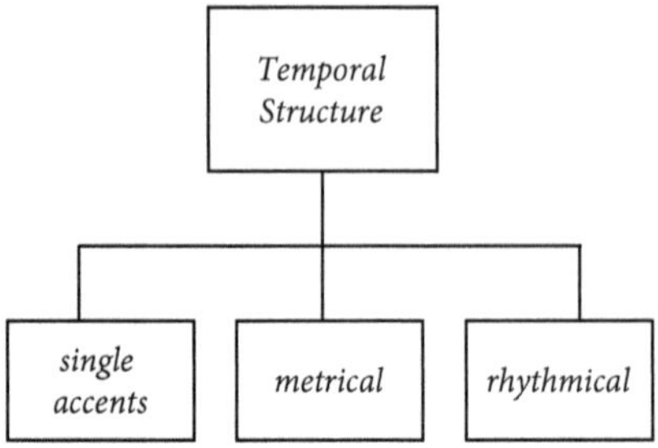

Fig. 14: Values of the category Temporal Structure

12.3 Definition of the Temporal Structure values

12.3.1 *single accents*

The *repetitive* unit comprises less than three subphases. Thus, the existence of a meter versus rhythm cannot be determined.

12.3.2 *metrical*

The *repetitive* unit comprises three or more sub phases and the duration between the subphases is equal.

12.3.3 *rhythmical*

The *repetitive* unit comprises three or more subphases and the duration between the subphases varies.

13 Supplementary category Target Location

13.1 Definition of the category Target Location

The Supplementary category Target Location specifies where a target is located. The target may be a position, an object, or a subject in the physical space or in the imaginary space, which is reflected in or created by gesture.

With reference to the neural organization of spatial attention, the location of the target is defined relative to the sagittal plane that is in line with the body midline. The body midline sagittal plane divides the body (body-internal space and body-surface) and the gesture/action space (body-external space) in two halves. Accordingly, four Target Location values are defined: (i) *right side:* the target is in the body-internal space, the body-surface, or the body-external space that is right to the body midline sagittal plane, (ii) *left side:* the target is in the body-internal space, the body-surface, or the body-external space that is left to the body midline sagittal plane, (iii) *body-midline:* the target is in the sagittal plane that is in line with the body midline, and (iv) *both sides*: in the to-be-coded unit, the target is / the targets are on both the right and left sides.

The precise definition of the target depends on the Function of the hand movement, as defined by the Function value.

For *egocentric deictics,* the target is the location the hand points to. For *egocentric deictics* with the Focus (value) *on body, on attached object, on separate object,* or *on person,* the target is where the body-surface, the attached object, the separate object or the person, respectively, is touched. For *in space–egocentric deictics* the spatial target is distant from the hand. It may even be in the other half of the gesture space than the gesture execution. As an example, the hand executes a *deictic–external space* in the right gesture space but the target of the pointing gesture is the left gesture space[24].

For *egocentric directions,* the spatial target is the location the hand directs at. *Egocentric directions* are almost exclusively *in space* and thus, the spatial target is distant from the hand. The destination of the direction or the route is the target.

24 The gesture space where the gesture is executed is assessed with the Supplementary category Execution Hemi-Space. Dissociations between the Execution Hemi-Space and the Target Location Hemi-Space provide valuable diagnostic information about neuropsychological impairment such as neglect.

For *pantomime–transitive*, the target is the imaginary counter-part that the gesturer pretends to act on, e.g. an imaginary object or environment. *Pantomime–transitive* gestures may include an imaginary tool that the gesturer uses to act on the imaginary counter-part. As an example, first the imaginary toothbrush (target 1) is grasped from an imaginary bathroom sink, then it is moved in front of the mouth (target 2) (in this example, based on the two different targets, two subunits are generated).

For *spatial relation–position* gestures, the target is the position that is created. In *spatial relation – route* gestures, the target is the destination of the created route or direction.

For *object-oriented actions*, the target is the object that is manipulated. For *on separate object*, *on attached object*, or *on person object-oriented actions*, the target corresponds to the Focus (value), i.e., the target is the separate object, the attached object or the person, respectively.

For *subject-oriented actions*, the target is most often a part of the body that is manipulated. For *within body*, *on body*, *on attached object*, or *on separate object subject-oriented actions*, the target corresponds to the Focus (value), i.e., the target is the muscles and joints, the part of the body, or the attached or separate object.[25]

To summarize, for *egocentric deictics* and *egocentric directions*, the target is the location the hand points to or directs at. For *pantomimes*, the target is the imaginary counter-part that is pretended to act on. For *spatial relation presentation* gestures, the target is the created position or destination. For *actions* the target is the part of the body (inner structures and surface) or the object/subject that/who is manipulated.

13.2 Selection of the units for the Target Location assessment

For a reliable assessment of the Target Location category the experimental setting should have a frontal view on the participant, in order to precisely estimate the body midline sagittal plane.

---

25 For *within body* and *on body subject-oriented actions*, the side where the target is (Target Location) may dissociate from the gesture/action hemi-space where the movement is executed (Execution Hemi-Space), if the target is a mobile part of the body that can be moved to the contralateral gesture space. As an example, the left hand may be moved to the right gesture/action hemi-space. If the left hand is touched by the right hand in the right gesture hemi-space, the Target Location value is *left side* and the right hand Execution Hemi-Space value is *ipsilateral* (i.e., the right gesture/action hemi-space).

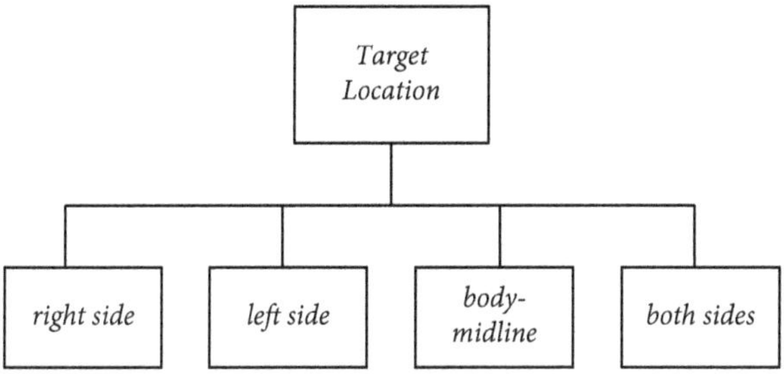

Fig. 15: Values of the category Target Location

A target, as defined above, can be identified in the following Function/Type values: *egocentric deictic-external target, egocentric deictic-You, egocentric deictic – body, egocentric deictic-self, egocentric direction-neutral,* egocentric *direction-imperative, egocentric direction – self-related, pantomime-transitive, spatial relation-position, spatial relation – route, object-oriented action, subject-oriented action,* and furthermore, if spatial relation information is included, also in *motion quality presentation.*

The Target Location assessment applies to the complex phase. In *phasic* and *repetitive*[26] units with one complex phase, there can be only one target. In *phasic* and *repetitive* units with two or more complex phases, there can be two or more targets. Thus, if the Target Locations differ between the complex phases of one to-be-coded unit, based on the Target Location assessment sub-units are created that match the complex phases. However, one complex phase is never divided further. This is an important rule because the value *both sides* is identical with the sum of the values *right side* and *left side*. Thus, any *both sides* unit would automatically be split up in a *right side* subunit and a *left side* subunit, if a complex phase could be split up.

13.3 Definition of the Target Location values

13.3.1 *right side*

The target is located in the body-internal space, the body-surface, or the body-external (gesture/action) space that is right to the body midline sagittal plane.

26 Note that in *repetitive* units, the Target Location assessment does not apply to the single subphases of the complex phase, but only to the complete complex phase.

Examples

- ♦ *phasic in space–egocentric deictic–external target*: The hand points to a target on the gesturer's right (right body-external space).
- ♦ *phasic on body–egocentric deictic–body*: The hand points to the right leg by touching it (right body-surface).
- ♦ *phasic in space–egocentric direction–neutral*: The hand indicates the direction to a distant target on the gesturer's right (right body-external space).
- ♦ *phasic in space–egocentric direction–imperative*: The hand indicates to someone to move to the right (right body-external space).
- ♦ *phasic in space–egocentric direction – self-related:* The hand displays a gesture as if moving an idea downwards to the right (right body-external space).
- ♦ *phasic in space–spatial relation–position:* The hand points to a position on an imaginary spatial map. The imaginary position is presented in the space that is right to the body-midline sagittal plane (right body-external space).
- ♦ *phasic in space–spatial relation–route*: The hand depicts a route with a destination on the right side on an imaginary spatial map. The destination is in the gesturer's right gesture space (right body-external space).
- ♦ *phasic on separate object–object-oriented action:* The hand grasps a pen that is right to the body midline sagittal plane (right body-external space).
- ♦ *phasic on separate object–object-oriented action:* An object that is on the gesturer's left side is grasped (Target Location value: *left side*) and is moved to the gesturer's right side (Target Location value: *right side*). In this example, the to-be-coded *phasic on separate object–object-oriented action* unit with two complex phases is divided into two subunits because of the Target Location assessment.
- ♦ *phasic on person–object-oriented action:* The hand touches a person on the gesturer's right (right body-external space).
- ♦ *repetitive within-body–subject-oriented action:* The right shoulder is moved in circles because of muscle tensions (right body-internal space).
- ♦ *repetitive on body–subject-oriented action:* The hand strokes the right leg (right body-surface).
- ♦ *phasic on attached object–subject-oriented action:* The hand plays with the earring of the right ear (right body-external space).

13.3.2 *left side*

The target is in the body-internal space, the body-surface, or the body-external space that is left to the body midline sagittal plane. Examples ♦ in analogy to *TL right side*

13.3.3 *body-midline*

The target is located in the sagittal plane that is in line with the body midline. Thus, the value *body-midline* refers only to a plane and not to a three-dimensional space. Accordingly, *body-midline* targets require spatially precise gestures and actions. As an example, in order to convey the information of a distant target being located at the body-midline sagittal plane, kinesically the longitudinal hand axis has to be in line with the body-midline sagittal plane, e.g. in a *deictic-external target* that refers to a target that is in line with the body midline, the longitudinal hand axis is in line with the body midline sagittal plane and the target is in the imaginary prolongation of the hand axis. In *spatial relation – position* gestures, the position created in the gesture space is in line with the *body midline.* In *egocentric direction* and *spatial relation – route* gestures, the target (destination) is in line with the *body-midline*[27].

Examples

- *phasic in space–egocentric deictic–external target:* The hand points to an object that is situated directly in front of the gesturer.
- *phasic on person–egocentric deictic–You:* The addressee stands right in front of the gesturer and the gesturer points to addressee's sternum by touching it. The gaze is directed at the addressee.
- *phasic on body–egocentric deictic–self:* The gesturer points to his/her own sternum and touches it. The gaze is directed at the addressee.
- *phasic in space–egocentric deictic–body:* The hand points to the navel. The gaze is directed at the navel.
- *phasic in space–egocentric direction–neutral:* The hand indicates the direction forward straight ahead.
- *repetitive in space–egocentric direction–self-related:* The hand with palm down is moved repeatedly downward in front of the gesturer's body midline, as if the gesturer indicates to him-/herself to calm down.
- *phasic in space–spatial relation–position:* The hand depicts a central position on an imaginary spatial map by creating a position in the gesture space that is in front of the gesturer's body midline.

---

27 Often also the movement path (upward, downward, forward, backward, or a blend of these directions) of the *egocentric direction* or *spatial relation – route* gesture is executed in the body-midline plane. As an example, the hand with palm down is held in front of the navel and then moved downwards several times as the gesturer indicates to him-/herself to calm down (*egocentric direction – self-related*). Here, the Target Location value is identical with the Execution Hemi-space value (both: *body-midline*).

- *phasic on separate object–object-oriented action:* The hand grasps a glass of water that is in front of the gesturer's body midline.
- *phasic on separate object–subject-oriented action:* The gesturer moves a cup of tea to the mouth in order to drink.

13.3.4 *both sides*

The value *both sides* comprises the *left side* and the *right side* of the body-internal space, the body-surface, and the body-external (gesture/action) space. As a target is one location, at first glance it may seem contra-intuitive that one location is on *both sides*. However, there are several possible constellations:

(i) The target is large and extends over the *right* and *left sides.*
(ii) In a bimanual *act apart* unit simultaneously each hand locates a target on each side.
(iii) In a bimanual *act on each other – subject-oriented action* unit both hands act on each other. The Target Location value is always *both sides,* as the surface of the right and left body halves are stimulated.

Examples

- *repetitive on body–egocentric deictic–body:* The hand points to and touches the right cheek and then in an identical manner the left cheek.
- *repetitive in space–egocentric deictic–external target:* The hand indicates first a target in the left hemi-space and then a target in the right hemi-space.
- *phasic in space – act apart symmetrical–egocentric direction–neutral*: Both hands direct simultaneously at two targets, one in the left hemi-space and one in the right hemi-space.
- *repetitive in space–egocentric direction–neutral*: The hand directs first at a distant target in the left hemi-space and then at a target in the right hemi-space.
- *repetitive in space–spatial relation–position*: The hand creates on an imaginary spatial map from right to left positions at equal distances, covering the right and the left gesture hemi-spaces.
- *repetitive on separate object–object-oriented action:* A large piece of paper is in front the gesturer's body. The hand draws first a circle on the left side and then in an identical manner on the right side.
- *repetitive on person–object-oriented action*: The hand touches a person, who stands directly in front of the gesturer, first on the left shoulder and then on the right.
- *repetitive on body–subject-oriented action:* The hand strokes the right cheek and then in an identical manner the left cheek.

- *phasic on attached object–act apart–subject-oriented action:* Each hand pulls on each earring.
- *phasic on body–act apart symmetrical–subject-oriented action:* Both hands stroke over the cheeks.
- *repetitive on body–act on each other symmetrical–subject-oriented:* The hands repetitively clap on each other.
- *repetitive within-body–act apart symmetrical–subject-oriented action*: Both shoulders are moved simultaneously in circles (e.g. because of muscle tensions).
- *repetitive on attached object–subject-oriented action:* The hand pulls on the earring of the right ear and then in an identical manner on that of the left ear.

14 Supplementary category Execution Hemi-Space

14.1 Definition of the category Execution Hemi-Space

The Supplementary category Execution Hemi-Space specifies the location where the hand displays the complex phase. Thus, in the context of this category, execution is defined as the display of the complex phase.

With reference to the neural organization of spatial attention, the location of the execution is defined relative to the sagittal plane that is in line with the body midline (same as for the Supplementary category Target Location). The body midline sagittal plane divides the body-external space (gesture/action space) in two hemi-spaces. A hemi-space is defined as the body-external space that is to the left or to the right of the body midline sagittal plane. Four Execution Hemi-Space values are defined: (i) *ipsilateral:* the laterality of the hand that displays the complex phase matches the laterality of the hemi-space, e.g. left hand executes in left hemi-space, (ii) *contralateral:* the laterality of the hand that displays the complex phase contrasts the laterality of the hemi-space, e.g. left hand executes in right hemi-space, (iii) *body midline:* the hand displays the complex phase in the sagittal plane that is in line with the body midline, and (iv) *ipsi-contra:* the hand displays the complex phase in both hemi-spaces.

While the category Execution Hemi-Space shares with the category Target Location the neuropsychologically grounded division of space by the body midline sagittal plane, the two categories differ regarding the fact that Target Location applies to the body-internal space, the body-surface, or the body-external space, while Execution Hemi-Space only refers to the body-external space. Furthermore, the Target Location values are defined with regard to an egocentric right–left orientation (Is the target on the left or on the right of the egocentric space?), while the Execution Hemi-Space values are defined with regard to the relation between the laterality of the moving limb and the laterality of the hemi-space (Is the execution on the ipsilateral or on the contralateral side of the limb?).

14.2 Selection of units for the Execution Hemi-Space assessment

For a reliable assessment of the Execution Hemi-Space category the experimental setting should have a frontal view on the participant in order to precisely estimate the body midline sagittal plane.

The Execution Hemi-Space can be assessed for all Function/Type values and furthermore, for all NEUROGES® units with a *phasic* or *repetitive* Structure, which per definition have a complex phase, as the Execution Hemi-Space assessment applies to the complex phase.

In *phasic* and *repetitive*[28] units with one complex phase, there can be only one Execution Space. In *phasic* and *repetitive* units with two or more complex phases, there can be two or more Execution Spaces. Thus, if the Execution Spaces differ between the complex phases of one to-be-coded unit, based on the Execution Hemi-Space assessment sub-units are created. However, one complex phase is never divided further. This is an important rule because the EHS value *ipsi-contra* value is identical with the sum of the values *ipsilateral* and *contralateral.* Otherwise, any complex phase that uses the ipsilateral and contralateral hemi-spaces (EHS value: *ipsi-contra)* would automatically be split up in an *ipsilateral* subunit and a *contralateral* subunit.

If, in bimanual units, the Execution Hemi-Space values for the right and left hands differ, the two hands are coded separately.

14.3 Definition of the Execution Hemi-Space values

14.3.1 *ipsilateral*

The laterality of the hand that displays the complex phase matches the laterality of the hemi-space. The knuckles (metacarpophalangeal joints) do not cross the body midline sagittal plane.

In unimanual right hand units, the right hand displays the complex phase in the right hemi-space. In unimanual left hand units, the left hand displays the complex phase in the left hemi-space. In bimanual units, the right hand displays the complex phase in the right hemi-space and the left hand in the left hemi-space.

Examples

- *phasic in space–egocentric deictic–external target*: The right hand displays the complex phase of an *egocentric deictic* in the right hemi-space.
- *phasic in space–act apart–egocentric deictic–external target*: The right hand displays the complex phase of an *egocentric deictic* in the right hemi-space

28 Note that in *repetitive* units, the Target Location assessment does not apply to the single subphases of the complex phase, but only to the complete complex phase.

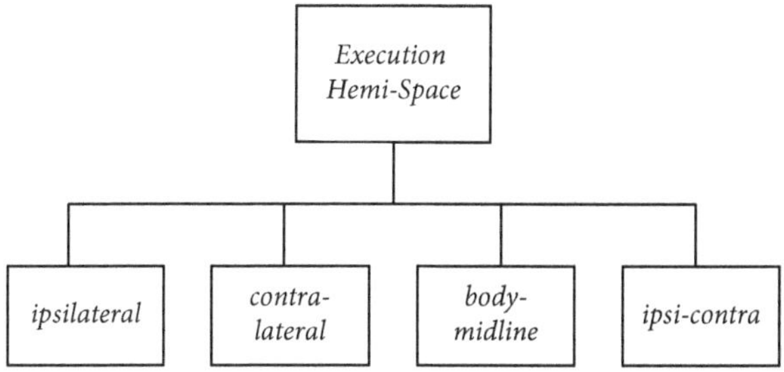

Fig. 16: Values of the category Execution Hemi-Space

while the left hand displays the complex phase of an *egocentric deictic* in the left hemi-space.

14.3.2 *contralateral*

The laterality of the hand that displays the complex phase contrasts the laterality of the hemi-space. The knuckles cross the body midline plane.

In unimanual right hand units, the right hand displays the complex phase in the left hemi-space. In unimanual left hand units, the left hand displays the complex phase in the right hemi-space. In bimanual units, the right hand displays the complex phase in the left hemi-space and the left hand in the right hemi-space.

Example

- *phasic in space–egocentric deictic–external target*: The right hand displays the complex phase of an *egocentric deictic* in the left hemi-space.

14.3.3 *body-midline*

The complex phase is performed in the sagittal plane that is in line with the body midline. Typically, the longitudinal hand axis is line with the body midline plane. If the hand axis is orthogonal to the body midline plane, the knuckles are in line with the body midline plane.

Examples

- *phasic in space–egocentric deictic–self*: The hand displays the complex phase of an *egocentric deictic* pointing to the sternum. The longitudinal hand axis is line with the body-midline sagittal plane.

- ♦ *phasic on body–act on each other–clap/beat:* Both hands clap on each other and hit each other at the body midline plane.
- ♦ *phasic on separate object–object-oriented action:* The hand draws with a pen a straight vertical line that is line with the body-midline sagittal plane, i.e., in front of the gesturer's body midline.
- ♦ *phasic on attached object–subject-oriented action:* The gesturer unzips a zipper that runs in line with the sternum.

14.3.4 *ipsi-contra*

The complex phase trajectory extends over the *ipsilateral* and *contralateral* hemi-spaces.

Examples

- ♦ *phasic in space–egocentric direction–external space:* The hand follows the line of a complete rainbow at the sky.
- ♦ *repetitive in space–egocentric deictic–external space:* The left hand displays a series of *egocentric deictics* in the left and right hemi-spaces.
- ♦ *phasic in space–spatial relation–route:* The hand traces a route that runs from the right to the left on an imaginary spatial map that the gesturer creates on the horizontal plane in front of his belly.

15 Supplementary category Referent

15.1 Definition of the category Referent

A referent is "the thing in the world that the word or phrase denotes or stands for" (Oxford Dictionary). Accordingly, in the Supplementary category Referent, the referent is the thing in the world that the gesture denotes or stands for. The "thing" may be a material object/subject or a non-material phenomenon.

The Supplementary category Referent registers whether the analyst assumes that the Referent of the gesture is (i) a material object/subject or (ii) a non-material phenomenon.

Experienced nonverbal behavior and gesture researchers usually have an intuition whether or not the Referent of a gesture is of material or non-material nature. However, thus far, little empirical research has been conducted to identify the movement criteria that coin the raters' intuition or to examine whether the raters' intuitive classifications are correct. Therefore, the Supplementary category Referent is a work-in-progress category and its values are hypothetical and need to be tested.

15.2 Selection of units for the Referent assessment

The Supplementary category Referent is assessed for the Function values *egocentric deictic, egocentric direction, pantomime, form presentation, spatial relation presentation, motion quality presentation*, and the respective Type values.

If there is a change of the Referent within the to-be-coded unit, which had been adopted from the Function or Type category assessment, then the Referent change demarcates subunits.

15.3 Definition of the Referent values

15.3.1 *material*

Short definition

GESTURES REFERING TO MATERIAL OBJECTS / SUBJECTS

Definition

The rater assumes that the gesture refers to material objects or subjects, their concrete spatial relations or physical motions or actions.

Gestures with the Referent *material* are executed precisely with regard to hand shape, hand orientation, gesture space use, path during complex phase, and efforts. The gaze is directed at the (imaginary) material entity that is indicated or created.

Examples

- *egocentric deictic–external target*:
  pointing to a house in the neighborhood
- *egocentric deictic–You,–self,–body* are always material.
- *egocentric direction–neutral:*
  indicating the direction towards the nearest city
- *egocentric direction–imperative:*
  indicating to the addressee to actually move her/his body or parts of his/her body into a specific direction, or to actually move an object into a specific direction, e.g. to move the bottle on the table into a specific direction
- *egocentric direction – self-related:*
  a ballet dancer rehearsing a choreography with mental training by performing the directions of body movement with his/her hands, e.g. for plié the hands moving down, for jumping the hands moving up.
- *pantomime–intransitive:*
  pretending ("as if") to swimming, or to perform a flic-flac like a circus artist
- *pantomime – transitive-active:*
  pretending ("as if") to brush the teeth, or to climb up a steep rock face
- *pantomime – transitive-passive:*
  pretending ("as if") to be pushed by another person
- *form–shape:*
  showing the shape of an apple by enclosing an imaginary apple; tracing the shape of the moon
- *form–size:*
  showing the height of one's child; showing the height of a mountain
- *spatial relation–position:*
  showing where on an imaginary map of London the Tower Bridge is located relative to Westminster Abbey
- *spatial relation–route:*
  showing on an imaginary map of London the route from Tower Bridge to Westminster Abbey
- *motion quality–manner:*
  showing a ball rolling; showing with a mento-heliocentric perspective how a circus artist performs a flic-flac; showing with a mento-heliocentric

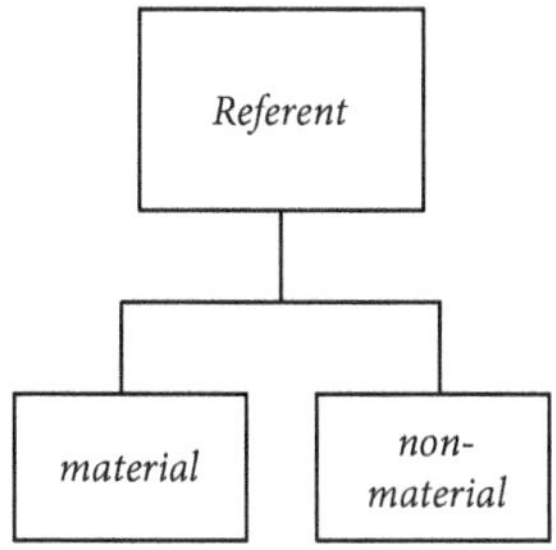

Fig. 17: Values of the category Referent

perspective the action of walking by moving the index and middle finger with finger tips oriented downwards

- ♦ *motion quality–dynamics*:
  showing a volcanic eruption; showing the sensory quality of a fur

Differentiate *material* from…

✎ *non-material*: Gestures that refer to *material* objects or subjects, their concrete spatial relations, or physical motions or actions are distinct and precise with regards to hand shape, hand orientation, gesture space use, path during complex phase, and efforts. The gaze is directed at the (imaginary) material entity that is indicated or created.

Conceptually similar gestures, e.g. an explosive relationship instead of an explosive volcano, may be used to refer to *non-material* phenomena. As compared to *material* gestures, their *non-material* counter-parts are more vague with regard to hand shape, hand orientation, gesture space use, path during complex phase, and efforts. The gaze is **not** directed at the imaginary non-material phenomenon that is indicated or created in gesture.

15.3.2 *non-material*

Short definition

GESTURES THAT REFER TO NON-MATERIAL PHENOMENA

Definition
Gestures with a *non-material* Referent refer to non-material phenomena. The non-material phenomena may be events, constructs, theoretical models, relations, mental processes such as mood and thoughts, etc. Included are gestures that refer to the gesturer's meta-perspective on his/her own process of thinking.

For researchers who want to specify the latter aspect of *non-material* reference, a more fine-grained differentiation is provided here. These *non-material own thoughts* gestures either implicitly reflect the logic structure of the thinking process (subtype: *own thoughts–ideographic*), the gesturer's evaluation of her/his own thoughts (subtype: *own thoughts–toning*), or the gesturer's acting with the own thoughts (subtype: *own thoughts–acting with*). *Own thoughts–ideographic* gestures are defined according to Efron (1941, p. 96): " …*ideographic*, in the sense that it traces or sketches out in the air the 'paths' and 'direction' of the thought pattern. [They] might also be called logico-topographic or logico-pictorial." Thus, ideographic gestures reflect the thinking process, i.e., the logical sequence in which the gesturer sets his/her thoughts, which thought develops from another one, etc. In line with Efron's term "logico-topographic" *ideographic* gestures are *spatial relation presentation* gestures. *Own thoughts–toning* gestures are gestural comments on the gesturer's verbal or gestural statement. They provide information about the reliability of the gestural or verbal statement such as "I am (not) confident about what I am saying here". *Toning* gestures are typically displayed at the start or at the end of a speech turn or a gesture sequence. *Toning* gestures are typically *motion quality presentation* gestures. In *own thoughts–acting with*, the gesturer acts with her/his thoughts as if they were objects, e.g. searches for them, throws them away, weights two ideas, etc. These gestures have an egocentric cognitive perspective, i.e. they are often *egocentric direction* or *pantomime-transitive* gestures. Researchers who want to register if the *non-material* referent refers to *own thoughts* technically note these codes in the tier Notes in NEUROGES®-ELAN.

In gesture, non-material phenomena are often depicted in analogy to material objects or subjects. However, as compared to gestures with a *material* Referent, their *non-material* counter-parts are more vague with regard to hand shape, hand orientation, gesture space use, path during complex phase, and efforts. The gaze is not directed at the presented non-material phenomenon.

Examples

- *egocentric deictic–external target:*
  pointing upward to heaven
- *egocentric direction–neutral:*
  indicating the direction towards heaven
- *egocentric direction–imperative:*
  indicating to the addressee to move his mental state into a certain direction, e.g. to calm down or to cheer up, or to move a thought, a plan, or an idea into a certain direction. As an example, the gesture indicates to the addressee to put down the idea, i.e., to forget about it.

- *egocentric direction – self-related:*
  performing a repetitive rotation in the wrist when desperately searching for a word

The gesture is an example of the subtype *own thoughts–acting with,* as it seems as if the gesturer tries to rotate a word out of his/her brain. The gesture is possibly akin to the *palm-out* gesture as thoughts are rotated out. However, while the *palm-out* gesture reflects the success of having brought out the idea and presenting it, the rotating gesture is performed to facilitate the process of bringing out thoughts.

The Structure of the unimanual gesture is *repetitive*, the Focus *in space*. The hand is flat and not tense, the palm is oriented toward the body. The path during complex phase is circular. The effort quality is sudden time, i.e., as if the gesturer tries to accelerate the thinking process. The head might be bowed and the gaze might be casted down (to improve concentration). In case of a right hand movement, there is a clockwise rotation, in case of the left hand a counter-clockwise one.

- *pantomime–intransitive:*
  pretending to stand on unstable grounds to depict loosing control
- *pantomime – transitive-active:*
  pretending to weigh two arguments with the hands when considering the pros and cons of a plan
  The weighing gesture is an example of the subtype *own thoughts–acting with*, as it indicates that the gesturer opposes and compares two ideas or arguments. The palms are oriented upwards and held like weighing scales and they move alternatingly up and down.
- *pantomime – transitive-passive:*
  pretending to be hit by something heavy when depicting being struck by bad news
- *form–size*:
  depicting a super event; or a big problem
- *form–shape*:
  depicting a perfect round evening
- *spatial relation–position:*
  depicting temporal positions, such as the past and the future; depicting political positions, such as the one of the right-wing politicians and that of the left-wing politicians
- *spatial relation–position:*

creating positions that represent family members and thereby revealing an implicit grouping of the family members

The gesture is an example of the subtype *own thoughts – ideographic,* if it reflects the gesturer's subjective implicit grouping of entities, e.g. the father and grandmother on the left side of the gesture space and the mother on the right side. In contrast, if the grouping matches the common sense and the semantics of the words, e.g. the left wing party is positioned on the left side and the right wing party on the right side, the subtype *ideographic* does not apply.

◆ *spatial relation–route:*

depicting a temporal course, e.g. the decline of the Roman Empire

◆ *spatial relation–route:*

creating a route that reflects the gesturer's implicit structuring of a working process

The gesture is an example of the subtype *own thoughts – ideographic,* if it reflects the gesturer's subjective implicit organization of a process, e.g. "I start with the vocabulary (marking position 1), then I learn the grammar (route to position 2), then I directly move to translating the text (direct route to position 3), and finally I repeat the vocabulary again (route back to position 1)".

◆ *motion quality–manner:*

depicting a revolution that starts rolling

◆ *motion quality–manner:*

depicting a situation that is unsteady with a waggling gesture

◆ *motion quality–manner:*

indicating that one is not sure about the own verbal oder gestural statement

The waggling gesture is an example of the subtype *own thoughts – toning,* if the gesturer uses it to indicate that his/her statement might not be reliable. In this case, the waggling gesture is displayed at the beginning or end of a gesture sequence or the verbal statement.

The Structure of the unimanual gesture is *repetitive,* the Focus is *in space*. The waggling gesture is a fast small supination–pronation movement of the hand with not more than 90° between the supination and pronation end positions. The hand shape is flat with the fingers spread without tension. The palm in oriented in the horizontal or sagittal plane. The path during complex phase is two-dimensional and semi-circular.

◆ *motion quality–dynamics:*

depicting an explosive dispute

16 Supplementary category Trigger/Motive

16.1 Definition of the category Trigger/Motive

The Supplementary category Trigger/Motive registers whether the analyst assumes that the trigger or the motive of the *subject-oriented action* is (i) to change the gesturer's physical state, (ii) to change the gesturer's visual appearance, or (iii) to regulate the mental state.

Experienced nonverbal behavior and gesture researchers usually have an intuition about the trigger or the motive of a *subject-oriented action*. However, thus far, little empirical research has been conducted to identify the movement criteria that coin the raters' intuition or to examine whether the raters' intuitive classifications are correct. Therefore, the Supplementary category Trigger/Motive is a work-in-progress category and its values are hypothetical and need to be tested.

16.2 Selection of units for the Trigger/Motive assessment

Function units with the value *subject-oriented action* are submitted to the assessment with the supplementary category Trigger/Motive.

16.3 Definition of the Trigger/Motive values

16.3.1 *physical regulation*

Short definition

ACTIONS TO CHANGE GESTURER'S PHYSICAL STATE

Definition

These are actions that aim at changing physical states, i.e., to give relief from unpleasant physical states or to produce pleasant states. They are reactions to somatosensory perceptions. Perceiving pain, being cold, being hot, etc. trigger *physical regulation* actions. Accordingly, these actions have a clear–typically for the rater identifiable–effect on the body, e.g. rubbing the skin, improving vision.

Note that these actions that originally serve *physical regulation* may become a habit and then serve *mental regulation* (see 16.3.3).

Movement form

Structure: *phasic, repetitive*

Focus: *on body, within body > on attached object, on separate object, in space*

Efforts: depending on the physical goal

Involvement of other parts of the body: -

Gaze: sometimes at the hand or the focus, respectively, e.g. at the hand that scratches the spot on the arm that itches

Other criteria: -

Note: the part of the body that is the focus of the *physical regulation* action
Examples (ordered according to StructureFocus)

- *Phasic or repetitive on body* is the most frequent StructureFocus in *physical regulation*, e.g. scratching because a mosquito bite itches; stroking when there is pain; removing the fringe from the forehead when it disturbs vision; holding the hands on the ears when it is too loud; holding the hand in front of the eyes when bedazzled; closing the nostrils with the fingers when it smells
- *Phasic or repetitive within body*, e.g. stretching the arms or rolling the shoulders to get relief from muscle tensions
- *Phasic or repetitive on attached object* is a rare StructureFocus in *physical regulation*, e.g. pulling the zipper when getting cold; adjusting glasses when they are really in an ineffective position; taking glasses out of the pocket and putting them on to improve vision
- *Phasic or repetitive on separate object* is a rare StructureFocus in *physical regulation*, e.g. putting off glasses when seeing better without them at near distance; drinking a glass of water when thirsty
- *In space* is an even more rare StructureFocus in *physical regulation*, e.g. fanning with the hand when being hot

Differentiate *physical regulation* from…

- *mental regulation*: In *physical regulation* the specific physical need that triggers the action can often be objectively identified, e.g. she folds her arms because she is cold. If the physical trigger requires it, the *physical regulation* action may be complicated including contortions such as scratching oneself on the back. In *mental regulation* actions no objective physical trigger can be identified. *Mental regulation* actions typically occur

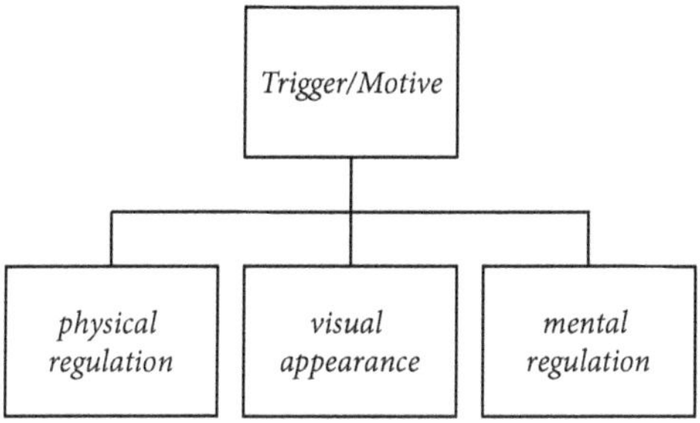

Fig. 18: Values of the category Trigger/Motive

as part of stereotypical behavioral patterns that are displayed repeatedly in the same psycho-social context, e.g. when someone is stressed, amused, embarrassed etc.

16.3.2 *visual appearance*

Short definition

ACTIONS TO CHANGE THE GESTURER'S VISUAL APPEARANCE

Definition

These are actions that change the gesturer's visual appearance. In general, the gesturer intends to improve the visual appearance in order to look more attractive. Only in shy subjects or in specific situations an individual might intend to look less attractive. Thus, most often *visual appearance* actions are preening behaviors and they have a social effect.

Visual appearance actions can be specific reactions to specific deviations in the visual appearance, e.g. the tie is not straight or the hair is not in place. However, *visual appearance* actions may also be displayed if no corrections of the visual appearance are necessary. In this case, they are rather displayed as an appeasement behavior indicating to the addressee that the gesturer wants to be beautiful for him/her and please him/her, e.g. stroking the hair behind the ear although the hair is in place.

Movement form

Structure: *phasic, repetitive*

Focus: *on body, on attached object*

Efforts: distinct use effort qualities

Involvement of other parts of the body: involvement of trunk possible

Gaze: sometimes at addressee

Other criteria: -

Note: the part of the body that is the focus of the *visual appearance* action
Examples (ordered according to StructureFocus)

- *Phasic or repetitive on body,* e.g. stroking hair back (repetitively) in order to look more attractive
- *Phasic or repetitive on attached object,* e.g. pulling the shirt (repetitively) over the belly in order to "officially" hide the belly but thereby to indirectly to attract the addressee's attention

Differentiate *visual appearance* from…

- *mental regulation*: *Visual appearance* actions are effective and specific in order to change the visual appearance. Often, the deviation in the visual appearance that motivates the action can be identified. If *visual appearance* actions are displayed as preening behavior, they are demonstrative and communicative.

In *mental regulation* actions no prior deviation in the visual appearance can be identified. M*ental regulation* actions typically occur as part of a stereotypical behavioral pattern that are displayed repeatedly in the same psycho-social context, e.g. when someone is stressed, amused, embarrassed etc.

16.3.3 *mental regulation*

Short definition

ACTIONS THAT STIMULATE THE BODY WITHOUT A RECOGNIZABLE PHYSICAL TRIGGER

Definition
These are actions that serve to regulate the gesturer's mental state, i.e., to work off energy, to stimulate, or to calm down. Two polar mental states that may elicit *mental regulation* actions are distinguished here: (i) hyperarousal, e.g. nervousness, stress; in this condition, *mental regulation* actions serve to calm down the gesturer; (ii) hypoarousal, e.g. boredom, tiredness etc. the gesturer has to cope with; in this condition, *mental regulation* actions serve to stimulate and activate.

No physical trigger, no visual appearance deficit nor social motive to improve the visual appearance is recognizable in *mental regulation* actions. Accordingly, the actions do not necessarily have a clear effect on the body or on the visual appearance. The most important feature of *mental regulation* – in contrast to *physical regulation* and *visual appearance* regulation–is that the individual displays the actions repeatedly in a stereotypical manner in the absence of objectively identifiable physical and visual appearance related triggers. Thus, in order to code the value *mental regulation*, the *subject-oriented action* should at least be observed twice in a stimulus set. If, while coding, the rater suspects that an action serves *mental regulation* but up to that moment (s)he only observed the behavior once, (s)he should first code the value *trigger/motive unknown* and then, if the behavior occurs for the second time, go back to the first tag and code *mental regulation.*

Movement form

Structure: *phasic, repetitive*

Focus: *on body, on attached object, on separate object, within body*

Efforts: depending on the action

Involvement of other parts of the body: -

Gaze: the gaze is typically **not** directed at the acting hand

Other criteria: Gesturers often display the *mental regulation* actions repeatedly in a stereotypical manner, often as part of a complex behavioral pattern, e.g. pulling on the necklace and smiling embarrassedly.

Note: the part of the body that is the focus of the *mental regulation* action
Examples (ordered according to StructureFocus)

- *Phasic on body*: stroking hair back because stressed
- *Phasic on attached object*: adjusting the watchstrap because of being embarrassed
- *Phasic on separate object*: putting a glass aside in order to gain time to respond to a difficult question
- *Repetitive on body*: scratching, rubbing because of being bored
- *Repetitive on attached object*: repetitively pulling on the necklace when embarrassed
- *Repetitive on separate object*: tapping with a pen on the table with impatience

16.3.4 *trigger/motive unknown*

As the Function category *subject-oriented action* refers to internal processes, i.e., physical states, mental states, and the wish to improve one's visual appearance, it may be difficult to reliably identify the internal trigger or motive. If the rater is insecure in his/her assumption concerning the gesturer's motive or trigger, (s)he chooses the value *trigger/motive unknown.*

List of Figures

List of Tables

References

Bressem, J. (2006). Formen redebegleitender Gesten-Verteilung und Kombinatorik formbezogener Parameter. Institute of German and Dutch Philology, Free University of Berlin, Master thesis, 117.

Bryjova, J., Munsch, S., Puder, J., Hoffmann, J. (2013). Die Reaktivität auf einen akuten Stressor und Emotionsregulationsmechanismen bei Kindern im Vorschulalter. Paper presented at the 8. Workshop Kongress für Klinische Psychologie und Psychotherapie, Universität Trier, Universität Trier, (9.–11. Mai).

Crovitz, H. F., Zener, K. (1962). A group test for assessing hand-and-eye dominance. America Journal of Psychology, 75, 271–276.

Cruz, R. F., lecture material based on Dell, C. (1995). A primer for movement description using effort-shape and supplementary concepts. New York: Dance Notation Bureau Press.

Darwin, C. (1872, reissued 2009). The expression of the emotions in man and animals. Oxford University Press.

Dell, C. (1979). A primer for movement description using effort-shape and supplementary concepts. New York: Dance Notation Bureau Press.

Densing, K., Konstantinidis, I., Seiler, M. (2017). Effect of stress level on different forms of self-touch in pre- and post adolescent girls. Journal of Motor Behavior. doi:10.1080/00222895.2017.1367640

Dvoretska, D. (2009). Kinetische Interaktion und Koordination. Humboldt-Universität Berlin, Diploma Thesis.

Dvoretska, D., Denissen, J., Lausberg, H. (2013). Kinesic turn taking and mutual understanding in interactive dyads. Paper presented at the TiGeR, Tilburg.

Dvoretska, D., Lausberg, H. (2013). Verbal and nonverbal intelligence show different patterns of hand movement. Paper presented at the 55th Conference of Experimental Psychologist, Vienna.

Dvoretska, D., Joraschky, P., Lausberg, H. (2014). Frühidentifizierung von Therapieabbrechern in der Psychotherapie. Paper presented at Deutscher Kongress für Psychosomatische Medizin und Psychotherapie, Berlin (26.–29. März).

Efron, D. (1941). Gesture and culture. The Hague: Mouton.

Ekman, P., Friesen, W. V. (1969). The repertoire of nonverbal behaviour: Categories, origins, usage, and coding. Semiotica, 1, 49–99.

Freedman, N. (1972). The Analysis of Movement Behaviour During the Clinical Interview. In A. W. Siegman and B. Pope (Eds.), Studies in Dyadic Communication, 153–175. New York: Pergamon.

Gabor, N., Vitinius, F., Obliers, R., Ritter, A., Lausberg, H. (2014). Gestural behaviour as an indicator for measuring the quality of a therapist-patient-relationship. Paper presented at the ICIP 2014, Université de Neuchatel.

Gabor, N., Vitinius, F., Obliers, R., Schreer, O., Masneri, S., Ritter, A., Lausberg, H. (2015). How the doctor's behaviour influences the patient's behaviour. Paper presented at the Deutscher Kongress für Psychosomatische Medizin und Psychotherapie, Berlin (25.–28. März).

Haaland, K. Y., Flaherty, D. (1984). The different types of limb apraxia errors made by patients with left vs. right hemisphere damage. Brain and Cognition, 3, 370–384.

Helmich, I., Lausberg, H. (2014). Hand movements with a phase structure and gestures that depict action stem from a left hemispheric system of conceptualization. Experimental Brain Research. doi:10.1007/s00221-014-4006-x.

Helmich, I., Lausberg, H., Sassenberg, U. (2011). Bewegungsverhalten als Indikator impliziter emotionaler Prozesse alexithymer und nicht-alexithymer Probanden (Poster). Paper presented at the 62. Jahrestagung des Deutschen Kollegiums für Psychosomatische Medizin (DKPM) und 19. Jahrestagung der Deutschen Gesellschaft für Psychosomatische Medizin und ärztliche Psychotherapie (DGPM). Deutscher Kongress für Psychosomatische Medizin und Psychotherapie, 23.–26.03.2011, Essen.

Helmich, I., Skomroch, H., Lausberg, H. (2014). Neuropsychological functions of hand movements and gestures change in the presence or absence of speech. Journal of Cognitive Psychology, 26(7), 740–753. doi:10.1080/20445911.2014.961925

Helmich, I., Simalla, N., Ollinger, N., Junge, R., Reinecke, K., Lausberg, H. (2018). Altered hand movement behavior in athletes with a history of a sport-related concussion. European Society for Cognitive and Affective Neuroscience (ESCAN 2018), Leiden, Netherlands, 19.–22.07.2018. Book of abstracts, p. 100.

Hermsdörfer, J., Mai, N., Spatt, J., Marquardt, C., Veltkamp, R., Goldenberg, G. (1996). Kinematic analysis of movement imitation in apraxia. Brain, 119, 1575–1586.

Heubach, T. (2016). Auswirkungen von kognitivem Stress auf das Handbewegungsverhalten – Können wir durch Handbewegungen während kognitiver Tests unsere Leistung steigern? German Sport University Cologne, Master thesis.

Hogrefe, K., Rein, R., Skomroch, H., Lausberg, H. (2016). Co-speech hand movements during narrations: What is the impact of right vs. left hemisphere brain damage. Neuropsychologia, 93, 176–188.

Holle, H., Rein, R. (2013). The Modified Cohen's Kappa: Calculating Interrater Agreement for Segmentation and Annotation. In H. Lausberg (Ed.), Understanding Body Movement. Frankfurt/Main: Peter Lang.

Holle, H., Rein, R. (2015). EasyDIAg: A tool for easy determination of interrater agreement. Behavior Research Methods, 47, 837–847.

Juszczyk, K., Ciecierski, K. (2016). Kinemo Software: Towards automated gesture annotation with ms Kinect. Paper presented at the MASI–Methodology for the Analysis of Social Interaction, Universität Würzburg.

Kendon, A. (1972). Some Relationships between Body Motion and Speech. In: A. Siegman and B. Pope (Eds.), Studies in Dyadic Communication, 177–210, New York: Pergamon Press, .

Kendon, A. (2010). Gesture – Visible Action as Utterance. Cambridge University Press.

Kestenberg, J. (1965a). The role of movement patterns in development I. Psychoanalytic Quarterly, 24(1), 1–36.

Kestenberg, J. (1965b). The role of movement patterns in development II. Psychoanalytic Quarterly, 24(4), 515–63.

Kestenberg, J. (1967). The role of movement patterns in development III. Psychoanalytic Quarterly, 26(3), 356–409.

Kestenberg, J., Sossin, M. (1979). The Role of Movement Patterns in Development II. New York: Dance Notation Bureau Press.

Kim, Z. H. (2016). Kulturelle Unterschiede in der Darstellung des eigenen Erlebens durch Beobachten des Balletts Giselle und des koreanischen Tanzes Sung-Mu: Ein Vergleich von Deutschen und Koreanern anhand des sprachbegleitenden Handbewegungsverhaltens. German Sport University, Doctoral Disseration.

Kim, Z. H., Lausberg, H. (2018a). Processing Emotional Expression in the Dance of a Foreign Culture: Gestural responses of Germans and Koreans to Ballet and Korean Dance. Journal of Movement Arts Literacy, 4(1, Art. 6).

Kim, Z. H., Lausberg, H. (2018b). Koreans and Germans: Cultural Differences in Hand Movement Behaviour and Gestural Repertoire. Journal of Intercultural Communication Research, DOI: 10.1080/17475759.2018.1475296.

Klatzky, R. L. (1998). Allocentric and Egocentric Spatial Representations: Definitions, Distinctions and Interconnections. In: C.

Freksa, C. Habel, K.F. Wender (Eds.), Spatial Cognition. LNCS (LNAI), 1404, 1–17. Heidelberg: Springer .

Kosslyn, S. M. (1980). Image and the Mind. Cambridge: Harvard University Press.

Kreyenbrink, I., Joraschky, P., Konstantinidis, I., Neumann, N., Lausberg, H. (2017). Nonverbales Verhalten von Patienten mit sozialen Phobien und ihren Therapeuten in psychodynamischen Psychotherapien (Teilprojekt SOPHO-NET). Zeitschrift für Psychosomatische Medizin und Psychotherapie, 63, 297–313.

Kryger, M. (2010). Bewegungsverhalten von Patient und Therapeut in als gut und schlecht erlebten Therapiesitzungen. German Sport University Cologne, Diploma Thesis.

Laban, R. (1988). The Mastery of Movement. Northcote House Publishers Ltd.

Lausberg, H. (2011). Das Gespräch zwischen Arzt und Patientin: Die bewegungsanalytische Perspektive. Balint Journal, 1, 15–24.

Lausberg, H. (Ed.) (2013). Understanding Body Movement. A Guide to Empirical Research on Nonverbal Behaviour. With an Introduction to the NEUROGES® Coding System. Frankfurt/Main: Peter Lang.

Lausberg, H., Davis, M., Rothenhäusler, A. (2000). Hemispheric specialization in spontaneous gesticulation in a patient with callosal disonnection. Neuropsychologia, 38, 1654–1663.

Lausberg, H., Helmich, I., Sassenberg, U. (2010). Bewusstheit von Emotionen: Bewegungsverhalten als Indikator impliziter emotionaler Prozesse bei alexithymen und nicht-alexithymen Probanden. Paper presented at the Deutscher Kongress für Psychosomatik und Psychotherapie. Abstract in Psychologische Medizin, Sondernummer zur 61. Arbeitstagung des Deutschen Kollegiums für Psychosomatische Medizin (DKPM) und 18. Jahrestagung der Deutschen Gesellschaft für Psychosomatische Medizin und Ärztliche Psychotherapie (DGPM), Berlin.

Lausberg, H., Helmich, I., Sassenberg, U., Petermann, K. (2016). Gender-Specific Implicit Emotional Processing in Alexithymic Individuals. Journal of Psychosomatic Research.

Lausberg, H., Kita, S. (2002). Dissociation of right and left hand gesture spaces in split-brain patients. Cortex, 38, 883–886.

Lausberg, H., Kita, S. (2003). The content of the message influences the hand choice in co-speech gestures and in gesturing without speaking. Brain and Language, 86, 57–69.

Lausberg, H., Kita, S., Zaidel, E., Ptito, A. (2003). Split-brain patients neglect left personal space during right-handed gestures. Neuropsychologia, 1595, 1–13.

Lausberg, H., Sloetjes, H. (2009). Coding gestural behavior with the NEUROGES®-ELAN system. Behavior Research Methods, 41(3), 841–849. doi:10.3758/BRM.41.3.841

Lausberg, H., Sloetjes, H. (2016). The revised NEUROGES®-ELAN system: An objective and reliable interdisciplinary analysis tool for nonverbal behavior and gesture. Behavior Research Methods, 48(3), 973–993. doi:10.3758/s13428-015-0622-z.

Lausberg, H., Zaidel, E., Cruz, R. F., Ptito, A. (2007). Speech-independent production of communicative gestures: Evidence from patients with complete callosal disconnection. Neuropsychologia, 45, 3092–3104.

Masneri, S., Schreer, O., Schneider, D., Tschöpel, S., Bardeli, R., Bordag, S., Auer, E., Sloetjes, H., Wittenburg, P. (2010). Towards Semi-Automated Annotations for Video and Audio Corpora. Conference proceedings of the 4th Workshop on Representation and Processing of Sign Languages: Corpora and Sign Language Technologies in conjunction with 7th Int. Conf. on Language Resources and Evaluation (LREC), Malta, June 22, 2010, 150–153.

McNeill, D. (1992). Hand and Mind. What gestures reveal about thought. Chicago: University of Chicago.

Meilinger, T., Vosgerau, G. (2010). Putting Egocentric and Allocentric into Perspective. In: C. Hölscher, et al. (Eds.), Spatial Cognition VII, LNAI 6222, 207–221. Springer: Verlag, Berlin: Heidelberg.

Neumann, N., Kreyenbrink, I., Reinecke, K., Lausberg, H. (2017). Hand rest positions of patients with social phobia and therapists in psychodynamic psychotherapy sessions (SOPHO-NET project). Journal of Multimodal Communication Studies, 4(1–2), 50–55. doi:10.14746/jmcs.

North, M. (1990). Personality Assessment through Movement. Plymouth: Northcote House Publishers.

Ochipa, C., Rothi, L.J.G., Heilman, K. M. (1994). Conduction apraxia. Journal of Neurology, Neurosurgery, and Psychiatry, 57, 1241–1244.

Oxford Dictionary

Postma-Nilsenová, M., Postma, E., Balsters, M., Krahmer, E., Schaafsma, J., Swerts, M., Vingerhoets, A., Mol, L. (2013). Automatic detection of hand/upper body movement and facial expressions as cues to feelings of exclusion. Paper presented at the Tilburg Gesture Research Meeting, Tilburg, The Netherlands

Raisig, S., Welke, T., Hagendorf, H., van der Meer, E. (2009). Insights into knowledge representation: The influence of amodal and perceptual variables on event knowledge from memory. Cognitive Science, 33, 1252–1266.

Rein, R. (2013). Using 3D Kinematics for the Analysis of Hand Movement Behaviour: A Pilot Study and some Further Suggestions. In: H. Lausberg (Ed.), Understanding Body Movement. Frankfurt a. M.: Peter Lang.

Reinecke, K. C. H., Dvoretska, D., Joraschky, P., Lausberg, H. (2018a). Non-verbal irregular movements during psychodynamic psychotherapy as a marker for comorbid depression in patients with social phobia. German Congress of Psychosomatic Medicine, Berlin, March 21- 24, 2018. E-book of abstracts, P – 134.

Reinecke, K. C. H., Neumann, N., Joraschky, P., Lausberg, H. (2018b). Kinesic Synchrony between Patient and Therapist in Psychodynamic Psychotherapies. 2nd Symposium on Embodied Interaction: Gesture, Touch and Embodied Meaning-making. University of Southern Denmark, June 26-27, 2018. Book of abstracts, pp. 58–60.

Salmaso, D., Longoni A. M. (1985). Problems in the assessment of hand preference. Cortex, 21, 533–549.

Sassenberg, U., van der Meer, E. (2010). Do we really gesture more when it is more difficult? Cognitive Science, 34, 643–664.

Sassenberg, U., Foth, M., Wartenburger, I., van der Meer, E. (2011). Show your hands–are you really clever? Reasoning, gesture production, and intelligence. Linguistics, 49(1), 105–134.

Seyfeddinipur, M. (2006). Disfluency: Interrupting Speech and Gesture. MPI Series in Psycholinguistics, 39, Nijmegen: Radboud Universiteid Nijmegen.

Skomroch, H., Lausberg, H. (2013). AUVIS–Audiovisuelles Data-Mining am Beispiel der Ereignis-Segmentierung in multimodalen Sprachdaten. Paper presented at the Kick-Off Workshop der eHumanities-Verbundprojekte Leipzig, 8./9. April 2013.

Skomroch, H., Lausberg, H., von Unterladstetter, V., Sandler, M., Strunk, J., Himmelmann, N. (2013). Aligning hand movement behaviour and intonation sequences. Paper presented at the Mapping Multimodal Dialogue (MaMuD), RWTH Aachen.

Slöetjes, H. (2013). Step by Step Instruction in NEUROGES® Coding with ELAN. In: H. Lausberg (Ed.), Understanding Body Movement: A Guide to Empirical Research on Nonverbal Behaviour: With an Introduction to the NEUROGES® Coding System. Frankfurt/Main: Peter Lang.

Wartenburger, I., Kühn, E., Sassenberg, U., Foth, M., Franz, E.A., van der Meer, E. (2010). On the relationship between fluid intelligence, gesture production, and brain structure. Intelligence, 38, 193–201.

Webster's dictionary

Wikipedia

www.ingramcontent.com/pod-product-compliance
Ingram Content Group UK Ltd.
Pitfield, Milton Keynes, MK11 3LW, UK
UKHW021921120926
8556IPUK00042BA/1112

9 783631 771723